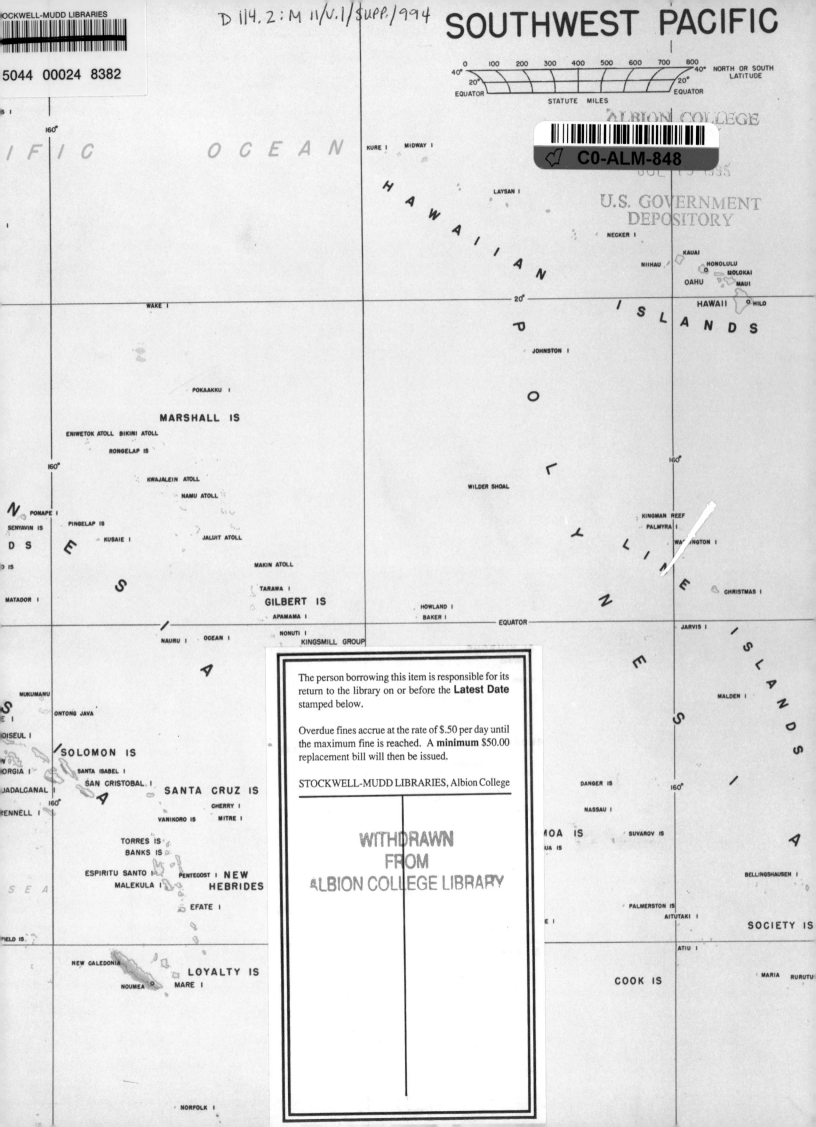

SOUTHWEST PACIFIC

D 114.2: M 11/V.1/SUPP./994

0 100 200 300 400 500 600 700 800 NORTH OR SOUTH LATITUDE
40° 40°
20° 20°
EQUATOR EQUATOR
STATUTE MILES

OCEAN
IFIC
160°

KURE I   MIDWAY I

HAWAIIAN

LAYSAN I

NECKER I

KAUAI
NIIHAU   HONOLULU
MOLOKAI
OAHU   MAUI

ISLANDS

20°   HAWAII   HILO

WAKE I

JOHNSTON I

P
O
L
Y
N
E
S
I
A

160°

POKAAKKU I

MARSHALL IS

ENIWETOK ATOLL   BIKINI ATOLL
RONGELAP IS
160°

WILDER SHOAL

KWAJALEIN ATOLL
NAMU ATOLL

KINGMAN REEF
PALMYRA I
WASHINGTON I

N   PONAPE I
SENYAVIN IS   PINGELAP IS
DS   E   KUSAIE I   JALUIT ATOLL
IS
MATADOR I

MAKIN ATOLL

CHRISTMAS I

TARAWA I
GILBERT IS
APAMAMA I

HOWLAND I
BAKER I   EQUATOR

NONUTI I
NAURU I   OCEAN I   KINGSMILL GROUP

JARVIS I

ISLANDS

MALDEN I

NUKUMANU
ONTONG JAVA

OISEUL I
ORGIA I   SANTA ISABEL I
SAN CRISTOBAL I   SANTA CRUZ IS
UADALCANAL I
160°
RENNELL I

SOLOMON IS

CHERRY I
VANIKORO IS   MITRE I

DANGER IS   160°
NASSAU I

TORRES IS
BANKS IS

ESPIRITU SANTO I   PENTECOST I   NEW
MALEKULA I   HEBRIDES
EFATE I

MOA IS   SUVAROV IS
UA IS

BELLINGSHAUSEN I

SEA

FIELD IS

PALMERSTON IS
E I   AITUTAKI I

SOCIETY IS

NEW CALEDONIA
LOYALTY IS
NOUMEA   MARE I

ATIU I

COOK IS   MARIA   RURUTU

NORFOLK I

Reports

of

General MacArthur

MacARTHUR IN JAPAN: THE OCCUPATION: MILITARY PHASE

VOLUME I SUPPLEMENT

PREPARED BY HIS GENERAL STAFF

Library of Congress Catalog Card Number: 66–60006

Facsimile Reprint, 1994

CMH Pub 13–4

FOREWORD

The *Reports of General MacArthur* include two volumes being published by the Department of the Army in four books reproduced exactly as they were printed by General MacArthur's Tokyo headquarters in 1950, except for the addition of this foreword and indexes. Since they were Government property, the general turned over to the Department in 1953 these volumes and related source materials. In Army and National Archives custody these materials have been available for research although they have not been easily accessible. While he lived, General MacArthur was unwilling to approve the reproduction and dissemination of the *Reports*, because he believed they needed further editing and correction of some inaccuracies. His passing permits publication but not the correction he deemed desirable. In publishing them, the Department of the Army must therefore disclaim any responsibility for their accuracy. But the Army also recognizes that these volumes have substantial and enduring value, and it believes the American people are entitled to have them made widely available through government publication.

The preliminary work for compiling the MacArthur volumes began in 1943 within the G–3 Section of his General Staff, and was carried forward after the war by members of the G–2 Section, headed by Maj. Gen. Charles A. Willoughby with Professor Gordon W. Prange, on leave from the University of Maryland, as his principal professional assistant. Volume II of the *Reports* represents the contributions of Japanese officers employed to tell their story of operations against MacArthur's forces. The very large number of individuals, American and Japanese, who participated in the compilation and editing of the *Reports* would make a complete listing of contributors relatively meaningless.

Volume I narrates the operations of forces under General MacArthur's command from the Japanese attack on Luzon in 1941 through the surrender in 1945. While service histories have covered much of the same ground in separate volumes, no single detailed narrative of General MacArthur's leadership as commander of the Southwest Pacific Area has yet appeared. Chapters dealing with the reconquest of Borneo, plans for the invasion of Japan, and the Japanese surrender make a distinctly new contribution. Volume I Supplement describes the military phase of the occupation through December 1948, reporting events not treated elsewhere in American publications. Volume II on Japanese operations brings together a mass of information on the enemy now only partially available in many separate works. Collectively, the *Reports* should be of wide interest and value to the American people generally, as well as to students of military affairs. They are an illuminating record of momentous events influenced in large measure by a distinguished American soldier.

Washington, D.C.
January 1966

HAROLD K. JOHNSON
General, United States Army
Chief of Staff

FOREWORD TO THE 1994 EDITION

I determined for several reasons to republish General MacArthur's reports to commemorate the fiftieth anniversary of World War II. First, the *Reports of General MacArthur* still stand as a detailed account from MacArthur's perspective of his operations against the Japanese in the Southwest Pacific Area. Second, the *Reports* offer a unique Japanese version of their operations in the Southwest Pacific that remains one of the few English-language descriptions of Imperial Army campaigns during World War II. Third, excellent illustrations, many of them original artwork commissioned for the *Reports*, plus superb maps give these volumes an enduring value for military historians and the American public. Finally, while General MacArthur remains a towering figure in American historiography, the passage of fifty years has dimmed the contributions of the U.S. Army units that first checked the Japanese southward advance in Papua New Guinea, then spearheaded the counteroffensive along the north New Guinea coastline that enabled MacArthur to make good his promise to return to the Philippines. The veterans of these campaigns, both men and women, deserve to be remembered for their contributions to the Nation in its time of greatest peril. These are General MacArthur's *Reports*, but they are also his testament to the American soldiers who served under his command.

Washington, D.C.
31 January 1994

HAROLD W. NELSON
Brigadier General, USA
Chief of Military History

PREFACE

". . . . I have noticed some impatience in the Press based upon the assumption of a so-called soft policy in Japan.

". . . . The first phase of the Occupation was of necessity based upon military considerations which involved the deployment forward of our troops and the disarming and demobilization of the enemy. This was coupled with the paramount consideration of removing former prisoners of war and war internees from the internment camps and evacuating them to their homes.

". . . . When the first phase was completed, the other phases as provided in the surrender terms infallibly followed in a prompt, complete and entire fulfillment of the terms of surrender.

". . . . Economically and industrially, as well as militarily, Japan was exhausted and depleted. Her governmental structure was controlled completely by the occupation forces and was operating only to the extent necessary to prevent social chaos, disease and starvation. . . . ."

DOUGLAS MACARTHUR

TABLE OF CONTENTS

CHAPTER I : PRELUDE TO OCCUPATION

Page

Concept of Operations : " Blacklist " 4

Initial Objectives of Occupation... 10

The Last Days : Capitulation 11

Organization for Occupation 12

Return of Surrender Delegation from Manila........................ 19

Japanese Reactions.. 23

Implementation of Operations " Blacklist " 24

The Eve of Occupation... 25

CHAPTER II : TROOP MOVEMENTS, DISPOSITIONS AND LOCATIONS

The Spearhead.. 28

Triumphal Entry 39

The Occupation Firmly Established 41

Sixth Army Occupation Movements 45

Japanese Reaction to Initial Occupation 47

Eighth Army Occupation is Completed 53

Communications, Procurement and Requisition..................... 55

Year-End Summary 56

The Beginning of the Second Phase 57

Service Unit and Supply Reorganization.............................. 58

British Commonwealth Occupation Force (BCOF) 62

The Occupation Stabilized.. 65

CHAPTER III : THE COMMAND STRUCTURE : AFPAC, FEC AND SCAP

Establishment of AFPAC : Army Forces in the Pacific............ 67

Establishment of SCAP : Supreme Commander or the Allied Powers.. 67

The Far Eastern Commission... 69

The Allied Council for Japan... 69

Organization of General Headquarters, SCAP 71

Functions of General Headquarters, SCAP 73

The Civil (Non-Military) Staff Sections, SCAP..................... 75

Foreign Diplomatic Missions 82

Establishment and Missions of FEC : Far East Command 82

Command Structure of General Headquarters, FEC................. 84

CHAPTER IV: RELIEF OF PRISONERS OF WAR AND INTERNEES

Page

SCAP Directives Regarding Prisoners of War 90

Formation of Recovery Teams 92

Preparation for Air Drops 94

Location and Supply of Prisoner of War Camps 96

Operation "Swift Mercy" 99

Recovered Personnel Section in Action 102

Operations of Medical Teams 109

Procedure Regarding Dead and Missing Prisoners of War 114

Final Processing of Prisoners of War in Manila 115

CHAPTER V: DEMOBILIZATION AND DISARMAMENT OF THE JAPANESE ARMED FORCES

The General Demobilization Program 117

Japanese Plans for Demobilization 120

Demobilization of the Japanese Home Forces 120

Demobilization of Overseas Forces 123

Reorganization of the Demobilization Machinery 126

Progress of Demobilization 127

The Process of Disarmament 134

Surrendered War Materiel: Disposition 136

Methods of Disposal 140

Return of Demilitarized Materiel to the Japanese 142

Disposal of Japanese Fleet Units 143

CHAPTER VI: OVERSEAS REPATRIATION MOVEMENTS

The Task 150

Policies 151

The Plan 151

First Phase: 17 Sep 45—28 Feb 46 152

Second Phase: 1 Mar—15 Jul 46 155

Third Phase: 16 July—31 Dec 46 158

Fourth Phase: 1 Jan 47—31 Dec 48 159

Evacuation of Japanese from South Korea 161

Return of Koreans 164

Pacific Ocean Areas 166

Philippine Islands 168

Ryukyu Islands 169

China Theater 170

Southeast Asia 176

Australian Areas 179

Soviet-Controlled Areas 179

Soviet Indoctrination of PW's 187

Summary: 1945—1948 191

CHAPTER VII: THE EIGHTH ARMY MILITARY GOVERNMENT
    SYSTEM   Page

    Concept of Military Government 194
    Formative Period 198
    Evolution of Organization : 1946—1948 201
    Social Affairs Division 203
    Economic Division 212
    Legal and Government Division 219
    Finance and Civil Property Division 222
    Procurement Demand 227
    General Conclusion 230

CHAPTER VIII: OCCUPATION SECURITY AND INTELLIGENCE
    MEASURES
    Assignment of Responsibilities 231
    Basic Plan for Civil Censorship.........................232
    Evolution of Civil (Occupation) Intelligence............233
        Civil Intelligence Section 233
        Operations Branch 233
        Civil Censorship Detachment 236
        441st Counter Intelligence Corps 241
        Public Safety Division 244
    Security Surveillance and Law Enforcement 254
    Internal Subversion 256
    Repatriation 258
    The Korean Minority Problem 260
    The Japan Communist Party.........................264
    Communist Infiltration of Repatriates 265

CHAPTER IX: AIR AND NAVY COMPONENTS
    Part I—Far East Air Forces : Initial Operations........268
    FEAF : Organization and Missions 270
    Maintenance of the Air Force in Japan 273
    Aerial Mapping and Other Activities 275
    Troop Carrier Aviation and International Air Traffic 275
    FEAF—Present and Future 275
    Part II—U. S. Naval Command in the Far East : Initial Operations 277
    COMNAVJAP : Organization and Missions.........278
    Fleet Activities, Yokosuka and Sasebo 281
    Mine-sweeping Operations 283
    SCAJAP—Merchant Shipping 286
    Repatriation 288
    Suppression of Illegal Traffic 288
    Miscellaneous Naval Activities : 1946—1948 289
EPILOGUE...291

ILLUSTRATIONS

Plate   Page
1   Organization of AFPAC, for " Blacklist " Operation, July 1945   3
2   " Blacklist " :   Concept of Phase I Operations   5
3   " Blacklist " :   Concept of Phase II Operations   8
4   " Blacklist " :   Concept of Phase III Operations   9
5   Senior Commanders of the Occupation Forces 13
6   USN Fleet Commanders at the Beginning of the Occupation........... 15
7   Surrender Negotiations at Manila... 18
8   Surrender Negotiations at Manila... 20
9   " Blacklist " :   Area of Initial Evacuation and Withdrawal of Major
       Japanese Units 22
10 Pre-occupation Party Arrives in Japan 26
11 The Occupation Begins, 30 August 1945...................................... 30
12 MacArthur Takes the Surrender, 2 September 1945 33
13 Surrender Day for the Japanese, 2 September 1945 37
14 Tokyo—The End of the Road, 8 September 1945 40
15 Prefectures of Japan :   The Principal Political Subdivisions............. 43
16 Location of Major Ground Units, 30 September 1945 46
17 Sixth U. S. Army Commander 48
18 GI :   Ambassador of Goodwill 50
19 Location of Major Ground Units, 31 October 1945 54
20 Location of Major Ground Units, 1 January 1946 59
21 The British Commonwealth Occupation Force, March 1946 61
22 Location of Major Ground Units, 6 December 1946 63
23 Organization of GHQ, AFPAC, 6 April 1945............................. 68
24 Area Controlled by SCAP 70
25 The Machinery of the Occupation of Japan from the Far Eastern
       Commission through SCAP to the Japanese People, December 1948.... 72
26 General Headquarters, Supreme Commander for the Allied Powers,
       31 December 1947 77
27 Foreign Diplomatic Missions and Agencies in Japan, September 1948...... 83
28 General Headquarters, Far East Command, December 1947................. 85
29 Territorial Subdivisions, FEC, December 1947 87
30 Senior Allied Commanders Released from Prisoner of War Camps 91
31 Prisoner of War Relief Missions 98
32 Barracks, Omori Prisoner of War Camp, Tokyo, 30 August 1945 101
33 Prisoner of War Camps in Japan, August—September 1945..............103
34 Red Cross Duties, September 1945 107
35 Released Prisoners of War, 5 September 1945 110
36 Organization of First and Second Demobilization Ministries,
       14 June 1946 121

Plate		Page
37	Disposition of Japanese Army Ground Forces in the Homeland at the Time of Capitulation, 18 August 1945	124
38	Japanese Army—Navy Air Dispositions, 15 August 1945	125
39	The Demobilization Organs of the Welfare Ministry, 1 June 1948	128
40	Organization of the Demobilization Board, June 1946—October 1947	129
41	Japanese Coastal Defenses, 18 August 1945	132
42	Japanese Airfields, 15 August 1945	133
43	Scrapping of Japanese Equipment, October 1945	137
44	Disposal of Weapons and Ammunition, October 1945	139
45	Disposal of Weapons and Ammunition, October 1945	141
46	Disposition of Major Japanese Fleet Units, 1 September 1945	144
47	The Japanese Light Cruiser *Ibuki* in Drydock at Sasebo—64 percent Scrapped, 14 March 1947	146
48	Japanese to be Repatriated, August 1945	148
49	Repatriation Begins	153
50	Shanghai to Yokosuka	156
51	Soldiers, Sailors and Displaced Civilians	160
52	Debarkation : Beppu and Uraga	163
53	From Port to Home	167
54	Flotsam of War : Displaced Civilians	171
55	Repatriates from China and Manchuria	175
56	Repatriation Shipping, October 1945—September 1948	177
57	Repatriates from Soviet Territory	180
58	Return to Home and a New Life	182
59	Repatriates from Soviet Prisoner of War Camps, 1949	185
60	Repatriates from Soviet Prisoner of War Camps, 1949	188
61	Japanese Press Expresses Opinion on Soviet Indoctrination of Repatriates, 1949	190
62	Principal Reception Centers and Repatriates Processed, September 1945—December 1948	192
63	Japan's Emperor and the New Democracy	196
64	Disposition of Military Government Units, January 1946	197
65	Organization of Military Government in Japan, July 1948	200
66	Military Government in Japan, January 1946—July 1948	202
67	Functions of Military Government Units in Japan, July 1948	204
68	Modernized Civil Education, March 1946	207
69	Control of Medical Supplies and Distribution of Army Rations	210
70	Rehabilitation of Industry	215
71	Blackmarket and Precious Metals	218
72	Women's Franchise : Milestone of Politics, April 1946	221
73	Field Inspection of Laboratories by Technical Intelligence Detachment, G-2, GHQ, FEC	225

Plate		Page
74	Military Government Team in Action, February 1948	228
75	Organization of Civil (Occupation) Intelligence Division, 15 October 1946	234
76	Censorship, July 1947	237
77	Comment Sheets Disseminated by CCD to User Agencies : Comparison between June 1947 and June 1948	242
78	441st CIC Districts and Field Detachments, 4 October 1948	245
79	Police Training Program, 1948	246
80	Crime Statistics and Police Effectiveness : 1924–1948	248
81	Fuchu Prison, Tokyo : Improvements Made, 1945–1947	250
82	Fire Prevention	252
83	Relationship of Counter Intelligence, Civil Censorship, Military Police and Military Government Detachments, 15 December 1948	253
84	Repatriation Interrogations, August 1948	259
85	Repatriation Interrogations, August 1948	261
86	Analysis of Population, Military and Police Strength by Prefecture, 15 December 1948	266
87	Fifth U. S. Air Force Zones of Responsibility, 1945—1947	269
88	Organization of FEAF Command and Headquarters Staff, 1947	272
89	Occupation Missions—FEAF	274
90	Pacific Military Airways, November 1948	276
91	COMNAVJAP : Task Organization, Task Force 96, 1947	279
92	Fleet Activities, Japan	282
93	Mine Situation in the Western Pacific, 20 February 1946	285
94	Moored and Influence Mines Swept, August 1945—April 1946	287
95	Japanese Newspaper Editorial Summarizes Four Years of Occupation, 1945—1949	292

CHAPTER I
PRELUDE TO OCCUPATION

From Melbourne, five thousand miles away[1] at the bottom of the world, General Mac-Arthur by mid-1945 had smashed his way back to the very outposts of the Japanese homeland itself: Buna, Biak, the Philippine Sea, Leyte—a tremendous itinerary of two and a half years against a fanatically resisting foe.

At the end of June, he paused to assemble his forces, grown from scattered, relatively green American troops[2] and a small but battle-hardened section of Australians, into a mighty concentration of power.[3] On the ground, in the air, and on the sea they were massing for what would be the final drive against the Japanese stronghold, the homeland archipelago.[4]

Enemy resistance was to be pulverized in an invasion drive that would begin in the fall of 1945 and be continued in a second phase in the spring of 1946. Operation "Olympic" would launch an amphibious assault by veteran Sixth Army troops against southern Kyushu to secure the needed beachhead.[5] Tremendous hammer blows by air and sea would soften up the formidable objective before the troops went in. Then, in Operation "Coronet," three corps including eight divisions of the Eighth Army, and two more corps of the First Army would be catapulted into the heart of the Tokyo Plain itself.

It was expected to be costly.[6] The enemy would be fighting in prepared positions. He would be fighting for his home, his family. He had nothing to gain by surrender, everything to lose by defeat.

The much publicized "invincibility" of the Nipponese soldier had been blasted, however, during the long campaign that started over the Kokoda Trail and had now reached a point within easy flight range of Tokyo. He bled and died like any other mortal, but of

---

1 For detailed account of major operations, see Vol. I of this series.

2 At the time of his arrival in Australia in March 1942, General MacArthur found approximately 25,000 American troops, mostly of service classifications, scattered from Western Australia to New Caledonia, a thousand miles east of the Australian mainland.

3 Initially, the Australian 6th Division, less two brigades, and the 7th Division. Both served in the Middle East.

4 GHQ USAFPAC, Opns Instns No. 4, Annex 3, "Troop Lists," 15 Aug 45 (S).

5 Operation "Downfall" was the over-all plan for the final conquest of Japan; "Olympic" was the first sub-division thereof, "Coronet" the second. (1) Rad CX-17032, CINCAFPAC to CINCPOA, 26 May 45. In CofS, GHQ 640 (Navy); (2) Conf of the CinC, USAFPAC and CINCPAC, Held at Manila, P I on 16 May 45. In CofS GHQ 653 (Navy).

6 In recommending courses of action to the War Department as early as April 1945, the CinC had noted that there would be an anticipated deficiency of some 36,000 hospital beds, even counting everything then available in the Pacific, should "Olympic" and "Coronet" be adopted. (Rad (TS) C-14442, CINCAFPAC to WARCOS, 20 Apr 45. In AFPAC 982.)

late it had been found that he would surrender.[7] Could it be that other tales of the seemingly immovable determination of the Japanese people from the lowest coolie to the Emperor himself, likewise had a basis more of propaganda than of fact? In other words, could there be a sudden collapse? Or even a total surrender of the Japanese military forces before the scheduled launching by General MacArthur of that final, costly drive into the very heart of the homeland? Every contingency had to be provided for.

While operations "Olympic" and "Coronet" delineated the vast concept of occupation by force, another plan just as complete and arranged for easy conversion from the basic concepts of "Olympic" and "Coronet," emerged from the Staff planning precincts of General Headquarters: this was Operation "Blacklist," General MacArthur's proposal to meet that other possibility, the sudden collapse or surrender of the Japanese Government and High Command. (Plate No. 1)

Operation "Blacklist" made its official but guarded appearance in top commands in July 1945; actually, it had been in the making since May of that year.[8]

The first edition was published 16 July and was presented four days later at a conference with ranking service representatives of the Pacific Ocean Areas at Guam.[9] General MacArthur based his plans on the assumption that it would be his responsibility to impose surrender terms upon all elements of the Japanese military forces within Japan, and that he would also be responsible for coordinating and enforcing upon the Japanese Government and High Command the demands of Allied commanders in other areas.

Operation "Blacklist" called for the progressive occupation of fourteen major areas in Japan and from three to six areas in Korea so that Allied forces could exert undisputed military, economic, and political control. These operations would employ twenty-two divisions and two regimental combat teams in addition to air and naval elements, utilizing all of the U. S. forces available in the Pacific Theater at the time. Additional forces from outside the theater would be required if occupation duties were to be assumed in Formosa or in China.

Operation "Blacklist" provided for maximum but discreet use of existing Japanese political and military organizations. These agencies still had effective control of the population, and they probably could be employed to advantage by the Allies. If the existing governmental machinery were swept away, the difficulties of control would be enormously multiplied and additional occupation forces would be needed.[10] The language

---

7   Toward the end of the war the Japanese were paying some attention to propaganda leaflets as well as "safe conduct" leaflets issued by FELO, the propaganda agency originally associated with Allied Intelligence Bureau (Vol. V, Int Ser, GHQ, FEC, *Operations of the Allied Translator and Interpreter Section* (R), Doc. App. VII. See also Vol. IV, Int Ser, GHQ, FEC, *Operations of the Allied Intelligence Bureau* (R), Sum of AIB Activ, p. 115.) In addition, between thirteen and fifteen hundred Japanese surrendered en masse July 1945 to the 93d US Division at Morotai when brought into that base by a US Navy escort which had intercepted the Japanese hospital ship *Tishibana Maru* actually loaded with troops and contraband instead of patients.

8   Rad C-15431, CINCAFPAC to AGWAR, 4 May 45. In G-3 GHQ Adm 381/61. GHQ was aware in top secret intelligence channels of current Japanese peace feelers through its embassy in Russia.

9   (1) Later revised. See GHQ USAFPAC, Basic Outline Plan for "Blacklist" Opns (2d ed), 25 Jul 45 (TS); (2) CINCPOA Memo for Record, 23 Jul 45 (TS). In G-3 GHQ Adm 380/6-3 P.

10   (1) GHQ USAFPAC, Basic Outline Plan for "Blacklist" Opns (2d ed), 25 Jul 45 (TS); (2) Rad C-25892 CINCAFPAC to CINCPAC, 16 Jul 45. In GHQ Adm 381/61; (3) Rad C-28793, CINCAFPAC to WARCOS, 27 Jul 45. In CofS GHQ WD 1088.

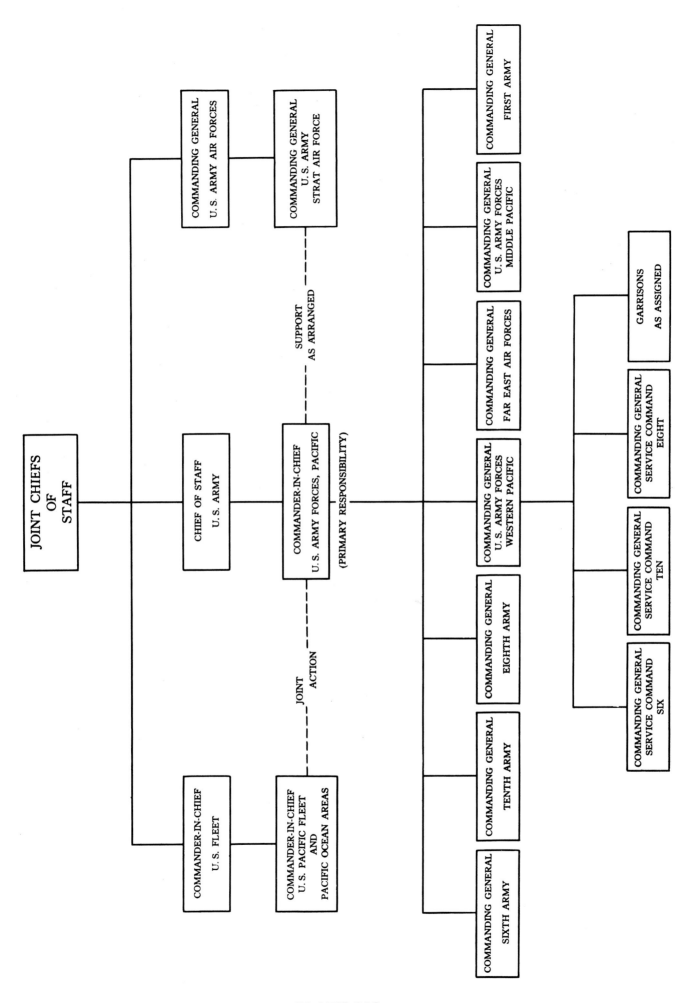

PLATE NO. 1

Organization of U. S. Army Forces, Pacific, for "Blacklist" Operations, July 1945

barrier alone represented an effective bar to administration.

A preliminary directive of the Joint Chiefs of Staff conformed generally to a collateral staff study prepared by Pacific Fleet Headquarters under the code term "Campus".[11] That study provided for entry into Japan by United States Army forces only after the Navy had made an emergency occupation of Tokyo and had completely deployed occupation forces in the principal parts. General MacArthur agreed that immediately after capitulation the United States Fleet should move forward, seize control of Japan's home waters, take positions in critical localities, and begin minesweeping operations, but this was considered to be merely a prelude for landings by strong, coordinated ground and air forces of the Army, prepared to overcome any possible opposition.

General MacArthur considered that naval forces were hardly designed to effect the occupation of an enemy country whose army was still in existence; the occupation should rather proceed along sound tactical lines, with each branch of the service performing its appropriate mission. General MacArthur objected to major reliance on airborne landings because they involved what he considered to be unwarranted hazards. He saw no reason for hasty or rash action. Occupation by a weak force might encourage local opposition, with serious repercussions among the bomb-shattered population.[12] It was estimated that there would be in excess of 1,700,000 regular combat servicemen to be disarmed in Japan proper and more than 3,200,000 civilian defense volunteers. In Korea about 270,000 regulars could be expected, while 35,000 civilian volunteers likewise would have to be disarmed.[13]

Concept of Operations: "Blacklist"

It was a basic policy in "Blacklist" to delegate authority and responsibility to designated army commanders and their corresponding naval task force commanders to the greatest extent consistent with central coordination by General Headquarters. However, the plan left nothing to chance. It could be assumed that at best there would be an attitude of non-cooperation in Japan and at worst, armed resistance in many parts of the main islands, despite such proclamations for the cessation of hostilities as would be required of the Emperor.[14] Consequently, the commitment of forces was stipulated to be sufficient to reduce completely any local opposition, to establish bases at the strategic points outlined, to seize control of the higher echelons of government in both Japan and Korea, and to immobilize the armed forces of Japan. It was planned to organize these strategic centers with utmost speed in order to make them service bases from which air and ground action could be brought to bear wherever the exigencies of the situation might require.

Second priority for occupation would be restricted to strategic points to establish control of remaining major political centers and avenues of sea communications.

A third priority for occupation would be concerned with areas for the establishment of control of food supply and of principal overland and coastwise communications.

---

11   Rad WX-17064/14, JCS to CINCAFPAC and CINCPAC, 14 Jun 45.

12   (1) CINCPAC to CINCPOA, Joint Staff Study "Campus," 9 Aug 45; (2) Rads C-29035 and C-28810, CINCAFPAC to WARCOS, 27 Jul 45.

13   GHQ USAFPAC, Basic Outline Plan for "Blacklist" Opns (3d ed), 8 Aug 45 (TS), p. 4.

14   GHQ USAFPAC, Opns Instns No. 4, Annex 4, Essential Elms of Enemy Info, 15 Aug 45 (S).

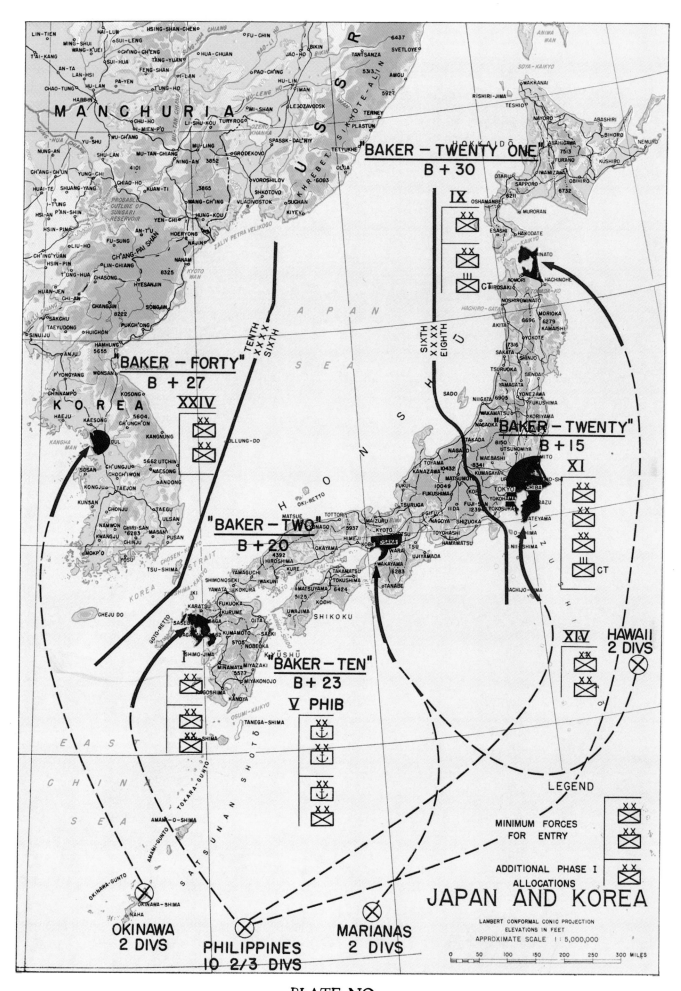

PLATE NO. 2

"Blacklist": Concept of Phase I Operations

Objectives selected for occupation in the three priorities or phases outlined were :[15]

PHASE   I—Kanto Plain, Sasebo—Nagasaki, Ko-
            be—Osaka—Kyoto, Keijo (Korea),
            Aomori—Ominato.
            (Plate No. 2)
PHASE   II—Japan: Shimonoseki—Fukuoka,
            Nagoya, Sapporo (Hok-
            kaido).
      —Korea: Fusan. (Plate No. 3)
PHASE III—Japan: Hiroshima—Kure, Kochi
            (Shikoku), Okayama, Tsu-
            ruga, Otomari, Sendai,
            Niigata.
      —Korea: Gunsan—Zenshu.
            (Plate No. 4)

Additional points under Phases II and III would be occupied by available troops as deemed necessary by army commanders in accomplishment of their missions.

The directed occupations would permit control of the political, economic, and military life of the two countries. The areas designated in Japan included 60 percent of the population, 80 percent of the industrial capacity and 48 percent of the food production. Those in Korea included 39 percent of the population, 18 percent of the industrial capacity, and 44 percent of the food production.

To accomplish Phase I objectives, it was planned in general to use the forces already designated in " Olympic " plus some elements from " Coronet." A total of 644,000 troops were earmarked as available. These included 251,800 of the Sixth Army and 308,700 of the Eighth Army.[16] (Of this total 83,500 were committed for the Korean Occupation.) There also were roughly 62,000 available from the Far East Air Forces (FEAF).[17]

---

15 GHQ USAFPAC, Basic Outline Plan for " Blacklist " Opns (3d ed), 8 Aug 45 (TS), p.8.

16 *Ibid*, Annex 3d (1).

17 Occupation units, target dates and objective areas for Japanese main islands only were as follows:

UNIT	ARMY	TARGET DATE	AREA
Elms XI Corps	Eighth	2 Sep	Tokyo
11th A/B Div	Eighth	15 Sep	Sendai
27th Inf Div	Eighth	3 Sep	Tokyo
1st Cav Div	Eighth	3 Sep	Tokyo
112th Cav RCT	Eighth	3 Sep	Tokyo
Americal Div	Eighth	8 Sep	Tateyama Bay
43d Inf Div	Eighth	13 Sep	Yokohama
Elms XIV Corps	Eighth	15 Sep	Yokohama
Elms IX Corps	Eighth	26 Sep	Hokkaido
77th Inf Div	Eighth	4 Oct	Otaru
81st Inf Div	Eighth	3 Oct	Aomori
158th RCT	Eighth	21 Oct	Yokohama
Elms X Corps	Sixth	3 Oct	Kure
24th Inf Div	Sixth	22 Oct	Kochi & Okayama
41st Inf Div	Sixth	3 Oct	Kure & Hiroshima
Elms V Amphib Corps	Sixth	22 Sep	Sasebo
5th Mar Div	Sixth	22 Sep	Sasebo & Nagasaki
32d Inf Div	Sixth	15 Oct	Fukuoka & Shimonoseki
2d Mar Div	Sixth	26 Sep	Nagasaki
Elms I Corps	Sixth	25 Sep	Osaka
33d Inf Div	Sixth	27 Sep	Kobe & Kyoto
6th Inf Div	Sixth	23 Oct	Osaka or Nagoya
25th Inf Div	Sixth	2 Oct	Nagoya

(From GHQ SCAP Daily Sit Rpt No. 15, 12 Sep 45.)

Operations to accomplish the three phases of occupation constituted the "B" or "Baker" series conducted by the United States Army Forces, Pacific, with individual operations designated by numbers within blocks of twenty assigned each Army concerned, and B-Day designated by the Commander in Chief for the initiation of the operations. "Baker" assignments were: Block 1 to 20, Sixth Army operations; Block 20 to 40, Eighth Army; Block 40 to 60, Tenth Army.[18]

"Baker-Sixty" was the alternate plan for "Baker-Twenty." "Baker-Twenty" required initial amphibious landings by XI Corps in the area of the Tokyo Plain (Kanto), followed by XIV Corps landings in northern Honshu. "Baker-Sixty" called for air landings by the 11th Airborne Division and the 27th Division in the vicinity of Tokyo, followed by XI Corps amphibious landings in the Tokyo Bay area.[19]

Utilization of the total forces at the command of General MacArthur to effect the Occupation was established as follows:[20]

United States Forces

a. *United States Army Forces, Pacific*
   Command of U.S. Army resources in the Pacific. (Except Alaskan Department, USASTAF and Southeast Pacific). Operations of U. S. Army Forces, "Blacklist" operations.
   Command of AFPAC Occupation Forces and imposition of surrender terms in assigned areas of responsibility. Approval of repatriation of Japanese Forces and nationals to
Japan proper. *Theater Command, SWPA.*

1. *Sixth Army*
   Landing forces, Kyushu, Shikoku, and Western Honshu area.
      Operations of Occupation Forces, same area.
      Preparation of Sixth Army elements from Western Pacific.
      Mounting of elements transported under Sixth Army control.

2. *Tenth Army[21]*
   Landing forces, Korea.
      Operations of Occupation Forces, same area.
      Preparation of Tenth Army elements from Western Pacific.
      Mounting of elements transported under Tenth Army control.

3. *Eighth Army*
   Landing forces, Northern Honshu, Hokkaido, Karafuto.[22]
      Operations of Occupation Forces, same area.
      Preparation of Eighth Army elements from Western Pacific.
      Mounting of elements transported under Eighth Army control.

4. *First Army (when available)*
      Preparations for further operations as directed.

5. *Far East Air Forces*
   Land-based air support, "Blacklist" operations.
      Troop carrier operations.
      Preparation of FEAF elements for displacement to Japan and Korea.
      Establishment of FEAF elements in designated locations.

6. *United States Army Forces, Middle Pacific*
      Preparation and mounting of U.S. Army Forces from Middle Pacific for CINCAFPAC as directed.
      Logistic support and administrative control of U. S. Army Forces in Middle Pacific.

---

18 GHQ USAFPAC, Basic Outline Plan for "Blacklist" Opns (2d ed), 25 Jul 45 (TS).

19 The decision to effect extensive landings by the 11th A/B Division was in consequence of General MacArthur's conviction that any show of naval landing strength should be accompanied by similar army forces which eventually would be better prepared and serviced to constitute a permanent occupying force. (Rad C-30508, CINCAFPAC to WARCOS, 3 Aug 45. In CofS GHQ WD 1099.)

20 GHQ USAFPAC, Basic Outline Plan for "Blacklist" Opns (3d ed), 8 Aug 45 (TS), pp. 10-11.

21 Occupation mission subsequently assigned to XXIV Corps.

22 The proposed occupation of southern Sakhalin (Karafuto) was purely speculative since high-level negotiations turning over Sakhalin and the Kuriles to the Soviets were not at that time known to theater commanders. This was one of the famous Yalta concessions.

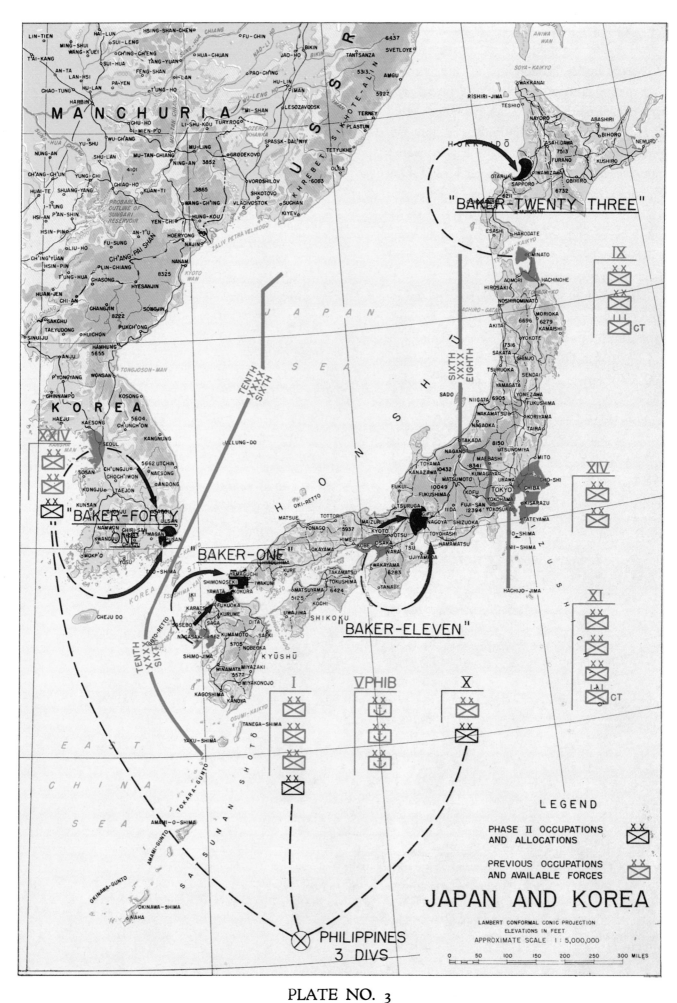

PLATE NO. 3

"Blacklist": Concept of Phase II Operations

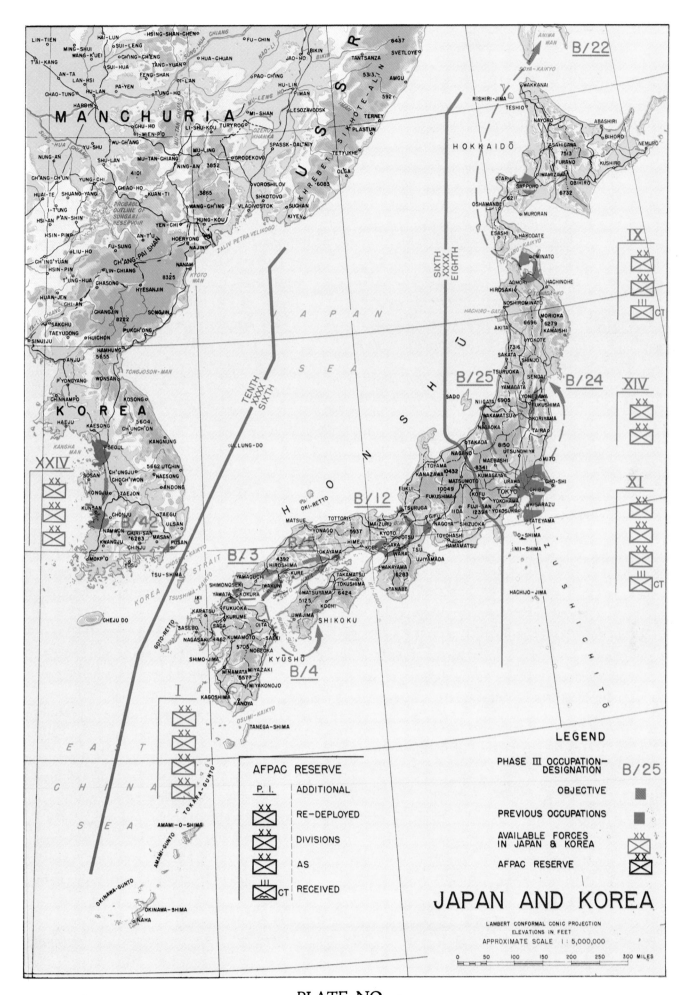

PLATE NO. 4

"Blacklist": Concept of Phase III Operations

7. *United States Army Forces, Western Pacific*
     Logistic support of U. S. Army Forces, Western Pacific.
         Logistic support of "Blacklist" operations.
     U.S. Garrisons, Western Pacific, as directed.
     Preparation and mounting of Base Service elements transported under USAFWESPAC control.
         Disposition of captured Japanese war material as directed.

8. *Naval Forces, SWPA*
     Preparation and mounting of Naval and Marine elements, SWPA, for CINCPAC.

b. *United States Pacific Fleet (as arranged)*
     Naval cover and support, "Blacklist" operations.
     Naval and amphibious phase, "Blacklist" operations, including Sixth, Tenth and Eighth Army operations.
     Preparation and mounting of U.S. Naval and Marine elements from POA.
     Theater Command, POA.

c. *United States Army Strategic Air Force (as arranged)*
     Transport of troops by air as arranged.
     VHB operations.

The Commander in Chief realized that there would need to be a considerable reorganization of AFPAC forces in order to properly strengthen the Occupation spearheads. Plans for such changes were drawn up and were to be announced within a few days.[23]

Initial Objectives of Occupation

The initial primary missons of the Occupation forces were set out as being the disarmament of the Japanese armed forces and the establishment of control of communications.[24]

These initial missions were purely military in character. From that point on, there would inevitably be a progressive fusion of the military with civil and political aspects of the nation which would also become the responsibility of the Commander in Chief. For some months, however, control would probably be direct and rigid. Accordingly, it was designated in the plan that army commanders would have assigned to them certain general and special tasks common to all occupation localities.[25] Under the heading of "General Tasks" the following were outlined:

a. Establishment of control of the armed forces and civil population in areas assigned and imposition thereon of prescribed terms of surrender requiring immediate military action.

b. Preparation for establishment of separate post-war governments and armies of Occupation in Japan Proper and Korea as subsequently directed.

The initial "Special Tasks" envisioned for army commanders were as follows:

a. Destruction of hostile elements which might oppose by military action the imposition of surrender terms upon the Japanese.

b. Disarmament and demobilization of Japanese armed forces and their auxiliaries as rapidly as the situation would permit. Establishment of control of military resources insofar as would be practicable with the means available.

c. Control of the principal routes of coastwise communication, in coordination with naval elements as arranged with the appropriate naval commander.

d. Institution of military government, if required, and the insurance that law and order would be maintained among

---

23 See Ch. III.
24 GHQ USAFPAC, Basic Outline Plan for "Blacklist" Opns (3d ed), 8 Aug 45 (TS), p. 8.
25 *Ibid*, pp. 12-14.

the civilian population. Facilitation of peaceful commerce, particularly that which would contribute to the subsistence, clothing and shelter of the population.

e. Recovery, relief, and repatriation of Allied prisoners of war and civilian internees without delay.

f. The securing and safeguarding of intelligence information of value to the United States and Allied Nations. Arrangement with the U. S. Navy for mutual interchange and unrestricted access by each Service to matters of interest thereto.

g. Suppression of activities of individuals and organizations inimical to the operations of the Occupation forces. Apprehension of war criminals, as directed.

h. Support of elements of the initial Occupation forces in the occupation of subsequent objectives, as directed.

i. Preparation for the imposition of terms of surrender beyond immediate military requirements.

j. Preparation for the extension of control over the Japanese as required to implement policies for post-war occupation and government, when prescribed.

k. Preparation for the transfer of responsibilities to agencies of the post-war governments and armies of occupation, when established.

Army commanders would issue their own detailed orders for the accomplishment of these general and special tasks. The orders would cover such matters as the safeguarding of cap-tured enemy combat materials, including documents, the proper securing of industrial properties against damage, and the preservation of public utilities.[26] It was emphasized that in view of the limited forces which would have to occupy a country of roughly eighty millions, army commanders would make all possible use of Japanese demobilized forces within the bounds of security, and would take all steps to insure that public servants, such as the civil police, railway workers, communication workers, utilities operators and public health officials, not only remained at their tasks but intensified their efforts to insure a continuation of all functions under what was certain to be a period of great stress.[27] It was imperative that discipline should be maintained, both among the armed forces of Japan and the civil population. Accordingly, provisions for enforcing the requirements of the Occupation authorities were made ; these were strictly in accordance with the established rules of land warfare, and were so specified.[28] Looting by Occupation forces and all other forms of violence against the habitants of the country were expressly forbidden.

The Last Days : Capitulation

General Headquarters was prepared to press the final act—occupation by force, or occupation by acquiescence.

Which would it be: Operation " Olympic " or Operation " Blacklist " ?

The possibility of surrender now was openly discussed in the world's capitals. On 27 July the Allied Powers called upon the Japanese

---

26 Operations Instructions No. 4 included specific detailed instructions which envisioned a comprehensive picture of conditions to be found and methods of dealing therewith.

27 Actually, upon entry of US Public Health and Welfare units, it was found to the astonishment of the commanders of these units that there existed no public health plan for Japan; responsibility appeared to be a matter of desultory community interest and action.

28 GHQ USAFPAC, Basic Outline Plan for " Blacklist " Opns (3d ed), 8 Aug 45 (TS), App. IV, Annex 5b, Enforcement of Surrender Terms.

Government through the Potsdam Declaration to cease the struggle, to throw out militarism and to invite the establishment of democratic processes under the direction of an Allied Commander in Chief to be named.

Tokyo was silent and remained silent. Apparently it would be " Olympic."

Then came 0800 of 6 August 1945 and the first atomic bomb unleashed against an inhabited place.[29] Three days later the Union of Soviet Socialist Republics declared war against the staggering empire. On the same day the second atomic bomb was dropped, this time against Nagasaki.

Stunned by these developments, and well aware that continued large-scale resistance would be impossible, the Japanese Government indicated receptiveness to the terms of the Potsdam Declaration.

General MacArthur shifted quickly to meet probable exigencies. He alerted Lt. Gen. Robert L. Eichelberger of the Eighth Army, Gen. Walter Krueger of the Sixth, Gen. Joseph W. Stilwell of the Tenth, and Lt. Gen. John R. Hodge of the XXIV Corps to hold their commands in readiness for the Occupation of Korea and Japan; in other words, to be prepared for the immediate implementation of " Blacklist," as somewhat augmented by a new edition put into the hands of Army commanders early in August.[30]

President Truman announced on 15 August the unconditional surrender by the Japanese Imperial Government. On the same day, General MacArthur was named Supreme Commander for the Allied Powers and was charged with taking all steps he deemed necessary and proper to effectuate the surrender terms with the least practicable delay.[31]

Simultaneously on that date two vital directives emanated from headquarters of the Supreme Commander in Manila. One cancelled Operation "Olympic" and ordered implementation of the initial phases of Operation " Blacklist." The other ordered the Emperor to take immediate effective steps for the cessation of hostilities and for the opening of radio communications between Manila and Tokyo.[32] With regard to the latter, exasperating and suspicious delays occurred and it was some days before a reliable channel was established. As soon as this was done, however, General MacArthur radioed a demand for the dispatch to Manila of a responsible Imperial Mission with full powers to receive details of the terms of surrender and to provide GHQ with pertinent information which would secure the safety of Allied prisoners of war, and eliminate any capability to resist occupation forces.[33]

Organization For Occupation

Simultaneously with the order to implement " Blacklist," SCAP initiated a thorough re-

---

29   For details of these historic days, see SWPA Ser, Vol. I, *The Campaigns of MacArthur in the Pacific.*

30   The final editions of " Blacklist " plan were dated 8 August 1945. The perfected and expanded plan was the product of a war-hardened, cohesive General Staff at the zenith of its efficiency. This would be no haphazard occupation, no " trial and error effort." The Commander in Chief's determination that history would regard the Occupation as an enlightened military effort by a Christian nation to assist rather than destroy a fallen foe, yet do so with firmness, efficiency and dispatch was reflected in the wealth of the directive planning outlined in the various annexes of " Blacklist." Foresight based on critical military studies and research into the customs and reactions of the Japanese was evident in the detailed measures to be taken by all commands in regard to counterintelligence, communications, engineering projects, military government, enforcement of surrender terms, control, disarmament and demobilization of the Japanese armed forces, and care and evacuation of Allied prisoners of war and civilian internees.

31   Rad (TS)WX-49042, WARCOS to CINCAFPAC, 14 Aug 45. In CofS GHQ AFPAC WD 1122 (TS).

32   See Vol. I, this series.

33   Rad Z-501, SCAP to Japanese Emperor, IJG, and IJ GHQ, 15 Aug 45.

Gen. Walter Krueger
Sixth U. S. Army
1943–1946

Lt. Gen. Robert L. Eichelberger
Eighth U. S. Army
1944–1948

Vice Adm. R. M. Griffin
Naval Forces Far East
1946–1948

Gen. Ennis C. Whitehead
Far East Air Forces
1945–1949

PLATE NO. 5
Senior Commanders of the Occupation Forces

organization of AFPAC forces to provide strength where it would be most needed by the Sixth and Eighth Armies and the XXIV Corps (then with the Tenth Army in the Ryukyus).[34]

The 11th Airborne Division had already passed to the control of the Commanding General of the Eighth Army, and had moved by air with full combat equipment from Lipa in Luzon to Okinawa, in a record time of forty-four hours. The Division was preparing to spearhead the invasion forces. Four days later, certain additional adjustments were made. The Eighth Army, which would occupy Japan alone from 28 August to 22 September, was given the IX and XI Corps, in addition to the XIV Corps which it already controlled.[35] The Sixth Army was increased primarily by the addition of the V Amphibious Corps, with its 2d, 3d and 5th Marine Divisions, located in Saipan, Oahu, Guam and Hawaii. General Krueger, Commanding the Sixth Army, also assumed control of the X Corps, the 6th Division from the Eighth Army, and the 98th Division from AFMIDPAC. Simultaneously, control of both these divisions passed to I Corps, already under the Sixth Army.

Control of the XXIV Corps on Okinawa passed from the Tenth Army to AFPAC, because it was to operate independently as the Occupation force in Korea south of the 38° parallel.

The total U. S. land and air forces now available to the Commander in Chief for Occupation operations and all other responsibilities in his area of command were as follows :[36]

(1) Sixth U. S. Army
Gen. Walter Krueger, U. S. Army
I and X Corps and V Amphibious Corps
(Marine)

6th, 24th, 25th, 33d, 41st and 98th Divisions, 2d, 3d and 5th Marine Divisions

(2) Eighth U. S. Army
Lt. Gen. Robert L. Eichelberger, U. S. Army
IX, XI and XIV Corps
27th, 43d, 77th, 81st and American Divisions, 1st Cavalry Division, 11th Airborne Division, 112th Cavalry RCT, 158 Infantry RCT.

(3) XXIV Corps
Lt. Gen. John R. Hodge, U. S. Army
7th, 96th and 40th Divisions.

(4) Tenth U. S. Army
Gen. Joseph W. Stilwell, U. S. Army
As constituted.

(5) First U. S. Army
Gen. Courtney B. Hodges, U. S. Army
As later constituted.

(6) Far East Air Forces
Gen. George C. Kenney, U. S. Army
5th, 7th and 13th Air Forces.

(7) United States Army Forces Middle Pacific
Lt. Gen. Robert C. Richardson, U. S. Army
As constituted.

(8) United States Army Forces Western Pacific
Lt. Gen. Wilhelm D. Styer, U. S. Army
As constituted.

General MacArthur assigned the responsibility for the security of the Ryukyus to ASCOM-I and directed AFWESPAC to assume combat responsibilities in the Southwest Pacific Area. The Commanding General of AFWESPAC established two commands to maintain security in the Philippines : the Luzon Area Command and the Southern Islands Area Command.

A recapitulation as of 15 August of the strength of combat and service troops committed exclusively to the Japan and Korea Occupa-

---

34 GHQ SCAP & USAFPAC, Mo Sum of Opns, Aug 45 (S).

35 Ibid.

36 GHQ USAFPAC, Opns Instns No. 4, 15 Aug 45 (S).

Adm. William F. Halsey
Third U. S. Fleet

Adm. Thomas C. Kinkaid
Seventh U. S. Fleet

Adm. Raymond A. Spruance
Fifth U. S. Fleet

Vice Adm. Frank J. Fletcher
North Pacific Force

PLATE NO. 6
U. S. N. Fleet Commanders at the Beginning of the Occupation

tion operations was as follows : [37]

XXIV Corps :

A.	Combat	62,724	
B.	Service	29,076	
	Total XXIV Corps		91,800

Sixth U. S. Army :

A.	Combat	122,355	
B.	Service	63,551	
C.	V Amphibious	93,522	
	Total Sixth U. S. Army		279,428

Eighth U. S. Army :

A.	Combat	156,691	
B.	Service	90,052	
	Total Eighth U. S. Army		246,743

Far East Air Forces :

A.	XXIV Corps Zone	10,669	
B.	Sixth Army Zone	35,654	
C.	Eighth Army Zone	42,810	
	Total Far East Air Forces		89,133
	Grand total for the operation		707,104

Air Corps units, exclusive of service elements, which might be called upon to sustain the operations either in combat or troop transportation missions and which were located within respective zones of responsibility were as follows : [38]

XXIV Corps : 475th Fighter Groups and one squadron of 317th Troop Carrier Group.

Sixth Army : Eighth and 348th Fighter Groups, the 375th and 443d Troop Carrier Groups and the Second Combat Cargo Group.

Army and Corps commanders were directed to organize Army service commands from troops to be made available to them from organizations envisioned for " Olympic " and " Coronet " operations.[39] The Commanding General of Sixth Army was to establish Army Service Command " O " (from " Olympic ") and General Eichelberger's Eighth Army was to be supplied and serviced by a similar unit, " C " (from " Coronet ").[40]

The Commanding General, AFWESPAC, was directed to release men and materials for these purposes as rapidly as possible.[41]

---

37 GHQ USAFPAC, Opns Instns No. 4, 15 Aug 45 (S), Annex No. 3, Tentative Troop List, Recapitulation, p. 61.

38 *Ibid.*

39 *Ibid*, Annex 5, Logistics.

40 Known as " USASCOM-O " and " USASCOM-C " respectively.

41 The complexity and magnitude of the supply problem was fully appreciated by GHQ. The Logistics Annex of the operations instructions creating USASCOM-O and USASCOM-C stated : " Because of the short time available for purposes of planning and organization logistically, these operations must be accomplished on the basis of availability of troops, materials, supplies, and transportation, rather than fulfilling planned requirements. Service troops are made available to commanders based on their availability at appropriate locations, and materials and supplies designed for support of troops in rear areas and loaded on ships to meet these requirements will be diverted to the occupied areas. As a result, supplies and materials arriving in occupied areas will not be those which would ordinarily be shipped to meet requirements for support of troops and for construction of specific facilities. It will therefore be necessary that commanders take advantage of all existing facilities found in occupied areas and accommodate construction of additional essential facilities to that which can be accomplished with materials located in the areas and those received in diverted shipping. Supplies as received will be unbalanced. Measures will be taken by this headquarters to obtain balanced stockages of supplies in occupied areas at the earliest practicable date. Service troops excess in one category will be employed to meet shortages in other categories. The maximum practicable number of service troops should arrive in the objective areas during the early phases of the Occupation, in order to better meet the needs of combat troops arriving later.

" Troops to be employed in this operation will be mounted with equipment and accompanying supplies which can immediately be made available to them upon announcement of 'B' Day. Commanders responsible for provision of equipment and accompanying supplies will take all possible measures to completely equip in advance all troops designated for these operations and to have available in the vicinity of staging areas accompanying supplies in quantities as indicated. . . . "

The Eighth Army was to lead the Occupation forces into Japan and was directed to execute " Baker 60 ".[42] This called for air landings in the vicinity of Tokyo by the 11th Airborne Division and the 27th Division (if required), followed by IX Corps amphibious landings in the Tokyo Bay area. The seaborne troops for Japan and Korea were scheduled to begin arriving after the formal surrender ceremony aboard the *USS Missouri* in Tokyo Bay, but the airhead would be secured by the 11th Airborne three days before the ceremony. The 27th Division had been alerted for airlift from the Ryukyus. The 4th Marine Regimental Combat Team (the Fleet Landing Force), was to occupy Yokosuka Naval Base, south of Yokohama, at the same time the 11th Airborne units were to establish their positions near Tokyo.[43]

Upon the Fifth Air Force would fall the chief responsibility for the tremendous air movements. To assist the Fifth Air Force, the Strategic Air Force was to release heavy bombers to the operational control of FEAF as requested by the latter. Strategic Air Force was also charged with dropping of food and supplies to prisoners of war and civilian internee camps. The Air Transport Command was to lend the bulk of its carrier planes as requested by FEAF and assigned by FEAF to Fifth Air Force. As aircraft which would carry in Occupation forces were turned around, they would be loaded with repatriated Allied prisoners of war requiring hospitalization. In addition, FEAF was charged with continuing its regular tasks of reconnaissance and photographing of Japan and Korea to facilitate the implementation of " Baker 60". A tentative series of " strategic " flights would be stepped up in frequency and size to constitute a show of force to discourage possible plots

on the part of recalcitrants. These flights would be restricted to critical areas south of 38° north. The U. S. Pacific Fleet was to provide air protection for naval forces, convoys and shipping.

The Thirteenth Air Force was to take over the Philippines area of responsibility, while the Seventh was to support the Tenth U.S. Army operations in the Ryukyus. The RAAF Command would continue to operate in the southern areas, particularly the Netherlands East Indies. Aircraft of the Seventh Fleet as well as Eighty-fifth Fighter Wing of the Air Defense Command would continue to operate in the Philippines area.[44]

The U. S. Pacific Fleet would be charged with the establishment of military government in the Marianas, Bonin, Volcano, Izu, and Kurile Islands and on Marcus Island.[4] At the same time it would have the responsibility for conducting the naval and amphibious phases of the occupation of Japanese territory by the United States Army Forces, Pacific. This would include provision of destroyer station ships along the entire convoy route from Okinawa to Honshu. The Third U.S. Fleet, under command of Admiral William F. Halsey, was to occupy Tokyo Bay and support Eighth Army landings. As has been stated, the *USS Missouri* of the Third Fleet, flying the pennant of Admiral Chester Nimitz, was to become the scene of the formal surrender ceremonies.[46]

The Fifth Fleet, under the command of Admiral Raymond Spruance, was to occupy and patrol sea approaches and coastal waters of Japan west of 135 degrees. Eventually it was to land elements of the Sixth Army in Kyushu, Shikoku, and western Honshu.[47]

The Seventh Fleet, under command of Admiral Thomas C. Kinkaid, was to be held to

42 Alternate plan for " Baker 20."
43 See n. 19.
44 Allied Hq, SWPA, Opns Instns No. 97, 22 Aug 45.

45 GHQ USAFPAC, Opns Instns No. 4, 15 Aug 45 (S).
46 GHQ SCAP & USAFPAC, Mo Sum of Opns, Sep 45 (S).
47 *Ibid.*

The Japanese delegation arrives at Nichols Field, 19 August 1945.

Col. S. Mashbir, Chief, Allied Translator and Interpreter Service (ATIS),
G-2, acts as interpreter during a pre-conference interval.

PLATE NO. 7
Surrender Negotiations at Manila

assist in staging, training, and mounting troops for the control of the coastal waters of China and Korea.[48]

The North Pacific Force, under Vice Admiral Frank J. Fletcher, was to be loaned for minesweeping operations between Honshu and Hokkaido.[49]

As had been the practice throughout the war in the Pacific, units of the British Commonwealth naval strength, particularly Australian ships which had distinguished themselves by their splendid war record with the American fleets, would be included in these critical Occupation operations.

Return of Surrender Delegation from Manila

Details for initial moves for the Occupation of Japan were outlined to the Imperial delegates which had arrived at Manila 19 August and had been in session with GHQ staff officers that and the succeeding day.[50] When they departed again for Tokyo, they carried with them four documents which outlined the requirements laid down by SCAP for the spearhead of occupation, for the formal surrender ceremonies, and for the subsequent reception of Occupation forces.[51]

In these documents SCAP stated that the acceptance of the surrender of the Japanese armed forces would occur in Tokyo Bay aboard a United States battleship on 31 August. To prepare for this, he indicated that an advance party would arrive by air at Atsugi airdrome near Tokyo, that United States Navy forces would arrive in Sagami Bay, immediately south of Tokyo Bay, and that naval forces would advance into Tokyo Bay. These movements were set for 26 August. Airborne forces accompanying the Supreme Commander were expected to land at Atsugi 28 August while, simultaneously, naval and marine forces were to land in the vicinity of Yokosuka Naval Base. The landing and establishing of airborne and naval forces would continue during the two days prior to the surrender ceremony.

The second document concerned the advance landing party and its point of entry. It specified that the immediate area surrounding the city of Tokyo was defined as the " Tokyo Bay Area."[52] This area comprised the region from Choshi north of Kumagawa, east of Ishioka, and southeast to Choshi. The boundary across the harbor entrance included the island of Nishima. Within the Tokyo Bay Area the portion from Otsuki eastward along the southern city limit line and extending across the Bay to Chiba and south of Amatsu, was defined as the " Area of Initial Evacuation." (Plate

---

48 *Ibid.*

49 *Ibid.*

50 This mission was lead by Lt Gen T. Kawabe, who had become Vice Chief of the General Staff in April. There were fifteen other members. They were met at Nichols Field by Maj Gen Charles A. Willoughby, ACofS, G-2, acting for SCAP, and Col Sydney F. Mashbir of Allied Translator and Interpreter Section, one of G-2's important subsidiary organizations which was to play a vital part in the conferences. For a complete report of these events see Vol. I, this series.

51 General title was: " Requirements of the Supreme Commander for the Allied Powers Presented to the Japanese Representatives at Manila, P. I., 19 Aug 45 ". The specific titles of the documents were (1) " Orientation, Agenda, and Requirements ", (2) " Requirements for Entry and Operations of an Advance Party Representing the Supreme Commander for the Allied Powers within the Tokyo Bay Area," (3) " Requirements for the Entry of the Supreme Commander for the Allied Powers and His Accompanying Forces," and (4) " Requirements for Entry and Operations of Initial Occupation Forces in Kanoya Area of Southern Kyushu ".

52 GHQ SCAP, Requirements of SCAP presented to the Japanese Representatives at Manila, P I, 19 Aug 45, Sec. II, " Requirements for Entry and Opns of an Adv Party Representing SCAP within the Tokyo Bay Area."

Conference for terms of Surrender opens. L to R, on the Japanese side, Capt. H. Yoshida, Capt. T. Ohmae, Rear Adm. I. Yokoyama, Lt. Gen. T. Kawabe, Mr. K. Okazaki, Maj. Gen. M. Amano, and Lt. Col. M. Matsuda; on the American side, Maj. Gen. L. J. Whitlock, Maj. Gen. R. J. Marshall, Rear Adm. F. P. Sherman, Lt. Gen. R. K. Sutherland, Maj. Gen. S. J. Chamberlin, Maj. Gen. C. A. Willoughby and Brig. Gen. D. R. Hutchinson.

Escorted by General Willoughby, the Japanese delegation arrives for conference. Ranking American officers await: Brig. Gen. D. R. Hutchinson, Maj. Gen. S. J. Chamberlin, Maj. Gen. R. K. Sutherland, and Rear Adm. F. P. Sherman, representing Admiral Nimitz.

PLATE NO. 8
Surrender Negotiations at Manila

No. 9)

The advance party would make preparations for the entry of the Supreme Commander and his accompanying airborne and naval forces into the Area of Initial Evacuation. The Japanese Imperial General Headquarters would be required to acknowledge to the Supreme Commander by 25 August safe conduct for the advance party which was to consist of about 150 persons, transported in planes with standard U. S. markings. This party was scheduled to land at Atsugi airfield. The Japanese would be required to provide for the following: security and preservation from harm of personnel, airplanes and equipment of the party while in the Area of Initial Evacuation; provision of every courtesy and facility to members of the party in the accomplishment of their mission; provision for suitable quarters and a police escort to insure absolute safety for each member of the party; the services of senior officers from the Japanese Army Air Headquarters, the Naval Air Headquarters, and the Japanese Army and Naval Headquarters, available to the commander of the advance party upon his arrival at Atsugi and prepared to provide such information as might be required as to facilities in the Area of Initial Evacuation; free communication by radio between the advance party and the Supreme Commander for the Allied Powers in Manila.

The Japanese Imperial General Headquarters was to evacuate all combatant units of the Japanese armed forces from the Atsugi airfield area, with the exception of civil police, which were to be maintained as necessary to prevent overt acts. The airdrome was to be in full operational condition. Notification would be required prior to 25 August as to the identity and frequency of the radio station in the Tokyo area with which the advance party could com-

municate in flight concerning time of arrival, landing instructions and other matters relating to the arrival of the party.

The third document, in addition to providing for the immobilizing and disarming of Japanese naval and air force units and installations, required provision for the safety of the United Nations prisoners of war and civilian internees pending the arrival of Occupation forces.[53] Camps were to be marked to enable Allied aircraft to identify them. The Yokosuka Naval Base was to be ready for occupation by 27 August. All combatant units of the Japanese armed forces were to be evacuated from the Area of Initial Evacuation and confined to the limits of their assigned bivouacs, with the exception of civil police; measures were to be guaranteed for the provision of adequate accommodations, billet and camp area facilities and utilities in the Area of Initial Occupation for the Supreme Commander and his accompanying forces.

It was directed that on the date scheduled for the arrival of General MacArthur in Japan, members of the Imperial General Staff would be available for conference with representatives of the Supreme Commander at Atsugi airfield upon arrival, and at such times and places thereafter as might be directed for the prompt settlement of all matters requiring attention. Guides and interpreters familiar with the Area of Initial Evacuation would be available.

General measures to be taken by 25 August by the forces of the Allied Powers were announced as follows: Allied aircraft would conduct daylight and night surveillance flights over Japan and Japanese controlled areas; Allied aircraft would drop supplies to the United Nations prisoner of war and internee camps; naval forces would occupy the coastal waters of

---

53 *Ibid*, Sec. III, " Requirements for the Entry of SCAP and His Accompanying Forces."

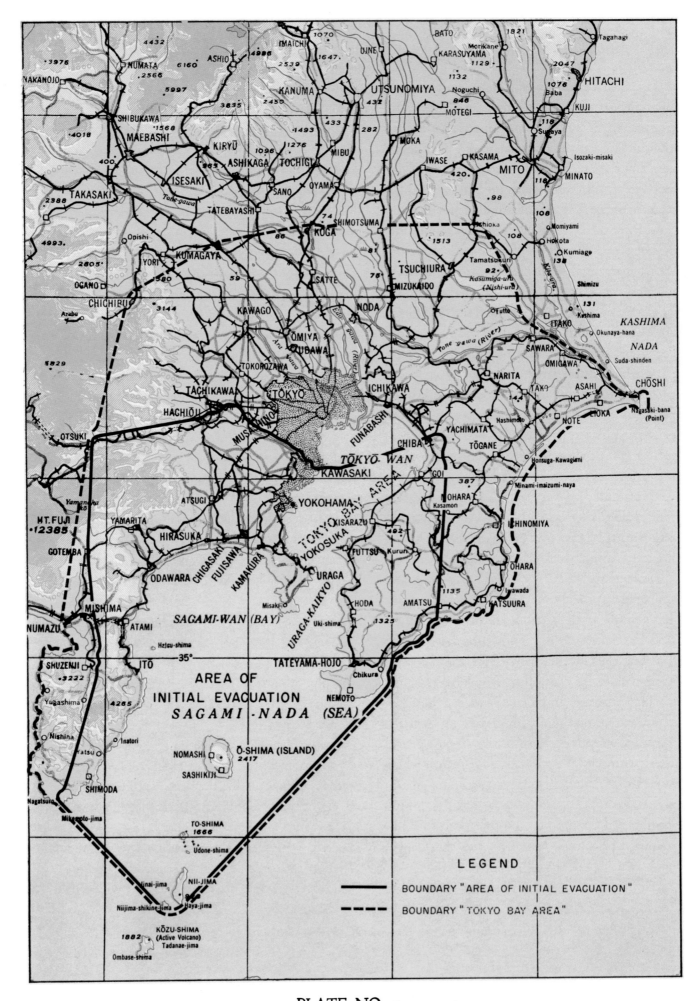

PLATE NO. 9

"Blacklist": Area of Initial Evacuation and Withdrawal of Major Japanese Units

Japan and Japanese controlled areas. Minesweeping operations by Allied naval forces were scheduled to be initiated in the ports of Osaka, Sasebo, Nagasaki, Takasu, Jinsen, Tsingtao, Canton, Shanghai, Hongkong, and Singapore. In these prescribed duties, the Allied forces would be unmolested.

The fourth document concerned the initial Occupation forces in the Kanoya Area of southern Kyushu.[54] It stipulated that an advance party, representing General Headquarters, would enter the area 1 September to prepare for the entry into the "Kanoya Area" of seaborne and airborne initial forces on the next day. The Japanese Imperial General Headquarters was directed to provide, by noon 30 August, guarantee of full security for entry into the Kanoya area of this advance party, consisting of twenty personnel, transported in two airplanes bearing standard U.S. markings. Exact time of arrival would be communicated to Kanoya radio station by direct message from the planes in flight. Ranking members of Japanese staffs were to hold themselves in readiness for conferences with high ranking American officers landing at Kanoya airfield.

Japanese Reactions

The return to Tokyo of the Manila envoys was delayed when one of the planes carrying the principals experienced engine trouble and had to be "ditched." The pilot was able to beach the plane so that, although all passengers were shaken up, none was hurt. It required most of the night, however, to arrange transportation to Tokyo and this interval was marked by considerable anxiety.[55] Prime Minister Prince Higashi Kuni sat up all night wondering "whe-

ther 'our invigorated *Tokko Tai*' (air attack units) had shot them down." If he was glad to hear that both planes were safe, he was far happier to learn that General MacArthur's terms for his nation were not so severe as he had feared.[56]

Higashi Kuni promptly took General Kawabe to the palace to make "a very minute report." According to Higashi Kuni, "The Emperor was quite relieved."[57]

General MacArthur's humane and considerate occupation policies unquestionably took Japan by complete surprise.[58] A *Domei* broadcast, 18 August, stating that the Allies had no intention of confiscating private property, reassured Japanese who had feared that Americans would follow the Japanese policy of looting civilian goods.

Immediately following the Emperor's surrender proclamation, officials of the Agriculture-Commerce Ministry and the Chief of the Tokyo Economics Board estimated that Japan's food supplies would be entirely dislocated because of expected heavy food requisitions by Occupation forces. *Yomiuri-Hochi* warned that the food requirements of the "tens of thousands" of Occupation troops would have a "great effect upon our present and future livelihood."[59]

When Japanese armies invaded foreign lands, the conquered populations, despite their poverty, had been expected to furnish not only full but even luxurious provisions for the invaders. Japan consequently looked upon General MacArthur as the precursor of a truly enlightened civilization.

Confidence in General MacArthur's justice went far toward reassuring Japanese who still credited pure wartime propaganda rumors.[60]

54 *Ibid*, Sec. IV, " Requirements for the Entry and Opns of Initial Occupation Forces in the Kanoya Area of Southern Kyushu."
55 Rad (S) 15 & 16, IJG to SCAP, 21 Aug 45.
56 Higashi Kuni, *My Memoirs* (Tohoshobo, 1947).
57 *Ibid*.
58 *Ibid*.
59 Tokyo, *Yomiuri-Hochi*, 18 Aug 45.
60 *Tokyo Shimbun*, 17 Sep 45.

Tokyo Shimbun, among others, deplored that wild gossip swept Japan. Of this kind *Yomiuri* reported : ....*within three days after surrender Tokyo citizens feared that :*

American soldiers would loot Japan.
Americans would rob Japan of all the food.
Women and girls would be violated.
All men would be killed.
What was left of Tokyo would be devastated.[61]

The American decision to reserve all Japanese food resources for the Japanese people and to supply the Occupation forces and their dependents with foodstuffs brought from America therefore produced a profound, completely unexpected, and highly favorable impression.[62]

During the next few days, while Japanese people were attempting to adjust their thinking to this new concept of enemy occupation, the weather became unfavorable and a series of typhoons lashed the home islands ; nevertheless, the people heard the drone of Allied aircraft overhead and from force of habit ran to their air raid shelters. There were no bombs ; instead, this was the beginning of the air force missions to drop relief supplies of food, medicine and clothing to the wretched Allied prisoners of war and civilians interned in camps in Japan. The missions continued despite extremely unfavorable weather which became sufficiently adverse to delay the implementation of " Blacklist " by forty-eight hours.

Implementation of Operations : " Blacklist "

General Eichelberger had moved his Eighth Army Command Post from the eastern coastal plain of Leyte to Okinawa on 26 August. On Okinawa both the 11th Airborne and the 27th Division were stalled on the scheduled airlift to Japan by the succession of typhoons.

All available troop transports of the Far East Air Force and dozens of the huge " Skytrains " and " Skymasters " of the Pacific Air Transport Command had been mobilized at Okinawa for this mammoth air operation—the greatest aerial movement during the Pacific war. The initial target date was officially postponed from 26 August to 28 August because of the adverse weather.[63]

Then the weather cleared and a cool, refreshing breeze, "very refreshing to the spirit," blew over the Kanto Plain.[64]

At Atsugi airfield near Tokyo, Japanese planes sat helplessly stripped of their propellers. A picked detachment of the Naval Security Corps, armed with clubs, guarded the Atsugi airfield where Lt. Gen. Seizo Arisue, Lt. Gen. Senichi Kamada, Captain Chuzaburo Yamazumi and Ken Tsurumi of the Foreign Office awaited the arrival of the American advance forces.

The heralds of that advance force, American Corsairs and Grummans, had appeared with the dawn of that historic day and continued to fly in strong formations over the entire Tokyo Bay and Atsugi area.

The first American formations flying from Okinawa were not expected until 0900, but half an hour earlier a twin-engined aircraft appeared in the skies from the south. It was a C-46 transport. The plane circled the field and then came in from the south to touch down upon the center runway at 0828. This plane was followed by fifteen others.[65]

From the leading plane debarked Colonel

---

61   Tokyo, *Yomiuri*, 19 Aug 45.
62   Higashi Kuni, *op cit.*
63   GHQ SCAP & USAFPAC, Mo Sum of Opns, Sep 45 (S).
64   Tokyo, *Yomiuri*, 29 Aug 45.
65   Maj Gen Seizo Arisue, in charge of the preparation of Atsugi airfield, reported in his unpublished " Memoirs of Atsugi " that for " some strange reason " this aircraft and the following ones came in downwind despite the fact that the Japanese had painstakingly erected an air sock for their guidance. The Americans probably preferred to take their chances with a slightly unfavorable wind than to nose helplessly into some prepared Japanese armoured trap.

Charles P. Tench, GSC, of the G-3 Section of GHQ, commanding the advance party.[66] Waiting automobiles conveyed Colonel Tench and party to the Japanese reception group.

General Arisue stiffly saluted Colonel Tench and, after introductions, the group entered a tent in the center of the field. General Arisue offered food, but Colonel Tench who had brought his own rations, declined with thanks.

Colonel Tench explained that his party consisted of approximately 150 officers and men and that their directive from the Supreme Commander was divided into four main divisions. It was as follows:

a. Reconnaissance of the Atsugi airdrome area to determine its suitability for the airborne operation to follow.

b. Establishment of required air installations and supplies to support initial phases of the air operations in the area as provided by the Commanding General, FEAF.

c. Supervision and coordination of improvements required at the Atsugi airdrome.

d. Establishment of communications with GHQ, AFPAC, without delay and reporting on suitability or non-suitability of the Atsugi airdrome for the purpose intended. All messages to be transmitted in code. Reporting over signal communications net additional information desired by the Commanding General, FEAF.

While this initial conference took place, soldiers debouched from the planes coming to earth every few moments, unloaded jeeps, and prepared to form exploratory parties. Colonel Hutchinson, who had been assigned as billeting officer, led the first of these on an inspection of the former Sagamigahara Air Unit barracks at the west end of the airfield. It was proposed by the Japanese that this barracks should serve as accommodations for the advance party. Other inspection teams immediately deployed over the entire airfield area.

A second flight of fifteen C-54's, C-46's, and C-47's arrived at 0935 and a third group of fifteen C-54's landed at 1100. These planes, carrying a total of 30 officers and 120 men wearing regular combat equipment were escorted by ten carrier-based Seventh Fleet F6F liaison planes flying from Sagami Bay.

The Japanese were amazed by the efficiency with which these Grumman fighters, landing on the grass, folded their wings " like cicadas," even while the planes were taxied into position.[67] The Japanese made no attempt to conceal the degree to which they were impressed by the speed with which the Americans motorized themselves and invested the entire field area. Their amazement was outspoken when within forty-five minutes after the leading planes had touched down, portable Signal Corps transmitters were on the air establishing communications with Okinawa. The last planes of the party brought fuel, lubricants, and maintenance equipment to make the intrepid little unit compact and self-sustaining until the anticipated arrival on 30 August of the main airborne force which would constitute the first of the Occupation troops for Japan.

The Eve of Occupation

While the air lift of the main initial force was in progress on 30 August, GHQ, AFPAC, issued an amendment to Operations Instruc-

---

66 Col Tench was followed by his immediate staff comprising Capt C. B. Jones, USN, Col E. K. Warburton, 5th AF, Cols C. R. Hutchinson and D. M. Dunne, CE, Cols S. S. Auchincloss and L. Park, SigC, and Maj F. Bowers, ATIS interpreter.

67 Tokyo, *Asahi Shimbun*, 29, 31 Aug 45; *Mainichi Shimbun*, 29 Aug 45.

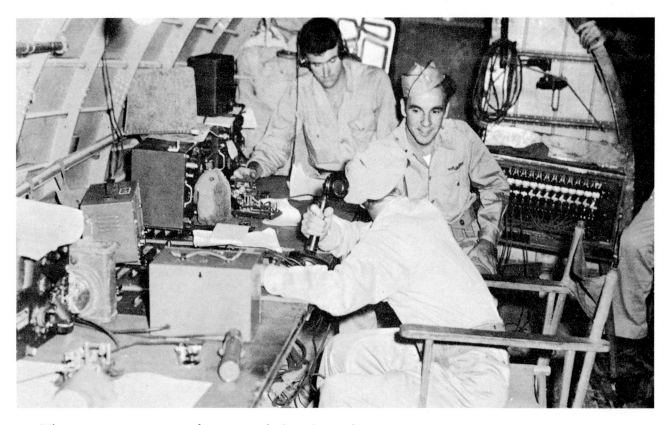

This communications plane served for three days as the only means of communication between the advance party at Atsugi and headquarters on Okinawa and in Manila.

The advance party at Atsugi Airfield, 28 August 1945.   Col. Charles P. Tench is met by Lt. Gen. Seizo Arisue.

PLATE NO. 10
Pre-occupation Party Arrives in Japan

tions No. 4, which materially altered the missions assigned to the Army commanders who soon would be arriving on the Nippon homeland. Instead of actually instituting "military government," Army commanders were to supervise the execution of the policies relative to government functions which GHQ, AFPAC, was to issue directly to the Japanese Government;[68] likewise the functions of the Armies with respect to the disarmament and demobilization of the Japanese armed forces were changed from "operational control" and direction to "supervision of the execution" of orders, as transmitted to the Japanese by GHQ, AFPAC. In contrast to the original concept the headquarters of the Japanese Government and its armed forces were required to shoulder the chief administrative and operational burden of disarmament and demobilization. The new plan was designed to avoid possible incidents which might result in a renewed conflict; no seizures or disarmaments were to be made by Allied personnel.[69]

Actually, with the arrival of the advance party, the toe-hold of occupation had been established. But less than 200 men with light weapons could hardly be described as constituting an occupation force in a country where three to four million soldiers of all classifications were still under arms, and as far as the Americans knew, were only precariously held in discipline by the proclamations of one man—the Emperor.

It was imperative that every effort be made to insure the early and safe arrival of the 11th Airborne force of some seven thousand men. An inspection of Atsugi revealed the necessity for the immediate construction of landing strips long enough to accommodate B-29s and C-54s which would be landing in rapid succession once the movement had started. Only one night could be devoted to this construction work involving strips one and one-half kilometers in length. Under the supervision of the small American force, the Japanese workmen recruited by the indefatigable General Arisue became efficient to a degree apparently never before experienced by the Japanese officers.[70] With the break of dawn, the work was near enough to completion to enable the advance party to signal GHQ at Manila for relay to Okinawa that everything was in readiness for the initiation of the real Occupation of Japan—the first by a foreign army in the recorded history of that nation.[71]

---

68   GHQ USAFPAC, Opns Instns No. 4, 15 Aug 45 (S), Amendment No. 12, Doc. App. IV. This type of military government is known as "passive" as contrasted to the "active" type introduced in Germany.

69   G-2, GHQ, was charged with the development and surveillance of plans for the demobilization and disarmament of the Imperial Forces, in view of expert knowledge of the internal structure of the Japanese Army. The first step was to be the abolition of the Imperial General Staff but the cautious retention of the Army and Navy Ministries which were Z of I agencies. (See Ch. II, p. 42.)

70   In his informal "Memoirs of Atsugi," General Arisue states: "I may say that through this all from the first to the final building of the runway, as long as I have been in the Army, I have never had to use my head and body for so long to such a great extent."

71   The communications unit established for this purpose actually was installed in the command plane in which Col Tench had arrived.

CHAPTER II

TROOP MOVEMENTS, DISPOSITIONS, AND LOCATIONS

The Spearhead

While the advance party secured Atsugi airstrip and made arrangements for the landing of additional troops, the 11th Airborne Division on Okinawa prepared itself for airlift to Japan. Its first echelon began landing at Atsugi early on the morning of 30 August, and troop and cargo-carrying aircraft continued to arrive at three-minute intervals throughout the day.

Immediately upon his arrival, Maj. Gen. Joseph M. Swing, Commander of the Division, conferred with Lieutenant General Arisue, making final arrangements for the arrival of General Eichelberger and later, General MacArthur.[1]

Simultaneously with the development of this airhead at Atsugi, elements of the Third Fleet anchored in Sagami Bay supported the landing of the 4th Regimental Combat Team of the 6th Marine Division at Yokosuka. The First and Second Carrier Task Forces (Task Forces 39 and 38) patrolled the coastal waters of the Empire, prepared to make a show of force

if necessary.[2] Forts and shore batteries on Futsu-saki, a narrow spit jutting out from the eastern shore into Uraga Strait, were occupied by small landing parties.[3] The main Fleet landing party went inland and established headquarters at Yokosuka Naval Base. While United States forces were securing these important points in the Area of Initial Evacuation, not a shot was fired, although the Marines, like their airborne counterparts at Atsugi, took no chances and were ready for immediate combat should there be the slightest attempt at deception by the Japanese. It soon became apparent that the Japanese had meticulously followed the requirements stipulated in Manila.[4] The area had been cleared of all military personnel except for a small detachment which policed and guarded the area. Coastal defenses and antiaircraft had been demilitarized and were marked with white flags which were visible for some miles. Courteous Japanese officers and guides were available for further instructions.[5]

In the missions outlined in "Blacklist," Eighth Army was assigned responsibility for occupying the Tokyo Bay area.[6] Therefore,

---

1   HQ Eighth US Army, G-3 Periodic Rpts, 29–30 Aug 45.

2   TF 38 and 39 covered both the amphibious and Atsugi air landings. (GHQ SWPA & USAFPAC, Mo Sum of Opns, Aug 45 [S], Naval Sum, p. 6.)

3   Occupational Monogr of the Eighth US Army in Japan, Vol. I, Aug 45 —Jan 46 (C), p. 17.   US and British flags were raised at 0100.

4   Since Japanese chains of command were still intact, the requirements of the CinC as laid down in Manila were implemented through them. Accordingly, specific directives to the Japanese armed forces in the Initial Evacuation Area were contained in a series of orders as follows : Imp GHQ, Army Sec Ord No. 1387, 21 Aug 45 ; Imp GHQ, Navy Sec Ord No. 52, 21 Aug 45, Dir No. 533, 22 Aug 45, Dir Nos. 534, 535, 536, 23 Aug 45, and Dir No. 538, 24 Aug 45.

5   Occupational Monogr of the Eighth US Army in Japan, Vol. I, Aug 45—Jan 46 (C), p. 17.

6   GHQ USAFPAC, Basic Outline Plan for "Blacklist" Opns (3d ed), 8 Aug 45 (TS).

upon landing at Yokosuka, the Marine forces came under the command of General Eichelberger. Hardly had the Marines established themselves when an infantry patrol from the 11th Airborne arrived from Atsugi to effect contact. The liaison patrol was from the 511th Parachute Infantry of the 11th Airborne, a unit which, after landing at Atsugi, had moved eastward to secure the Yokohama dock area in preparation for large scale amphibious landings in that vicinity.

Throughout the morning and early afternoon of 30 August the big transport planes continued to arrive in steady succession at Atsugi. When General Eichelberger arrived approximately six hours after the first troops, his paratroopers sent up a great shout of welcome. He waved back to them saying, " This is the beachhead where I was supposed to land in the invasion of Japan. General MacArthur gave me this area. I certainly never expected to get here by plane without a shot being fired."[7] General Swing briefly reviewed the situation for him and introduced General Arisue. They discussed plans for the reception of General MacArthur and his party expected later that afternoon. General Arisue suggested that he act as guide, but the Eighth Army Commander directed him to proceed at once along the proposed route to check security measures and then to remain in Yokohama.[8]

Near the adminstration building on the far side of the Atsugi airfield, some anxious-to-please Japanese armed guards were saluting every American who passed within yards of them. Meanwhile, regiments of the 11th Airborne were establishing their headquarters near the airfield. Units of the forward echelons of GHQ and Headquarters, Fifth Air Force, were arriving by plane and were loading equipment to be used for an operating headquarters into the nondescript trucks which the Japanese had assembled. " Manpower " was as important as " horsepower," as one after another of the worn-out vehicles broke down on the road between Atsugi and Yokohama. For the first time, the occupying forces could see for themselves to what straits the Japanese nation had been reduced by the prolonged and exhausting war.

Shortly before 1400 there was a stir of excitement. A strong contingent of newspapermen, photographers, and newscasters swarmed to witness the arrival of the Supreme Commander. As the General stepped from the plane he was greeted by Generals Eichelberger and Swing and cheering veterans of the 11th Airborne Division to whom he said : " Melbourne to Tokyo was a long road but this looks like the payoff."[9]

General MacArthur paused only a few moments at the airfield, then stepped into a

---

7 As General Eichelberger alighted, a sergeant of the 187th Para-glider Infantry turned to one of his men and was heard to say : " Do you know when the last time I saw that Joe was ? We were the lead battalion walking up the road to Tagaytay Ridge last February. We were hurrying to take Manila from the south. I looked over my shoulder and there was this big guy wearing a helmet with three stars. A few of the boys were talking to him, so I eased over too. He's a swell egg. All of a sudden this jeep comes wheeling up the road. It was General Swing. He stood up and yelled at us, " Hey—break it up—disperse—keep moving—let's go. What's the matter with you men ? There are Jap snipers all over the place.' We kind of broke up a little and there was Eichelberger standing there grinning, so he yells back ' that's the idea, Joe, that's the spirit, good advice, keep them scattered.' Yeh, I still think with a couple of breaks we could have been sleeping in the Manila Hotel by the time the 1st Cav hit town." (Occupational Monogr of the Eighth US Army in Japan, Vol. I, Aug 45—Jan 46 [C], p. 18.)

8 General MacArthur had ordered that there be no formal Japanese reception party. Gen Arisue was designated as liaison officer, between the US headquarters and the remnant Japanese staffs.

9 GHQ SWPA & USAFPAC, Mo Sum of Opns (S), Aug 45, p. 12.

General R. L. Eichelberger, at right, with Maj. Gen. J. M. Swing, Commander, 11th Airborne Division, receives the report of Japanese officers at Atsugi airfield, during the initial landings.

General Eichelberger greets General MacArthur at Atsugi airfield.

PLATE NO. 11
The Occupation Begins, 30 August 1945

waiting automobile to go on to Yokohama where temporary General Headquarters were being established. General Arisue had assured General Swing that requirements presented to the Japanese emissaries in Manila had been fulfilled and the route was safe.[10] The fifteen miles of roadway between the airfield and the New Grand Hotel were lined with thousands of armed Japanese soldiers and policemen. They stood at attention but faced away from the road, an additional security measure which was customarily used only for the movements of the Japanese Imperial family. In spite of these elaborate preparations, the Americans took no chances. The Honor Guard Company of the 3d Battalion, 188th Para-glider Infantry, had taken the precaution of guarding the entire length of the Atsugi—Yokohama road.

Units of the forward echelon of GHQ managed to move most of their equipment to the Yokohama Customs House for the establishment of GHQ. But before unpacking was thoroughly under way, orders were given to unpack only the essentials needed to carry on for a few days. It was General MacArthur's intention to move his staff and his headquarters to the capital itself as soon as reports had been received on suitable sites for billets and offices. Eighth Army Headquarters staff likewise set up a temporary arrangement preparatory to moving into the Customs House which it was to occupy when GHQ transferred to Tokyo.

By the end of the day, 4,200 troops and 123 planes had completed the move from Okinawa.[11] Weary troopers dropped their gear in assigned areas and the rattle of mess

kits replaced all other sounds. It was a peaceful sound and one which few men of the 11th Airborne Division had expected would characterize their descent upon the home soil of Japan.

At the New Grand Hotel the Supreme Commander had his evening meal in the company of news correspondents and his ranking generals. It was a democratic gathering and the meal was a simple one—hamburgers and grapes.[12]

The weather turned against the Occupation plans during the night. Okinawa dispatched only eight airloads for Atsugi airfield; nevertheless, this lift was sufficient to bring forward the remaining elements of the 511th Parachute Infantry, and the regiment was able to establish its command post that day in Yokohama. There were now more than 2,000 occupation troops within the confines of the city.

In spite of the bad weather, ground operations continued. Patrols ranged out to Asano and Yokohama docks, through the bombed industrial city of Kawasaki and up to the Tama River on the outskirts of Tokyo. No incidents were reported. The 187th and 188th Para-glider Infantry Regiments dispatched men to scout the Hayama—Misaki area (guarding the entrance to Tokyo Bay) and west along Sagami Bay as far as Odawara.[13] They reported these areas completely cleared. Everywhere women and children ran into hiding, while men and boys saluted and bowed at the approach of the paratroopers. There was no sign whatever of civil disturbance or Japanese resistance. During the afternoon a reinforced company from the Third Fleet Landing Force occupied Tateyama Naval Air Sta-

---

10 Requirements of SCAP Presented to Japanese Representatives at Manila, PI, 20 Aug 45, Doc II, Requirements for Entry and Opns of an Adv Party Representing SCAP within the Tokyo Bay Area.

11 Occupational Monogr of the Eighth US Army in Japan, Vol. I, Aug 45—Jan 46 (C), p. 20.

12 Personal notes of Carl Mydans, correspondent, *Time* and *Life* magazines.

13 Occupational Monogr of the Eighth US Army in Japan, Vol. I, Aug 45—Jan 46 (C), p. 20.

tion on the east side of Tokyo Bay. It was anticipated that this area would be occupied by the 112th Regimental Combat Team. To prepare for this, the Marine unit planned a reconnaissance of the whole area on the following day.

The first airshift of occupation troops within Japan took place on 1 September. The reconnaissance troop of the 11th Airborne Division was transported by plane across Tokyo Bay and to Kisarazu airfield where it secured both the field and surrounding installations.[14] Meanwhile, the 1st Cavalry Division and 112th Cavalry RCT, under the XI Corps, arrived in Sagami Bay and prepared to land the 1st Cavalry at Yokohama on 2 September, and the RCT at Tateyama (Chiba Peninsula) on 3 September.[15]

The Japanese had been repeatedly told through official communiques during the course of the war that American naval strength had been reduced to impotency. Consequently, the tremendous collection of seapower anchored in Tokyo Bay in preparation for the official surrender ceremonies must have been a shocking and sobering sight.[16] By evening preparations were complete for the ceremonies which were to take place at 0900, 2 September 1945, aboard the USS *Missouri*.

Occupation operations did not pause even for that historic event. An umbrella of 400 B-29's and more than 1500 fleet carrier planes circled above the bay. At the same time, while the surrender document was being signed aboard the battleship,[17] Task Force 33 arrived in Tokyo Bay with the first elements of XI Corps. By noon the leading elements of this force, which was under the command of Maj. Gen. William C. Chase, began to debark. Approximately 3,000 men were landed and by early evening the convoy to the assigned divisional assembly areas of Hara-Machida had begun. The 112th Cavalry RCT also arrived with the leading elements of XI Corps but remained afloat until the following morning.[18]

That historic day witnessed numerous other developments of vital importance to the Occupation. Immediately after the signing of the surrender document, the Supreme Commander issued Military and Naval General Order Number 1 to the Japanese. It was based upon the "United States Initial Post Surrender Policy for Japan"[19] and confirmed the general

14 *Ibid*, p. 21.

15 HQ XI Corps FO 23 had provided for alternate landings for the 12th Cavalry, one on Sagami Bay beaches, and the other at Yokohama docks. Since the docks were found to be in good repair, the unit was ordered to prepare for landing there.

16 The first US ship to enter Yokohama harbor was USAHS *Marigold*, carrying the 42nd General Hospital. Included with the concentration of US warships were the British battleships *Duke of York* and *King George V* and two Australian cruisers accompanied by two destroyers. (HQ Eighth US Army, CWS Hist Rpt, Mil Occupation of Japan through Nov 45, pp. 12—13.)

17 The actual signing by General MacArthur occurred at 0908 and four minutes earlier by the Japanese representatives. (GHQ SWPA & USAFPAC, Mo Sum of Opns [S], Sep 45, p. 2.)

18 Occupational Monogr of the Eighth US Army in Japan, Vol. I, Aug 45—Jan 46 (C), p. 29.

19 This policy, which had concurrence of the State Department, had been announced by the President and given wide circulation throughout the world, (GHQ USAFPAC PRO Release No. 227, 23 Sep 45.) It specified that the ultimate objectives of the Post Surrender Policy were to insure that Japan would not again become a menace to the peace and security of the world, and to bring about the eventual establishment of a responsible government which would respect the rights of other states and would support the objectives of the US as reflected in the ideals and principles of the charter of the United Nations. Democratic processes would be instituted in determining the type of government the Japanese desired and the ideals of a democratic social and political order would be promulgated. The document specified that there would be military occupation to destroy despotic power in the land, disarm the country, free prisoners of war and internees, and carry out all such other operations as SCAP might direct. (See Ch. III for organization and operations of SCAP.) The Japanese people would be expected to comply completely with a program of announced regimentation in order to effect a rehabilitation of the economic structure of the land so that the population would be able to maintain itself within a reasonable time. This clause was to come into prominence later when certain of the Allied Powers challenged the right of SCAP to forbid strikes by government employees engaged in such vital fields as transportation and other public utilities upon which the day-to-day welfare of the people directly depended.

Japanese Delegation, headed by Foreign Minister Shigemitsu and
General Umezu, on board *USS Missouri* in Tokyo Bay.

General MacArthur takes position before a microphone as the Japanese general signs
the Surrender Document. In the rear of the Supreme Commander stands Lt. Gen.
Jonathan Wainwright, defender of Corregidor until its fall in May 1942.

PLATE NO. 12
MacArthur takes the Surrender, 2 September 1945

requirements which had been outlined to the Japanese emissaries at Manila two weeks previously. The order called upon the Imperial General Headquarters "... by direction of the Emperor and pursuant to the surrender to the Supreme Commander for the Allied Powers...", to order the Japanese forces to surrender themselves and their arms to designated representatives of SCAP in various parts of the Pacific Theater and China.[20] The Japanese police force was initially exempted from the general disarmament and was ordered to remain on duty for the preservation of law and order, for which it would be held responsible. The Japanese Government was directed to provide detailed information about the armed and economic resources of the country. The safety and well-being of prisoners of war and civilian internees was specifically demanded and all pertinent records were required immediately. The Japanese were to be prepared to deliver all such persons to Allied authorities.

To permit maximum concentration upon the immediate occupation problems in the Japanese main islands and Korea, responsibility for implementation of surrender and subsequent operations in all other Pacific areas was considered outside the province of SCAP. The following commands were dissolved: Allied Land Forces, Allied Naval Forces, and Allied Air Forces. For surrender purposes the British Empire assumed control of certain portions of the Southwest Pacific Area, the Netherlands East Indies, and Australian and New Zealand Forces in the East Indies, south of the Philippines and Manus Island.

Immediately after the surrender ceremonies were concluded, Eighth Army Headquarters authorized the dispatch of several "mercy teams," organized in early August for the recovery of Allied prisoners of war and internees. These units landed at Atsugi on 30 August and established themselves in Yokohama, impatiently awaiting the order which would permit them to fan out rapidly through the surrounding areas to begin their work.[21]

In order to avoid incidents which might develop from operations of these teams and to insure that the Japanese population would quickly learn precisely what was expected of them, GHQ, SCAP, did not depend solely upon General Order Number 1. People were informed directly through existing newspaper and radio facilities.[22] This action was also expected to serve as an automatic and effective check against the recurrence of militaristic or ultra-nationalistic propaganda. After screening by the Counter Intelligence Corps, civilian personnel recommended by the Japanese as being trustworthy and pro-democratic in their beliefs were retained to assist in dissemination of news and information from GHQ. Initially *Domei* and *Joho Kyoku* news agencies and the Japan Broadcasting Corporation were utilized and administered by GHQ.[23] Orders were issued that all Japanese outbound international

---

20 In developing the general agenda of the surrender negotiations in Manila, G-2/G-3 had already laid the groundwork for the demobilization of the Japanese forces in the Home Islands, which represented the major immediate problem for the Occupation.

21 Occupational Monogr of the Eighth US Army in Japan, Vol. I, Aug 45—Jan 46 (C), p. 21. Actually Navy units had "jumped the gun" (Halsey) in the matter of recovering PW's. For a detailed account of these activities and all others associated with the recovery of prisoners of war see Ch. IV. The Monograph quoted above credits Eighth Army with recovering a total of 23,985 persons.

22 This action was in keeping with a policy jointly concurred in by State, War, and Navy Departments as well as by the OWI, and radioed to SCAP a week previously. (Rad W-52702, WARCOS to CINCAFPAC, 22 Aug 45.)

23 *Ibid.*

news services to unoccupied areas would originate from Tokyo. GHQ, SCAP, would authorize through its established agencies the use of all world news and pictures published or broadcast in Japan. News releases would be supplied by the Office of War Information in continental United States. Japanese radio stations picked up OWI broadcasts directly from San Francisco, Hawaii, Saipan, and Manila.[24]

Japanese radio and newspapers might freely use news originating within Japan provided:[25]

1. Nothing was disseminated prejudicial to public order and safety, including criticism of surrender terms and Allied control measures.

2. No suggestion was imparted of disunity in Allied Powers policy toward Japan.

3. No praise or pity was expressed for Japanese taken into custody by Allied authority.[26]

4. No promises were attributed to Allied Power, excepting basis of direct textual quotations from official documents reported without comment or interpretation.

5. Files of all publications were maintained for Allied inspection.

It was decided also that motion picture shows would be temporarily suspended pending review by censorship authorities.[27]

Eighth Army assumed responsibility for the Area of Initial Evacuation but functioned through the Japanese Government. The task of allocating areas, facilities, and equipment to occupation agencies was also placed under its jurisdiction. The only exceptions to this arrangement were the Yokosuka Naval and Air Bases which were assigned to the Navy. Boundaries were later fixed by agreement between the Eighth Army and the Navy. The Eighth Army Commander allocated the Atsugi airdrome and surrounding territory to the Far East Air Forces, and made available to General Headquarters those facilities requested through its representatives.

On 30 August GHQ, AFPAC, issued an amendment to the last operations instructions. This amendment materially altered the missions assigned to the Army commanders. Instead of actually instituting " military government," Army commanders were to supervise the execution of the policies relative to government functions which GHQ, AFPAC, was to issue directly to the Japanese Government.[28] Likewise, the functions of the armies with respect to the disarmament and demobilization of the Japanese armed forces were changed from operational control and direction to supervision of the execution of orders, as transmitted to the Japanese forces by GHQ, AFPAC. In contrast to the original concept, the Japanese Government and its armed forces were required to shoulder the chief administrative and operational burden of disarmament and demobilization.[29] The new plan was designed to avoid possible incidents which might result in spo-

---

24 *Ibid.*

25 *Ibid.* News releases were subject to mild censorship through CCD (Civil Censorship Detachment), an operating agency of the theater G-2.

26 The fact of seizure could be reported.

27 (1) See Ch. VIII. (2) GHQ FEC, Int Ser, Vol. VIII, *Operations of the Counter Intelligence Corps in SWPA and Occupied Japan* (S), and Vol. IX, *The Civil Intelligence Section: Occupation Phase, 1945–48* (S). This series was distributed to Service schools primarily.

28 GHQ USAFPAC, Opns Instns No. 4, Aug 45 (S), Amendment 12.

29 G-2 GHQ was charged with the development and surveillance of plans for the demobilization and disarmament of the Imperial Forces, in view of expert knowledge of the internal structure of the Japanese Army. The first step to be taken was to abolish the Imperial General Staff but to retain (with qualifications) the Army and Navy Ministries which were essentially Zone of Interior administrative agencies and demilitarize them progressively, as required.

radic conflict.

On 3 September, GHQ, SCAP, issued Directive Number 2.[30] It was a comprehensive document, the basic authority for the Occupation of Japan by Allied Forces. Among its numerous provisions was an order to the Japanese Imperial Government and the Japanese Imperial Headquarters, to comply with all the outlined requirements, to assure prompt and orderly establishment of the Occupation forces, and to establish specific controls over disarmament and demobilization of Japanese armed forces.[31]

To facilitate the Occupation of Japan by the two United States Armies, this Directive specified that the boundaries of the First Japanese Army (Group) would be adjusted to coincide with those of the Eighth U.S. Army. Similarly, the boundaries of the Second Japanese Army (Group) would coincide with those of the Sixth U.S. Army. As specified by the Directive, the Commanding General of the First Japanese Army (Group) reported to General Eichelberger for instructions. General Eichelberger directed him to notify all Japanese military commanders and civilian officials that, beginning with 6 September, they could expect United States reconnaissance parties to travel throughout their areas. Following this, the occupying troops would move in. Seventy-two hours' advance notice of a reconnaissance party's arrival in a particular area and forty-eight hours' notice of the movement of troops would be given. These detailed arrangements would permit the Japanese commanders to disarm their units prior to arrival of occupation forces and to restrict them to barracks or camp areas, thus reducing the possibility of any clashes.

The Commanding General of the Second Japanese Army (Group) reported to the Sixth U.S. Army Commander. At the same time, a senior representative of the Chief, Japanese Imperial Naval General Staff, reported to a designated naval representative for instructions covering the entry of United States naval forces into Japanese and Korean waters and naval establishments.

The 112th Cavalry Regimental Combat Team landed at 0930 on 3 September near Tateyama Bay naval air station and established control over coastal defenses. Immediate contact was made with the 11th Airborne Division reconnaissance troop which was patrolling north to Chiba and south to Tateyama. Control of the 112th Cavalry RCT passed to the 11th Airborne Division.

Four years of bitter warfare had taught the American soldier that appearances where Japanese were concerned could be fatally deceptive. As patrols pushed out to the Yokohama—Tateyama area, carbines were ready and faces were grim, despite the fact that Japanese men and boys continued to salute respectfully. Here is what an official situation report had to say of the period:[32]

No hostile military or civilian action during period as 112th RCT landed Tateyama where 1,600 armed troops were reported: Jap Army, Navy and State Dept officials met our forces and agreed to stipulation of the surrender. 11th A/B Div and Fleet Landing Force continued to patrol area of responsibility with no reported unusual incidents. CIC Detachment and Japanese Civil Police completed investigation of 2 Jap civilians found dead vicinity Grand Hotel, Yokohama, 1 Sep. Japanese Police satisfied deaths not result any American action.

---

30   See Ch. V.

31   G-2 was charged with the GHQ staff supervision of plans and execution as developed by the Japanese authorities, in regard to demobilization and disarmament of the Imperial Forces in Japan. G-3 and US Navy took over repatriation movements of contingents abroad. See Ch. V.

32   GHQ USAFPAC, G-2 Daily Sum, No. 1, 5 Sep 45 (S), p. 1.

Prayers at the Imperial Palace.

Prayers at Yasukuni Shrine, Tokyo.

PLATE NO. 13
Surrender Day for the Japanese, 2 September 1945

The next day witnessed an event unique in Japanese political history. While troops continued to unload in Tokyo Bay, an emergency session of the Diet was called to hear the Emperor's address and Prime Minister Prince Naruhiko Higashi-Kuni's explanation of the developments which led to the Imperial decision to surrender. The Emperor's opening address to the Diet was significant. It was the first time he gave direct orders to his subjects. The address was lucid and free of ambiguous terms. Previously, the Imperial rescript had merely stated acceptance of the Potsdam declaration. The people knew only that the instrument of surrender had been signed by representatives of the Emperor. Now the Emperor told them in person that, in his desire to improve Japan's difficult position, he had ordered capitulation. Thus, even in defeat, the unique traditional relationship of the " Emperor-head of the Japanese Nation-family " had been preserved. Peaceable fulfillment of Allied demands could mean continuation of this relationship. At the same time, it was hinted that this privilege might be lost if the Allied demands were not peaceably fulfilled. The Emperor ordered the people to abide by the terms of surrender and to work toward regaining the trust and faith of the world. He stressed the need for coolness, self-discipline, and assistance to soldier's families and others who suffered as a result of the war. To the Japanese this was a clear directive to work in peace, an indication that a new chapter in the life of the nation was beginning. It is interesting to note that although the term " surrender " was not used in the Imperial address, it occurred frequently in the local press.[33]

While the Emperor was addressing the Japanese people, Lt. Gen. Charles P. Hall's XI Corps Headquarters finished unloading and opened in Yokohama. The 8th Cavalry Regiment (1st Cavalry Division) passed to control of the Commanding General, XI Corps, and relieved the 11th Airborne Division of guard duty on the perimeter along the inner Yokohama Canal and at vital installations in Yokohama proper.[34] The 12th Cavalry Regiment moved to the Tachikawa area, west of Tokyo, and occupied Chofu, Yokota, Showa, and Tachikawa airfields, completing United States control of all important airfields on the Kanto Plain.[35] Meanwhile, elements of the 11th Airborne continued to arrive at Atsugi despite unfavorable weather. Service troops of the Far East Air Forces and the first battalion of the 127th Infantry (32d Division) landed at the Kanoya airdrome on 4 September. They occupied the area south of Tokyo.[36] On 5 September, reconnaissance parties from the XI Corps and 1st Cavalry Division penetrated Tokyo in preparation for the main movement of troops planned for 8 September. The 1st Cavalry Division thus claimed to be the first unit in Tokyo.

The weather continued to be unfavorable and the remaining elements of the 11th Airborne on Okinawa were forced to postpone departure for Atsugi until the following day. On 6 September the 11th Airborne closed at Okinawa. No casualties had been reported in the movement of the 11th Airborne between Okinawa and Atsugi, but fifty-nine men had been killed and nine seriously injured in crashes

---

33 GHQ USAFPAC, G-2 Daily Sum, Sep 45 (S).

34 HQ Eighth US Army, G-3 Periodic Rpt, 2–3 Sep 45.

35 Occupational Monogr of the Eighth US Army in Japan, Vol. I, Aug 45—Jan 46 (C), p. 30.

36 GHQ SCAP & USAFPAC, Mo Sum of Opns, Sep 45 (S), p. 3. The 32d Division was assigned to Sixth Army which was not yet scheduled for occupation movements. The Division was still in the Philippines; the 127th Infantry thus became the first Sixth Army combat unit to enter Japan.

between Luzon and Okinawa.[37] Troop carrier planes began moving elements of the 27th Division.[38] By evening of 7 September the air movement of the 27th Division from Okinawa to Atsugi had assumed sizeable proportions. Approximately 25 percent of the strength of the 105th Infantry Regiment had arrived. The forward command post of the Division closed at Okinawa and opened at Hiratsuka.

Triumphal Entry

The initial landing at Atsugi was the first occupation of Japanese soil by American troops. However, the event which was to symbolize the real defeat of Japan was the entry of the Supreme Commander and his forces into Tokyo, the final step on a long trail.

At 0800 on 8 September a motor convoy left the assembly area of 1st Cavalry Division at Hara-Machida and turned toward Tokyo. Among other vehicles was a jeep which carried General Chase, the Division Commander. Unfortunately for all those of the Division who had so thoroughly earned the right to be "first" in Tokyo, the bulk of the Division was carrying out occupation duties and not many units could be spared for the mission. Only the band, the second squadron of the 7th Cavalry Regiment, the 302d Cavalry Reconnaissance Troop, and one veteran representing each of the other non-participating troops were included for the formal entry.

North and east the convoy sped. The cavalrymen moved through pine-covered hills, pock-marked with caves dug by the Japanese. They passed through Hachioji, almost obliterated by United States air attacks. Only scattered corrugated metal shacks, some steel and concrete safes and vaults, a few tall stacks, and forlorn, fire-blackened ruins remained of what had been a thriving industrial city of 60,000 people. Along the Chofu Highway Japanese children waved, shouted, bowed or saluted. It was difficult to believe that this occasion emblematized conquest. The convoy seemed more like a triumphant parade of troops returning home to receive the victor's plaudits.[39]

The cavalcade halted at the city limits. General Chase alighted from his jeep and stepped across the line. As soon as he was seated again in his jeep, the convoy resumed its movement. The U.S. Army was in Tokyo.[40]

A few hours later, at a simple ceremony in front of the American Embassy, General MacArthur gave the following order to General Eichelberger: "Have our country's flag unfurled and in the Tokyo sun let it wave in its full glory, as a symbol of hope for the oppressed and as a harbinger of victory for the right."[41] The guard of honor presented arms and the officers saluted, as the Stars and Stripes waved over Tokyo, Japan's capital city—humbled, charred, and flattened in defeat.

The Commanding General, XI Corps became responsible for the city of Tokyo, a task delayed for several days to allow the Japanese to disarm the troops within the capital. During the day, the 2d Cavalry Brigade Headquarters and the 7th Cavalry Regiment moved to Tokyo, establishing their bivouac area on the Yoyogi Parade Ground adjacent to the Meiji Inner Shrine. Elements of the 132d Infantry of the Americal Division had arrived at Yokohama,

---

37 GHQ USAFPAC, G-2 Daily Sum, No. 5, 9 Sep 45 (S).
38 Occupational Monogr of the Eighth US Army in Japan, Vol. I, Aug 40—Jan 46 (C), p. 30.
39 *Ibid*, pp. 30–32.
40 *Ibid*.
41 *Ibid*.

General MacArthur with Maj. Gen. Wm. C. Chase, followed by Admiral Wm. F. Halsey and Lt. Gen. R. L. Eichelberger enter the American Embassy grounds, Tokyo, for the official raising of the American flag.

Salute to the flag in the American Embassy grounds.

PLATE NO. 14
Tokyo—The End of the Road, 8 September 1945

and were en route to their assembly area two miles southwest of Hara-Machida.[42]

The 187th Para-glider Infantry of the 11th Airborne Division continued to guard Atsugi airfield and vicinity and relieved elements of the 1st Cavalry Division at Hara-Machida Military Academy and Ordnance School. During the course of guard duty around the field an incident occurred which was initially thought to be the first clash with Japanese civilians. Approximately 100 men attempted to loot warehouses at the northeast corner of the airfield. Troops of the 187th broke up the attempt and arrested three persons. Another resisted arrest and was killed. An immediate investigation revealed that the offenders were not Japanese but Koreans.[43]

The Occupation Firmly Established

With the United States troops in Tokyo, the Occupation became an accepted fact to the Japanese people. There were no hostile or subversive moments, only a curious interest on the part of all classes of Japanese as new units moved through the streets of Yokohama and Tokyo. The Japanese press in general maintained an attitude which was almost that of a host.

With the exception of the 8th and 12th Cavalry RCT's, on security duty in the Yokohama—Tachikawa area, remaining units of the 1st Cavalry moved from Hara-Machida into Tokyo on 9 September.

The Americal Division continued its debarkation during 9 and 10 September and established its command post northwest of Hara-Machida. Nearly all of the division artillery was established in the Yokohama area, while more than 60 percent of the 164th Infantry was billeted in the vicinity of Tachikawa.

Good weather had favored large-scale air movements from Okinawa and seventy-four planes arrived at Atsugi carrying personnel and equipment of the 27th Division. The regimental headquarters of the 105th Infantry had been established at Odawara and rail transportation had been marshalled for the movement of the incoming troops on 10 September.[44] On the same day Task Force 35, bearing Eighth Army representatives, entered Katsuyama Bay on the Uraga Peninsula east of Tokyo, and a landing was made at Katsuura. Considerable army and navy equipment was found in good condition and no incidents were reported.

By 10 September primary security duties were taken over by the Americal Division which, with the exception of a battalion of the 164th Infantry, had completed unloading and moving from the docks. Elements of the Division relieved 1st Cavalry units on duty in Tachikawa and Chofu airfield areas and in the Yokohama area. At Hara-Machida the 182d Infantry of the Americal Division replaced elements of the 11th Airborne which was to be transferred to Sendai. Soon thereafter the advance party of the 11th Airborne departed for Sendai. The air movement of the 27th Division from Okinawa went on without interruption during the day, while the 105th Infantry, which had arrived earlier, moved by rail from Atsugi to Odawara. Meanwhile the 106th opened a temporary command post at Zama.

At the initiation of G-2, SCAP directed that the Imperial General Headquarters should be

---

42 *Ibid*, p. 32.

43 HQ Eighth US Army, G-3 Periodic Rpt No. 10, 9 Sep 45 (R).

44 *Ibid*.

dissolved not later than 13 September.[45] It had served its immediate purpose. The pattern of the Occupation in the Initial Evacuation Area, as outlined in the original surrender documents, was assuming definite shape. The Eighth Army, charged with execution of General Order Number 2, was ready to expand its area of operations. Radiation movements of several subordinate units were carried out:[46] (1) XIV Corps landed at Sendai on 15 September and opened its headquarters on the 18th; (2) 11th Airborne and 27th Divisions transferred control of and responsibility for their current assigned areas to XI Corps; (3) 11th Airborne Division began rail and motor movement to Sendai on 14 September, occupied Miyagi Prefecture and opened its command post on 1 October at Sendai; (4) control of both divisions passed to XIV Corps; (5) farther north, the 81st Division, IX Corps, landed in the Aomori area on 27 September; (6) elements of the 77th Division landed on 15 October at Otaru and secured the city with its port facilities, occupied Sapporo, and as troops became available, extended control throughout the island of Hokkaido.[47]

In the same order were included a number of other instructions generally in keeping with the prudent policy of avoiding friction. Among them were discreet reminders to commanders that the moves were still operational in character. It directed that all units be continuously in a state of combat readiness. Each commander charged with initial occupation of an area was directed to dispatch a reconnaissance party at least forty-eight hours in advance for verification of Japanese compliance with existing directives. No subordinate commander was allowed to issue directives to the Japanese military authorities. He submitted his request to Eighth Army Headquarters for specific instructions, which were then sent from that headquarters to the Japanese. Considerable attention was given to dress, conduct, discipline, and military courtesy of the troops. All commanders were ordered to take positive steps to protect shrines, objects of art, historic and religious monuments; Imperial residences and buildings; and all embassies, consulates, and buildings belonging to any of the United Nations.[48]

Nearly all of the 1st Cavalry Division was established in Tokyo by 13 September. On 14 September, the final plane load of 27th Division troops arrived at Atsugi. Elements of the 43rd Infantry Division moved to Kumagaya, northwest of Tokyo. The Eighth Army's area of responsibility was extended by CINCAFPAC to include the entire prefecture of Nagano. Patrols by the newly-arrived 27th Division were operating in the Hadano area. The same day, elements of Headquarters XIV Corps began unloading in the Sendai area. XI Corps was informed by Eighth Army that its area of responsibility would include the prefectures of Chiba, Ibaraki, Tochigi, Saitama, Tokyo, Gumma, Nagano, Yamanashi, and Kanagawa (excluding the Yokosuka Naval Base).[49] (Plate No. 15)

During the period 17–20 September, expan-

---

45 SCAPIN 17, 10 Sep 45. This measure indicated the close G-2 surveillance of general policy matters connected with the demobilization of the Japanese Armed Forces. The Japanese General Staff was an operational entity for strategic decisions; it was not required for the administrative processes of repatriation, demobilization and disarmament: such matters were within the purview of the Ministries of War and Navy which were retained temporarily.

46 Occupational Monogr of the Eighth US Army in Japan, Vol. I, Aug 45—Jan 46 (C), p. 38.

47 *Ibid.*

48 *Ibid*, pp. 38–39.

49 *Ibid*, p. 39.

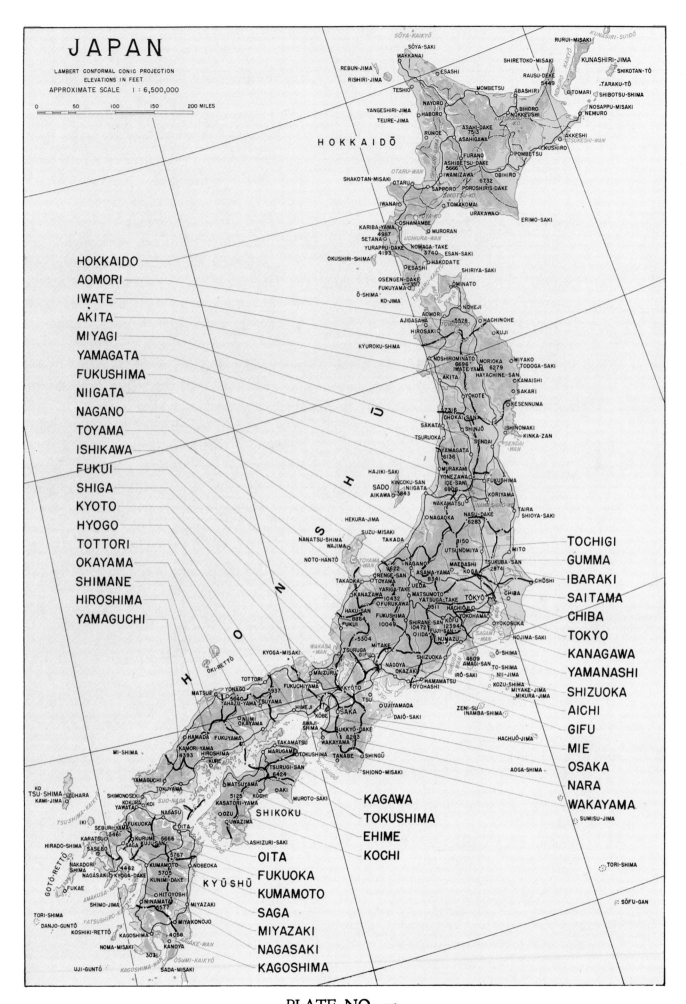

JAPAN

LAMBERT CONFORMAL CONIC PROJECTION
ELEVATIONS IN FEET
APPROXIMATE SCALE 1 : 6,500,000

0   50   100   150   200 MILES

PLATE NO. 15
Prefectures of Japan : The Principal Political Subdivisions.

sion and readjustment continued within the Initial Occupation Area.[50] The 43rd Division sent elements in to relieve the 164th Infantry Regiment at Irumagawa airfield. The 11th Airborne Command Post opened in Matsushima in northern Honshu on 17 September. Fifth Air Force troops began to relieve infantry units at airfields. On 20 September the 4th Marine Regiment assumed the responsibility for all areas and missions formerly assigned the Fleet Landing Force which reverted to the control of the 6th Marine Division. The 27th Division moved from Muratsuka to occupy Kashiwazaki, Takada, Korizama, Fuchishima, Sanjo, and Nagaoka in the Niigata area on 20 September.[51]

On 20 September advance elements of the 97th Division arrived in Tokyo—the first division from the European Theater of Operations in Japan. The 97th was ordered to relieve the 43rd Division which prepared to return to the Zone of Interior.[52]

In compliance with instructions from General Eichelberger, an advance party of staff officers of IX Corps, 81st Division, and 77th Division arrived in Yokohama on 2 September. After conferring with the Eighth Army staff,

the advance party left by plane for Ominato, and from there proceeded by motor to Aomori. There they conferred with the prefectural governor, the chief of police, and the senior army commander of the area. The party found that the Japanese had complied with the surrender terms and that the landing area was cleared of all Japanese troops.[53] Arrangements were made for troop billets, transportation, and office space for IX Corps units scheduled to occupy Hokkaido. Only minor disturbances occurred during this visit. They were caused by Chinese and Korean laborers. Officers of the advance party visited the laborers' camps and quieted the Chinese and Koreans by assuring them that plans were already under way for their evacuation home.[54]

XIV Corps was directed to assume control of the 11th Airborne Division and the 27th Division and to take over occupation responsibilities within the Corps zone of occupation on 27 September.[55] The Eighth Army would continue to be responsible for moving elements of the 11th Airborne Division and the 27th Division into the zone of occupation of the XIV Corps until they were established in their areas.[56] The Occupation of Japan meanwhile

---

50   On 17 September, General MacArthur moved his GHQ from Yokohama to Tokyo. Beginning at 0800 a fleet of 50 trucks shuttled back and forth between Yokohama and Tokyo transporting 600 officers and 1,400 enlisted men. Japanese residents stared in amazement as columns of trucks which seemed to continue for miles, rumbled to a stop near the side-entrance of the Dai Ichi building. In the vacated rooms of the building, Japanese electricians were still stringing wires while ten special units were cleaning the building. No formal ceremonies took place. The only outward sign that this building was to be the site of GHQ was that two guards stood at each entrance. The entire program was completed by 1700.

51   GHQ SCAP & USAFPAC, Mo Sum of Opns, Sep 45, p. 5.

52   *Ibid*, p. 8.

53   Occupational Monogr of the Eighth US Army in Japan, Vol. I, Aug 45—Jan 46 (C), p. 40.

54   *Ibid.*

55   Amendment to Eighth US Army FO No. 32, eff 27 Sep 45. (XIV Corps Rpt No. 1 on the "Blacklist" Opn, 20 Aug—30 Sep 45.)

56   The 27th Infantry Division, having left personnel on Okinawa and having lost a sizeable group by redeployment to the US, had only approximately 66 percent of its organizational strength in the objective area. By 28 September all elements of 27th Division had closed in their respective areas as assigned by the Division Commander, but a large Division rear echelon of assigned replacements, together with the Division's heavy equipment, was on Okinawa or en route to Japan under control of Eighth Army.

had proceeded so well that shipments of all combat elements of Corps troops (except combat engineers) were cancelled.

Before the end of September, IX Corps units landed in force in northern Honshu.[57] 81st Division troops landed on 25 September and established Division headquarters in Aomori. Regimental command posts were located as follows: the 321st Infantry at Tsuchiya, the 322d Infantry at Hirosaki, and the 323d Infantry at Hachinohe. (Plate No. 16)

With the exception of the 158th Regimental Combat Team, which was scheduled to occupy Utsunomiya (northwest of Tokyo) in October, Eighth Army's occupation of Honshu was virtually completed by the end of September. The main and supporting movements had taken place with smoothness and dispatch, something that had not been anticipated. Not one serious incident marked the movement of thousands of Eighth Army troops into Honshu. All areas were under firm control. Units of the IX, XI, and XIV Corps carried out their missions without trouble. They operated routine security patrols, seized and secured critical Japanese installations and made local checks on the demobilization of the Japanese armed forces. The progressive destruction of enemy ammunition and materiel was also supervised. In a surprise move at the end of the month, troops and CIC units established guards over all Japanese financial institutions and strong rooms. The banks were closed, pending a detailed inspection by SCAP technical experts.[58] In the midst of these activities the 43rd Division, the first to be returned to the Zone of Interior, sailed from Yokohama on 28 September.

Sixth Army Occupation Movements

Because the initial occupation under Eighth Army had gone so smoothly, it was possible to accelerate Sixth Army occupation assignments. Originally it was planned for Sixth Army moves to be initiated only after the Eighth Army had completed its assignments under "Blacklist," and the desire of Japan to accept the surrender terms had been established beyond all doubt. Although no sizeable Sixth Army landings were planned until October, main preliminary moves began on 25 September.[59]

General Krueger's area of responsibility was divided into three zones. I Corps, commanded by Maj. Gen. Innis P. Swift, was to occupy the Osaka—Kyoto—Kobe zone. This zone included thirteen prefectures and extended south from the Eighth Army boundary to a point between Kobe and Okayama. The central zone of the Sixth Army area was adjacent to the I Corps zone and comprised the remainder of southern Honshu (except the Shimonoseki tip) and the island of Shikoku. Maj. Gen. Franklin C. Sibert's X Corps was given responsibility for this area, which became the second zone. The third zone, which included the Shimono seki tip of Honshu and the island of Kyushu,

---

57 This was not the first US occupation movement at that northern port. On 9 September elements of the North Pacific Fleet entered Mutsu Bay and occupied the naval base and airfield at Ominato. Mine sweepers cleared the Bay, and several cruisers and destroyers were available to provide naval gunfire support if needed. Two CVE's provided air cover.

58 Occupational Monogr of the Eighth US Army in Japan, Vol. I, Aug 45—Jan 46 (C), p. 56.

59 The first Sixth Army troops to arrive in Japan occupied Kanoya airdrome in southern Kyushu in company with FEAF troops. The unit was the 1st Battalion, 127th Infantry, 32d Division. The Battalion reverted to Division control during November. An advance echelon of Sixth Army HQ of 19 officers and 2 enlisted men under Brig Gen H. W. Kiefer arrived at Wakayama, Honshu, 19 September, to initiate implementation of GO No. 2. (Sixth US Army Rpt on Occupation of Japan, 22 Sep—30 Nov 45, p. 23.)

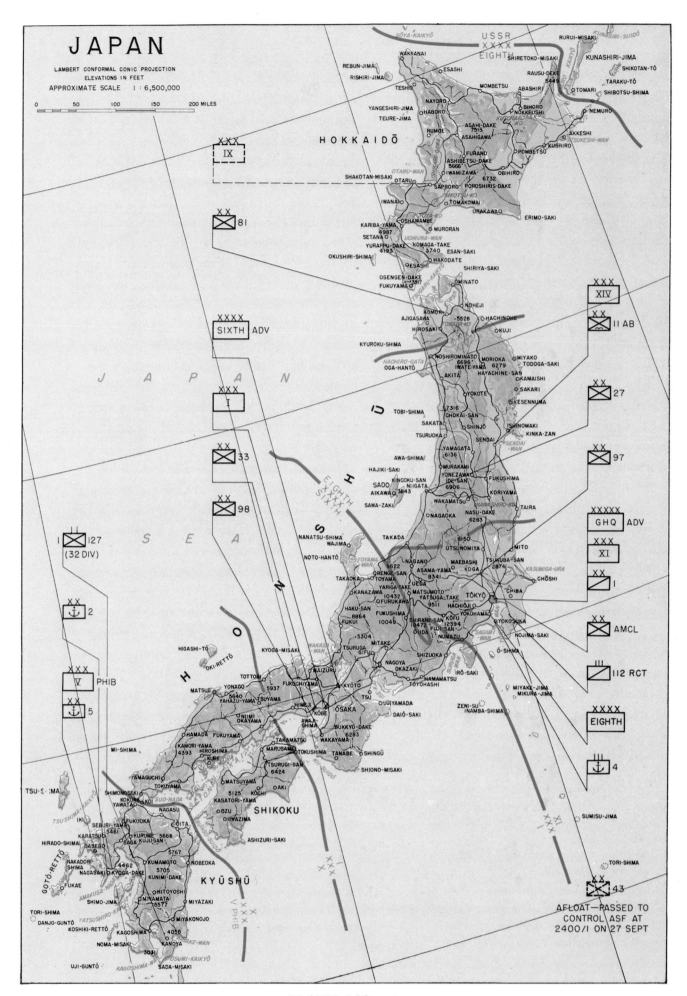

PLATE NO. 16

Location of Major Ground Units, 30 September 1945

was assigned to the V Amphibious Corps commanded by Maj. Gen. Harry Schmidt, USMC.

The leading elements of the 5th Marine Division landed at Sasebo (Kyushu) on 22 September, and on the following day the 2d Marine Division went ashore at Nagasaki. After these key objectives had been occupied, the 2d Marine Division expanded south of Nagasaki to assume control of the Nagasaki, Kumamoto, Miyazaki, and Kagoshima prefectures. In the meantime the 5th Marine Division expanded east to the prefectures of Saga, Fukuoka, Oita, and Yamaguchi.[60]

Headquarters Sixth Army landed at Wakayama on 25 September and opened at Kyoto two days later. Two of the three divisions of I Corps, the 33d and the 98th, arrived on 25 and 27 September respectively.[61] The 32d Infantry Division was not scheduled to move from the Philippines to Japan until October.

There was every indication by the beginning of October that the Occupation was proceeding satisfactorily. Although there was good cooperation on the part of both the Japanese population and the officials of the government,[62] it was necessary to move Sixth Army troops into their zones of responsibility in order to make the Occupation complete. In view of complete Japanese cooperation, modifications of the original " Blacklist " plan were possible in expediting the Occupation. Paragraphs of that order regarding possible resistance were eliminated.[63]

When General Krueger (Sixth Army) assumed command of ground forces in the zones of responsibility of V Amphibious Corps and I Corps on 24 and 27 September respectively, he established his headquarters in Kyoto. I Corps was to control the Osaka—Kyoto—Kobe area; X Corps, the central portion of the Sixth Army Zone; and V Amphibious Corps, the extreme southern part.

All movements of Sixth Army units were of dual nature: occupation and adjustment for early inactivation of the veteran Sixth. After this was accomplished, transfer of low-point troops into Eighth Army and deployment of high-point troops to the Zone of Interior for discharge or reassignment would follow.[64]

Japanese Reaction to Initial Occupation

The Japanese reaction to the initial occupation was so favorable that the Supreme Commander issued an official statement in September in which he estimated the total occupation force could be cut to 200,000 men by 1 July 1946.[65] This seemed unbelievable and some

---

60 Sixth US Army Rpt on Occupation of Japan, 22 Sep—30 Nov 45.

61 *Ibid*, p. 18.

62 By 1 October 1945 the demobilization of Japanese armed forces was approximately 87 percent complete. See Ch. V.

63 Sixth US Army Rpt on Occupation of Japan 22 Sep—30 Nov 45, FO 75, 21 Aug 45.

64 The " point system " provided for the early return of men who had 85 or more points. According to a memo issued by G-3 GHQ, 6 September 1945, sub: Readjustment, 80,000 high-point personnel would be returned during the first month of occupation. Between September and the end of 1945, 390,000 would be scheduled for return. General MacArthur requested that there be 25,000 replacements each month during November and December. (Rad [S] C-15173, CINCAFPAC to WARCOS. 26 Sep 45. In G-3 GHQ Adm 370.) All of this was in conformity with the plans of the War Department to reduce the total army to approximately 2,100,000 by 1 July 1946. The War Department was under great pressure from Congress. In the various theaters including the Pacific, the amazed citizens of occupied countries saw American soldiers participating in open protest rallies, demanding early action on their return to the ZI.

65 Occupational Monogr of the Eighth US Army in Japan, Vol. I, Aug 45—Jan 46 (C).

Gen. Walter Krueger as he appeared in
the field in 1945

Gen. Walter Krueger arrives in Tokyo for
a visit with the Supreme Commander.

PLATE NO. 17
Sixth U.S. Army Commander

American magazines and newspapers were quite antagonistic, claiming that the statement had been made for effect only and was not in the best interests of safety. Nevertheless, the "man on the ground," the American soldier, was inclined to believe it.

Calming a nervous populace called for discipline and friendliness. General MacArthur's troops proved themselves equal to the task. American personal kindness and official consideration were wholly unexpected by the Japanese. Those factors went far toward building good relations with an emotionally disturbed people. Beginning with the first hours of the Occupation, the old authoritarian background of the Japanese contrasted with the free, liberal philosophy of the American forces. Adjustments had to be made and sometimes led to misunderstanding and confusion.

Japan, accustomed to close control from the top and always indifferent to independent thinking from those in lower strata, had no criteria by which to initiate or to judge the value of the original measures so strongly desired by the occupation authorities. Adjustment, however, proved far less difficult than had been anticipated. This was partly due to the apparent eagerness of the Japanese to adapt themselves to occidental methods, although a great deal of credit must be given to the shrewd advance planning of General MacArthur.

Japanese ideas of how their conquerors would react once Japan was occupied were based on former Japanese Army policy in the conquered Asiatic and Pacific Ocean areas. In those areas the native populations, regardless of their own food shortage, were always expected to feed the Japanese troops. Mindful of their army's policy and in anticipation of food requisitions by the Occupation forces, the Kanagawa prefectural authorities laid in a store of onions, potatoes, fruit, and meat. Since all intelligence surveys had correctly reported an acute shortage of food in Japan, Occupation personnel expressed considerable surprise at this abundance. When a member of the reception committee explained that the food had been "requisitioned," one of the United States officers made it clear that no such special consideration was desired. This attitude, wholly at variance with Japanese Army practices abroad, produced an immediate, favorable effect upon Japanese public opinion. The Japanese were further impressed by early reports of tolerant treatment of the Japanese by our soldiers.

Two days after the surrender, twenty truckloads of flour, rolled oats, canned goods, and rice arrived at the Yokosuka municipal office as relief supplies for the local people. The next day eleven more trucks appeared with medical supplies, blankets, tea, and other goods. Mayor Umezu, completely overwhelmed by this unexpected generosity, expressed his deep appreciation.[66] Simultaneously, American soldiers on patrol or sightseeing in trucks and jeeps circulated throughout the occupied areas. Amused by the Japanese children, they handed out chocolate bars, hard tack, chewing gum, and candy drops.[67]

There were other humane actions, as in the case of three American soldiers who gave first aid to a girl knocked down and severely injured by a Japanese street car. The soldiers were further reported to have hailed a passing army vehicle and to have taken the injured girl to a hospital. This act was greatly appreciated by the Japanese.[68]

Units temporarily billeted in the Yokohama Museum and the Yokohama City Library created a very favorable impression. Just before

66 Tokyo, *Nippon Times*, 7 Sep 45.
67 *Ibid.*
68 *Tokyo Shimbun*, 11 Sep 45.

GI with Japanese children.

Shopping on the Ginza.

PLATE NO. 18
GI: Ambassador of Goodwill

leaving, they carefully cleaned the rooms, gathered up all the trash, and buried waste and refuse in a neighboring lot.[69]

The friendly boyishness of the new arrivals who, when strolling along the Ginza for the first time, polled the numerous street stall eating places to ask for milk[70] amused the Japanese and eased the tension. These minor incidents exemplify what appealed to the " face saving " tradition-bound nature of the Japanese people.

To forestall any incidents which might be caused by exuberant, irresponsible soldiers seeking souvenirs, all commanding officers were instructed to take necessary precautions. Considering the fact that the majority of occupation troops were combat veterans, relatively few incidents marred the initial occupation. The Japanese received the victors submissively following the Emperor's mandate. They had accepted the Americans cautiously and were eventually impressed by the complete absence of systematic looting and violence which many had fully expected. The one factor which had an immediately noticeable effect on the people of Japan was the spontaneous generosity of the Americans.

There was no lack of a realistic attitude on the part of the Occupation authorities. This was an occupation of enemy country, and fanatics were known to exist and circulate. For this reason, ten check points, manned jointly by Japanese policemen and Eighth Army troops, were established around the initial occupation zone. The police, stationed outside the zone, stopped all passers-by to make sure that no armed individuals penetrated. The troops remained for the most part within their area and arrested those who acted suspiciously. Cooperation between the Occupation forces and Japanese civil police was thus early established.[71]

The Japanese press, which at first had been inclined to be dubious about American behavior, now voiced unanimous praise.[72] Japanese authorities, in striving faithfully to avoid unpleasant incidents which might lead to violence, urged their people to act prudently, decorously, and with composure, " thereby displaying the true essence of the Yamato race."[73]

This took several forms. Initially, the Japanese publicists and officials recommended passive acceptance of Occupation authority, and avoidance " as far as possible " of all but the most essential business relations with Americans. This, it was pointed out, was not due to hostility between the two peoples but to the unavoidable fact that customs differences and language barriers posed almost insuperable obstacles to normal social relations.[74] As a further means of lessening conflict they began to intensify efforts to widen the use of English. This was not an easy task. English had been frowned upon during the war, school courses in the language had been discontinued, and in many places casual use of English had been regarded as a sign of disloyalty. Nevertheless, as soon as surrender was proclaimed, efforts

69   *Ibid*, 6 Sep 45.

70   *Ibid*, 9 Sep 45.

71   The so-called Public Safety Division (PSD), an operating agency of G-2, was established early to initiate and supervise certain police reforms ; this section utilized US experts of the caliber of Mr. L. J. Valentine, former police Commissioner of New York City.   See Ch. VIII.

72   Tokyo, *Yomiuri* and *Tokyo Shimbun*, which had been the worst offenders, completely reversed their attitude.

73   Tokyo, *Nippon Times*, 1 Sep 45.   There should have been no doubt in the official mind :   the carefully calculated treatment of the Japanese delegation in Manila set an official psychological pattern that was immediately persuasive.

74   Tokyo, *Yomiuri*, 23 Aug 45.

were made in every town and village to revive the study of the language.[75] Specifically, the police advised the Japanese to stop worrying, to disregard rumors, and to report to the police all problems arising between Japanese and foreigners.[76] Newspapers, using a well worn Japanese method, warned that the eyes of the world were upon Japan and that calmness was to be maintained.[77] One newspaper, blandly assuming that. "...coquetry is the cause of trouble....," warned women against the use of heavy lipstick, rouge and eyebrow pencil. It also urged Japanese to be cautious of the type of English used on the streets. "Do not loiter in the streets nor follow the troops, and do not try to purchase anything from soldiers...." was probably its most significant advice.[78] *Yomiuri* and *Tokyo Shimbun* were the most consistent of all Japanese newspapers in warning Japanese women against improper costumes or behavior.[79] After cautioning girls against walking unattended even in the daytime, *Yomiuri* added: "Even when called upon by foreign soldiers saying 'hello' or 'hey', intermingled with their broken Japanese, women will pay no attention and will avoid all contact with them."[80] The press and the people alike were soon to learn that even in the few instances when women were molested, the offenders were punished.

Washington suggested that restrictions should be placed upon associations of Occupation personnel with the Japanese population only in the event that the Occupation authorities considered such restrictions necessary.[81]

General MacArthur, who had lived in the Orient for many years, was reluctant to make an issue of a delicate problem. The subject was therefore handled with tolerance, restraint, and discretion.

Recognizing early that restoration of good relations depended largely upon the correctness of Japanese behavior, and that this in turn called for proper understanding of American psychology, Japanese newspapers stressed the need for promoting good relations. Lack of information concerning American ideals and methods was cited as a chief obstacle in promoting mutual confidence.[82] Although this was a complete reversal of form according to their former pronouncements, it was not too surprising. The Japanese psychology was quite pliable where their country's future was concerned.

The Japanese eagerly sought contacts with American soldiers. They made strenuous efforts to facilitate proper social relations. Tokyo municipal police prepared a chart of entertainment places and distributed it to all policemen, officials, and others who might be asked to direct Occupation troops to such resorts. Various associations worked out elaborate plans for restaurants, recreation centers, theaters, dance halls, and other entertainment facilities. Rather than depend on Japanese recreation plans (some of which were not approved by Occupation authorities), clubs and snack bars were provided by the American Red Cross and Army Special Services. Special Services also took over numerous hotels, theaters, parks, golf

---

75   *Tokyo Shimbun* reported, 23 September, that railway employees in Tokyo Station were required to attend a morning drill in English language conversation.

76   Tokyo, *Nippon Times*, 1 Sep 45.

77   Ibid.

78   Tokyo, *Yomiuri*, 7 Sep 45.

79   (1) *Tokyo Shimbun*, 19 Aug 45; (2) Tokyo, *Yomiuri*, 23 Aug 45.

80   Tokyo, *Yomiuri*, 23 Aug 45.

81   Rad WX 56906, Wash to CINCAFPAC, 30 Aug 45.

82   Tokyo, *Yomiuri*, 26 Aug 45.

clubs, and other facilities, providing a variety of supervised recreation for Occupation personnel.

By the end of September, Japan's defeat had become a reality to her people. For the first time in her long history Japan had become a nation completely dominated by a foreign power. The firm hand of General MacArthur was controlling and guiding the Japanese nation and the people seemed responsive and cooperative. The large task of demilitarization of factories and resources had begun. War criminals were being arrested and held for trial. Ammunition, weapons, and other military material were being moved to depots to be inventoried and eventually destroyed. All these things the Japanese people had initially accepted, and continued to accept submissively, if not favorably.

Eighth Army Occupation is Completed

A responsibility of the IX Corps, occupation of Hokkaido began 4 October when the 306th Regimental Combat Team of the 77th Division made the initial landing. The remainder of the Division proceeded by water convoy and landed at Otaru the following day. The 307th Regimental Combat Team immediately took control at Sapporo. On 7 October, Headquarters IX Corps landed and Maj. Gen. Charles W. Ryder assumed command of all IX Corps troops.[83] The last major organization to move in the Eighth Army zone of occupation was the "Bushmaster" unit, 158th Regimental Combat Team, which occupied Tochigi Prefecture.[84] Thus, by the middle of October, roughly seven weeks after the first troops of the 11th Airborne Division landed at Atsugi airfield, Operation "Blacklist" was virtually completed as far as the Eighth Army was concerned. All important areas were controlled either by assigned troops or by active patrols.[85] (Plate No. 19)

Hardly had the troops reached their objectives, when extensive movements of high point troops to the Zone of Interior began a second phase of Eighth Army movements within Japan. The Americal Division relinquished control in Tokyo and Kanagawa Prefectures (except Yokosuka Naval Base area) to the 1st Cavalry Division, and in Yamanashi Prefecture to the 97th Division. The 97th Division also relieved the 27th Division in Niigata and Fukushima Prefectures and assumed operational control of the 158th Regimental Combat Team in Tochigi Prefecture. The 1st Cavalry assumed responsibility for Yamanashi Prefecture, formerly under the 97th.[86] Closing its long Pacific campaign record, XIV Corps returned to the United States with the 27th Division in December. In January, the 11th Airborne Division took over the northern tip of Honshu, relieving the "Wildcats" (81st Division). Its control was further extended in March to include Hokkaido, thus relieving the 77th Division.

---

83 Occupational Monogr of the Eighth US Army in Japan, Vol. I, Aug 45—Jan 46 (C), p. 42.

84 *Ibid*, p. 42. Originally scheduled to go on to northern Japan as part of the IX Corps command, soldiers of this unit entered Yokohama Harbor instead on 13 October for their first glimpse of the goal for which they had been destined when organized at Panama. On 14 October the combat team assumed responsibility for the occupation of Tochigi Prefecture.

85 Troop movements only; the tremendous task of administering the terms of the surrender had hardly begun, and would continue as long as the Occupation itself was maintained under SCAP.

86 Occupational Monogr of the Eighth US Army in Japan, Vol. I, Aug 45—Jan 46 (C), pp. 104-5. Preparing for the inactivation of the 112th and 158th RCT's in January 1946, and with approval from Army, 22 December, XI Corps directed that the 1st Cavalry Division relieve the 112th on 2 January and that the 97th Division relieve the 158th on 5 January.

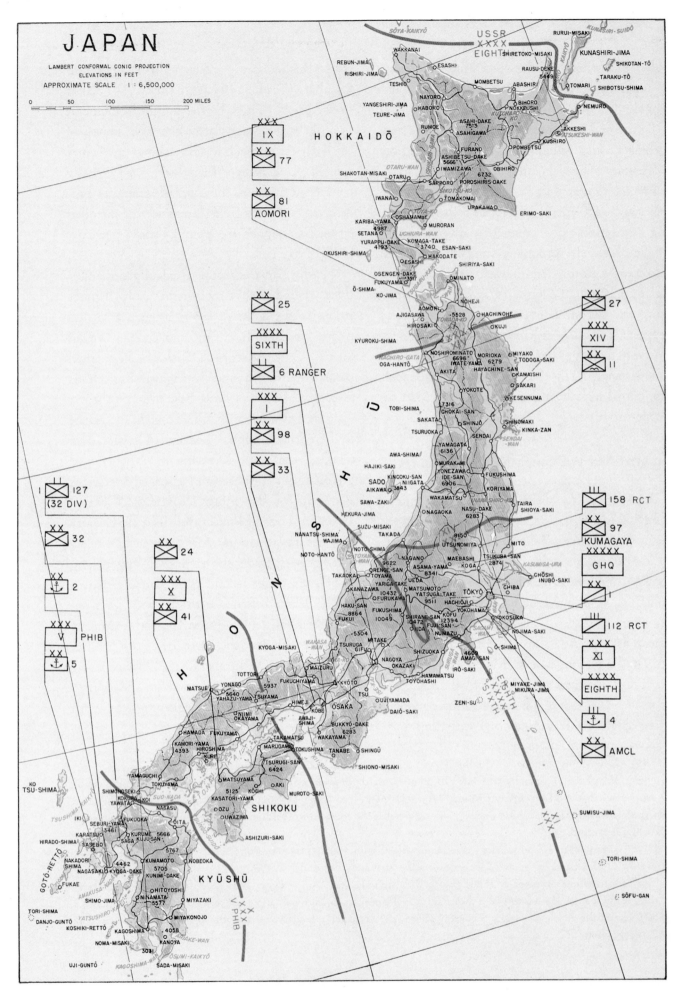

PLATE NO. 19
Location of Major Ground Units, 31 October 1945

Communications, Procurement and Requisition

The initial work of Signal Corps units required not only installation and maintenance of communications over the island of Honshu as the number of Occupation troops increased weekly, but also necessitated survey and overhaul of worn Japanese equipment to determine ways and means of blending this into a swiftly growing communications network. Bombings of Japan had caused destruction of about 25 percent of all wire communications. An additional 25 percent had reached a low state of efficiency through overloading and poor maintenance. In Tokyo only 50,000 of the original 200,000 instruments were in service. In all of Japan it was estimated that approximately half of all the instruments in use at the beginning of the war were buried in the debris.[87]

There was no difficulty in procuring billets and office space during the initial occupation. The 11th Airborne Division took over barracks vacated by Japanese soldiers. For several days, the paratroopers and the 1st Cavalry men moved from one installation to another in their respective assigned sectors and occupied whatever space was available. But with the arrival of additional troops and the heavier concentration of forces in the half-gutted Tokyo—Yokohama area, the problem became acute.

There arose an immediate need for an orderly, supervised system which could provide billeting space and bivouac areas with the least possible delay. The problem had been anticipated, however, and the advance party which landed at Atsugi on 28 August carried instructions from General Headquarters for the establishment of the Eighth Army Area and Facilities Allocation Board. On 2 September an advance party of seven officers organized the Board in Yokohama in order to coordinate demands on the Japanese for procurement of facilities. This original small section was greatly enlarged when most of the personnel of the Eighth Army Field Artillery Section, headed by Brig. Gen. Eugene McGinley, were placed on temporary duty with the Allocation Board. Its maximum strength was forty-five officers and twenty enlisted clerks.[88]

To handle efficiently the volume and variety of requests submitted, the Board was organized into four sections: Billeting and Housing, Area and Storage, Records, and Coordination and Planning. A fifth section was later added to assume control of the Tokyo area, excluding the part which General Headquarters had already acquired for its own use.[89]

Japanese officials played an important role in many phases of the Occupation and the work of the Allocation Board was no exception. The Yokohama Liaison Office, created to simplify and coordinate routine administrative

---

87 Occupational Monogr of the Eighth US Army in Japan, Vol. I, Aug 45—Jan 46 (C), p. 101.

88 Divisions and other units assigned occupation duties outside the Tokyo—Yokohama area requisitioned their billets and bivouac areas through the Allocation Board, but this was done mainly for the purpose of keeping central records. Actually, there was little possibility of conflict in the outlying areas, because only one unit was in occupational control of a single area. For example, after an advance party of a corps had made reconnaissance with the aid of local officials, the corps submitted a requisition, with accompanying overlays, for approval of the Allocation Board. At first much delay resulted from slow action on the part of the Yokohama Liaison Office. It was necessary that this office learn from the local civil officials many miles away whether the use of facilities requested could be turned over to the Americans without serious loss, from the Japanese point of view, to the community. Later this condition was remedied by designating representatives in all the prefectures who could make spot decisions for the Liaison Office. (Occupational Monogr of the Eighth US Army in Japan, Vol. I, Aug 45—Jan 46 [C], pp. 64–65.)

89 Ibid, p. 65.

matters, was a subordinate echelon of the Japanese Facilities Agency. The office operated in compliance with the provisions of an Eighth Army administrative order.[90] The same order directed that all billeting space, barracks, camp areas, port facilities, transportation, and many other major installations would be allocated by the Board, based on requirements submitted by subordinate units.[91]

Year-End Summary

Beginning with a mere handful of men late in August, the Eighth Army moved three corps, seven combat divisions, and supporting service troops into Japan within less than a month. By October a total of 232,379 Eighth Army men were in the country.[92] The Sixth Army in its zone of responsibility had an approximately equal number. However, this was the high water mark and already the tide was turning the other way. It was apparent to careful observers that the capitulation of Japan was as comprehensive as it was real. Consequently, General MacArthur's mid-September estimate that an army of 200,000 would be adequate to garrison the islands was now widely acclaimed.

General MacArthur was impatient with critics who mistook the Occupation policy of allowing the Japanese considerable freedom in rebuilding the country economically and politically as a sign of softness. In a significant press release dated 14 September he stated :[93]

I have noticed some impatience in the press based upon the assumption of a so-called soft policy in Japan. This can only arise from an erroneous concept of what is occurring.

The first phase of the occupation must of necessity be based upon military considerations which involve the deployment forward of our troops and the disarming and demobilization of the enemy. This is coupled with the paramount consideration of withdrawing our former prisoners of war and war internees from the internment camps and evacuating them to their homes. Safety and security require that these steps shall proceed with precision and completeness lest calamity may be precipitated. The military phase is proceeding in an entirely satisfactory way. Over half of the enemy's force in Japan proper is now demobilized and the entire program will be practically complete by the middle of October. During this interval of time safety and complete security must be assured.

When the first phase is completed the other phases as provided in the surrender terms will infallibly follow. No one need have any doubt about the prompt, complete and entire fulfillment of the terms of surrender. The process, however, takes time. It is well understandable in the face of atrocities committed by the enemy that there should be impatience. This natural impulse, however, should be tempered by the fact that security and military expediency will require an exercise of some restraint. The surrender terms

90 HQ Eighth US Army, Adm Ord No. 15. (Occupational Monogr of the Eighth US Army in Japan, Vol. I, Aug 45—Jan 46 [C], p. 65.)

91 GHQ pursued the same policy. A Japanese Liaison Group was organized under G-2 to parallel the corresponding Japanese Government Central Liaison Office. The entire range of governmental contact was handled through this channel, as a buffer unit. It must be noted that in this period the bulk of GHQ had remained in Manila as the customary rear echelon; the tremendous problems of the initial crucial months from the fall of 1945 to the spring of 1946, were handled by the small forward echelon. G-2 entered the picture repeatedly because it was the only source of linguist talent and possessed inherent expert knowledge of the Japanese civil and military structure.

92 Occupational Monogr of the Eighth US Army in Japan, Vol. I, Aug 45—Jan 46 (C), p. 107.

93 GHQ USAFPAC Press Release, 14 Sep 45. The Occupation fell into two inescapable phases: (a) demobilization and disarmament and (b) political reform and economic rehabilitation. Impatient onlookers, safe from direct military contact, agitated for the second phase, completely ignoring the military risks of the first. Unlike the battered Germans in Europe, the Japanese Army in the Home Islands was entirely capable of combat; potential reactions had to be carefully weighed.

are not soft and they will not be applied in kid-gloved fashion.

Economically and industrially, as well as militarily, Japan is completely exhausted and depleted. She is in a condition of utter collapse, her governmental structure is controlled completely by the occupation forces and is operating only to the extent necessary to insure such an orderly and controlled procedure as will prevent social chaos, disease and starvation.

The over-all objectives for Japan have been clearly outlined in the surrender terms and will be accomplished in an orderly, concise and comprehensive way without delays beyond those imposed by the magnitude of the physical problems involved.

It is extremely difficult for me at times to exercise that degree of patience which is unquestionably demanded if the long-time policies which have been decreed are to be successfully accomplished without repercussions which would be detrimental to the well-being of the world but I am restraining myself to the best of my ability and am generally satisfied with the progress being made.

The inconsistencies of armchair strategists, clamoring for repressive measures while weakening U. S. troops through accelerated demobilization became obvious in all theaters. Fortunately, General MacArthur's accurate psychological appraisal of the Japanese system enabled him to handle a contradictory situation. It was possible to utilize the Japanese government structure to the extent necessary to prevent complete social disintegration, insure internal distribution, maintain labor, and prevent calamitous diseases or wholesale starvation. With the Occupation well under way it was General MacArthur's opinion that the purposes of the surrender terms could be accomplished with only a small fraction of the men, time, and money originally projected.

Following the newly adopted Congressional policy of greatly reducing the armed forces, plans were developed for deactivation and redeployment. The result was that by the end of the year, General Eichelberger's command (Eighth Army) was under 200,000[94] and was still going down. Meanwhile, the Occupation continued at an undiminished pace, quietly and efficiently.

The first four months of the Occupation were also a period in which great changes were brought about in the social, political, and economic life of Japan.[95] Beginning with the famous " Bill of Rights " directive in the second month of the Occupation, SCAP had issued a steady stream of orders to the Japanese Government designed to destroy those influences in Japan which had led her into war, and to establish a democratic form of government. Political prisoners were liberated; the secret police force was dissolved; Shinto religion was separated from the state; the Emperor renounced his divinity; women's suffrage was promulgated; the educational system was revised; trade unions were legalized; and scores of other political and social reforms were launched. All of this required supervision and surveillance on the part of military occupation personnel.

The Beginning of the Second Phase

With the opening of 1946, a new phase in the Occupation of Japan began. Activities during the first months, from the landing at Atsugi in August to the end of the year 1945, consisted primarily of movements to occupy Japan and the deployment of large numbers of combat troops prepared equally to fight or favor, the recovery of Allied prisoners and

---

94   Occupational Monogr of the Eighth US Army in Japan, Vol. I, Aug 45—Jan 46 (C), p. 108.

95   This period saw the creation of several predominantly civil agencies under SCAP in contradistinction to normal staffs under FEC. Among the earliest to begin to function were: Government Section (GS), Economic & Scientific Section (ESS), Public Health & Welfare (PH&W), and Civil Intelligence Section (CIS).

internees, the establishment of Occupation facilities, and the disarming and demobilizing of the Japanese armed forces.

From a military standpoint, the new phase would be concerned primarily with the maintenance of immediate objectives and the entering upon long-range objectives of the Occupation. Both would be accomplished with a greatly reduced and constantly adjusting military force, yet one capable of meeting all emergencies, even combat, if necessary.

Among internal military problems confronting the Occupation, one of the most important was redeployment and deactivation of troops. Sixth Army was relieved of occupation duties on 31 December 1945, and General Eichelberger assumed command of all occupation army troops.[96] At that time his Eighth Army consisted of five corps, eleven divisions, a number of lesser tactical units, and hundreds of service organizations. (Plate No. 20) The total strength was 18,123 officers and 223,383 enlisted men.[97] This seemed to guarantee Eighth Army a personnel pool adequate to cope with its assigned mission, but by this time the United States' demobilization program had developed the tremendous momentum which reached its peak in January 1946. Actually there was more shipping available to the Zone of Interior than there were soldiers to fill it. Consequently, the point system, which had already undergone revision downward, was again modified.[98] Following this change of the point system, Eighth Army lost 48,830 commissioned and enlisted personnel in January. The 1,385 replacements received hardly offset this loss, and the Eighth Army strength dropped sharply to 194,061 by the end of January.[99]

The 11th Replacement Depot at Okazaki and the 4th Replacement Depot at Zama shipped the soldiers home through the ports of Nagoya and Yokohama respectively. During January both depots reported the return of the " 100,000th homeward-bound soldier."[100]

The Air Force strength in January was listed at 30,799.[101] The Fifth Air Force with its base at Irumagawa was charged with the responsibility for air operations in Japan; the Fifth Fighter Command, based at Itazuki in Kyushu, covered southern Japan; and the Fifth Bomber Command, also at Irumagawa, controlled northern Japan.

Service Unit and Supply Reorganization

During January the largest single unit operating under Sixth Army was USASCOM-C[102] which was originally the service of supply for Eighth Army under the old " Coronet "

---

96 Inactivation of Sixth US Army took place on 26 January 1946.

97 Occupational Monogr of the Eighth US Army in Japan, Vol. II, Jan—Aug 46 (C), p. 20.

98 The current troop movements were revised to release all officers with 67 army service record points or with 45 months of service as of 30 April, and all enlisted men with 45 points or 30 months of service as of that date. Then, to provide absolute assurance that all available space would be used, authority was granted to call officers with 65 points or 42 months as of that date, should such action prove necessary.

99 Occupational Monogr of the Eighth US Army in Japan, Vol. II, Jan—Aug 46 (C), p. 21.

100 At Okazaki the January record showed 1,425 officers and 33,304 enlisted personnel returned to the US. At Zama the total for the month came to 43,506, of which 296 were returned by air and 43,210 by water transportation. In all, 78,235 individuals were started homeward in January through these depots. Eighth Army losses for the month made up less than two-thirds of this total, the difference being accounted for by readjustment of personnel from GHQ, Fifth Air Force, Merchant Marine and other services in Japan. (Occupational Monogr of the Eighth US Army in Japan Vol. II, Jan—Aug 46 [C], p. 21.)

101 Ibid, pp. 22—23.

102 Ibid, p. 30.

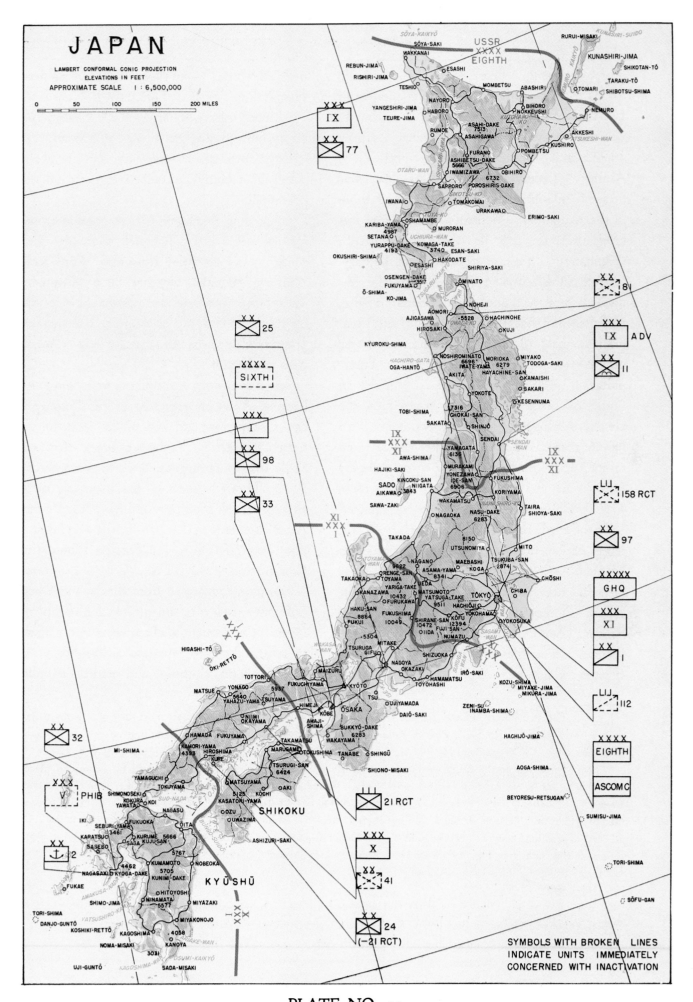

PLATE NO. 20
Location of Major Ground Units in Japan, 1 January 1946

operations plan. There were nearly 110,000 troops in this unit, the result of a merger of USASCOM-O and USASCOM-C (the respective "Olympic" and "Coronet" supply organizations of the Sixth and Eighth U.S. Armies). Inactivation of surplus units was undertaken immediately, particularly of those in the Kure area. Control of that region was transferred to the British Commonwealth Occupation Force at the end of January. USASCOM-C was concerned with the immediate improvement of water systems, housing, airdrome and hospital installations, and communications. Over-all communications traffic increased 30 percent in one month. Transportation problems increased as supplies en route for Sixth Army were diverted to the already overloaded Eighth Army ports.[103] To handle these assignments in the face of rapid military reshuffling, the Army began to employ Japanese nationals. More than 2,800 of them were employed at the Yokohama central pier.

In the Medical Service, five general hospitals, three station hospitals, and three evacuation hospitals were inactivated during January. General hospitals were maintained in the Tokyo—Yokohama area and at Sapporo, Sendai, Kyoto, and Kobe. Typical of the personnel difficulties encountered by all medical services, which were expected to carry on at peak efficiency,[104] were those of the 42d General Hospital at Tokyo. This unit, housed in the St. Lukes International Medical Center, had an authorized strength of 144 officers and 450 enlisted men as of 1 January, but its actual strength was only 130 officers and 171 enlisted personnel.[105]

It became necessary to use combat troops for services when personnel shortages grew acute. For example, the 68th Antiaircraft Artillery Brigade, together with Automatic Weapons Units, was made responsible for the operation and supply of Aomori and Sugamo prisons, where accused Japanese war criminals were confined.[106]

Large quantities of supplies were accumulated because of the unexpectedly peaceful nature of the Occupation and the sharp reduction of troop strength.[107] Although every effort was made to reroute cargoes which were not needed in the Theater, much of the incoming cargo had to be unloaded to withdraw needed items. After inventory and selection, the surplus supplies were referred to the Foreign Liquidation Commission of AFWESPAC for disposition.

Supplies confiscated from the Japanese were ordinarily useless or unsuitable for occupying forces. Consequently, channels were organized to return them to Japanese authorities. All stores of food, clothing, and medical supplies

---

103 The 3d Military Railway Service reported nearly 140,000 troops and 600,000 short tons of freight moved during January. The 11th Major Port in Yokohama broke all records in January by handling an average of 6,284 long tons daily. (Occupational Monogr of the Eighth US Army in Japan, Vol. II, Jan—Aug 46 (C), p. 32.)

104 It was during the spring of this year that the worst epidemic in the post-war world hit Japan and placed serious demands on the Medical Corps. In the Kobe—Osaka area, typhus and smallpox reached epidemic proportions among the civilian population in February, when 3,000 typhus cases were reported; at the peak, in March, 7,841 persons died of typhus and 6,069 of smallpox. In one instance 377 new typhus cases were reported in Osaka in one day. Of 10 cases of smallpox among American soldiers, all died. Strict medical control measures were instituted and in April the authorities could announce that the epidemic had been brought under control. (Occupational Monogr of the Eighth US Army in Japan Vol. II, Jan—Aug 46 [C], p. 55.)

105 *Ibid.*

106 *Ibid*, p. 36. Other units of the 68th Brigade furnished security guards for the 11th Major Port, 71st QM Depot, Yokohama Ordnance Base Depot, the Engineer Depot, and other USASCOM-C installations.

107 Occupational Monograph of the Eighth US Army in Japan, Vol. II, Jan—Aug 46 (C), p. 73.

Lt. Gen. R. L. Eichelberger and Lt. Gen. H. C. H. Robertson, BCOF, inspect Kure dock area.

General Eichelberger inspects the Australian Guard of Honor at Kure,
British Commonwealth Occupation Force Headquarters.

PLATE NO. 21
The British Commonwealth Occupation Force, March 1946

were distributed as equitably as possible when and where they were most needed. As far as practicable, scrap from combat equipment was converted into domestic articles which reappeared on the Japanese market. Destructive munitions were dumped.[108]

Occupation troops were constantly uncovering caches of precious metals and gems, which either were of Japanese origin or were looted from invaded countries. On 14 January Eighth Army troops in Chiba Prefecture found sixty two tons of silver in one cache. In another instance the Civil Intelligence Section of G-2 recovered 46,000 carats of industrial diamonds seized mainly from the optical plants of occupied territories, particularly the Netherlands East Indies.[109]

British Commonwealth Occupation Force (BCOF)

Following agreements reached between British Commonwealth and United States Government representatives in Washington late in 1945,[110] and between Australian authorities and SCAP in December, the first elements of BCOF arrived in Japan by air 8 February.

These were headquarters staff personnel. The following day a naval shore party arrived. It was not until 13 February, however, that the first sizeable unit came in. This was the 34th Australian Infantry Brigade, consisting of 1,200 troops, which landed and was established at Kure the same day. On 20 February Headquarters, BCOF, opened at Kure.[111] Six days later Lt. Gen. J. Northcott, the Commander, arrived.[112]

Iwakuni airfield in Yamaguchi Prefecture was made Headquarters of the BCOF Air Group, which was under the operational control of the Fifth U.S. Air Force. Air Vice Marshal C.A. Bouchier opened the headquarters of the British Commonwealth Air Group there on 1 March 1946. The following week, the 81st Wing, Royal Australian Air Force, flew in from Borneo. Other air units included the 14th Squadron of the Royal New Zealand Air Force which arrived on 24 March. By 24 April the preceding units were joined by the 11th and 17th Squadrons, RAAF, and the 4th Squadron, Royal Indian Air Force.

BCOF ground forces continued to arrive throughout the spring and summer of 1946 until they reached their troop strength in

---

108 Between 1 October 1945 and 30 August 1946, occupation troops disposed of nearly 866,000 tons of munitions of all types. Of this total, nearly 140,000 tons of explosives were returned to the Japanese for commercial use. (Occupational Monogr of the Eighth US Army in Japan, Vol. II, Jan—Aug 46 [C].)

109 Additional material concerning this subject may be found in GHQ FEC, G-2 CIS Records.

110 The British Government proposed a combined force from the United Kingdom, Canada, Australia, New Zealand and India to consist of a brigade group (regimental combat team) and elements of Air Force and Navy from each country. The Australian Government agreed to provide 1 brigade group, 3 air fighter squadrons and certain warships. New Zealand volunteered a brigade group, an air fighter squadron and small naval units. The United Kingdom Government's contribution was to be 1 brigade group, 2 air fighter squadrons and selected warships of the British Pacific Fleet. Canada, because of her commitments in Europe could not contribute towards the British Commonwealth Force. It was decided that Australia should provide the bulk of the headquarters and the commander of the Force, which would be under the direct operational control of SCAP. However, the commander of the Force would be responsible to the Joint Chiefs of Staff in Australia (JCOSA). Agreements between Britain and India resulted in a decision to combine 5 Brigade (UK) and 268 Brigade (India) under British command. The senior regiment was the Royal Welsh Fusiliers. New Zealand's contribution was the 9th New Zealand Infantry Brigade renamed 2d New Zealand Expeditionary Force, Japan. The Australian units had fought in the Middle East and SWPA, while the United Kingdom and Indian troops had a splendid fighting record together in the Burma campaigns. The New Zealand Brigade had a distinctive record in the North African Campaign. (BCOF Hist, 1948, Part 1.)

111 HQ BCOF was moved to Eta Jima, an island near Kure, 16 May. (BCOF Hist, 1948, Part II.)

112 Lt Gen H.C.H. Robertson assumed command of BCOF on 7 June 1946.

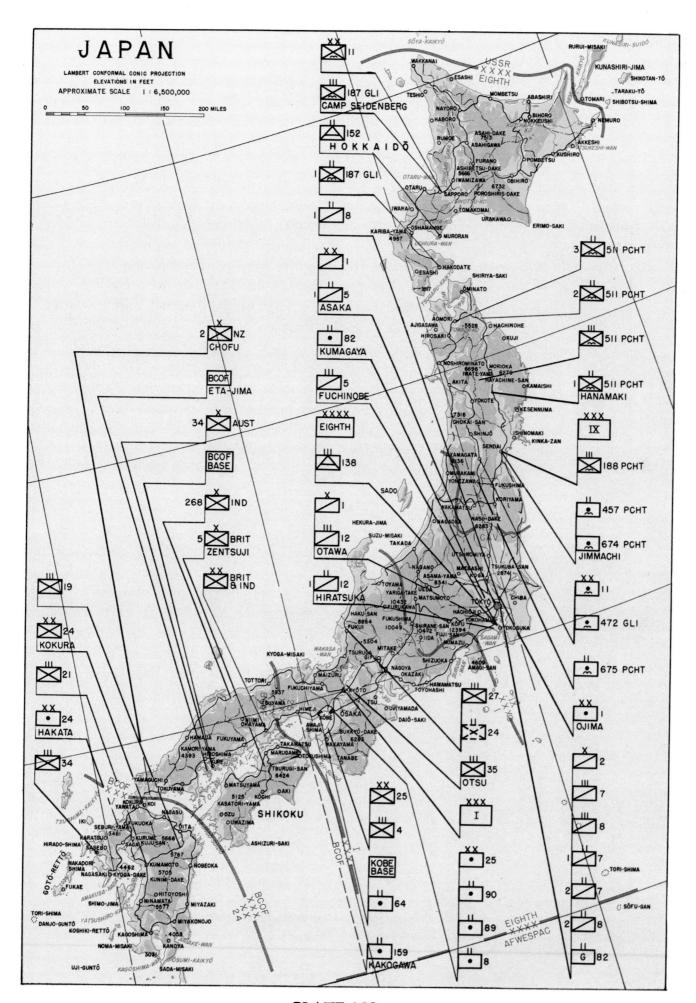

PLATE NO. 22
Location of Major Ground Units, 6 December 1946

August with a total of 36,154 officers and men.[113] On 25 March the Occupation took on a distinctive international aspect when headquarters of the British and Indian Division, under Maj. Gen. D. Tennant Cowan, arrived at Hiro. On the same day the 5th British Infantry Brigade arrived, moving on the 24th of the month from Hiro to Kochi (Shikoku).

The military role of BCOF, under the direction of SCAP, included the following functions: the safeguarding of all Allied installations, and of all Japanese installations awaiting demilitarization; the demilitarization, disposal, and military control of Japanese installations and armaments.[114] In March, BCOF progressively relieved I Corps troops in Shimane, Yamaguchi, Ehime, Kochi, Tokushima, Kagawa, Tottori, and Okayama Prefectures, and the island of Shikoku. The operation was completed by 10 June.

Liaison between GHQ, SCAP, and BCOF was maintained through the establishment in Tokyo of a headquarters known as British Commonwealth Sub-Area, Tokyo. This headquarters became responsible for the administration of all British subjects, military and civilian, stationed in the capital.

In order to assure the British Commonwealth Force greater participation in the Allied " show of strength," BCOF troops were ordered to Tokyo in April to share the responsibility of guarding the Imperial Palace and other honor assignments with troops of the 1st Cavalry Division. The first Commonwealth unit selected for Tokyo duty was the 34th Australian Infantry Brigade.[115]

The BCOF troops in Tokyo provided a colorful relief to the solid background of the numerous American forces engaged in general duties. With these relatively small, well-drilled units participating in many ceremonies, BCOF greatly impressed the Japanese. The frequent parades, including one "trooping of the colors" in front of the Imperial Palace by the 2d Battalion of the Royal Welsh Fusiliers, were among the most interesting and colorful functions of the Occupation. The daily change of guard at the palace was watched with interest by Japanese and Americans alike.[116]

The usual occupation duties were lightened somewhat for BCOF in its area of responsibility in October 1946 when the last of repatriation centers in that area was closed because only small numbers of repatriated Japanese arrived. BCOF, however, fell heir to a troublesome problem—the illegal entry of Koreans into Japan. Although the solution of such smuggling was placed in the hands of the Japanese Government by SCAP, complete supervision by BCOF was necessary in its area. There was need for close operational coordination—involving the use of air, land, and sea forces to properly patrol the coastal areas and apprehend violators. Cooperation between BCOF and I Corps was developed early and continued.[117]

---

113 Occupational Monogr of the Eighth US Army in Japan, Vol. II, Jan—Aug 46 (C), p. 41.

114 (1) BCOF Hist, 1948, Part I. (2) FO No. 35 was published by HQ Eighth US Army, 7 March 1946. This directed BCOF to: (a) Progressively assume responsibility for all occupation missions except military government, in the area assigned them on dates mutually agreed upon by the General Officers commanding I Corps and BCOF; (b) provide necessary troops to assist MG units in performance of their missions; (c) provide troops for military operations other than the occupation of its zone; (d) assume responsibility for supervision of operation of repatriation centers located in the zone of occupation. (Occupational Monogr of the Eighth US Army in Japan, Vol. II, Jan—Aug 46 [C] p. 41.)

115 BCOF Hist, 1948, Part II.

116 The US divisions in Japan inaugurated a rotation roster so that representative units of each division would be given an opportunity to share in Honor Guard duties and to see Tokyo; the plan became effective in August 1946.

117 BCOF Hist, 1948, Part V.

Provost courts were established in the BCOF area in May for the purpose of handling all types of cases of United Nations nationals who were not connected with the military forces. BCOF reported "a remarkable lack of crimes against personnel of the Armed Forces."[118]

The Intelligence Corps of BCOF was made responsible for the disposition of enemy equipment. The one large disposal operation took place on Okuno Shima, where the principal Japanese chemical warfare arsenal had been functioning from 1925 to 1945. The elimination of dangerous chemicals and decontamination in this area, known as Operation "Lewisite," took over six months to complete. At the end of this hazardous operation, over 18,000 tons gross weight of war gasses and vesicants had been destroyed, and much valuable information had been collected on Japanese preparations for chemical warfare.

I Corps Realignments: With the introduction of BCOF troops into the Kure area, I Corps' area of responsibility was split—25th Division was located in central Honshu, north of the BCOF zone, while the 24th Division occupied the southern part of the island. By mid-year the shifts necessary to allow BCOF to assume its duties were completed. The 24th Division left Shikoku and Tottori Prefectures to relieve the 2d Marines on the west coast of Kyushu. By the end of August, this Division occupied all Kyushu. The 25th Division was replaced by BCOF in Okayama. By the end of August, 25th Division occupied all of the Kinki region, operating its patrols from head-quarters at Osaka."[119]

The 2d Marine Division was to be relieved of occupation duties as rapidly as compensatory shifts could be made. After BCOF troops arrived, the area af responsibility for the Marines was gradually decreased through the indirect action of BCOF substituting for the 24th Division. For the latter, in turn, gradually began to relieve the 2d Marine Division.[120] The 24th finally replaced the Marines on 15 June.[121]

The Occupation Stabilized

Early in 1946, with the reduction of strength, troop lists were revised, and the number of units reduced. By mid-year, Eighth Army consisted of I Corps with the 24th and 25th Divisions, IX Corps with the 1st Cavalry and 11th Airborne Divisions, and the necessary service organizations and base commands. The deployment of major tactical units in zones of responsibility was stabilized by July 1946. No major, and only a few minor, changes in troop lists or locations of units occurred during the remaining months of 1946 or in 1947.[122] (Plate No. 22)

By the end of 1946, most of the combat veterans had been returned to the Zone of Interior and had been replaced largely by draftees inducted near the end of the war or afterward. Many of them arrived in Japan with incomplete basic training; camps were built and special training programs were instituted. Units were so critically short of

118 *Ibid,* Part VI.

119 Occupational Monogr of the Eighth US Army in Japan Vol. II, Jan—Aug 46 (C), p. 46.

120 *Ibid,* p. 50. By mid-year the 19th Infantry relieved the Marines in Oita and Miyazaki Prefectures. The 2d Marine Regiment moved to Sasebo at this time.

121 On 15 June the 8th Marine Regiment departed from Kyushu and reverted to control of CG, Fleet Marine Force, Pacific, for disposition; on 5 July elements of the 5th Marine Regiment left Kyushu under the same conditions while the remaining elements followed shortly thereafter. (Eighth US Army, G-3 Periodic Rpts No. 67, 22 Jun 46; No. 69, 6 Jul 46.)

122 Occupational Monogr of the Eighth US Army in Japan, Vol. III, Sep 46—Dec 47 (C), pp. 5–6.

personnel that much of this took the form of on-the-job training. Within ten months the bulk of these young draftees were replaced by Regular Army enlisted men, increasing the trend toward a more stabilized peacetime organization. From the military standpoint, local duties became routine. Except for guard duty and disaster relief work, the primary duties of a combat army disappeared.

The Occupation pattern had developed sufficiently to have its characteristics remain fairly constant after 1946. The decline in strength of military forces was contrasted by the rise in the number of civilian specialists and other employees sent in from the Zone of Interior or hired locally to carry on the Occupation. Although the administration of the Occupation was still in the hands of the military, its operation became increasingly a function of the Japanese civil sections operating under General MacArthur in his capacity as the Supreme Commander for the Allied Powers.

CHAPTER III

THE COMMAND STRUCTURE: AFPAC, FEC AND SCAP

Establishment of AFPAC: Army Forces in the Pacific

The conquest of the Philippines completed the principal mission of the Commander in Chief of the Southwest Pacific Area.

On 4 April 1945 a command directive was issued by the Joint Chiefs of Staff for the guidance of commanders in the Pacific Theater. This directive stated that the over-all objective in the war against Japan was to be brought about at the earliest practicable date by establishing sea and air blockades, by conducting intensive air bombardments and destroying Japanese air and naval strength, and by invading and seizing objectives in the industrial heart of Japan. General MacArthur was designated as Commander in Chief, Army Forces in the Pacific, (CINCAFPAC) and all U.S. Army resources in the Pacific (less SE Pacific Area and Alaskan Department) were placed under his control.[1]

On 6 April, the War Department ordered the above consolidation:[2]

Effective at once U.S. Army Forces in the Pacific is established. Short title AFPAC. U.S. Army Forces in the Pacific will consist of those forces presently assigned U.S. Army Forces in POA. General of the Army MacArthur is designated Commander-in-Chief, U.S. Army Forces in the Pacific (CINC-AFPAC), in addition to his present assignment. Transfer of forces will be accomplished in accordance

with instructions issued by JCS already.

On the same day General MacArthur issued General Order Number 1, GHQ, AFPAC, which established AFPAC and placed it under his command. Four months later the Japanese surrendered.

The command structure of AFPAC remained static throughout the initial phases of the Occupation and furnished the military background for the development of SCAP, the next evolutionary step in the high command. (Plate No. 23)

Establishment of SCAP: Supreme Commander for the Allied Powers

At Potsdam in July of 1945, the heads of the governments of the United States and the United Kingdom agreed upon the terms of the surrender ultimatum to be offered Japan. Following this agreement, the Potsdam Declaration, concurred in by China and subsequently approved by the Union of Soviet Socialist Republics, was issued on 26 July. The Japanese capitulation proclamation included acceptance of the terms of this declaration.

On 14 August General MacArthur was designated " Supreme Commander for the Allied Powers " (SCAP) pursuant to an international agreement among the above four governments. This instrument accorded the General an extraordinary range of authority:[3]

---

1   Rad WX 62733 (TS), JCS to MacArthur, 4 Apr 45.   In C/S GHQ SWPA, WD 956 (S).
2   Rad WX 63939, Washington to Distr, 6 Apr 45.   In C/S GHQ SWPA, WD 959 (S).
3   (1) Rad W 48672 (TS), WARCOS to CINCAFPAC, 13 Aug 45.   In C/S GHQ SWPA, WD 1119 (S).

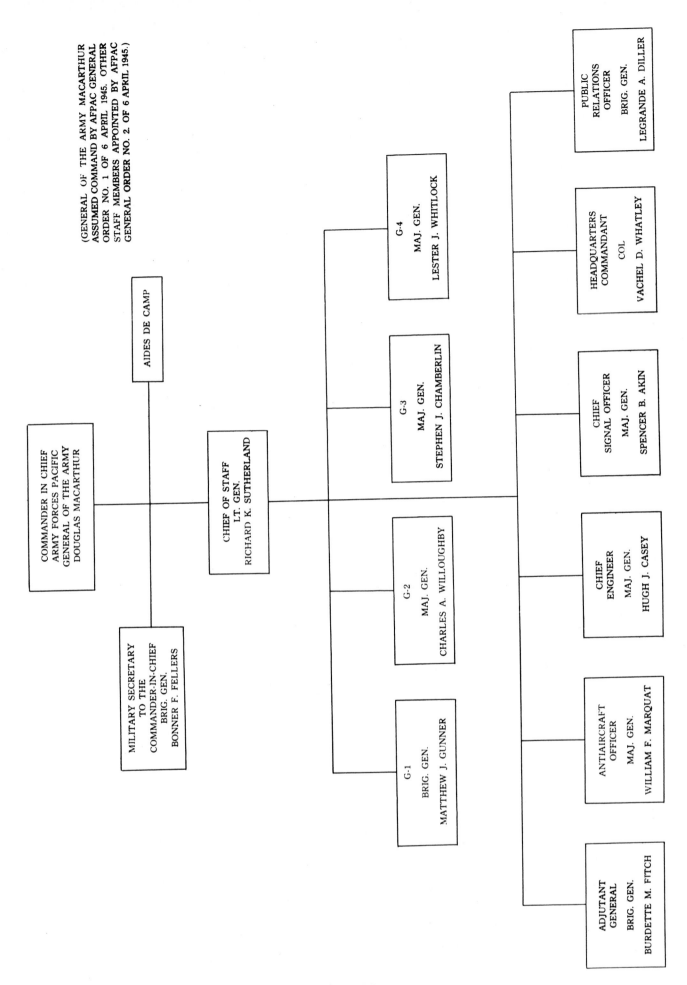

(GENERAL OF THE ARMY MACARTHUR ASSUMED COMMAND BY AFPAC GENERAL ORDER NO. 1 OF 6 APRIL 1945. OTHER STAFF MEMBERS APPOINTED BY AFPAC GENERAL ORDER NO. 2 OF 6 APRIL 1945.)

COMMANDER IN CHIEF ARMY FORCES PACIFIC GENERAL OF THE ARMY DOUGLAS MACARTHUR

AIDES DE CAMP

MILITARY SECRETARY TO THE COMMANDER-IN-CHIEF BRIG. GEN. BONNER F. FELLERS

CHIEF OF STAFF LT. GEN. RICHARD K. SUTHERLAND

G-1 BRIG. GEN. MATTHEW J. GUNNER

G-2 MAJ. GEN. CHARLES A. WILLOUGHBY

G-3 MAJ. GEN. STEPHEN J. CHAMBERLIN

G-4 MAJ. GEN. LESTER J. WHITLOCK

ADJUTANT GENERAL BRIG. GEN. BURDETTE M. FITCH

ANTIAIRCRAFT OFFICER MAJ. GEN. WILLIAM F. MARQUAT

CHIEF ENGINEER MAJ. GEN. HUGH J. CASEY

CHIEF SIGNAL OFFICER MAJ. GEN. SPENCER B. AKIN

HEADQUARTERS COMMANDANT COL VACHEL D. WHATLEY

PUBLIC RELATIONS OFFICER BRIG. GEN. LEGRANDE A. DILLER

PLATE NO. 23

Organization of General Headquarters, Army Forces in the Pacific, 6 April 1945

From the moment of surrender, the authority of the Emperor and the Japanese Government to rule the state will be subject to you and you will take such steps as you deem proper to effectuate the surrender terms.

You will exercise supreme command over all land, sea and air forces which may be allocated for enforcement in Japan of the surrender terms by the Allied Forces concerned.

While the Occupation of Japan was still in progress, the U. S. Joint Chiefs of Staff issued a "Basic Directive for Post-Surrender Military Government in Japan Proper";[4] this directive reiterated General MacArthur's authority as SCAP and defined policies for his guidance in the Occupation and the control of Japan. It described Japan as consisting of four main islands: Hokkaido (Yezo), Honshu, Kyushu, Shikoku, and about 1,000 smaller adjacent islands. (Plate No. 24) Later directives extended the area south to 30° north latitude.[5]

SCAP was granted authority to establish direct military government if necessary;[6] he was, however, to exercise his power, as far as compatible with the accomplishment of his mission, through the Emperor of Japan and the Japanese Government.[7] This authority determined the administrative character of the Occupation. Direct military government, similar to the type operating in Germany, was not established in Japan. The Japanese Government was permitted to exercise normal powers in matters of domestic administration; certain changes in governmental machinery and personnel were made to insure that requirements of the Occupation were met.

The Far Eastern Commission

Although in its basic concepts the Occupation of Japan was undertaken on behalf of the principal Allied Powers, in its practical aspects, it was essentially a United States operation. It did assume a more Allied character, however, with the establishment of the Far Eastern Commission in Washington and the Allied Council for Japan in Tokyo. These two organs were agreed upon in a meeting of the Foreign Ministers of the United States, United Kingdom, and U.S.S.R. at Moscow in December 1945, and were subsequently approved by China.[8]

The Far Eastern Commission was established as a high policy-making body for the Occupation of Japan. It consisted of representatives from eleven nations: China, the United Kingdom, the United States, Union of Soviet Socialist Republics, France, the Netherlands, Canada, Australia, New Zealand, India, and the Philippines. The Commission formulated policies, principles, and standards for accomplishing the terms of the surrender; it reviewed, upon the request of any member, directives issued to the Supreme Commander or action taken by him involving policy decisions within the jurisdiction of the Commission; and it considered such other matters as might be assigned to it by agreement among the participating governments. However, the Commission had no authority to make recommendations for territorial adjustments nor to conduct military operations.[9]

The Allied Council for Japan

The Allied Council for Japan was initially

---

4 JCS Dir 1380/15, 3 Nov 45 (TS).
5 GHQ SCAP Occupation Instns No. 5, 1 Jan 48.
6 JCS Dir 1380/15, 3 Nov 45, sub: Basic Dir for Post Surr Mil Govt in Japan Proper.
7 USAFPAC Opn Instns No. 4, 29 Nov 45 (Rev) (R), Annex 8, Mil Govt.
8 Rad WCL 32355, Washington to CINCAFPAC ADV, 28 Dec 45.
9 Communique of Moscow Conference, 27 Dec 45.

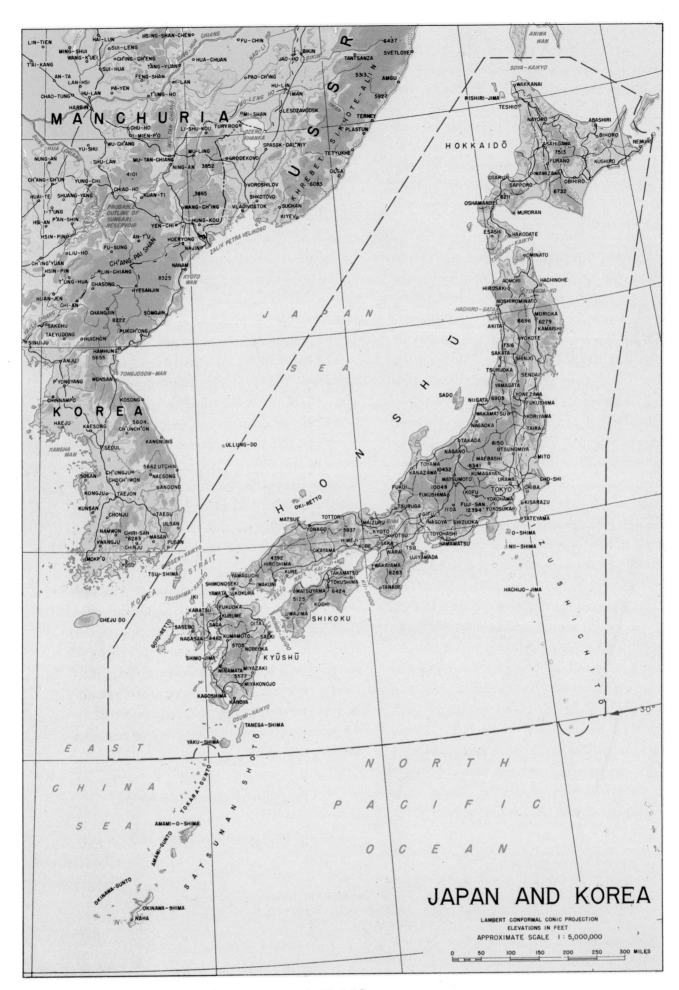

JAPAN AND KOREA

LAMBERT CONFORMAL CONIC PROJECTION
ELEVATIONS IN FEET
APPROXIMATE SCALE 1 : 5,000,000

0   50   100   150   200   250   300 MILES

PLATE NO. 24
Area Controlled by SCAP

an advisory body. It was located in Tokyo and consisted of four members : the Supreme Commander (or his Deputy), who was Chairman and United States Representative ; a representative each from the Soviet Union and China ; and a member representing jointly the United Kingdom, Australia, New Zealand, and India.[10] The Council met every two weeks "to consult with and advise" the Supreme Commander on the implementation of the terms of surrender, the occupation and control of Japan, and any supplementary directives ; it exercised certain limited authority.

The Supreme Commander carried out the terms of the basic directive and supplementary interim directives of the U. S. Joint Chiefs of Staff. Policies adopted by the Far Eastern Commission were transmitted to him through the Joint Chiefs of Staff. SCAP issued the necessary orders and directives to the Japanese Government and to the Occupation forces, and insured that these orders were put into effect.

Despite the fact that he was directly responsible to the U. S. Joint Chiefs of Staff, he consulted and advised the Allied Council for Japan on matters of substance in the execution of policy decisions of the Far Eastern Commission.

In the event that a member of the Council disagreed with the Supreme Commander's proposed action regarding the execution of policy decisions of the Far Eastern Commission, concerning a change in the regime of control, fundamental changes in the Japanese constitutional structure, a change in the Japanese

Government as a whole, or related matters, the Supreme Commander did not issue final orders until there was agreement with the Far Eastern Commission.[11] (See Plate No. 25 for visual presentation of relationships discussed.)

Organization of General Headquarters, SCAP

After the appointment of General Mac-Arthur as Supreme Commander,[12] a General Headquarters for SCAP was established with origins in the then existing GHQ, AFPAC (U. S. Army Forces in the Pacific) ; GHQ, AFPAC, and GHQ, SCAP, were physically combined and, for practical reasons, a number of staff sections, agencies and individuals continued to perform dual roles for SCAP and AFPAC. There was, however, a distinct demarcation between the authority and responsibility of SCAP and CINCAFPAC. SCAP's authority was limited to Japan, whereas CINCAFPAC commanded all Army Forces in the Pacific area.

The Supreme Commander exercised authority over all land, sea, and air forces which were then assigned to Japan. These forces included the British Commonwealth Occupation Force (BCOF)—the only representative Allied force present—the U. S. naval forces, and U. S. air forces. The Eighth U. S. Army was the actual Army of Occupation[13] and was charged with the tactical mission of implementing and enforcing SCAP directives.

The Supreme Commander exercised control

---

10   Rad WCL 32355, Washington to CINCAFPAC ADV, 28 Dec 45.

11   Other than the foregoing, the Allied Council had no obvious relationship to the Far Eastern Commission. There have been recognizable instances, however, in international press releases, in which the timing of publicity indicated that certain foreign powers simultaneously presented the same subject, agenda, comment or argument in the Council and in the Commission.

12   Rad W 48672 (TS), WARCOS to CINCAFPAC, 13 Aug 45.   In C/S GHQ SWPA, WD 1119 (S).

13   The Sixth US Army occupied the islands of Kyushu, Shikoku, and the western half of Honshu from 22 September to 31 December 1945, at which time control passed to the Eighth US Army. The Sixth Army was inactivated on 26 January 1946.   (8th Info and Hist Sv, Sixth Army Occupation of Japan, 22 Sep—30 Nov 45.)

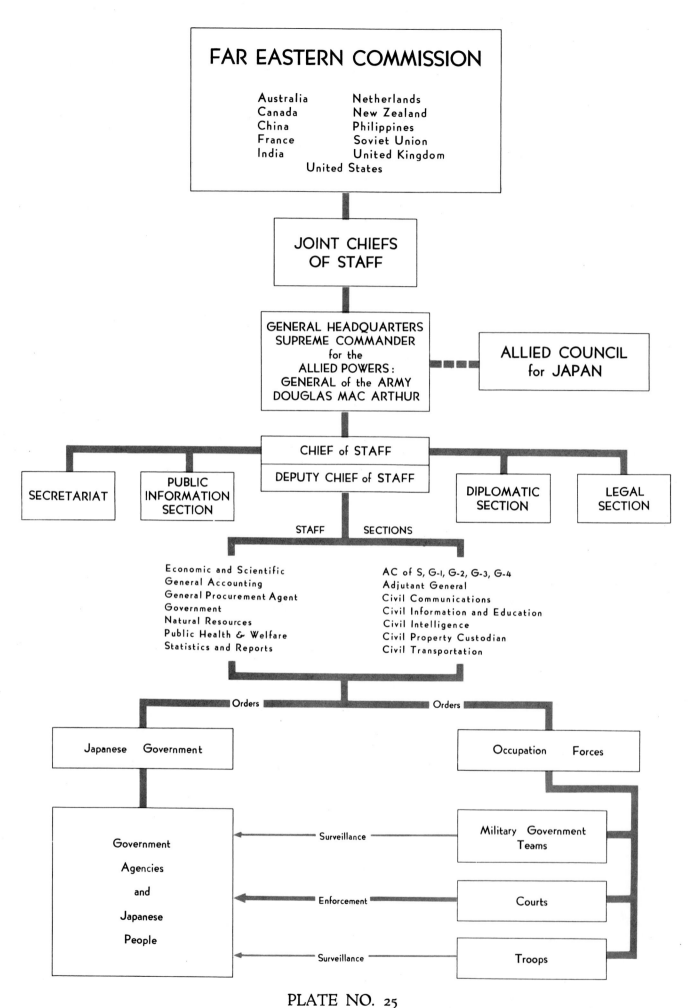

FAR EASTERN COMMISSION

Australia   Netherlands
Canada   New Zealand
China   Philippines
France   Soviet Union
India   United Kingdom
United States

JOINT CHIEFS OF STAFF

GENERAL HEADQUARTERS SUPREME COMMANDER for the ALLIED POWERS: GENERAL of the ARMY DOUGLAS MAC ARTHUR

ALLIED COUNCIL for JAPAN

CHIEF of STAFF
DEPUTY CHIEF of STAFF

SECRETARIAT   **PUBLIC INFORMATION SECTION**   **DIPLOMATIC SECTION**   **LEGAL SECTION**

STAFF   SECTIONS

Economic and Scientific
General Accounting
General Procurement Agent
Government
Natural Resources
Public Health & Welfare
Statistics and Reports

AC of S, G-1, G-2, G-3, G-4
Adjutant General
Civil Communications
Civil Information and Education
Civil Intelligence
Civil Property Custodian
Civil Transportation

Orders   Orders

Japanese Government

Occupation Forces

Government Agencies and Japanese People

Military Government Teams

— Surveillance →

Courts

— Enforcement →

Troops

— Surveillance →

PLATE NO. 25

The Machinery of the Occupation of Japan from the Far Eastern Commission
through SCAP to the Japanese People, December 1948.

of the Japanese people through the normal administrative organs of the Japanese Government. The established form of communication was a memorandum for the Japanese Government (known as a SCAPIN), authenticated by the Adjutant General, and dispatched through the Liaison and Coordination Office, an administrative agency in the Prime Minister's Office.[14] The Liaison and Coordination Office then transmitted the memorandum to the proper ministry or other agency of the Japanese Government for necessary action. To insure Japanese compliance with the directives of the Supreme Commander, two methods were used : transitory inspections by representatives of the staff sections of GHQ, and continuous observation and surveillance by the Occupation forces.[15] In order to accomplish these aims, the Eighth Army utilized the military government teams which had been organized, prior to the surrender, for possible use in establishing direct military government in Japan.[16]

The General Staff Sections, AFPAC, performed certain limited duties for SCAP.[17] For example, the G-1 for AFPAC was also the G-1 for SCAP; the General Staff, however, did not coordinate the activities of the SCAP Civil Sections except in matters affecting the Occupation forces from a specific military point of view.[18]

There were other equally important enforcement and surveillance agencies operating on a national scale from the outset of the Occupation : Counter Intelligence, Censorship, Public Safety, the Military Police and local Provost Marshal.

Functions of General Headquarters, SCAP

General Headquarters, SCAP, functioned along the lines of a conventional military staff, but since SCAP was charged with the primary mission of steering the Japanese nation and people along the lines of SCAP directives, its staff structure was designed to meet requirements of Japanese civil affairs in all phases of human activity.

Operations instructions, SCAP, were carried out by the Eighth U. S. Army[19] and, when practicable, through the CG, FEAF, and COMNAVJAP. The Supreme Commander exercised jurisdiction over the air forces allocated to the Occupation through the CG, FEAF;[20] the latter also had operational control over BCOF's air contingent.[21]

BCOF was integrated in and under the operational control of the Eighth U. S. Army

---

14 The Japanese Central Liaison Office also maintained a representative in the grade of *Chokunin* (Minister) in the G-2 Foreign and Japanese Liaison Section. The ever-increasing problems of interpretation and translation were handled by wartime ATIS (Allied Translator and Interpreter Service) which adjusted its operations to meet Occupation conditions.

15 (1) SCAP Staff Memo No. 7, 13 Feb 46 ; (2) SCAP & USAFPAC Staff Memo No. 56, 10 Dec 46.

16 (1) See Ch. VII ; (2) SCAP Occupation Instns No. 4, 20 Sep 46 (R).

17 GHQ SCAP Cir No. 14, 26 Dec 46, par. 2.

18 Several of the SCAP Civil Sections were headed by officers who remained chiefs of Staff Sections of GHQ AFPAC ; for example, Gen Willoughby was Chief of Civil Intelligence Section (CIS) as well as G-2 for GHQ, SCAP and AFPAC ; Brig Gen G.I. Back was Signal Officer of AFPAC as well as Chief of the Civil Communications Section ; Gen F.S. Besson was Transportation Officer for AFPAC as well as Chief of the Civil Transportation Section.

19 SCAPIN 436, 13 Dec 45, sub : Regrouping and Consolidation of Occupation Forces in Japan (GC).

20 (1) SCAP Occupation Instns No. 1, 13 Sep 45 (S) ; (2) JCS Dir 1259/27, 11 Dec 46 ; (3) Rad ZX 29678, CINCAFPAC to CG's Conc, 30 Dec 46 ; (4) GHQ FEC Cir No. 1, 1 Jan 47.

21 (1) SCAP Occupation Instns No. 3, 12 Feb 46 (R) ; (2) USAFPAC G-3 Opns Rpt No. 1415, 22 Feb —1 Mar 46.

and received operational orders in the same manner as United States forces.[22] The Commanding General, BCOF, however, had direct access to the Supreme Commander on matters of major policy of his force.[23] BCOF was administered and supported logistically by the British Commonwealth and had direct communication with the British Commonwealth Joint Chiefs of Staff in Australia.[24]

The Supreme Commander exercised command of naval forces allocated to the Occupation through COMNAVJAP. Actually the headquarters of COMNAVFE (Commander, U. S. Naval Forces, Far East) and COMNAVJAP were physically combined. COMNAVJAP controlled the coastal waters of Japan, commanded all naval activities ashore in the Occupation area, and exercised operational control of all naval forces, both U. S. and Allied, assigned to the Occupation of Japan.[25] COMNAVJAP also controlled activities of Japanese shipping through SCAJAP (Shipping Control Authority for the Japanese Merchant Marine).[26] SCAJAP played an important role in the general repatriation movements.

As naval representative of SCAP,[27] COM-

NAVJAP was responsible for the disposal and scrapping of the Japanese Navy;[28] repatriation of Japanese and other foreign nationals;[29] mine-sweeping in Japanese waters;[30] the supervision of the Japanese Merchant Marine;[31] and declaration and disposal of surplus naval property.

The Military Government teams which the Eighth Army used to insure Japanese compliance with SCAP directives were spread throughout Japan to cover the principal centers of population and industry.[32] The Army commander, however, was not limited to these teams in his supervision, but used tactical troops in surveillance missions when necessary.[33]

Progressive steps were taken to enforce SCAP's orders. First, the Japanese Government was held responsible for its actions and for the enforcement of laws, ordinances, and regulations which were promulgated to carry out the instructions of SCAP. Secondly, juridical enforcement was effected by the military occupation courts. They had sole jurisdiction with Japanese courts over any act prejudicial to the objectives of the Occupation.[34] Ultimate enforcement rested with the Occupation troops.

---

22 (1) SCAP Occupation Instns No. 3, 13 Feb 46; (2) Eighth Army Rad EX 34063 FB, 4 Mar 46. (GHQ SCAP, Hist of the Non Mil Aspects of the Allied Occupation of Japan, 2 Sep 45—1 Jan 47, p. 4.)

23 SCAP Occupation Instns No. 3, 12 Feb 46.

24 *Ibid.*

25 SCAP Occupation Instns No. 4, 20 Sep 46.

26 SCAP Occupation Instns No. 5, 1 Jan 48.

27 Rad 200157, COM5thFLT to COMNAVJAP, 20 Mar 46. (GHQ SCAP, Hist of the Non Mil Aspects of the Allied Occupation of Japan, 2 Sep 45—1 Jan 47, p. 5.)

28 SCAP Occupation Instns No. 4, 20 Sep 46.

29 *Ibid.*

30 *Ibid.*

31 *Ibid.*

32 Rpt of the MG Sec, GHQ USAFPAC, 5 Aug—2 Oct 45. (GHQ SCAP, Hist of the Non Mil Aspects of the Allied Occupation of Japan, 2 Sep 45—1 Jan 47, p. 6.)

33 As a corollary, the 441st CIC, an operating agency of the AC of S, G-2, in his dual role as Chief, CIS, SCAP, deployed immediately into the field detachments, on initial landing in 1945, and maintained a complete coverge throughout Japan in each prefecture.

34 (1) SCAPIN 756, 19 Feb 46, sub: Exercise of Criminal Jurisdiction; (2) SCAPIN 853, 25 Mar 46, sub: Exercise of Criminal Jurisdiction; (3) SCAPIN 1218, 19 Sep 46, sub: Amendment of Memo on Civil and Criminal Jurisdiction.

The Civil (Non-Military) Staff Sections, SCAP

Before the Japanese surrender in August 1945, a Military Government Section was established in GHQ, AFPAC, to administer occupied Japan.[35] This section with its subordinate units was to take over the Government of Japan in every phase of activity. It assumed the duties of preparing plans for direct military government of Japan.[36] Personnel specially trained for military government were assigned to the Military Government Section and to the Sixth and Eighth Armies, where they performed staff functions at army, corps, and division levels and were organized into units for use at the prefectural and local levels.[37]

On 28 August 1945 Military Government activities of army and corps commanders were limited to a few specified functions and the following policies were set forth:[38]

(1)   SCAP will issue all necessary instructions directly to the Japanese Government.

(2)   Every opportunity will be given the Government and people of Japan to carry out such instructions without further compulsion.

(3)   The Occupation Forces will act principally as an agency upon which SCAP can call, if necessary, to secure compliance with instructions issued to the Japanese Government and will observe and report on compliance.

A 6 September basic Occupation policy directive ordered that:[39]

. . . in view of the present character of Japanese society and the desire of the United States to attain its objectives with a minimum commitment of its forces and resources, the Supreme Commander will exercise authority through Japanese Governmental machinery and agencies, including the Emperor, to the extent that this satisfactorily further United States objectives.

Certain supervisory activities of the Military Government Section were then transferred to the newly established Economic and Scientific and Civil Information and Education Sections of General Headquarters, AFPAC.[40]

On 26 September the Chief of Staff, AFPAC, announced that:[41]

(1)   So long as the system of enforcing the Potsdam Declaration and the surrender terms through the Japanese Government worked satisfactorily, there would be no direct military government in Japan.

(2)   A number of special staff sections would be established by General Headquarters, SCAP, to advise the Supreme Commander on non-military matters in relation to the occupation of Japan.

(3)   The Military Government Section, General Headquarters, USAFPAC would be discontinued and its remaining personnel transferred to the several new staff sections or to the military government of Korea.

The Supreme Commander established General Headquarters, SCAP, on 2 October 1945[42] with general and special staff sections, using

---

35   USAFPAC GO No. 92, 5 Aug 45 (R).

36   USA FM 27–5, par 22, defines the duties assigned to the MG sections of a theater staff.

37   Rpt of the MG Sec, GHQ USAFPAC, 5 Aug—2 Oct 45.

38   USAFPAC Opns Instns No. 4, 28 Aug 45 (S), Annex 8, Mil Govt. (GHQ SCAP, Hist of the Non Mil Aspects of the Allied Occupation of Japan, 2 Sep 45—1 Jan 47, p. 6.)

39   SWNCC 150/4, 6 Sep 45.   Subsequent basic Occupation directives repeated the substance of this provision. (GHQ SCAP, Hist of the Non Mil Aspects of the Allied Occupation of Japan, 2 Sep 45—1 Jan 47, p. 7.)

40   USAFPAC GO No. 170, 15 Sep 45 ; No. 183, 22 Sep 45 (R).

41   Rpt of the MG Sec, GHQ USAFPAC, 5 Aug—2 Oct 45 (C).   (GHQ SCAP, Hist of the Non Mil Aspects of the Allied Occupation of Japan, 2 Sep 45—1 Jan 47, p. 6.)

42   GHQ SCAP GO Nos. 1 and 2, 2 Oct 45.

the G-1, G-2, G-3, G-4, and Adjutant General's Sections and the Public Relations Office of U. S. Army Forces, Pacific[43] to perform their respective functions for SCAP.[44]

Ten special staff sections were activated on 2 October: the Economic and Scientific, Civil Information and Education, Natural Resources, Public Health and Welfare, Government, Legal, Civil Communications, Statistics and Reports, and Civil Intelligence Sections, and the Office of the General Procurement Agent.[45] Those subsequently established were the Office of Civilian Personnel, International Prosecution Section, General Accounting Section, Civil Property Custodian, Diplomatic Section, and Civil Transportation Section.[46]

The Civil Intelligence Section was discontinued on 3 May 1946 and its duties assumed by the Assistant Chief of Staff, G-2.[47] On 29 August it was reactivated[48] but continued under operational control of G-2 in his dual capacity as Chief of Theater Counter Intelligence.

The SCAP Sections (Plate No. 26) corresponded in general to the technical branches of the Japanese civil government with which they were associated.[49] They were responsible for making recommendations to the Supreme Commander on policies and actions which would implement the terms of the surrender and the directives received from higher authorities. They carried on continuous research and analysis and maintained close liaison with their counterparts in the Japanese Government.[50] They operated directly under a Deputy Chief of Staff who was assisted by an Executive for Administrative Affairs and an Executive for Economic and Industrial Affairs.

These staff sections of SCAP Headquarters were charged with responsibility for initiating action on Occupation matters, and with continuing necessary staff action to follow the assigned tasks through to completion.[51] In cases where several staff sections had a major interest in a problem, the initiating section was responsible for accomplishing intra-staff liaison to bring about complete and coordinated action. In effecting this liaison, staff sections were directed to make liberal use of personal contact and other informal methods.[52]

The International Military Tribunal for the Far East (IMTFE) was not a part of the Headquarters, but a related operating agency. It was established by the Supreme Commander on 19 January 1946 for the just and prompt trial and punishment of major war criminals in the Far East. It consisted of judicial representatives of nations who were members of the Far Eastern Commission. The Supreme Commander was charged with reviewing the proceed-

---

43   Of which he was Commander in Chief.   (SCAPIN 2; Dir No. 2, Office of SCAP, 3 Sep 45.)

44   SCAP Cir No. 14, 26 Dec 46, inclosing organization chart of GHQ SCAP.

45   SCAP GO Nos. 3, 4, 5, 6, 7, 8, 10, 11, 12, and 13, 2 Oct 45.

46   SCAP GO No. 16, 14 Nov 45; No. 20, 8 Dec 45; No. 4, 24 Jan 46; No. 10, 8 Mar 46; No. 18, 18 Apr 46; No. 35, 7 Sep 46.

47   GHQ SCAP GO No. 22, 3 May 46.

48   GHQ SCAP GO No. 34, 29 Aug 46.

49   SCAP sections have no exact counterparts in a normal military staff.   Their establishment was caused by conditions peculiar to the Occupation and they played an important part in the outstanding success of the control and rehabilitation of a nation of over 77 million people.

50   When necessary, the General Staff sections of GHQ, AFPAC, furnished administrative, logistic, and service support to SCAP civil staff sections and agencies.

51   SCAP Staff Memo No. 6, 28 Nov 45.   (TS) (GHQ SCAP, Hist of the Non Mil Aspects of the Allied Occupation of Japan, 2 Sep 45—1 Jan 47, p. 9.)

52   *Ibid.*

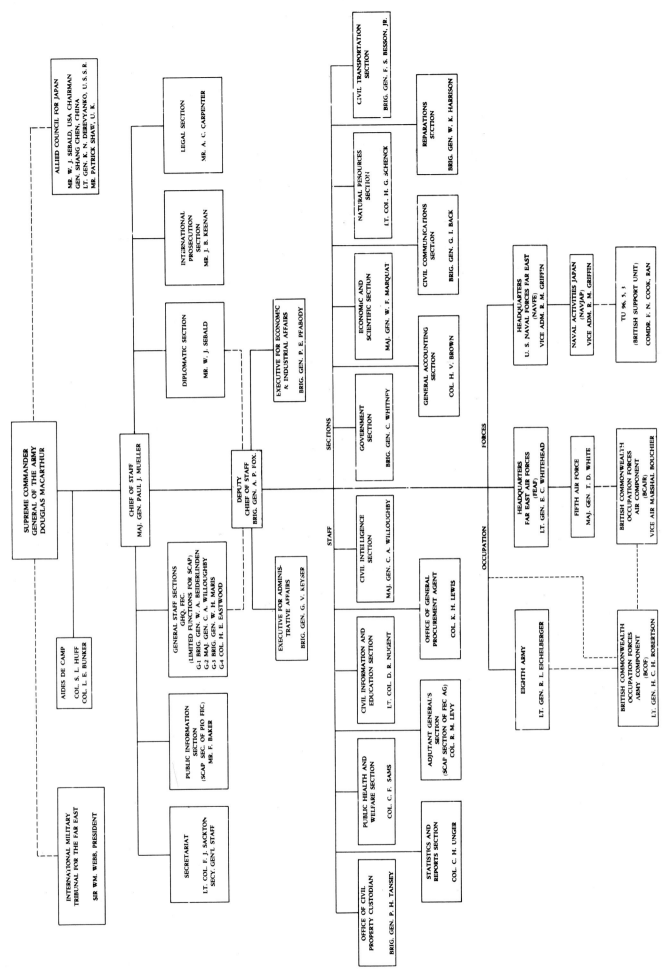

PLATE NO. 26

General Headquarters, Supreme Commander for the Allied Powers, 31 December 1947

ings of the Tribunal on the completion of its work and with the execution of its judgments.[53]

The International Prosecution Section was established as a special staff section to prepare for trial and prosecute all cases involving crime resulting from planning, preparing, initiating, or waging of a war of aggression or a war in violation of international treaties and agreements, or participation in a common plan or conspiracy for the accomplishment of any of the foregoing.[54]

The Legal Section was established as a special staff section to advise the Supreme Commander for the Allied Powers on: general policies and procedures with respect to war crimes in categories other than the international aspects, which are commonly known as violation of the laws or customs of war, and to supervise the prosecution of war criminals accused of such offenses; general policies and procedures with respect to Occupation courts; and legal matters of a general nature. This section investigated such war crimes as mentioned above, prepared such cases to be tried, established and maintained a central registry of all Japanese war criminals and suspects and made recommendations pertaining to their apprehension and incarceration (this comprised all categories of war criminals). It recommended composition of military courts, commissions or other tribunals for the trial of Japanese war criminals accused of violation of the laws or customs of war, and the rules and procedures for the guidance thereof, and recommended composition of military courts, commissions or other tribunals for the trial of persons accused of violation of the rules and regulations of the Occupation orces, and the rules and procedures for the guidance thereof.[55]

The Diplomatic Section, an outgrowth of the Office of the United States Political Advisor for Japan, was an integral section of GHQ, SCAP.[56] It dealt with international affairs pertaining to Japan. The Section controlled relationships with foreign diplomatic representatives and supervised other U. S. State Department agencies in Japan.[57] As chairman and member for the United States on the Allied Council for Japan, the chief of the Diplomatic Section was also deputy for the Supreme Commander.

The Economic and Scientific Section was established as a special staff section which was responsible for developing economic, industrial, financial, and scientific policies to be pursued in Japan in order to implement the Potsdam Declaration.[58] Its functions consisted of making recommendations towards maximum production and equitable distribution of essential goods among the civil population and the maximum production of supplies required by the occupying forces. It coordinated the activities of commercial, technical, and industrial missions from the United States and Allied nations which were concerned with the economic, industrial, financial, or scientific rehabilitation of Japan.[59] The Economic and Scientific Section also advised the Supreme Commander on Japanese labor policies and programs, including labor relations and labor unions; employment and employment exchanges; wages, salaries, and hours; protective

---

53 GHQ SCAP GO No. 20, 26 Apr 46.

54 GHQ SCAP GO No. 20, 8 Dec 45.

55 GHQ SCAP GO No. 21, 9 Dec 45.

56 Note the previous intervention of G-2 Foreign Liaison: September 1945 to March 1946.

57 GHQ SCAP GO No. 18, 18 Apr 46.

58 GHQ SCAP GO No. 3, 2 Oct 45.

59 G-2 maintained a remnant of its wartime Technical Intelligence Teams (5250th Tech Int Co) which worked on numerous projects for ESS.

labor legislation; and labor procurement for the Occupation forces.[60]

SCAP's mission in the economic field in Japan was an integral part of the total Occupation objective, namely, to insure that Japan would not again, alone or jointly with other powers, commit aggressive warfare. In an attempt to carry out this mission, three major lines of action were followed in the economic field: the industrial and scientific disarmament of Japan, the democratization and reform of the economic structure, and the restoration of the Japanese general economy on a self-supporting basis. Since Japan could feed herself only by exporting manufactured products, her economy was closely geared to foreign trade. American aid was limited to the most urgent requirements necessary to avoid disease and unrest in the harrassed population. American appropriation made possible the importation of food, fertilizer, petroleum products, and medicines. With the exception of cotton, Japan had no funds to import raw materials.

In March 1947 ESS was granted the power to issue licenses to approved foreign concerns desiring to conduct business in Japan. Such licenses incorporated restrictions which were necessary to assure compliance with all existing regulations.[61] On 15 August 1947, private foreign trade representatives were permitted to enter Japan.

As a still further potential stimulus to foreign trade, SCAP projected a plan to use Japanese-owned gold and silver as a base for acquiring foreign credits. This was achieved by creating the "Occupied Japan Export-Import Revolving Fund" which was to be used as a credit base for financing importation of raw materials for processing and exporting. This credit base was first utilized on 13 May 1948 when one government and three private banks pledged to finance a 60,000,000 dollar credit. The Economic and Scientific Section was responsible for advising the Supreme Commander on policies and programs relating to the custody, operation, management, and control of this fund.[62]

The Natural Resources Section. Although Japan claimed that the basic reason for her aggression in the Far East was economic, the chief cause being the desperate need for raw materials, the ironic result was further depletion of her meager resources. To establish favorable economic conditions, which would help prevent the revival of militarism, it was necessary to increase Japan's resources to satisfy her needs and to democratize her institutions.

The Natural Resources Section was established as a special staff section to advise SCAP on agricultural, forestry, fishery, and mining (including geology and hydrology) policies and activities in Japan.[63] It arranged for and co-ordinated surveys and reports; located source data in Japan relating to agriculture, forestry, fishing and mining in countries formerly occupied by Japan; and recommended measures to insure the development, exploitation, production, processing, and distribution of basic industry products required for rehabilitation of the national economy.

The Civil Intelligence Section maintained a national system of intelligence and information coverage through its law enforcement and surveillance agencies. This section was the operating agency for counterintelligence and general security functions within the command and was primarily responsible for the dissolu-

---

60 GHQ SCAP GO No. 33, 29 Aug 46.

61 GHQ SCAP GO No. 3, 19 Mar 47.

62 (1) GHQ SCAP GO No. 12, 15 Aug 47; (2) GHQ SCAP Cirs No. 9, 15 Aug 47, and No. 15, 11 Dec 47.

63 GHQ SCAP GO No. 6, 2 Oct 45.

tion and surveillance of ultra-nationalistic and militaristic organizations. It was charged with public safety matters in Japan, including police, prison, maritime safety, and fire control systems, and also maintained censorship of Japanese information media, mail, and telecommunications.[64]

The Government Section was responsible for policies pertaining to the internal structure of civil government in Japan.[65] It investigated and reported to the Supreme Commander any modifications and reforms of civil government in Japan. It made recommendations regarding the demilitarization and decentralization of the Japanese Government as well as elimination of feudal and totalitarian practices. It investigated, reported, and made recommendations regarding laws, policies, practices, procedures, and other factors in the personnel administration of the Japanese Government, in order to develop democratic precepts, integrity, and efficiency in its administration.

The Civil Communications Section's functions were to rehabilitate and operate civil signal and postal communications in Japan.[66] It arranged for and coordinated surveys and reports on existing teleradio and postal communications systems and on laboratories and educational institutions which were adapted to the study of problems relating to signal communications facilities and conditions.

The Public Health and Welfare Section was required to initiate policies relating to public health and welfare problems.[67]

The primary consideration in public health and welfare activities was to achieve a level of health and welfare among the civil population which would prevent widespread disease and unrest likely to interfere with the Occupation. The major problem in attempting to achieve this goal was the lack of trained and qualified Japanese personnel to conduct the various programs at national, prefectural, and local levels. Also, there were not enough personnel among military government teams to supervise SCAP-directed national programs. A complete public health organization, from the Ministry of Welfare down to and including the health center level, was established throughout Japan. This called for many educational and training programs to instruct Japanese officials in modern public health and welfare practices. The improvement of public health and the development of welfare activities was an integral part of the program designed to help develop civic responsibilities.

The Civil Information and Education Section had the job of formulating policies for public education, religion, and other sociological problems of Japan.[68] It concentrated on educational and sociological reforms, with particular reference to the democratization of the national school system. It made recommendations to insure the elimination of doctrines of militarism and ultra-nationalism, including juvenile military training, from all elements of the Japanese educational system.[69] It also insured the protection, preservation, and salvage of works of art and antiquity, cultural treasures, religious articles, libraries, museums,

---

64 See Ch. VIII. In general terms, this section operated in a manner analagous to the American FBI. Adapted to Occupation conditions its activities became important in view of the rise of international communism.

65 GHQ SCAP GO No. 10, 23 Jun 47.

66 GHQ SCAP GO No. 6, 13 Apr 48.

67 GHQ SCAP GO No. 7, 2 Oct 45.

68 GHQ SCAP GO No. 27, 3 Jun 46. G-2 linguist agencies furnished a complete daily coverage of the Japanese press, as an aid to public opinion digests.

69 Through the collateral intervention of CIS in the control and surveillance of ultra-militaristic and subversive elements.

archival repositories, religious buildings, and historical monuments.

The Civil Transportation Section's duties consisted of making plans for the use and rehabilitation of water and land civil transportation facilities of Japan, except for operating responsibilities assigned to Commander, Naval Activities, Japan.[70] The Civil Transportation Section, in conjunction with the Economic and Scientific Section, established requirements and priorities in raw materials and industrial capacity necessary to provide the facilities and equipment for the transportation system in order to serve the essential needs of the internal economy of Japan.

The Statistics and Reports Section was responsible for the collection, tabulation, and presentation of statistical and other special and routine reports which pertained to the non-military aspects of the Occupation of Japan.[71]

The General Procurement Agent coordinated, controlled and issued regulations governing the procurement of supplies, equipment, materials, services, real property, and facilities in Japan in order to prevent competition in procurement. It provided for the equitable allocation of supplies, equipment, materials, real property and facilities, and services; standardized procedures for procurement; and effected equitable allocation of Japanese resources. The General Procurement Agent was also responsible for liaison with the Central Liaison Committee of the Japanese Government.[72]

The General Accounting Section was responsible for general policies and procedures pertaining to financial accounting matters and maintained records covering the financial aspects of the Occupation.[73]

The Office of the Civil Property Custodian advised on general policies and controlled and disposed of enemy and Allied properties and assets under its jurisdiction.[74] This office recommended and established procedures, and executed approved programs for the blocking and impounding of property which was acquired by Japan under duress, wrongful acts of confiscation, dispossession or spoilation. Lastly, it was responsible for the maintenance of complete records and accounts of all confiscated property and its disposal.

The Reparations Section planned the program for processing Japanese industrial assets considered available for claim and removal as reparations.[75]

The Reparations Technical Advisory Committee was established as a consultative committee to assist the Supreme Commander in the development of technical and administrative procedures to assure an orderly removal of reparations goods from Japan and in settling problems between countries arising over claims.[76] The Chairman of the Committee was the Chief of the Reparations Section. The other members of the Committee were chiefs of the Reparations and Restitutions Delegations which represented the Far Eastern Commission.

The Restitution Advisory Committee was established to assist the Supreme Commander in matters dealing with the disposition of property found in Japan and identified as having been located in an Allied country and removed to Japan by fraud or coercion by the Japanese or their agents.[77] The Restitution Advisory Committee consisted of a chairman and one member from each of the Reparations and Restitution Delegations representing nations in

70 GHQ SCAP GO No. 35, 7 Sep 46.
71 GHQ SCAP GO No. 6, 18 Apr 47.
72 GHQ SCAP GO No. 5, 2 Oct 45.
73 GHQ SCAP GO No. 4, 24 Jan 46.

74 GHQ SCAP GO No. 10, 8 Mar 46.
75 GHQ SCAP GO No. 8, 8 May 47.
76 GHQ SCAP GO No. 9, 21 May 47.
77 GHQ SCAP GO No. 5, 13 Apr 48.

the Far Eastern Commission who desired to participate. The Civil Property Custodian was Chairman of the Committee.

Foreign Diplomatic Missions

In addition to the administrative and advisory staffs authorized for the members of the Allied Council of Japan, a number of foreign diplomatic representatives, pre-war embassies, legations and agencies were accredited to SCAP rather than to the Japanese Government. (Plate No. 27) These diplomatic agencies served as channels of communication on operational and administrative matters between their governments and SCAP. Certain functional representatives, distinct from these missions, worked directly with SCAP in handling matters which pertained to restitution and reparations, as well as to foreign trade, on a government to government basis.[78]

Establishment and Missions of FEC: Far East Command

On 1 January 1947 a GHQ, FEC, order established the Far East Command, with General MacArthur as Commander in Chief.[79] This command was established as an interim measure for the immediate post-war period, with particular consideration to the tactical requirements for protracted occupation of former enemy areas. It was, in fact, an adaptation of the then existing AFPAC organization, with no change in the GHQ staff. It

was simply the old staff continuing under a new name, with many of its officers remaining in the same relative positions.

The Far East Command included the United States forces in Japan, Korea, the Ryukyus, the Philippines, the Marianas and the Bonins.[80] General MacArthur exercised unified command over all forces allocated to him by the Joint Chiefs of Staff and Allied Powers; however, it was at this time that the Army Forces in the Middle Pacific (AFMIDPAC) passed from his control.

The Commander in Chief, Far East Command, (CINCFE) was made responsible for United States occupation functions in Japan and in Southern Korea, and United States military duties in the Philippines. He was also responsible for security of the Far East Command, including the protection of sea and air communications, United States policy within the limit of his command, and support of the Commander in Chief, Pacific, in his mission. Lastly, he was charged with making plans and preparations in case of a general emergency. He was to provide for the safety of United States forces in Korea and China; oppose enemy advances; secure Japan, the Ryukyus, the Marianas, and the Bonins; and discharge United States military responsibilities in the Philippines.[81]

In the event of an emergency declared by General MacArthur, United States forces in China were to come under his control.[82] He was also assigned operational control of the facilities and local forces in the Marianas and

---

78   SCAP instituted a Foreign Liaison Section, under control of G-2, through which communications with diplomatic missions and the Japanese Government were initially handled. ([1] SCAP Staff Memo No. 41, 9 Jun 46, sub: Official Relations and Contacts with the IJG, with Staff Secs of GHQ, and with US Occupational Forces; [2] SCAP Staff Memo No. 49, 27 Jun 46, sub: Channels of Communication with Foreign Govts.)

79   GHQ FEC GO No. 1, 1 Jan 47. The order was in accordance with JCS Dir 1259/27, 11 Dec 46, sub: Unified Command Plan.

80   GHQ, FEC Opns Instns No. 2, 1 Feb 48 (S).

81   *Ibid.*

82   *Ibid.*

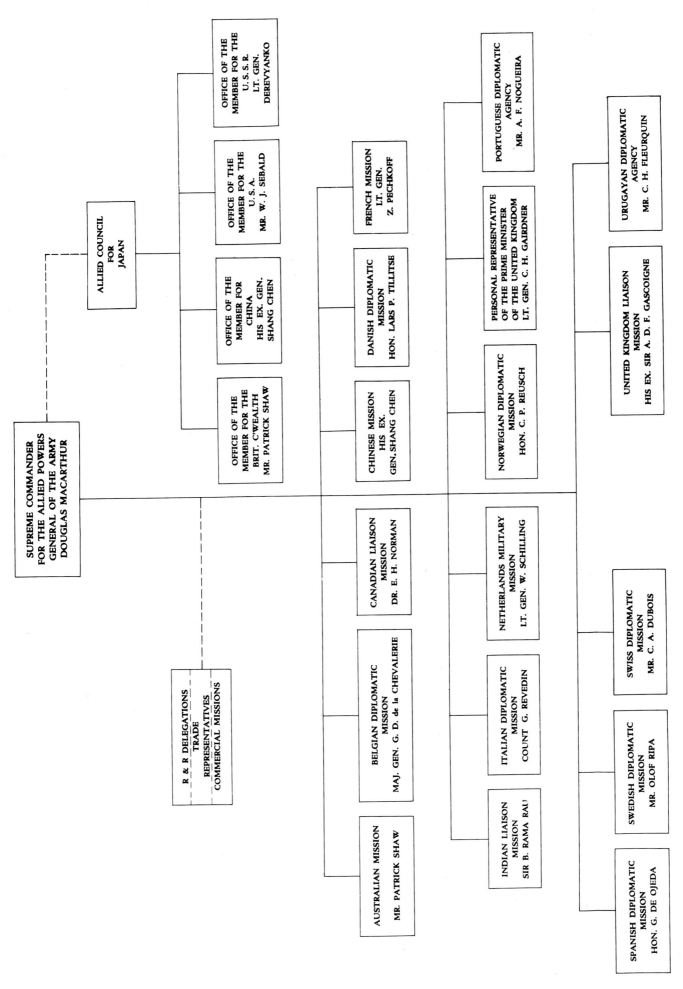

PLATE NO. 27

Foreign Diplomatic Missions and Agencies in Japan, September 1948

Bonin Islands;[83] this change was significant because the control did not include responsibility for the military and civil government of these islands, nor any responsibility for naval administration and naval logistics.[84] The overall plan, however, did make General MacArthur responsible for their security; local forces and their facilities were assigned to his operational control to assist him in discharging his mission.[85]

Command Structure of General Headquarters, FEC

The organization through which CINCFE administered and controlled the far-flung tactical establishment of FEC was a General Headquarters. It consisted of a conventional high-level military staff, with the addition of a Joint Strategic Plans and Operations Group. There was also an increase in the number of special staff sections. (Plate No. 28)

The Joint Strategic Plans and Operations Group became an important staff element in the exercise of unified command. It consisted basically of three small, co-equal Ground, Navy and Air Staff Groups which furnished planning teams for joint intelligence, joint operations and joint logistic planning. The Group was small, and its functions were limited to the preparation of joint plans for possible major emergencies.

The bulk of General Headquarters was located in the Administrative and Executive Group, which consisted of a conventional high-level General Staff and a Special Staff. This Group handled the major part of CINCFE's military operational functions, including those administrative aspects of joint command pertaining to the peacetime missions of the three services.

It should be mentioned again that the nature and duties of the General and Special Staff Sections did not change with the order creating the Far East Command. The change was merely in nomenclature—for example, G-3, GHQ, AFPAC became G-3, GHQ, FEC.

The primary mission of the Far East Command was to support the Occupation of Japan and Southern Korea.[86] A major portion of the Far East Command, including the British Commonwealth Occupation Force, carried out Occupation missions in Japan under the direct control of SCAP.[87] The command structure of the Far East Command and the allocation and distribution of forces was dictated by the

---

83 *Ibid.*

84 *Ibid.*

85 (1) JCS Dir 1259/27, 11 Dec 46 (C), sub: Unified Command Plan; (2) Rad WX-87793, Washington to CINCAFPAC, 17 Dec 46.

86 GHQ FEC Opns Instns No. 2, 1 Feb 48 (S). In addition, the FEC was assigned the following missions: (a) Discharge of US military responsibilities in the Philippines, under the terms of a Military Assistance Agreement and a Military Bases Agreement negotiated in March 1947. These responsibilities included the roll-up of wartime bases in the Philippines and the disposition of supplies accumulated there for the support of a full-scale offensive against Japan. (b) Maintenance of the security of the FEC, including the protection of sea and air communications. (c) Support of US policy within the scope of CINCFE's command responsibility. This mission involved carrying out the terms of numerous property sale and transfer agreements, the conduct of military government in the Ryukyus, and the conduct of a program of mapping land areas in and adjacent to the FEC, the latter in accordance with international agreements which provided for making such maps available to the Allied governments concerned. However responsibility for civil and military government functions in the Marianas-Bonin-Volcano Islands was specifically excluded from CINCFE's mission and assigned to the Pacific Command under the CinC, Pacific and US Pacific Fleet. The Pacific Command comprised the forces throughout the Pacific other than FEC forces. (d) The conduct of an extensive program of mapping and procurement of terrain intelligence in accordance with international agreements (See "c" above) Field operations covered the establishment of ground control and execution of aerial photography for mapping and charting Japan, Korea, Ryukyus, Philippines, Netherlands East Indies, and other areas in the South and Southwest Pacific.

87 JCS Dir 1259/27, 11 Dec 46 (C), sub: Unified Command Plan.

84

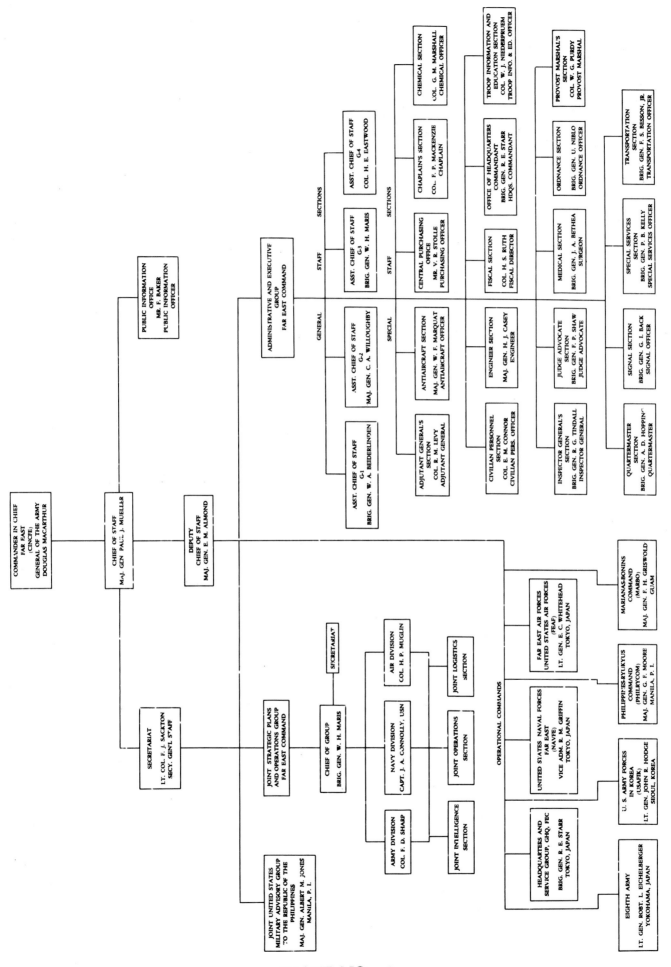

PLATE NO. 28
General Headquarters, Far East Command, December 1947

missions and the military geography of the area. (Plate No. 29)

By far the largest number of United States Ground Forces allocated to CINCFE were assigned to the Eighth Army, the major command charged with the tactical mission of occupying Japan. United States forces under the Eighth Army were divided into two corps—the IX Corps and the I Corps, each consisting of two divisions. The British Commonwealth Occupation Force came under General Mac-Arthur's operational control in his capacity as Supreme Commander and was assigned to Eighth Army. The XXIV Corps, consisting of two United States divisions, occupied Korea and was designated as U. S. Army Forces in Korea (USAFIK).

Generally speaking, the Far East Command was divided into an " Occupation Area " and a " Support Area," with major ground combat elements located in the Occupation Area. The remaining ground troops, primarily service troops and Philippine Scouts, were distributed among the major ground headquarters in the Support Area, and the Ryukyus, Philippines and Marianas—Bonins Commands. All of these, like Eighth Army and XXIV Corps, were army components. There was no over-all headquarters for the ground elements within the Far East Command, and the four separate ground commands reported directly to CINC-FE.

Because of their greater mobility, command of naval and air forces within the theater fol-lowed a somewhat different pattern, making it mandatory that control for each of these services be centralized in a single commander. The Commander, Naval Forces, Far East, (COMNAVFE) controlled all naval forces assigned to CINCFE and exercised his authority through appropriate subordinate naval headquarters.[88] The Commanding General, Far East Air Forces, (CG, FEAF) was responsible for all air forces assigned to the Far East Command,[89] including operational control of the British air contingent in Japan. He exercised his power through three Air Force headquarters and Headquarters, 1st Air Division. Within the over-all air and naval commands, the subordinate structure conformed to the geographical areas where the naval and air bases were located.

CINCFE controlled all ground forces and activities in the Ryukyus, including Military Government, through the Commanding General, Ryukyus Command. The over-all objective of the Military Government administration in the Ryukyu Islands was to maintain exclusive United States control in this area until such time as the international status and the future administration of these islands was determined.[90]

The Philippine Command had only a small force, maintained primarily as a supervisory echelon for the direction of the activities of the Philippine Scouts.[91] The Scouts, although still retaining a number of combat unit designations, performed guard duty over surplus property

---

88 SCAP Occupation Instns No. 5, 1 Jan 48.

89 *Ibid.*

90 Specific objectives of the Ryukyus Command were: (a) Liquidation of political, social, and economic ties with the Japanese mainland. (b) Restoration of standards of living consistent with those existing prior to the war by: physical restoration of damaged property and facilities; continued improvement of health and sanitation; institution of a sound program of economic development of trade, industry, and agriculture along lines which would insure that the profits and benefits thereof accrued to the native inhabitants and which would assist them in achieving the highest possible level of economic independence; and establishment of an educational program adapted to native capabilities and to local environment.

91 SCAP Occupation Instns No. 2, 1 Feb 48.

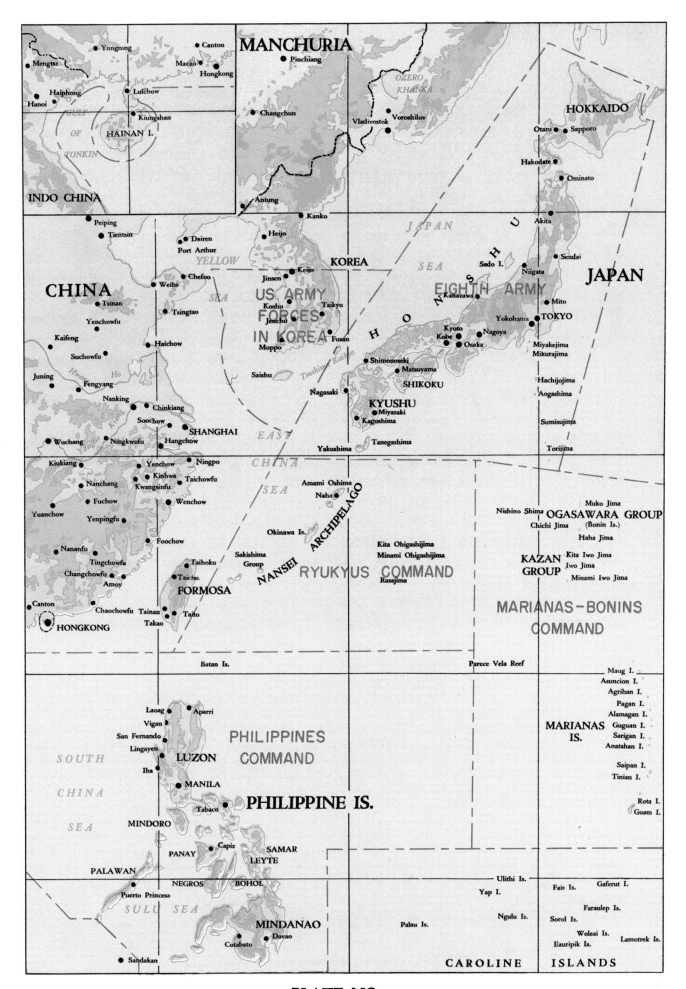

PLATE NO. 29
Territorial Subdivisions, Far East Command, December 1947

and provided the bulk of the troop labor.[92]

CINCFE also had jurisdiction over all United States Ground Forces in the Marianas—Bonins Area, known as the Marianas—Bonins Command (MARBO).[93] MARBO consisted almost entirely of service troops, including some scouts.

Subordinate Navy echelons were located in the same areas as the ground commands. In Japan, COMNAVFE had a dual assignment as Commander, Naval Activities, Japan (COMNAVJAP). In the Philippines, COMNAVFE commanded the local naval forces through the Commander, Naval Forces, Philippines (COMNAVPHIL).[94] The Commander of the Marianas Islands (COMMARIANAS) was under COMNAVFE for the operational control of local naval forces and under CINCPAC for those naval functions which did not come under CINCFE.[95] These functions included responsibility for the civil government of Guam, the United States trusteeship over the mandated islands, and the Naval Military Government in the Volcano Islands. Since the last two groups had been previous possessions of Japan, they were not included in the trusteeship agreement. COMMARIANAS also commanded naval forces in the Caroline and Marshall Islands and reported in this capacity directly to CINCPAC. Military and naval

government in the Marianas—Bonins area was specifically excluded from CINCFE's mission,[96] and COMMARIANAS came directly under CINCPAC and the U.S. Pacific Fleet for these functions. United States trusteeship over the former Japanese mandated islands was administered through naval channels and was not a function of CINCFE.

The subordinate echelons of the Far East Air Forces also corresponded to the principal land areas. Since the primary mission of the ground forces in the Marianas—Bonins Area was the support of the air forces, the Commanding General, 20th Air Force, was also placed in command of the ground forces. In his first capacity he reported to CG, FEAF, and in his second role, he reported directly to CINCFE.

Under the established structure, the unified command of air, ground, and naval elements was exercised only by CINCFE. However, in an emergency, local commanders were to assume jurisdiction over all Far East forces within their areas and execute previously prepared plans. This arrangement insured unified action in an emergency and, at the same time, left the command structure flexible enough to permit independent employment of air and naval forces.

---

92 Under the terms of the Philippine Military Assistance Agreement, signed March 1947, the US, subject to a mutual agreement to be arrived at later, was committed to furnish unspecified military assistance to the Republic of the Philippines in the training and development of armed forces, and in the performance of other services which might devolve upon the Republic under its international agreements. It was specified in the Agreement that the US would furnish equipment and technical supplies for training, operations and certain maintenance of a Philippine armed force of such strength and composition as might mutually be agreed upon. The Joint Chiefs of Staff formulated a policy as to the general extent to which the US would aid in its development. No clear-cut agreement as to the size of such a force had been reached between the two governments as of the end of December 1948.

Also specified in the Military Assistance Agreement was the establishment of a U. S. Military Advisory Group composed of Army, Navy, and Air officers whose duty it was to assist and advise the Republic on military and naval matters. This Group, known as " USMAG ", was set up at Manila and placed under the command of CINCFE. However, since, by the terms of the Agreement, it had to deal through the local State Department officials on all policy matters, and, since the extent of US aid was governed by policies established in Washington, CINCFE could exercise little control over its activities.

93   GHQ FEC Opns Instns No. 2, 1 Feb 48 (S).

94   *Ibid.*

95   *Ibid.*

96   *Ibid.*

CHAPTER IV

RELIEF OF PRISONERS OF WAR AND INTERNEES

Allied prisoners of war in Japanese custody, including merchant seamen, are (to be) repatriated at the earliest possible date consistent with military operations. The urgency of this mission is second only to military operations and to the maintenance of the forces of occupation.[1]

Thus read the operational instructions implementing Operation "Blacklist," the basic plan for the occupation of Japan and Korea on the surrender of the Imperial Japanese Government. Within a few hours after the first reconnaissance party of Americans arrived at Atsugi airfield to initiate the pre-surrender requirements, the first Allied prisoners of war became free men. Three weeks later virtually all those held as prisoners on the Japanese mainland had been evacuated and were on the way back to their homes. The speed of liberation from all prison camps in Honshu, Hokkaido, and Shikoku within the first two weeks of September put the Eighth Army weeks ahead of the most optimistic estimates made for this enterprise.[2]

Prior to the cessation of hostilities there was considerable concern in General MacArthur's Headquarters about the fate of the prisoners of war and civilian internees. The care and evacuation of these persons were im-portant objectives in the specific plans which senior staffs were directed to "develop and maintain in an advanced state of readiness, as a matter of urgent priority."[3]

One of the major missions outlined in "Blacklist" was to locate United Nations prisoners of war and internees, to provide them with adequate food, shelter, clothing and medical care, and to register and evacuate them to rear areas.[4]

As defined by "Blacklist," the term "United Nations prisoners of war" included all persons held in Japanese custody, who were or had been members of, or accompanied or served with, the armed forces of any of the United Nations; captured members of the armed forces of countries occupied by Japan, as well as those who had served with the merchant marine of any of the United Nations, were also included. All of these categories, under terms of the Geneva Convention, should have been treated as prisoners of war even though not recognized as such by Japan; at the same time, "Blacklist" designated a civilian internee as a person "without a military status, detained by the enemy, who is not a national of the Japanese Empire as constituted on 10 July 1937."[5]

The general term did not include personnel

---

1 GHQ USAFPAC, Basic Outline Plan for "Blacklist" Opns (3d ed), 8 Aug 45 (TS), Annex 5f, Care and Evacuation of Allied PW's and Civ Internees.

2 Occupational Monogr of the Eighth US Army in Japan, Vol. I, Aug 45—Jan 46 (C), p. 28.

3 (1) GHQ USAFPAC, Basic Outline Plan for "Blacklist" Opns (2d ed), 25 Jul 45 (TS). "Blacklist" operations had been in the making since May 1945 and went to top commands in July of that year. The 1st edition was published 16 July 1945 and presented at Guam 4 days later at a conference of ranking service representatives. (2) Rad (TS) C-15431 CINCAFPAC to AGWAR, 4 May 45. In G-3 GHQ Adm 381/61 (TS).

4 GHQ USAFPAC Basic Outline Plan for "Blacklist" Opns (3d ed), 8 Aug 45 (TS), par. 2e, Common Tasks, p. 13.

5 *Ibid*, Annex 5f, App 1.

who, although formerly held in Japanese custody as prisoners of war, had accepted release from the status in exchange for employment by Japan. Persons in this category, after definite identification, were to be dealt with as displaced persons.

The "facts and assumptions" of "Blacklist," though a pre-surrender document, proved generally correct:

Best estimates indicate that there are approximately 36,000 (Allied) personnel of various categories located in approximately 140 camps. In most instances this personnel will be in extremely poor physical condition requiring increased diet, comforts and medical care. Poor housing and sanitary conditions will require immediate large scale transfers to best available facilities to be preemptorily commandeered. Complete reclothing will be imperative. Records in general will be incomplete for both survivors and deceased.[6]

SCAP Directives Regarding Prisoners of War

Document I of the "Requirements of the Supreme Commander for the Allied Powers Presented to the Japanese Representatives at Manila, P. I., on 19 August 1945", called for the Japanese surrender delegation to be prepared to furnish all available information pertaining to "prisoner of war and civilian internment camps and places of detention, wherever located, within Japan and Japanese controlled areas." The location and status of Generals Jonathan M. Wainwright and Arthur E. Percival, top-ranking United States and British prisoners of war, were specifically required.

The Japanese emissaries at Manila presented an agreement to return prisoners of war and internees immediately. They asked to be notified as soon as possible as to where and when the Allied Nations would have the necessary ships for the prisoners' repatriation, and indicated that the following ports had been selected as embarkation points: Hakodate, Niigata, Aomori, Fushiki, Tsuruga, Sendai, Yokohama, Nagoya, Kobe, Shimonoseki, Nagasaki, and Hakata. They further stated that a committee comprised of members of the Prisoner of War Information Bureau, Army and Navy Ministries, and the Foreign Office had been formed. The committee was to make preparations to return Allied prisoners, with assistance from the Swiss and Swedish Legations and the International Committee of the Red Cross in Japan.[7]

Elaborating on the prior demand, the earliest SCAP directives to the Japanese Government prescribed a speedy release of the prisoners.[8] On 2 September, SCAP General Order Number 1 ordered:

(1) The safety and well-being of all United Nations Prisoners of War and Civilian Internees will be scrupulously preserved, to include the administrative and supply services essential to provide adequate food, shelter, clothing and medical care until such responsibility is undertaken by the Supreme Commander for the Allied Powers.

(2) Each camp or other place of detention of United Nations Prisoners of War and Civilian Internees together with its equipment, stores, records, arms, and ammunition, will be delivered immediately to the command of the senior officer or designated representative of the Prisoners of War and Civilian Internees.

(3) As directed by the Supreme Commander for the Allied Powers, Prisoners of War and Civilian Internees will be transported to places of safety where

6 *Ibid*, Annex 5f, par. 2 (GHQ USAFPAC Opns Instns No. 4 (S), Annex 12, 15 Aug 45, gives an estimate "... 36,000 Allied personnel...located in approximately 140 camps...")

7 Documents Submitted to SCAP by the Japanese Mission to Negotiate Surrender, Manila, PI, 19 Aug 45, Repatriation of POW's and Internees.

8 SCAP Dir No. 1, 2 Sep 45, enclosing SCAP GO No. 1, and No. 2, 3 Sep 45.

Gens. Jonathan M. Wainwright and Arthur E. Percival
after release from PW Camps in Manchuria.

Maj. Gen. E. P. King at Nichols Field,
Manila, on his way to the United States.

PLATE NO. 30

Senior Allied Commanders Released from Prisoner of War Camps.

they can be accepted by Allied authorities.

(4)   The Japanese Imperial General Headquarters will furnish to the Supreme Commander for the Allied Powers, without delay after receipt of this order, complete lists of all United Nations Prisoners of War and Civilian Internees, including their locations.

A day later, Directive Number 2 instructed the Japanese Imperial Government to dispatch instructions for all prisoners of war and civilian internees without delay. The prisoners were to be assembled at the earliest opportunity and the following statement was to be read to them in English and in such other languages as might be required:

The formal surrender of Japan to the Allied Powers was signed on 2 September 1945. General of the Army Douglas MacArthur has been named Supreme Commander for the Allied Powers. United Nations Forces are proceeding as rapidly as possible with the occupation of the Japanese Home Islands and Korea. The relief and recovery of Allied Prisoners of War and Civilian Internees will be accomplished with all possible speed.

Pending the arrival of Allied representatives the command of this camp and its equipment, stores, records, arms and ammunition are to be turned over to the Senior Prisoner of War or a designated Civilian Internee, who will thenceforth give instructions to the Camp Commander for maintenance of supply and administrative services and for the amelioration of local conditions. The Camp Commander will be responsible to the Senior Prisoner of War or designated Civilian Internee for maintaining his command intact.

Allied representatives will be sent to this Camp as soon as possible to arrange for your removal and eventual return to your homes.

This directive also authorized the requisitioning of government or military stocks

to insure that the prisoners and internees would receive rations equivalent to the highest scale locally available to Japanese armed forces or civilian personnel. All of the prisoners were to be furnished the best medical care possible, together with all necessary medical supplies, and adequate shelter, clothing, and bathing facilities.

Complete lists of all prisoners of war and civilian internees (showing name, rank or position, nationality, next of kin, home address, age, sex, and physical condition) were to be prepared and dispatched to the Supreme Commander for the Allied Powers. Extracts from available records on deceased or transferred prisoners of war and civilian internees, showing substantially the same data (including data of death and burial site, or transfer and destination), were also to be furnished.

Formation of Recovery Teams

Every military unit arriving in Japan in the days just before and after the formal surrender ceremony on 2 September 1945 played its particular role in the recovery of the prisoners of war and civilian internees.

GHQ, AFPAC, had been given the responsibility to operate and train the necessary liaison, recovery, and final processing teams which would be required to speedily liberate the prisoners.[9] The Recovered Personnel Detachment had organized and trained teams to accompany field forces in the anticipated invasion of Japan.[10] This project was a joint mission of the Adjutant General and the Commanding General, Special Troops, GHQ. Meanwhile, a liaison team of three officers and three enlisted men (one each from the United States, British, and Netherlands Forces) had been

---

9   GHQ USAFPAC, GO No. 103, 11 Aug 45, Estab of the Recovered Pers Det.
10   (1) GHQ USAFPAC, Basic Outline Plan for "Blacklist" Opns (TS) (3d ed), Annex 5f, 8 Aug 45   (2) GHQ USAFPAC, Opns Instns No. 4 (S), 15 Aug 45, Annex 12.

trained for duty with each of the two armies and six corps which were scheduled to make the initial entry into Japan."

The recovery teams (approximately seventy) were set up on the basis of one for each 500 prisoners of war and civilian internees. Each team was composed of two officers—one United States and one British. Twelve additional recovery teams were held in reserve to be attached when needed.[12] The final processing teams were to be assigned to the four recovered personnel disposition centers or collecting points proposed for Japan and Korea. Every team was composed of nine officers and twenty enlisted men, and included one officer and one enlisted man from Great Britain, Australia, Canada, and the Netherlands.

The job of locating the prisoners was delegated by GHQ to the commanding generals of the Sixth and Eighth Armies and the XXIV Corps, within their respective areas. Each was charged with the following duties:[13]

(1)   Locate, care for and safeguard all Allied recovered personnel.

(2)   Provide billets, food, clothing, comforts and medical care.

(3)   Accomplish initial processing of subject personnel....[14]

(4)   Establish recoveree disposition centers near ports of embarkation or landing fields as may be required.

(5)   Evacuate recovered personnel to recoveree disposition centers established by Commanding General, AFWESPAC, in the Philippines.

(6)   Collect, preserve and forward all records that may be captured pertaining to recovered personnel.

(7)   Exact from the Japanese Government and

military command maximum resources and facilities available to assist in the accomplishment...(of the above).

(8)   Assume operation of Allied prisoner of war and internment camps located within their respective areas.

(9)   Utilize first available air, motor, or water transport to expedite evacuation.

Duties of the Commanding General, AFWESPAC, were outlined in the same document, as follows:

(1)   Provides supplies and equipment required by recovery and processing teams.

(2)   Provides Commanding Generals, Sixth and Eighth Armies and XXIV Corps with ample clothing and equipment for prisoners of war and internees including women and children; subsistence of proper type and quantity; medical supplies and facilities to insure adequate medical care of the recoverees.

(3)   Establishes and operates a final processing center in the Manila area, consisting of one replacement depot augmented by one British and one Australian processing unit comparable to a Replacement Battalion.

(4)   Provides messing detachments, supplies and equipment and administrative facilities at final disposition center.

(5)   Receives, billets, and provides rations, clothing and medical care for recovered personnel in recoveree disposition centers established in the Philippines.

(6)   Furnishes air, motor or water tranportation as may be needed in the movement of recoverees within his area of responsibility.

(7)   Processes and evacuates from the Philippines prisoners of war and civilian internees after clearance by this [AFPAC] headquarters and as arranged with

---

11   Eighth Army, IX, XI, and XIV Corps; Sixth Army, I, X and V Amphib Corps. XXIV Corps went to Korea.

12   Actually each additional recovery " team " consisted of one Dutch enlisted man and was used whenever Dutch repatriates were involved.

13   GHQ USAFPAC, Opns Instns No. 4 (S), 15 Aug 45, Annex 12.

14   USAFPAC, Cir 19, sub: Adm of Recovered Mil Pers Other Than Phil Army, covered forms to be filled out by PW's providing information on treatment, atrocities, etc.   Cir 20 made similar provision for civilian personnel. (GHQ USAFPAC Cir 19 & 20, 9 Jul 45, Incl 1, RPD Forms 44 & 23.)

the governmental authorities concerned.

The planned process of evacuation for Americans, British, Canadians, and Australians was from the camps to recovered personnel disposition centers, to the final processing center, and thence to their destinations. Nationals of the other United Nations were to be held in the final disposition centers until provision could be made by their respective governments for their return home.

Highest priority on transportation was directed, with movement by air to be used to the maximum. Priority was given for the evacuation and repatriation of the sick and wounded, but there was no discrimination because of rank, service, or nationality.

In early August numerous messages regarding the relief and release of internees and prisoners of war were transmitted between Tokyo and Washington via Bern.[15] The Recovered Personnel Sub-section was then transferred from Manila to Okinawa in preparation for moving to Japan.[16]

Preparation for Air Drops

Meanwhile, the reported conditions of starvation rations, disease, and maltreatment of the men and women in Japanese camps[17] spurred military authorities to arrange for immediate relief measures to ease the last days of incarceration.[18] It was estimated that thirty days would be required for complete evacuation of Japan, and that many lives could be saved by supplying food, clothing, and medical supplies during the interim.[19] Air transport was chosen as the most feasible method of providing the necessary supplies. The original plan called for Far East Air Forces planes, based on Okinawa and in the Philippines, to share the air supply task with Marianas-based B-29's. Just as the program was about to be initiated, the entire project was assigned to the Twentieth Air Force and prisoner of war supply missions were executed from 27 August to 20 September 1945.[20]

The spearhead of the Tokyo shuttle arrived at Kadena Airfield (Okinawa) in mid-August. They were planes of the Air Transport Command which were to carry the 11th Airborne Division north to Tokyo for the Occupation and bring back the former American prisoners to Okinawa on their way to the States. The Air Transport Command crews, which came from all over the world for this epoch-making operation, shuttled their planes between Tokyo and Okinawa. They were called in from "Snowball": the Presque Isle, Maine-to-Paris

---

15 The communications addressed to the Japanese Government by the Department of State concerning the treatment of American PW's and civilian internees totaled approximately 240 from 7 December 1941 to 2 September 1945.

16 Occupational Monogr of the Eighth US Army in Japan, Vol. I, Aug 45-Jan 46 (C). Col M. H. Marcus and Lt Col E. E. Graham headed the Recovered Personnel Division, AGO GHQ USAFPAC, Manila.

17 (1) From collection of various regulations regarding PW's and issued by PW Int Bur, 22 Nov 43. (2) "The answer of the Japanese Government to the Red Cross regarding the treatment of POW's is that Japan has not ratified the treaty regarding treatment of POW's." (IPS Doc No. 2197, 24 Jun 46 p. 3.)

18 "In the event of unconditional surrender or sudden collapse of the Japanese Govt and Imperial High Command, it is proposed to immediately air drop emergency supplies to prisoners of war and civilian internees of the United Nations held in known Japanese camps....Supplies to be flown from bases in the Philippines and Ryukyus nonstop...." (Rad(TS) C-32871, CINCAFPAC G-4 to CG China Theater, 12 Aug 45. In G-3 GHQ Adm 384. 1/13-2.)

19 "...Swiss representative of International Red Cross reports all POW camps desperately in need of food. Recommend plane drops particularly sugar, chocolate, candy, condensed milk...." (Rad [TS] 281101/z, COM3rdFLT to SCAP, 29 Aug 45. In G-3 GHQ Adm 383.6 [TS].)

20 HQ 20th AF, Tac Mission Rpt, Mission No. POW, 27 Aug—20 Sep 45 (C).

run; from "Crescent": the Wilmington, Delaware-to-India run; and from North Africa via India and the Philippines.

Because of the nature of the project, it was decided that only general planning would be done at Twentieth Air Force Headquarters. Specific planning on routes, loading, and dates of missions was to be done by the wings engaged in the operation.[21] An important factor in planning the operation was the availability of food, medical supplies, and cargo parachutes. It was obvious that if the Twentieth Air Force were to carry out the supply drops quickly, all supplies must be packaged and made available in the Marianas. The food and medical supply requirements for the program were set up on the basis of thirty days' supply for 69,000 persons. (This figure included the Japanese Home Islands, Korea and China.) Arrangements were made through the Western Pacific Base Command for all supplies to be made available at Saipan. This was made possible by borrowing on stores and provisions which had been accumulated for the planned invasion of Japan. Since 63,000 cargo parachutes were required for the project and only 11,000 were available in the Marianas, it was necessary to obtain additional ones from the Philippines.

After determining where and in what quantities the necessary supplies could be delivered, loading and dropping tests were conducted by the Operational Engineering Section in order to make detailed plans. Throughout the course of these tests, it was found that a 10,000 pound load consisting of forty individual drop units was the capacity of a B-29. The best altitude during the initial dropping was determined to be between 500 and 1,000 feet; while the most practical speed for the drops was established at approximately 165 miles per hour.

After the first three days of operation, however, it was decided that the established altitude was too low, and crews were briefed to drop bundles above 1,000 feet. This height allowed for better functioning of parachutes, and avoided causing injuries among prisoners and destruction of supply bundles.[22] To facilitate identification, all aircraft engaged in these operations were marked "PW Supplies" in letters three feet high under each wing.

Plans were made to drop supplies in increments of three, seven, and ten-day units. The three-day supplies were to include juices, soups, clothing and medical supplies. The seven-day packages would contain additional medical supplies and food of a more substantial nature. The ten-day supplies were to consist of almost all food, with some medical supplies. A fourth increment of additional supplies would simply repeat the three-day unit bundles. Instruction leaflets for allocation and use of supplies were included, and each aircraft was to take

---

21 *Ibid.*

22 This was evidenced by the following extracts from GHQ SWPA Daily Sum and G-2 Est of the Enemy Sit (TS), 20 Aug—4 Sep 45: (a) "COM3rdFLT RA 33 Japan, 30 Aug 45: PW's are tremendously appreciative of food drops. Pilots are urged to select nearby areas for drops, as some packages without parachutes have been plummeting through roofs." (b) "JAP GOV'T X 345, 30 Aug 45: Referring to information on civilian internee camp number 25, it was learned that...accidents happened as a result of the dropping of the supplies to the camps by Allied aircraft on 27 and 28 August....Some casualties were caused, although details are still unavailable, within Tokyo prisoners camp No. 4 at Naoetsu and prisoners camp No. 7 at Hanaoka and other places. A drum was dropped at three places in the central area of Tokyo in the vicinity of which no prisoners or internees camps are located. It seems that these accidents were mostly due to the faulty attachment of the dropped material to the parachute, causing the former to come off from the latter when dropped, or the failure of the parachute to open because of the extremely low altitude from which the material was dropped...." (c) "JAP GOV'T 453: PW Supply-dropping B-29's Cause Casualties: 4 Sep 45: 'Several' B-29's dropping PW supplies in Higashi Maizuru City (Maizuru area) wounded several persons. Request that future supply drops be only made to POW camp at Miyazu."

photos of the operation whenever conditions permitted.

Normally every plane was to carry supplies sufficient for 200 persons for the particular three, seven, or ten-day period. But for camps of 1000 or more population, aircraft were slated for special loads which would provide for greater efficiency in packaging.[23]

On 18 August 1945 medical supplies for 31,000 people had been assembled, packed, and stored on Guam while quartermaster stores for 50,000 people were assembled, packed, and stored on Saipan. All these supplies were prepared for air-dropping to PW's and internees held by the Japanese.[24]

Location and Supply of Prisoner of War Camps

The most perplexing problem in planning these operations was determining the location and population of the camps to be provided. On 16 August 1945 the Commanding General, USASTAF, radioed Commander in Chief, AFPAC, that an official current list of PW camps and civilian internee centers from Japanese Government sources was urgently needed for the efficient execution of the assigned air drop mission. The camp designation, the number of PW's present, general location, and geographic coordinates were requested. Evacuated camp sites were to be named and located, since the currently available information on this subject was considered too unreliable for the successful execution of airdrops. Because population figures for many of the camps could be only estimates, it was inevitable that there would be cases of over-supply and under-supply. A study prepared by the MIS-X Section of GHQ on 14 August indicated locations, conditions, and strengths of Japanese prisoner of war camps.[25] The only positive intelligence on these camps was intermittently furnished by the International Committee of the Red Cross; however, since that agency was allowed to visit relatively few camps in Japan, conditions listed in its reports could not be considered representative. All other camp intelligence came from a variety of sources; much of it was obtained from interrogations of Japanese prisoners and had to be assessed accordingly.[26]

According to the principles established by the Geneva Convention, the International Committee of the Red Cross was to be notified of the location of all PW camps. Since the Japanese did not consider themselves bound to these principles, it was only after the surrender that this organization was able to obtain access to Japanese prison camp records. In cooperation with Allied authorities, Dr. Marcel Junod, who had been active in International Red Cross activities throughout the war, established a plan for rapid evacuation of prisoners of war and civilian internees. Conditions in Japan, camp strengths as of the latest reports, and plans for evacuation were outlined in a

---

23   HQ 20th AF, Tac Mission Rpt, Mission No. POW, 27 Aug—20 Sep 45 (C).

24   Rad (TS) NR: 2302, COMGEN USASTAF to COMGEN FEAF, 18 Aug 45. In G-3 GHQ Adm 383–6/1/TS.

25   GHQ USAFPAC—MIS-X (a G-2 operating agency), Locations and Strengths of POW and Civ Internment Camps in Japan, 14 Aug 45.

26   Captured Pers and Mat Br, G-2 WD. Principle sources included NEFIS (Netherlands East Indies Forces Int Sv), AIB (Allied Int Bur), ATIS (Allied Translator and Interpreter Sv, G-2), and what information MIS-X (Mil Int Sv), AFPAC, had been able to obtain through intensive interrogations of released prisoners in the PI CINCPAC/ POA, AGAS (Air Ground Aid Sv). See G-2 GHQ FEC Int Ser, Vol. IV, *Operations of the Allied Intelligence Bureau (R)*; Vol. V, *History of the Allied Geographical Section (R)*.

radio message via Washington.[27]

On 29 August, in compliance with SCAP's request for further information, the Japanese radioed that they were trying their best to collect the required data concerning the Allied prisoners of war. They complained, however, that it was practically impossible in so short a time to complete the comprehensive investigation demanded since communications with various places either had been severed or were extremely difficult.[28]

The first official Japanese compilation of prisoner of war camps, known as the "Yellow List" and containing the names of seventy-three camps, was made available to the Twentieth Air Force on 27 August 1945. After coordi-

nating the location of these camps with those listed in "Blacklist", aircraft of the 314th Bombardment Wing were dispatched to verify the location of camps on the Japanese home islands of Honshu, Shikoku, and Kyushu.[29] This reconnaissance established the existence and location of several additional encampments.

When the ground forces began occupation of all strategic areas in Japan, the necessity for air surveillance lessened, and the Far East Air Forces turned their efforts toward deploying air units to Japan for occupation duties and the continued dropping of supplies.[30] During the period from 27 August to 20 September, aircraft of the 58th, 73rd, 313th, 314th, and 315th Bombardment Wings flew 900 effective

---

27 "...Following information received from Tokyo...in order to facilitate repatriation POW and civilian internees Far East. Organization 7 groups delegates Intercross and protecting power who are authorized to go to 7 main camps in Japan, namely Hakodate, Sendai, Tokyo, Nagoya, Osaka, Hiroshima, and Fukuoka in order to supervise conditions concerning evacuation POW and CI from internment centers to debarkation centers... Japanese delegation who left for Manila communicated these intentions to Allied Headquarters and acceptance by the Japanese Government of these measures. Junod established contact with all delegates and other interested by group giving all instructions ....Junod asked Japanese Government to increase immediately food rations all POW especially CI. Orders have already been given. Junod established plan with authorities for evacuation of POW and CI which will be ready August 24th. He believes that in view of conditions massive regrouping of prisoners in ports of embarkation impossible but he proposes evacuation of nearer camps to the ports and gradual transportation from faraway camps toward nearby camps which have been previously vacated. This will assure maximum security in feeding of POW and prevent crowding. Transportation towards camps and ports by train 80 percent 3rd class, 20 percent 2nd class, reserved for sick and officers. In consideration of the great number of sick people Junod has spoken to have necessary hospital ships available. Evacuation of CI complicated by great numbers who are residents Japan and occupied territories. Would like to transmit to Junod opinions Governments concerned.... Approximate strength or numbers of POW transmitted to Allied General Headquarters by Japanese Government on June 30 1945: Hakodate 1,579, Sendai 3,844, Tokyo 5,848, Nagoya 3,357, Osaka 4,541, Hiroshima 3,155, Fukuoka 10,457, total in Japan proper 34,509....Total occupied territories, 69,346 general total POW, 103,855, of whom 11,572 sick. Approximate strength of CI in April: Tokyo 36, Kanagawa 66, Hyogo 163, Nagasaki 41, Saitama 56, Fukushima 140, Hokkaido 24, Miyagi 35, Hiroshima 44, Aichi 35. Total in Japan 640.... This list does not mention civilian internees under Military control. More detailed and more recent lists follow. Would like to have opinion of Governments concerned to enable us to inform Junod Tokyo who will re-transmit to all delegates Far East. Coordinating action interested powers seems indispensable for satisfactory execution of above plan. We ask that all Allied Commands Far East be informed of this plan, and contact our delegates on the spot to assure fast application of necessary measures. We put at disposal Allied authorities all our delegates. If another plan already established and applied would be grateful to be informed so that we may advise Junod. Would like very much to receive ultimate lists of repatriates established by Allied authorities. Same text sent to London delegates." (Rad NR: 1946, Washington to CINCAFPAC, China, India, 24 Aug 45. G-3 Adm 383.6 [S])

28 (1) Rad (S) 3094, COMGEN USASTAF to COM G-5, 26 Aug 45. In G-3 GHQ Adm 383/6 (S); (2) GHQ SWPA Daily Sum and G-2 Est of the Enemy Sit (TS), 29 Aug 45.

29 HQ 20th AF, Tac Mission Rpt No. POW, 20 Sep 45 (C).

30 GHQ SCAP and USAFPAC Mo Sum of Opns (S), Sep 45.

Sendai PW Camp No. 3 Relief Mission flown by 20th Air Force, 12 September 1945.

Japanese unloading supplies dropped by air at Omori PW Camp near Tokyo, 30 August 1945.

PLATE NO. 31
Prisoner of War Relief Missions

sorties and dropped 4,470 tons of supplies. Successful drops were made to 158 camps.[31]

The Navy was notified of these relief operation plans and furnished air-sea rescue facilities, consisting of surface vessels on permanent stations along the routes flown.[32]

Operation "Swift Mercy"

In the outer bay just beyond Yokosuka, elements of the Third U. S. Fleet, under command of Admiral William F. Halsey, had awaited the signal which would allow them to enact the Navy's role in the Occupation mission.[33] On 21 August Admiral Halsey had radioed Commander in Chief, Pacific Advance,

that beginning on the day of initial landings his command was prepared to provide for and screen a considerable number of Allied prisoners of war and internees. In Tokyo Bay area the Third Fleet had immediately available three hospital ships, thirty doctors, ninety corpsmen, and clothing and food for 3,000 men. By the first of September the Navy expected to have additional small ships, twenty doctors, sixty corpsmen, and food and clothing for 4,000 men.[34]

The Swiss representative of the International Committee of the Red Cross, with Task Force 31, anchored off Yokosuka, meanwhile reported that many of the PW's were sick (150 were seriously ill in Shinagawa camp hospital) and

31	FINAL STATISTICS ON PW CAMP PROJECT*:									
Wing	A/C Sched	Air Borne	Eff Sorties	Non-Eff Sorties	Tons Ldd	Tons Drpd	Tons Jettisoned	Tons Rtd	A/C Lost	Casualties
58	76	75	60	15	359	282	10	67	2	12
76	581	580	472	108	2932	2370	99.3	463	4	39
313	231	222	190	32	1192	1018	11.3	163	1	14
314	62	62	61	1	248	244	10	4	0	0
315	126	127	117	10	610	556	0	54	1	12
	1076	1066	999	166	5341	4470	120.6	751	8	77

* Totals include camps in China, Korea, and Formosa for which separate statistics unavailable. (HQ 20th AF, Tac Mission Rpt No. POW, 27 Aug—20 Sep 45 (C).)

32 *Ibid.* Surface vessels were stationed between the following points during the period of these missions: Marianas to Iwo Jima, Iwo Jima to Honshu, Okinawa to Honshu.

33 (1) Rad (TS) 200245/z, COM3rdFLT to CINCPAC ADV, 21 Aug 45. In G-3 GHQ Adm 383.6 (TS); (2) Rad (C) 240219/z, COM3rdFLT to SCAP, 25 Aug 45; (3) GHQ SCAP & USAFPAC Mo Sum of Opns (S), Sep 45.

34 On 25 August, General MacArthur had advised Admiral Halsey that ". . . it is not believed advisable for Third Fleet to undertake any unilateral action re assistance and evacuation prisoners of war Tokyo Bay area. Action being taken by this headquarters to effect coordination in this matter." (Rad [C] 251457, SCAP to Halsey, 25 Aug 45. In G-3 GHQ Adm 383-6/1/S.)

Admiral Halsey proposed that immediate action be taken and, in a radio to General MacArthur 29 August, stated that: ". . . all facilities under my command are available to you and to the CG Eighth Army for the immediate extension of urgent care, assistance and evacuation of the Allied POW's in eastern Honshu. Suggest that the liaison officers of the Eighth Army be sent to me at Yokosuka in order that I may initiate and expedite this task in accordance with your policies. . . . Have a tactical organization ready with all the available information and prepared to act. Propose for the most expeditious action: 1. Send medical assistance and food with Red Cross and Japanese liaison to Tokyo Bay waterfront camps promptly reporting to CG Eighth Army and to you on conditions found. 2. Receive released POW's on board hospital ships and APA's in Tokyo Bay for evacuation to points CG Eighth Army directs. 3. Send on 3 Sep with 8th Army liaison party 1 LSV, 1 APA, with appropriate escorts and minesweepers to an East Coast port in the Sendai area to contact camps in that area, extend medical assistance and evacuate to points CG Eighth Army directs. 4. Establish transient hospital, clothing, and supply station for POW's at Yokosuka for use as required." (Rad [TS], Halsey to MacArthur, 29 Aug 45. In G-3 Adm 383-6.)

that all camps were in desperate need of food. The Red Cross Committee also furnished information on 200 aviation personnel, in extremely bad condition at Omori camp on the waterfront. The urgency of the situation was confirmed by extensive photographic coverage of PW camps, which showed prisoners signalling to planes for food and medical supplies.[35] From the Japanese it was learned that there were supposedly 6,125 Allied PW's in the Tokyo area, of which 417 were bedridden. This distressing situation was further confirmed by two British marines who were rescued by a patrol boat near Sagami Bay anchorage. They had escaped from Kawasaki prison camp, a one-story wooden barracks where there was a critical lack of food, medicine, and clothing. The hopeless predicament of prisoners in Tokyo waterfront camps indicated that their release was one of prime urgency. Medical care was badly needed and had the highest priority. Obviously, there was no reason to assume that the Tokyo area was an exception but that conditions in inland camps were equally bad, a strong reason to handle the problem on an over-all basis rather than piecemeal evacuations on a possibly preferential basis; as a matter of fact, the inland camps required the handling of 30/40,000 internees.

In view of these reported conditions, on 29 August, Admiral Halsey was authorized by Admiral Nimitz to take prompt action regarding the PW's.[36] Within a short period the evacuation of waterfront camps was under way. The first prisoners to be evacuated were from Omori, Shinagawa, and Ofuna camps.[37] Commander Task Group 30.6 radioed to Commander Third Fleet:[38]

There has never been a blacker hellhole than the POW hospital we are now evacuating one-half mile north of mooring. Approximately 500 have now (30 August) been processed to Benevolence including fracture, open wounds, concussions, burns and in general the worst malnutrition imaginable. Bestial beatings were common especially at Ofuna, inquisitorial den of brutism. The cheers of POW as our boat hove into sight brought tears to our eyes. Operations are proceeding according to plan. The bath, medical care, chow, interview, and clean bed routine is a merciful machine of efficiency.... Preliminary list of POW will be sent Commander 3rd Fleet in morning.

A touching scene greeted rescuers at the camp near Yokosuka Naval Base. There, more than 1,000 emaciated and starving Allied war prisoners were taken aboard the USS *Ancon*.

---

35 Messages Painted on PW Camps included: " SOS, " " 406 Prisoners," " 503 Men Here," " Have Hospital Cases Here," " Drop Radio Please," " Thanks Yanks, Aussies," " PW US PW 1734 Men," " Men from Corregidor, Bataan Thank Wasp." " Hong Kong Men Thank You," " All Left This Camp." (HQ 20th AF, Tac Mission Rpt, Mission No. POW, 27 Aug—20 Sep 45 [C].)

36 Upon receiving Admiral Halsey's report of conditions in waterfront camps, Admiral Nimitz sent an urgent message to General MacArthur: " In view of circumstances outlined urge that you immediately authorize Halsey to take immediate action to contact POW and to take such action as necessary for alleviating their condition and moving them into American jurisdiction. In order that the intolerable conditions outlined by him may be corrected in minimum time and to provide for possible failure or delay in communications, COM3rdFLT is hereby authorized, if no reply is received from you by 1300 Tokyo time today, to initiate such local action as to POW's as humanitarian considerations require." (Rad [C] 281830, CINCPAC ADV to SCAP, 29 Aug 45. In G-3 GHQ Adm 383-6 /1/S.)

SCAP radioed his concurrence, stating that evacuees should be returned to AFWESPAC, Manila. (Rad [C] 290339, SCAP to CINCPAC ADV, 29 Aug 45. In G-3 GHQ Adm 383-6.)

37 "... On the evening of 29 August 1945, a U. S. Naval Landing unit of about 150 men under the command of a Rear Admiral, broke into the Shinagawa camp of the Allied War Prisoners, Tokyo, and forcibly led away the prisoners...." (Rad [C] CA51551, CINCAFPAC ADV to CINCPAC, 1 Sep 45. In G-3 GHQ Adm 383.6 [C].)

38 Rad 292310Z, COM TG 30.6 to COM3rdFLT, 30 Aug 45. In G-3 GHQ Adm 383.6.

Close-up of Barracks, Omori Prisoner of War Camp.

Leon S. Johnston of Atlanta, Georgia, and Harry R. Sanders of
Terre Haute, Indiana, interned for over three years at Omori Camp.

PLATE NO. 32
Barracks, Omori Prisoner of War Camp, Tokyo, 30 August 1945

Among them were the gallant survivors of Wake and Bataan who had withstood long months of solitary confinement and threats of death. At least 80 percent of them were suffering from malnutrition;[39] all of the prisoners at Omori and Shinagawa camps, except for the few who were of recent capture, were suffering from the same deficiency, a majority of them seriously. Many were medical and surgical cases. The conditions in these two camps had been abominable and the treatment extremely brutal. The third camp, Ofuna, had been the *Gestapo* center of Japan.

Recovered Personnel Section in Action

As stated previously, the Occupation ground forces had also made careful plans for their part in the evacuation program. The Recovered Personnel Sub-section of G-1, Eighth Army, had made systematic arrangements for the liberation of prisoners as rapidly as possible;[40]

seventy recovery teams had been organized and assigned to the Sixth and Eighth Armies and the XXIV Corps. In addition, nine liaison teams, in which the British, Canadian, Australian, and Netherlands Governments were represented, were attached to army and corps headquarters.

After V-J Day, teams were immediately dispatched to prison camp areas in Japan where they released, processed, and arranged transportation for 32,624 prisoners of war, all of them liberated within a period of three weeks.[41]

The Recovered Personnel Section (28 teams) arrived in Yokohama on 30 August 1945 with the advance airborne echelon of Eighth Army Headquarters.[42] Advance planning proved invaluable in coordinating airdrops of food, clothing and medical supplies for immediate relief to the prisoners; although some changes became necessary since the Japanese had made extensive transfers of prisoners after 30 June 1945.[43] It should be noted that there were also

---

39   *The Red Cross Courier*, October 1945.

40   See pp. 100 ff.

41   PRISONERS OF WAR RELEASED, AUGUST—SEPTEMBER 1945:

AREA	BASE CAMP	NO. SUB-CAMPS	U. S.	BRITISH	DUTCH	OTHERS	TOTAL
Hakodate	Bibai	4	505	828	208	56	1597
Sendai	Kurozawajiri	11	1638	863	480	585	3566
Tokyo	Omori-Ku	21	2728	1361	1208	772	6069
Nagoya	Nagoya-Shi	11	1596	1127	472	141	3336
Osaka	Shinden	12	1914	1444	529	819	4706
Hiroshima	Ashima	9	523	1463	477	493	2956
Fukuoka	Fukuoka	18	2391	2583	3799	1621	10394
7	7	86	11295	9669	7173	4487	32624

(USAFWESPAC Semi-Ann Rpt, 1 Jun-31 Dec 45.)

42   Until 12 July 1945, G-1 Section administered problems dealing with recovered personnel through section and base commanders; thereafter, staff supervision was exercised through Recovered Personnel Division, Adjutant General's Office, actual operation having been turned over to the Replacement Command. (USAFWESPAC Semi-Ann Rpt, 1 Jun—31 Dec 45, p. 24.)

43   One report stated that approximately 11,000 British and American PW's had been transferred from the Tokyo area to Yamaguchi Prefecture in the Ube area. Nearly 3,000 of these had last been reported working in coal-mines near Onda, west of Ube. (GHQ USAFWESPAC MIS-X Sec Rpt, Locations & Strengths PW & CI Camps in Japan, 14 Aug 45.)

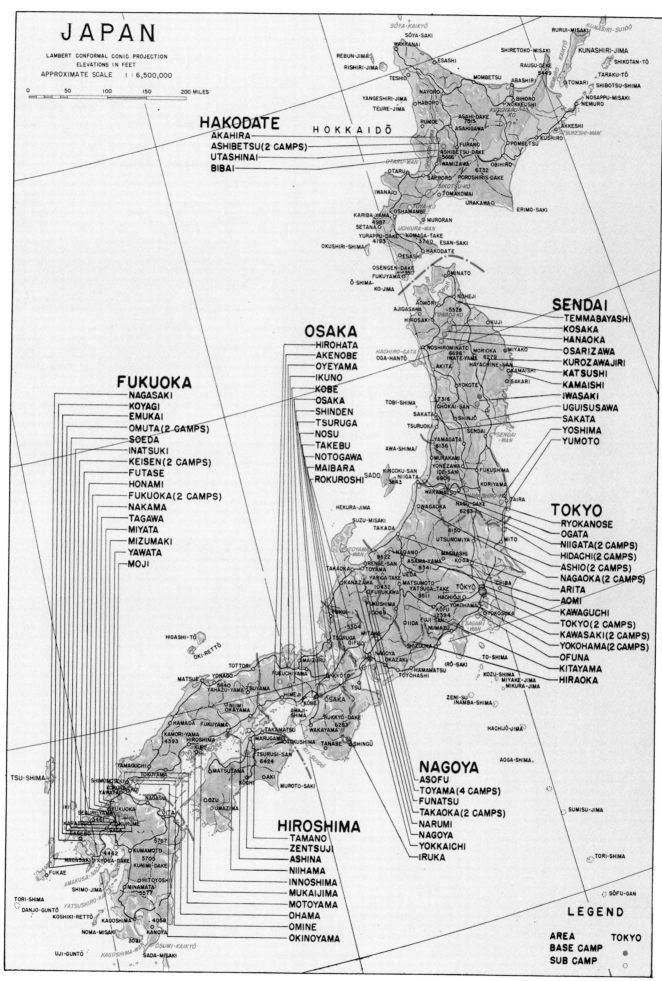

JAPAN

LAMBERT CONFORMAL CONIC PROJECTION
ELEVATIONS IN FEET
APPROXIMATE SCALE 1 : 6,500,000

0   50   100   150   200 MILES

HAKODATE
AKAHIRA
ASHIBETSU(2 CAMPS)
UTASHINAI
BIBAI

HOKKAIDŌ

SENDAI
TEMMABAYASHI
KOSAKA
HANAOKA
OSARIZAWA
KUROZAWAJIRI
KATSUSHI
KAMAISHI
IWASAKI
UGUISUSAWA
SAKATA
YOSHIMA
YUMOTO

OSAKA
HIROHATA
AKENOBE
OYEYAMA
IKUNO
KOBE
OSAKA
SHINDEN
TSURUGA
NOSU
TAKEBU
NOTOGAWA
MAIBARA
ROKUROSHI

FUKUOKA
NAGASAKI
KOYAGI
EMUKAI
OMUTA(2 CAMPS)
SOEDA
INATSUKI
KEISEN(2 CAMPS)
FUTASE
HONAMI
FUKUOKA(2 CAMPS)
NAKAMA
TAGAWA
MIYATA
MIZUMAKI
YAWATA
MOJI

TOKYO
RYOKANOSE
OGATA
NIIGATA(2 CAMPS)
HIDACHI(2 CAMPS)
ASHIO(2 CAMPS)
NAGAOKA(2 CAMPS)
ARITA
AOMI
KAWAGUCHI
TOKYO(2 CAMPS)
KAWASAKI(2 CAMPS)
YOKOHAMA(2 CAMPS)
OFUNA
KITAYAMA
HIRAOKA

NAGOYA
ASOFU
TOYAMA(4 CAMPS)
FUNATSU
TAKAOKA(2 CAMPS)
NARUMI
NAGOYA
YOKKAICHI
IRUKA

HIROSHIMA
TAMANO
ZENTSUJI
ASHINA
NIIHAMA
INNOSHIMA
MUKAIJIMA
MOTOYAMA
OHAMA
OMINE
OKINOYAMA

LEGEND

AREA   TOKYO
BASE CAMP
SUB CAMP

PLATE NO. 33
Red Cross Duties, September 1945

many internees confined in places other than prisoner of war camps.[44]   The accuracy of PW strength figures was further reduced by wholesale movements of Allied PW's from camps in heavily bombed coastal areas.   To add further to the confusion, the Japanese Government had placed restrictions, despite vigorous protests, upon the activities of representatives of the Swiss Government and the International Red Cross Committee.   This action made it more difficult for the American authorities to have a full and accurate picture of the conditions under which many prisoners were held by the Japanese. Most civilian internees were held in camps which were visited by neutral representatives, but practically nothing was known of the whereabouts or welfare of military personnel who were held in camps which the neutral representatives were not permitted to inspect.[45] Soon after the Occupation began, the Japanese Government reported to SCAP that there had been ninety-four PW camps in Japan.   Noticing that several camp names in the affidavits from former prisoners were not among those listed, the Chief of Legal Section's Investigation Division sent out investigators to comb Japan. They returned with the names and locations of

thirty-three additional PW camps, including the infamous Ofuna camp and interrogation center operated by the Japanese Imperial Navy.[46]   As revised information about locations and needs of individual camps reached the Recovered Personnel Subsection, it was compiled and passed on to FEAF. Such information brought prompt action : planes went swooping over freshly located Japanese prison stockades to drop food and supplies often on the very day the new locations were reported. (Plate No. 33)

An American surgeon, inmate of one of these camps gave a graphic account of the reactions of the prisoners of war :[47]

Six tiny black specks appeared in the sky. Flying low over rugged mountain ranges, these planes wove back and forth in single file, following the course of the river. At a height of five thousand feet they roared over camp. ...Three hundred ragged prisoners ran up and down the little compound waving their arms hysterically and yelling themselves hoarse, trying to attract their attention. On the roofs of the barracks we had painted in huge orange letters " P. O. W.", on a black background. We had laid out gray blankets forming the same letters on a strip of white sand outside the camp. ...The flyers missed the signs, covered by the heavy ground mist which settled over the tiny valley in the early morning.

---

44   TABLE OF PERSONS DETAINED UNDER OTHER THAN MILITARY JURISDICTION

JURISDICTION	LOCATION	PERSONS	PRINCIPAL NATIONALITY
Ministry of	Metropolitan Police HQ	36	American, British, others
Internal	Kanagawa-Ken, Totsuka	19	Australian, others
Affairs	Kanagawa-Ken, Yamakita	47	British, Canadian, others
	Hyogo	163	American, British, others
	Nagasaki	41	British, Canadian, others
	Saitama	56	Canadian, British, others
	Fukushima	140	British, Greek, others
	Hokkaido	24	American
	Miyagi	35	Dutch, American
	Hiroshima	44	Dutch
	Aichi	35	Dutch, Italian
TOTAL		640	

(Documents Submitted to SCAP by the Japanese Mission to Negotiate Surrender, Manila, 19 Aug 45, p. 87.)

45   (1) GHQ USAFPAC MIS-X Sec reported on 14 August 1945 that there were 25 civilian internment camps in Japan, with a total of 1,362 internees, 166 of these being Americans.   (2) Dept of State Press Release No. 653, 4 Sep 45.

46   GHQ FEC PIO Press Release, 10 Jun 48.

47   Alfred A. Weinstein, M D, *Barbed-Wire Surgeon* (New York, 1948), pp. 293-4.

104

They disappeared over the horizon as we moaned and cussed. An hour later we heard the drone of motors in the west. They appeared again, lower this time, their black wings shining in the morning sun. Down through a cleft in the mountain range the flight leader dove straight for the enemy camp, waggling his wings. We howled, cheered, and pounded each other. Tears of joy streamed down our faces. Hearts thumped with happiness as we saw the white star in its blue circle on the wings of the plane.

The planes followed one after another at a level of a thousand feet. They circled round and round the hidden valley, checking wind currents and trying various approaches to the little camp. Finally the flight leader made his run, clearing the pine trees on the overhanging mountain range by feet. Down he dove steeply to a level of three hundred feet above camp. A black object hurtled down from the plane; an orange parachute fluttered open. A suspended fifty-five-gallon drum pendulumed back and forth three times and dropped with a thud in a clearing fifty feet square, between the Nip administration building and the galley—a bull's eye! The plane pulled out of its dive, clearing the barracks, and climbed rapidly to top the opposing hills. One after another the planes roared down and dropped their loads. One food packet landed in the doorway of the galley. The parachute of another failed to open. Its drum plummeted to the ground and buried itself deeply in the mud near the bank of the river. Something red fluttered down. The men high-tailed

it. There was a note stuck in a sandbag which had a long, red cloth streamer. It read: "Hello, Folks: The crew of the U.S.S. Randolph send their best. Hope you enjoy the chow. Keep your chin up. We'll be back."

Our first contact with American forces in three and a half years!...

Liberated prisoners were taken from camps in the interior to Yokohama where hospital ships, billeting accommodations, and food supplies were available. Twenty-eight specially trained AFPAC recovery teams, each composed of an officer and three enlisted men, were attached to the Eighth Army for this mission.[48] Some of the teams moved into the interior before demilitarization of the Japanese armed forces, in order to seize camp records before they could be destroyed by camp commanders. Diaries, records of deaths, and information on atrocities (later used in the trials of war criminals) were seized by these teams. Other recovery teams boarded Navy vessels to aid in evacuation of camps near the coast.[49]

Eighty-six Red Cross field men arrived with the first occupation troops, and four Red Cross girls attached to the 42d General Hospital arrived in Tokyo Bay on the USAHS *Marigold*.[50] These American Red Cross repre-

---

48 On 26 August 1945, 9 officers and 16 enlisted men, making up Recovery Teams Nos. 62, 63, 64, and 65 and liaison personnel of the US, Australian, and Dutch armed forces, reported for duty with the XIV Corps and were placed under the jurisdiction of the IG Section for the movement of the occupation forces into Japan. The activities of the IG Section were to include the supervision and coordination of all recovery work by the teams attached to the XIV Corps. In addition to their normal task of handling Allied prisoners of war and their processing and evacuation, these teams were assigned the task of examining all former camp sites in their assigned area, after the release of the prisoners. (XIV Corps, Rpt No. 1 on the "Blacklist" Opn, 20 Aug-30 Sep 45 [R], p. 9.)

49 Occupational Monogr of the Eighth US Army in Japan, Vol. I, Aug 45—Jan 46 (C).

50 (1) The first US ship to enter Yokohama was the USAHS *Marigold*, carrying the 42nd General Hospital. (Med Hist of 42d Gen Hosp, Ann Rpt of Activ for 1945, gives this date as 30 August 1945; however, Occupational Monogr of the Eighth US Army in Japan, Vol. I, Aug 45—Jan 46, gives the date as 31 August.) (2) The first medical unit to arrive in Japan was the 5th Portable Surgical Hospital, which landed with elements of the 11th Airborne Division, 28 August. (Occupational Monograph of the Eighth US Army in Japan, Vol. I, Aug 45—Jan 46 [C], p. 216.) (3) Early in September the Surgeon's Section (I Corps) had been informed of the desirability of having an officer from its section go to Japan, with an advance echelon for the purpose of evacuating Allied PW's. G-4 of Corps accepted the recommendation of the Surgeon that one evacuation hospital participate in this advance operation. The 54th Evacuation Hospital, then located at Urdenata, Luzon, was alerted and within 24 hours had loaded out on an LST. The 70th Replacement Depot which accompanied the advance echelon received medical augmentation which enabled them to accomplish their mission. (HQ Eighth US Army, CWS Hist Rpt, Mil Occupation of Japan through Nov 45, pp. 12–13.)

sentatives were among the first visitors from the outside to talk to prisoners of war at Kawasaki camp Number 1, where medical care was most critically needed. Most of the prisoners captured earlier at Guam, Bataan and Corregidor had been imprisoned for more than three years. Many of them had died from abuse and hunger and deprivation during their long confinement; however, those who had survived were in a slightly improved condition, due to the earlier air drops of food, clothing and medical necessities.[51]

In camp Number 3 at Maibara, sixty-five miles northeast of Osaka, the prisoners had spent their noon hours diving for mussels to provide the only nutritious food obtainable during their long imprisonment; as in all the other camps, they had been forced to sustain life on watery soup, scanty greens, and barley gruel. Mount Futabi Camp, near Kobe, contained civilian workers who had been taken prisoner at Guam and had been interned for three and a half years.[52] United States veterans of Wake Island and Bataan also emerged from these Japanese prison camps. They listened dazedly to the conversation of the American medical men who cared for them. Buried in prison camps for three years, they had no idea that the United States had twelve million men under arms and that Germany had surrendered. Not even the name of Harry Truman meant anything to them. They listened to unfamiliar expressions and names of battles, planes, and army units about which they knew nothing. Year after year, men had vanished into Japan without a trace—the men of Singapore, of Hong Kong, of Bataan, of Wake, of the ships sunk at sea, and of the planes shot down in combat. Only a few had received Red Cross packages; practically all their guards had engaged in graft; they had been beaten and kicked, had been forced to bow and to obey endless petty rules invented by their captors.[53] For stubbornly rebellious prisoners and airmen from whom the Japanese hoped to extract information there was a special treatment. They were sent to Ofuna, a camp for unregistered prisoners, where they endured months of solitary confinement and torture.[54] The fate of prisoners who became sick was hardly better.

51 *The Red Cross Courier*, Oct 45.

52 *Ibid.*

53 *Time Magazine*, 3 Sep 45.

54 (1) Secretary of State James Byrnes made public on 5 September a 10,000-word report on the maltreatment of American PW's by the Japanese Army in which he said: "Persons who mistreated PW's in violation of the Geneva Convention Land Warfare and International Law ought to be punished severely. In this respect, Japanese war criminals will be held responsible to the utmost as was the case in Germany."

The State Department report is based on about 200 protests presented to Japan since the outbreak of war by former Secretary of State Hull, former Secretary of State Stettinius, and former Ass't Secretary of State Grew. Many of them have been withheld from publication on the ground that the war was in progress. In the report in question, the names of those who are responsible for the maltreatment of Allied prisoners of war are enumerated. (Tokyo, *Asahi Shimbun*, 8 Sep 45.)

(2) According to a Manila report, prisoners of war who arrived there on their way home have told the press as follows regarding treatment by the Japanese Army: Without any provocations, the Allied PW's were beaten badly. High Allied officers were humiliated, and the Japanese Army schemed to ferment division of opinions among the lower ranks of the Allied troops. B-29 flyers were especially maltreated. Food and medicines were not satisfactorily provided for the Allied prisoners. In many instances, Allied patients died because diagnosis was refused until they were at the stage when operations were necessary. All kinds of sickness were prevalent among the PW's: malaria, dysentery and TB were common diseases. These were due to lack of proper diet and treatment. TB patients were made to stand in the cold outdoors, and Japanese guards would pour water over them every half an hour. In spite of the Geneva Convention, officers were put to forced labor. (Tokyo, *Asahi Shimbun*, 12 Sep 45.)

Lt. Gen. H. Tamura, Chief, Japanese PW Intelligence Bureau, points out camps to Col. R. R. Coursey, G-1, GHQ, Col. A. E. Schanzie, G-1, Eighth Army, and IRC delegates Dr. M. Junod and M. Strahler.

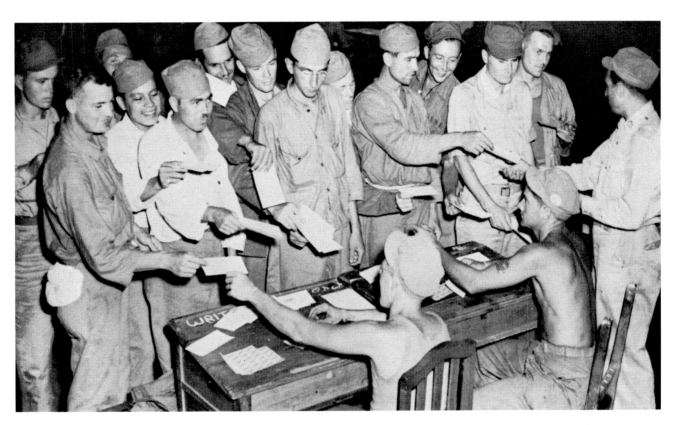

At Atsugi Airfield, Allied prisoners of war released from Toyama Camp bring letters to the American Red Cross table for postage and mailing back home.

PLATE NO. 34
Red Cross Duties, September 1945

The majority of these men, when sent to the dirt-floored buildings of Shinagawa, lone hospital for 8,000 prisoners near Tokyo, simply went to their deaths.[55] There was a complete lack of sanitation. Patients slept on flea-infested mats without blankets. The operating tables were bare boards. A number of the prisoners died as a result of being used as guinea pigs for incredible experimentation.[56]

Prisoners were promptly evacuated from camps where these apalling conditions existed to relay points from which they could be sent to processing centers and then home. In order to bring in necessary ships for loading, mine sweepers were ordered in to clear the various ports used. Ambulances, trucks, food and medical supplies were rushed to the various loading areas. Principal landing places were Kochi for Shikoku, and Omuta in Shimbara, Kaiwan for Kyushu and western Honshu camps,

---

55   PRISONER OF WAR INTERNMENT CAMPS IN JAPAN PROPER:

LOCATION OF CAMPS	AGGREGATE PW'S RELEASED	NUMBER OF PATIENTS
Hakodate	1,597	67
Sendai	3,566	495
Tokyo	6,069	417
Nagoya	3,336	288
Osaka	4,706	305
Hiroshima	2,956	199
Fukuoka	10,394	899
Total	32,624	2,670

(Documents Submitted to SCAP by the Japanese Mission to Negotiate Surrender, Manila, 19 Aug 45 [C], Part I, p. 97. Aggregate from footnote 41 supra. The surrender data were too low.)

56 (1) *Time Magazine*, 17 Sep 45. (2) Evidence presented in the War Crimes Trials held in Yokohama described the fate of captured American fliers held by Western Army of Kyushu after April 1945. (Interview with Mr. Paul K. von Bergen, Legal Sec, GHQ SCAP, 13 Jun 49) Kyushu Imperial University was located a few miles away from Western Army Headquarters in Fukuoka City. With the consent of authorities of Western Army and under the observation of staff officers, several fliers were taken from their cells to the medical college where they were used for medical experiments. While there were modern, adequate operating facilities available, the fliers were actually vivisected in an old, wooden, dirty room used by medical students in the studies of autopsy and anatomy, on a tin covered table used by the students to dissect corpses. At the time the army was particularly interested in obtaining a blood substitute. In this instance sea water was used on the prisoners: blood was drained and sea water injected until the victims bled to death. New techniques in the removal of lungs were attempted. Instruction on the practical technique of stomach resection was demonstrated. In one instance a slit was made in the heart muscle, then sutured, after which the suture was removed so that other surgeons could practice. In one or more operations a complete liver was removed. There was at least one brain operation. After the prisoners were killed, other medical scholars dissected the corpses and obtained specimens including the brain.

On the night of 19 June 1945, Fukuoka City had its one air raid after which the remaining eight plane crash survivors were taken out into the compound and decapitated in retaliation. On or about 10 August 1945, approximately eight prisoners were taken to Aburayama and used in the training of the guerrilla squad, a unit of specially selected young officers training to lead the civilians in a last ditch stand, in *karate*, a hand-to-hand combat technique in which fliers were punched and kicked in vital areas. One prisoner was subjected to bow and arrows, and all of them ultimately to decapitation.

On 15 August 1945, after the broadcast of the Imperial rescript of the Emperor, the remaining seventeen American captives held were summarily decapitated in the fear that otherwise they would have been able to disclose the previous atrocities.

The fliers were reported to the Occupation authorities as having died in the Fukuoka and Hiroshima bombings and in an incident where, after the 15th of August, a plane of the special attack corps came from Tokyo, took up the remaining prisoners and suicide crashed into the Bay.

except Kagoshima and Nagasaki which were accessible locally.[57] After 1 September the movement of prisoners was rapid, and on 6 September General Eichelberger requested evacuation and processing facilities for 1,600 prisoners of war at Hakodate and for 3,802 at Sendai.[58] On 10 September eight Allied ships arrived in Shiogama and began loading personnel for evacuation early the following morning.[59]

After years of unbelievable suffering, released prisoners of war often had their former Japanese captors at their mercy, since control of each camp was turned over to a senior officer or civilian prisoner. To their everlasting credit, most of the prisoners refrained from revenging themselves. In several instances, some of them did all in their power to aid those Japanese who had shown them kindness during their long period of confinement. Many of them gave articles of food and clothing from their own inadequate supply to their former jailers.[60]

Operations of Medical Teams

To supplement the work of the Recovery Teams, the Eighth Army Surgeon organized four medical teams which were sent to various camp areas to care for the sick and alleviate suffering. These arrived in Yokohama, from Okinawa, on 30 August 1945. After physical examination, the prisoners were formed into groups and escorted to Yokohama. One team was assigned to Navy Task Force 36 and made two mercy trips, utilizing the USNHS *Rescue* for hospital cases. The first mission covered the Hamamatsu area near Nagoya, where approximately 3,850 prisoners were processed; 15 percent of them required hospital care. The second troop covered the Sendai and Kamaishi area, where about 3,000 prisoners were found.[61]

A second team proceeded to the Kobe area by rail and established headquarters in Kobe Prison House Number 2. This territory had originally been assigned to Sixth Army, but due

---

57 Rad 030730/z, GUAM to CINCAFPAC, 3 Sep 45. In G-3 GHQ Adm 383.6/1 (S).

58 (1) Rad DX71517, CG 8th Army to CINCAFPAC ADV, CINCAFPAC, COMNORPAC W CINCPAC 3rd FLT CTG 30.6, 6 Sep 45. In G-3 GHQ Adm 383.6 (S); (2) Rad 051525/T, CG 8th Army to COM3rdFLT, 6 Sep 45, In G-3 Adm.

59 Tokyo, *Asahi Shimbun*, 12 Sep 45.

60 (1) "The prisoners did something else which I shall always remember. Making up bundles of their old Red Cross shoes, blankets, and clothes, these starved men went into the villages and out in the countryside to find the squalid huts in which lived the Jap foremen who had befriended them on their work details. They knew these small-timers hated the Jap military and monopolistic industrial machine. They knew their families were facing another hard winter. They gave these Jap civilians their pitifully shabby collection of clothes." (Weinstein, *op cit*, pp. 290–1.) (2) "A Good Deed by US POW's: A railway accident occurred at Sasago on the 6th with some casualties. Immediately after the accident, a train bearing 80 American POW's arrived at the Sasago station on its way from Kayano to Yokohama. The railway officials were worried over a possible delay in the POW transportation, but on learning of the accident the POW's proposed to help those in need and a dozen men, getting out of the train, began giving first aid to the wounded with what medical supplies they had with them. In the meantime, other POW's opened canned foods and gave them to the wounded. Offering their own blankets, these POW's made impromptu beds for the wounded.

"When the repairs were completed and the POW train was about to pull out of the station, canned goods, blankets, coats, overcoats, etc., were thrown out of the windows one after another to help out the injured.

"At the request of the Kofu Railway Control Section (that) their thanks be conveyed to the POW's, Transportation Ministry, Kobiyama, was instructed to obtain grapes, well known product of Kofu, to present to the POW's as a token of gratitude." (Tokyo, *Asahi Shimbun*, 12 Sep 45.)

61 HQ Eighth US Army, Office of Surg, Med Rpt on the Occupation of Japan for Sep 45, Annex 4, Incl d.

Prisoner of war, newly arrived at Yokohama Central Station, is carried to an ambulance by medics of the 1st Cavalry Division, XI Corps.

Recently arrived prisoners of war relax outside a warehouse on docks at Yokohama.

PLATE NO. 35
Released Prisoners of War, 5 September 1945

to the urgency of the situation, areas assigned to Eighth Army were extended in order to bring speedy relief.[62] By 7 September the team had cleared 7,500 evacuees from thirteen camps in the vicinity and had them enroute to Yokohama. This group also handled all litter cases from the International Committee of the Red Cross in Kobe, where the Japanese had collected the seriously ill patients from the nearby stockades. Ninety percent of these patients were in advanced stages of tuberculosis.[63] Processing in the Kobe area was completed by a third team which evacuated approximately 6,900 prisoners from 6 to 20 September.

The fourth team operated from 10 to 20 September and processed 1,600 prisoners in five separate camp areas on the island of Hokkaido. Traveling thence from Yokohama, they were the first Americans to land on an airstrip near Chitose City. Headquarters of the team were set up in the Chitose Naval Air Training Base, and all evacuees were transported to Yokohama by plane.[64]

In the turmoil of the first days of the Occupation, one of the earliest of many conferences at Headquarters (Yokohama) was held by the Eighth Army Surgeon on 1 September 1945. In this meeting plans were perfected for evacuating prisoners of war who required hospitalization and evacuation. It was decided that all recoverees should be screened by the medical staff of USAHS *Marigold*, anchored in Yokohama harbor. The repatriates were classified in three categories: (1) Those found to be acutely ill and requiring extended hospitalization were to be assigned to the *Marigold* for direct transportation to a hospital in the United States. This group was to include United States service and civilian personnel and Canadians if they so desired. (2) Those who were found to be not only acutely ill, but also in need of a period of rehabilitation were to be

62 "Reurad NR 311012–Z. Urgency of situation indicates advisability of immediately extending evacuation of prisoners of war to 6th Army and 5th Flt areas. 8th Army and 3rd Flt working jointly to evacuate those within 8th Army and adjacent Honshu area to screening point at Yokohama. 6th and 8th Armies assisted by 3rd or 5th Flt units and regardless of Army and Fleet boundaries to extend opns to include all of Honshu, Kyushu, and Shikoku. It is desired that POW and civilian internees evacuated from western Honshu, Shikoku, and Kyushu be evacuated to Okinawa. Navy hospital ship to be made available at Okinawa for sceening purposes as majority of this personnel is Allied and destined for Manila, Australia and NEI. Naval vessels carrying Army contact teams to approach ports suitable for evacuation to naval vessels at pre-arranged ports. Army teams available at Yokohama now. Request conference earliest at Yokohama for complete planning with fleet representatives as designated by you. Plan discussed with Fleet Liaison who concurs. In view of reported conditions especially in Kyushu it is desirable to place rescue teams there simultaneously and at earliest practicable date." (Rad ZAX 5029, SCAP ADV to CINCAFPAC, 3 Sep 45. In G-3 GHQ Adm 383–611/S.)

63 Occupational Monogr of the Eighth US Army in Japan, Vol. I, Aug 45—Jan 46, (C).

64 "Subject evacuation of POW and civilian internees from western Honshu, Shikoku and Kyushu. Request 5th Fleet use Ports of Wakanoura and Nagasaki. Task Group with hospital ship to proceed Wakanoura to receive personnel transported there by rail from camps western Honshu and Shikoku. Ten recovery teams from 8th Army will proceed by destroyer from 3rd Fleet to join task group at Wakanoura and execute initial processing and 2d Task Group with hospital ship proceed to Nagasaki for similiar action and 6th Army to provide 10 recovery teams at Okinawa to be picked up by Nagasaki Task Group and hospital ship to evacuate North American bed cases to Marianas and other British nationals in accordance with arrangements to be made with CINCBPF and ambulatory except Navy to be evacuated to Okinawa then to Manila via air and surface vessels and hospital ship to Okinawa no longer required and notify SCAP, 8th Army and 3rd Fleet date of rendezvous at Wakanoura and notify SCAP, 8th Army and 6th Army date of arrival ship at Okinawa to receive recovery teams and personnel to be evacuated estimated 10400 at Nagasaki, 10600 at Wakanoura and standard procedure now effective with 3rd Fleet and 8th Army will furnish 5th Fleet and 6th Army representative for guidance upon ship arrival." (Rad ZAX, SCAP to GHQ Manila, 6 Sep 45. In G-3 GHQ Adm.)

transferred to a hospital ship (possibly the USNHS *Rescue*) for transportation to the Marianas Islands for the required period of rehabilitation. (3) Ambulatory cases not requiring hospitalization or treatment were to be flown to various points, as indicated by results of the screening process.[65]

Processing for Home : Before the above plan could be launched, circumstances of rapid evacuation of the camps necessitated some revisions. The 42d General Hospital, which had arrived in Tokyo Bay on August 1945 aboard the *Marigold*, assumed the processing of liberated PW's and civilian internees.[66] Facilities were established for this purpose in warehouses in the Yokohama dock area on 3 September, and twenty-four hours later the first group of evacuees went through the processing routine. Despite the three types of processing involved—medical, factual, and dispositional—this famous hospital unit eventually was able to handle three persons per minute.

Four phases made up the processing routine. Upon arrival at the Yokohama Central Station, the former prisoners found that every effort was made to make them feel at home. General Eichelberger was there as often as possible to extend his warm personal greetings.[69] The welcoming committee, composed of a group of officers and nurses, distributed candy, cigarettes, and other luxuries to the arrivals and escorted them to the hospital area. A division band from either the "Americal" or the 1st Cavalry was on hand to brighten the occasion with popular American tunes. After the evacuees reached the hospital area, all undesirable equipment and clothing was discarded; salvageable articles were sent to the Quartermaster Depot. A hot, substantial meal was served to all incoming groups, a measure of practical psychological value, inasmuch as most of them had been traveling from fourteen to sixteen hours without food. During several twenty-four-hour periods in these busy days, the mess served as many as 3,500 meals.[68]

After this reception, evacuees were taken to a decontamination room where they disrobed completely. Each individual was then required to take a shower, while at the same time his clothing and personal effects were sprayed with DDT. An army nurse interviewed each one, recorded his temperature, pulse, respiration, and complaints, as well as other personal data. A complete physical examination followed. Non-patients were given an issue of new clothing and proceeded to the General Headquarters processing area, where the required War Department data were obtained. They were then classified for various types of evacuation, according to status. Litter cases were carried to a separate area, served a meal, disrobed, bathed, given a physical examination and admitted directly to a hospital ship.[69] War

65 HQ Eighth US Army, Office of the Surg, Med Rpt on the Occupation of Japan for Sep 45.

66 Processing (of liberated PW's) began on 4 September 1945 and ended on 21 September 1945. The average number processed per day was 1033 with as many as 2450 in one 24 hour period. A total of 17,731 PW's were processed through this hospital unit. (Med Hist of 42d Gen Hosp, Ann Rpt of Activ for 1945, 24 Jan 46.)

67 Occupational Monogr of the Eighth US Army in Japan, Vol. I, Aug 45—Jan 46, (C).

68 HQ Eighth US Army, Med Rpt on the Occupation of Japan for Sep 45, Annex No. 4, Incl d.

69 "We clambered aboard the U. S. S. *Rescue* and were promptly told to strip and throw our lice-covered rags overboard. Into a steam-filled shower room we crowded. Oh, the first heavenly thrill of plenty of soap and piping-hot water squirting through the needle valves of the shower! We scrubbed and scrubbed our bodies, peeling off one layer of filth after another. We squirmed with pleasure under the jets. As we left the showers, medics with flit guns sprayed our heads and bodies with DDT while we pirouetted slowly, arms raised. In freshly washed pajamas sweet with cleanliness we walked through a line of docs who checked us over quickly. On the softest mattress, between the whitest sheets I have ever seen, I slipped into bed in the hundred-bed ward. . . .

"Better than food was the God-sent feeling of safety. We had been living at the mercy of barbarous, hair-trigger

Department data were obtained from these individuals by supplemental processing teams aboard the hospital ships. As passenger manifests were made up, each group was evacuated by air or water. All ambulatory cases left Japan within twenty-four hours of arrival in Yokohama.[70]

Radio reports were prepared daily and sent to Commander in Chief, Army Forces Pacific, Tokyo; Commander in Chief, Army Forces Pacific, Manila, and the Adjutant General, Washington, which meant that relatives in the United States and in other United Nations were usually given the news of recovery within a few days. Machine records showing the nationality, branch of service, date and place of recovery, and physical condition were made. These rosters enabled many servicemen of the Allied Powers to gain information that relatives and former comrades were alive and had been freed from the prison camps. Copies of this roster were furnished to Commander in Chief, AFPAC Advance, in Tokyo, the U. S. Navy, and the Marine Corps. One copy went to representatives of the International Committee of the Red Cross for transmittal to Geneva.[71]

A grand total of 17,531 prisoners and internees were processed through the 42nd General Hospital during the eighteen-day period it operated in this capacity. The evacuees included people from the United States, Great Britain and Ireland, Canada, Australia, New Zealand, India, the Netherlands, Greece, France, Spain, Iceland, Finland, Italy, Malay, Guam, China, Norway, Hawaii, Czechoslovakia, Mexico, Burma, Poland, Malta, and Portugal.[72]

The 608th Medical Clearing Company (Sep), under directions of the Eighth Army Surgeon, served as a holding station at Atsugi airfield and arranged for air transportation. Americans and Canadians were flown to Guam, Saipan, or Manila.[73] Nationals of other countries went by air to Okinawa, and from there flew to Manila. Rapid preparation of passenger lists and coordination with the Air Transport Command made it possible to fly as many as 1,600 individuals in one day by C-54's from Atsugi to Okinawa and thence to Manila.[74] Similar numbers were evacuated to Guam aboard U. S. Navy vessels. By 21 September the processing of prisoners of war and civilian internees had largely been completed and the 42d General Hospital ceased operations as the processing agency. This work was then assumed by the 608th Medical Clearing Company (Sep) and the 30th Portable Surgical Hospital, both located at Atsugi airfield, but relatively few recoverees remained to be taken care of.[75] In all, the Eighth Army freed and evacuated 23,985 persons.[76]

---

69 (contd.) personalities for so many years that the gentleness and kindness we were shown was enough to make us sob silently in our pillows. Terms like 'freedom of speech,' 'trial by one's peers,' 'the right of redress,' 'habeas corpus,' were no longer a series of glib words that rolled off the tongue. They had a flowing, vivid quality to the liberated prisoners who had existed for years without the protection of these monuments of civilization. They were music to our ears. We could never forget their significance." (Weinstein, *op cit*, pp. 296–7.)

70 Occupational Monogr of the Eighth US Army in Japan, Vol. I, Aug 45—Jan 46, (C).

71 Eighth US Army, G-1 Rpt, 1945.

72 HQ Eighth US Army, Office of the Surg, Med Rpt on the Occupation of Japan for Sep 45, Annex 4, Incl d.

73 (1) Rad 060535/z, CinC BPF to CinC Hong Kong, 7 Sep 55; (2) Rad 081117/z, CinC BritPacFlt to COMGEN AFWESPAC, 9 Sep 45; (3) Rad 060533/z, SHA No. 404 to GHQ Manila, 9 Sep 45; (4) Rad 140211/z, VABPF to COM3rdFLT, 15 Sep 45. In G-3 GHQ Adm 383.

74 "1648 Allied Recovered Prisoners of War evacuated by air to Okinawa 7 Sep 45 signed Eichelberger." (Rad 71531, Eighth A ADV to Navy Okinawa, 9 Sep 45. In G-3 GHQ Adm 383.6).

75 HQ Eighth US Army, Office of the Surg, Med Rpt on the Occupation of Japan for Sep 45, Annex 4, Incl d.

76 Americans, 8,946; British, 7,613; Canadians, 1,751; Australians, 1,455; Dutch, 3,301; other nationals, 919. (Occupational Monogr of the Eighth US Army in Japan, Vol. I, Aug 45—Jan 46 [C].)

Procedure Regarding Dead and Missing Prisoners of War

All former prisoners of war camp sites were examined. During the investigation of these camps, Japanese officers, doctors, and employees of mining companies were interviewed. Records and documents were secured. They included lists of prisoners, reports on prisoners who had died at the camps, hospitalization reports, authorization to dispose of bodies, receipt for ashes of those who had died and had been cremated, photographs of camps, camp regulations, employment of prisoners, food, clothing, housing, and general welfare. Effort was made to determine cause of death and to obtain a full report if death was not due to natural causes. In one instance it was learned that thirty-two prisoners of war were killed or died as a result of shelling and bombardment by the Allied Navy. In many instances it was found that available records and documents had been removed when the prisoners were released.[77]

On 30 September 1945 SCAP issued a memorandum to the Imperial Japanese Government regarding regulations of prisoners of war. The memorandum directed that articles and money of the dead prisoners, whether possessed by the military personnel in charge of camps, government offices, hospitals, or dressing stations, must be sent to the Prisoners' Information Bureau. It demanded a prompt report as to what action had been taken to secure the personal property of all deceased prisoners. The report was also to include evidence of funds, such as credits for money held by or on deposit with any agency or representatives of the Imperial Japanese Government;[78] and all sums due but not paid to a prisoner of war for services rendered prior to his death. In the event that the above outlined action was not taken regarding a deceased prisoner's property, it was to be marked to show the prisoner's name, rank, serial number, nationality and branch of service, as well as the name of the camp where he had been confined. The belongings were then to be delivered to the headquarters of the major Allied military force occupying the zone or district where the items were found. After delivery was made, a report was to be sent to SCAP. This report was to include a roster showing all information listed above for every deceased prisoner of war and civilian internee.[79]

In a further effort to account for all missing prisoners of war, not located in camps by the recovery teams and not listed among the dead in camps, the Adjutant General's Office sent another memorandum to the Imperial Japanese Government on 26 November 1945 requesting additional information.[80] Recovery teams also attempted to acquire all possible information on deceased prisoners who had been cremated. The customs of the Japanese did not allow for the proper burial of the dead, and consequently the problems were much greater than anticipat-

---

77 XIV Corps, Rpt No. 1 on the "Blacklist" Opn, 20 Aug—30 Sep 45 (R), p. 9.

78 "An officer among the Prisoners of War can give his services out of his own volition but he will not be paid for his labor. The amount of pay for a POW general will be 35 yen less than that for a Japanese general; 30 yen less for POW field officer; and 27 yen less for company officer. Surplus money of POW's will be turned over to the National Treasury." (IPS Doc No. 2197, 24 Jun 46. In PW Info Bur.)

79 Memo, SCAP for IJG, AG 383.6, 30 Sep 45.

80 This memorandum requested information regarding Japanese vessels sunk while carrying Allied prisoners of war or internees, the name of the ship, port of embarkation, date, place and circumstances of sinking and a nominal roll of prisoners of war or internees who had died of illness or from other causes while aboard Japanese vessels. (Memo, SCAP for IJG, AG-560, 26 Nov 45.)

ed. The varied problems confronting the Quartermaster Section in this task included the investigation of prisoner of war camps, the recovery of air crashes, and the disposition of the remains of all deceased persons. Diaries of prisoners, conferences with prisoner camp commanders, and interrogations of other Japanese were chief sources of information for lists of the dead and their location. For personnel not accounted for, further investigation was carried on by Graves Registration personnel.[81] This search for the dead was carried out simultaneously with the evacuation of the living.

Final Processing of Prisoners of War in Manila

Evacuees from Japan were processed in Manila before leaving for home. From the moment these former prisoners came under the control of American forces everything possible was done to add to their comfort. They were given an enthusiastic and warm welcome, and an attempt was made to comply with all of their requests.

The mission of receiving, processing, and looking after these people was given to the Replacement Command. Here recreation programs, a central registration file, and communication centers were established. Messages from home were delivered as quickly as possible.[82] British, Australian, and Canadian male personnel and later the Dutch were assigned to the 5th Replacement Depot; women, children, and family groups were sent to the Women's Replacement and Disposition Center for processing. To provide adequate

medical facilities and care for recovered Allied military personnel, a 1500-bed general hospital was attached to the Replacement Command. In addition, two infirmaries and a number of dispensaries were operated in two reception centers near Manila. A medical processing group was set up at Nichols Field for the preliminary separation of former prisoners into two groups : those needing hospitalization and those able to proceed directly to the depots.

Five thousand beds were held in reserve in the Manila area, 500 of them for women and children at the 120th General Hospital at Santo Tomas University, and the remainder at the Mandaluyong Hospital Center. A total of 2,000 beds were also held in reserve at bases in northern Luzon. These bed credits were based upon the assumption that 45,000 freed persons would be processed through the Philippines. The allotment proved to be more than adequate.[83] Clothing, equipment, and post exchange supplies were issued free; well earned promotions were given and decorations awarded; accrued pay accounts were settled; and entertainment and Red Cross recreation activities were provided. By utilizing air travel to the greatest possible extent, transportation to their homes was arranged with little delay.

Of the 28,786 evacuees received by 30 September 1945, 12,286 were repatriated. From October to December approximately 3,000 additional persons arrived. By this time repatriation shipments had progressed so satisfactorily that by the end of October there remained only a few hospital cases, together with 6,529 Dutch personnel. The latter remained only because of the uncertain political situation in the Netherlands East Indies. By

---

81   Occupational Monogr of the Eighth US Army in Japan, Vol. I, Aug 45—Jan 46 (C).

82   Gen Jonathan Wainwright was the first person to receive a 1616 message form. It was delivered when he reached Manila on 30 August. (*The Red Cross Courier*, October 1945.)

83   31,617 recoverees had been received in the Philippines through 31 October; only 183 remained in need of hospitalization on that date, a total of 2,676 having been hospitalized during the preceding period.

the end of the year a total of 31,879 former prisoners had been processed with but a few hundred still under the jurisdiction of the Replacement Command.[84]

Thus, in the short period of four months, most of the Allied prisoners of war and civilian internees had been restored to their families. Through careful preparation, the efficient execution of plans, and the full cooperation of all personnel concerned, " Blacklist's " rescue mission proved most successful.

---

84   USAFWESPAC Semi-Ann Rpt, 1 Jun—31 Dec 45, p. 8.

CHAPTER V

DEMOBILIZATION AND DISARMAMENT OF
THE JAPANESE ARMED FORCES

The General Demobilization Program

There must be eliminated for all time the authority and influence of those who deceived and misled the people of Japan into embarking on world conquest, for we insist that a new order of peace, security and justice will be impossible until irresponsible militarism is driven from the world.... The Japanese military forces, after being completely disarmed, shall be permitted to return to their homes with the opportunity to lead peaceful productive lives.[1]

These principles enunciated in the Potsdam Declaration formed the basis for the elimination of military power and the initial plans for the demobilization of the Japanese armed forces incidental to occupation movements. Upon the return of the surrender delegation to Japan in August 1945, a complex demobilization machinery went into high gear: the rapid, orderly repatriation, demobilization and disarmament of the Japanese armed forces, at home and abroad, began immediately.

In view of the Theater G-2's detailed knowledge of the strength and dispositions of the Imperial Japanese Forces and the internal structure of the General Staff and other military organs after four years of intimate combat association, the intelligence section was given a prominent role in the surrender negotiations. In the agenda of the conference, the basic conditions were laid down for demobilizing and disarming the Imperial Forces. G-2 was directed to supervise the initial demobilization and disarmament plans of the Japanese Government, to exercise GHQ supervision of subsequent developments thereunder, and to render periodical progress reports.

On the day of surrender, the Imperial Japanese Forces totaled 6,983,000 troops, an aggregate of 154 army ground force divisions, 136 brigades,[2] and some 20-odd major naval units.[3] Army and Navy forces stationed within the home islands numbered 3,532,000; air force units were then integral parts of the Army and Navy. The balance of the Japanese forces were spread in a great arc from Manchuria to the Solomons, and across the islands of the Central and Southwest Pacific.[4]

Accurate and reliable figures on total strengths at the time of surrender were unavail-

---

1 Potsdam Declaration, 26 Jul 45, pars. 6 and 9.
2 GHQ SCAP, Progress of Demob of the Japanese Armed Forces, 31 Jul 48, p. 9.
3 GHQ SCAP, Final Rpt, Progress of Demob of the Japanese Armed Forces, 31 Dec 46 (R), Incl 61.
4 *Ibid.*

LOCATION OF JAPANESE FORCES, 31 December 1946:

	HOME ISLANDS	OVERSEAS*	TOTAL
Army (incl Air comps)	2,353,000	3,172,000	5,525,000
Navy (incl Air comps)	1,179,000	279,000	1,458,000
Totals	3,532,000	3,451,000	6,983,000

*Forces in the Kuriles and Karafuto are included in the overseas strength.

able for some time. Original figures presented to General MacArthur's headquarters required continuous adjustment; and as repatriation progressed, it became apparent that hundreds of thousands of men, included in initial Japanese strength estimates, had perished prior to the conclusion of hostilities.

In the over-all picture, enormous military risks were involved in landing initially with "token" United States forces. The Japanese mainland was still potentially a colossal armed camp, and there was an obvious military gamble in landing with only two and a half divisions, then confronted by fifty-nine Japanese divisions, thirty-six brigades, and forty-five-odd regiments plus naval and air forces. The terrific psychological tension was dissolved by the relatively simple formula of preserving the existing Japanese Government, and utilizing its normal agencies to effect the complicated processes of disarmament and demobilization.

The program for the accomplishment of this tremendous task was initiated under the provisions of several key directives in August—September 1945.[5] Immediate responsibility for demobilization was vested in the Imperial General Headquarters and the Japanese Army and Navy Ministries, in order that their technical and administrative skill could be exploited to the maximum degree. Supervising and planning this complicated operation required careful coordination on the part of the Occupation forces and ultimately involved practically all General Staff sections[6] and several Japanese

---

[5] SCAP Dir No. 1, 2 September 1945, ordered immediate dissemination and compliance with GO No. 1, 2 September 1945, which outlined the methods for surrendering of Japanese armed forces in Japan and abroad, named SCAP representatives to accept the surrender of troops, and ordered immediate disarming of all Japanese troops.

SCAP Dir No. 2, 3 September 1945, Part II, Japanese Armed Forces, outlined in detail controls and procedures concerning disarmament and demobilization of Japanese armed forces deemed necessary to insure orderly compliance with terms of surrender. The Imperial Japanese GHQ was ordered to conduct a speedy and orderly demobilization of all Japanese forces and outline specific procedures to be followed.

GHQ USAFPAC Operations Instructions No. 4 (S), 31 August 1945, Appendix 11, SCAP Control, Disarmament and Demobilization of Japanese Armed Forces, outlined instructions to the commanding generals of the Sixth and Eighth Armies. In general, these instructions were to establish a system of surveillance and inspection, effect coordination of movement of Japanese troops, and aid in the transfer of arms and equipment to insure rapid and complete demobilization and disarmament.

[6] Functions of the responsible staff sections and agencies were as follows:

Development of Basic Plans .... G-2, GHQ, SCAP; Japanese War & Navy Ministries
Control of Army Demobilization .... Japanese War Ministry: First Demob Bureau
Control of Navy Demobilization .... Japanese Navy Ministry: Second Demob Bureau
GHQ Control of the First Demobilization Bureau .... G-2, GHQ, SCAP
GHQ Control of the Second Demobilization Bureau .... COMNAVFE: SCAJAP*
Disposal of Armament and Equipment .... G-4, GHQ, SCAP
Periodic Reports on Demobilization .... G-2, GHQ, SCAP
Repatriation Movement .... G-3, GHQ, SCAP
Operation of Repatriation Centers .... Japanese Welfare Ministry
Control of Repatriation Shipping .... COMNAVFE: SCAJAP
Operation of Repatriation Shipping .... Second Demobilization Bureau
Periodic Reports on Repatriation .... G-3, GHQ, SCAP
Control and Disposal of Armament .... G-4, GHQ, SCAP
Collection of Armament and Equipment in the Field ....Sixth and Eighth US Armies; COMNAVFE; FEAF

* SCAJAP (Shipping Control Authority for the Japanese Merchant Marine) was under the control of COMNAVFE.

118

agencies.

Certain civil sections were also drawn into this complex picture in connection with various phases of the demobilization operation. For example, the Public Health and Welfare Section of GHQ, SCAP, cooperating with G-3, was instrumental in developing effective repatriation quarantine policies, a step which prevented the dangerous epidemics so often associated with mass movements of people.[7]

To effect coordination and facilitate progress of the demobilization and disarmament program, each local Japanese commander was ordered to report to the senior U. S. Army commander in his area for command instructions; the Japanese staff was required to produce such information as locations of regiments and all larger units, tables of organization, actual strength figures, status of demobilization, and locations and names of commanders of demobilization depots. When this information was checked against the same information submitted by the Japanese Imperial General Headquarters[8] some discrepancies were noted; for example, the Japanese failed to report twenty-three units of the 100th Air Brigade located at Takamatsu airfield on Yura Island (Shikoku District). However, through local surveillance by Occupation troops, complete demobilization was quickly carried out.[9]

Orders published by the Sixth and Eighth U. S. Armies implemented SCAP Directives Numbers 1 and 2. In essence they called for existing agencies (such as the Japanese military, naval, and civilian police, and the senior naval and military commanders) to disarm all personnel found with weapons. These agencies were also charged with expediting the transportation of Japanese military and naval personnel to their homes and directing the local authorities in the storing of surrendered arms and munitions and undertaking reconnaissance to insure that Occupation orders were being obeyed.[10] Only the local Japanese police were permitted weapons considered necessary to maintain law and order.

In the initial Occupation phase, the infantry regiment became the chief instrument in the local supervision of demobilization. The entire plan for the imposition of surrender terms was based on the presence of infantry regiments in all Japanese prefectures. The outline of Occupation duties was fairly well established by SCAP and AFPAC instructions. The Sixth and Eighth Armies assigned prefectures to corps, divisions, and regiments. The specific number of prefectures assigned was determined by

---

7 " The following instances are cited as being indicative of the magnitude of the quarantine problem and the value of strict procedures enforced by the Supreme Commander for the Allied Powers. The occurrence of 711 proven cases of cholera and 479 carriers aboard 114 vessels resulted in 232,907 persons being detained in quarantine. Two hundred fifty-five cases of typhus fever were found among repatriates on some 52 vessels, most of which arrived from China, Manchuria and Korea. Two hundred seven cases of smallpox were discovered on 54 vessels from China and Manchuria. At no time has there existed in this program any threat of danger among the Occupation forces." (GHQ SCAP, PH&W Rpt, 31 Jul 48, p. 38.)

8 SCAP Dir No. 2, 3 Sep 45, Part II, par. 4.

9 8th Info & Hist Sv, HQ Sixth Army, Sixth Army Occupation of Japan, (undated) p. 58.

10 When the Sixth Army entered Japan, approximately 80 percent of the Japanese armed forces in the area of entry had been demobilized. The active troops, in most cases, were employed as guards for military installations and as administrative personnel in the demobilization and disarmament program. The Japanese commander, in collaboration with the chief of police, submitted lists of all Japanese installations and inventories of materiel within the area for consolidation and forwarding to SCAP. As soon as the US Army accepted custody of Japanese military installations, the Japanese authorities were informed that there was no further need for the guard and service personnel who were then relieved and subsequently demobilized. See Ch. II.

population density, industries, and military installations. Usually regimental zones of responsibility comprised a single prefecture.

The Japanese had not waited for the Allied forces to appear before they started to disband their Army and Navy: in September-October 88 percent of the Army was demobilized. The Occupation troops soon found the bulk of their activities directed towards supervising disposition of war material. The demobilization program functioned smoothly and efficiently on its own momentum and reports to GHQ were monotonously uniform: "No disorders; no opposition; cooperation continues."

Japanese Plans for Demobilization

The over-all plan for the completion of the Japanese demobilization program, prepared by the Chiefs of the Military and Naval Affairs Bureau provided for the transformation of the existing Japanese Army and Navy Ministries into Ministries of Demobilization, on 1 December 1945. (Plate No. 36) The two Demobilization Ministries were to be staffed by civilians and organized much in the same way as the already existing Japanese civil ministries. As the demobilization program decreased in scope, the Demobilization Ministries were to be further changed into small bureaus, tentatively by 1 April 1946. It was estimated that the General Staffs of the Army and Navy and the Department of Military Training could be dissolved by mid-October; the only professional personnel to be retained were those necessary to carry on essential business, liaison, and information for the Occupation forces. The naval recommendations included estimated dates for complete repatriation of all Japanese then serving outside the Empire, minesweeping, and completion of administrative problems such as operation of hospitals, ports, and shipyards.

These plans, submitted mainly in chart form, were approved by SCAP on 10 October.[11] There were certain inferential conditions: the dates listed in the plan would be regarded as absolute maximum, not to be exceeded; Japanese authorities would exert every effort to advance specific dates whenever possible.

Demobilization of the Japanese armed forces fell naturally into two major categories, the demobilization of the forces in the home islands and the forces overseas. The Japanese Navy Ministry (later the Second Demobilization Ministry) was given the mission of transporting all repatriates to Japan. Upon their arrival in the homeland they were channeled through either army demobilization or navy demobilization channels, depending upon their individual status. Demobilization of the overseas forces depended entirely upon chronology of repatriation to Japan.

Demobilization of the Japanese Home Forces

At the time of surrender, the command structure within the Empire was organized into two major branches, Army and Navy, both, however, under Imperial General Headquarters. The Army, which consisted of fifty-seven infantry divisions, two armored divisions, thirty-six brigades, the Emperor's personal guards, and the four anti-aircraft divisions was grouped into several major commands as follows: First General Army (Group): Eleventh, Twelfth, and Thirteenth Area Armies, stationed in northern Honshu, Aomori to Nagoya; Second General Army (Group): Fifteenth and Sixteenth Area Armies, stationed in southern Honshu, Nagoya to Shimonoseki, and Shikoku and Kyushu; and the Fifth Area Army which was directly under the Imperial GHQ, stationed in Hokkaido, Karafuto, and the

11   SCAPIN 137, 10 Oct 45, sub: Demobilization, Japanese Armed Forces.

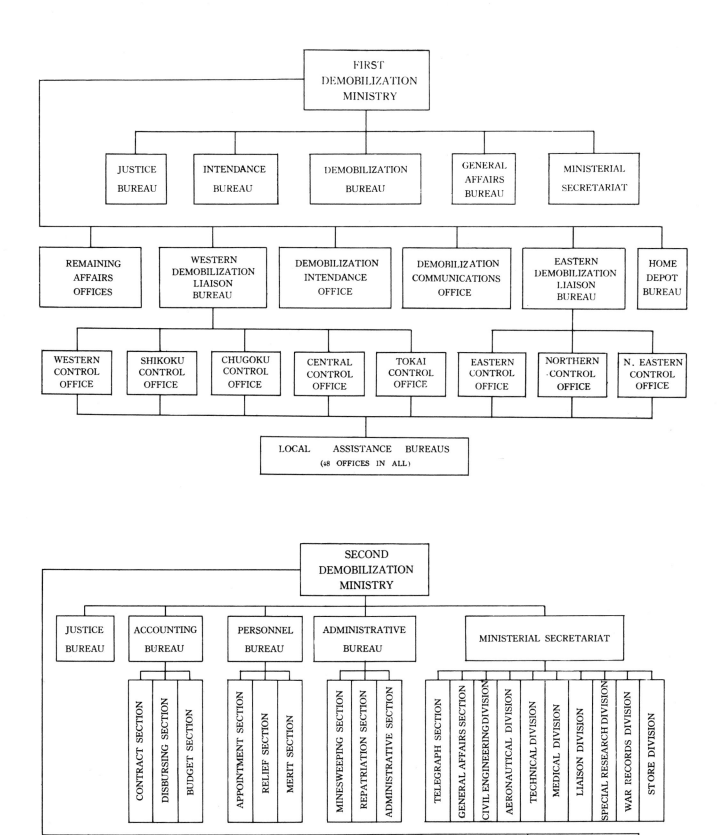

PLATE NO. 36

Organization of First and Second Demobilization Ministries, 14 June 1946

Kuriles. (Plate No. 37) For convenience in effecting demobilization, the Japanese boundary between Army Groups was altered to conform to the established boundary between the Sixth and Eighth U. S. Armies.[12]

A new but temporary command function of "Demobilization Commissioner" was created. The commanding generals of the First and Second General Armies (Groups) functioned as senior commissioners. Under the Ministers of War and Navy and the Chief of the General Staff, all commanders of units down to and including divisions operated as "commissioners"; while lower echelon commanders did not rank as commissioners, they were responsible for the demobilization of their own units. Under this organizational framework, the Japanese War Ministry completely demobilized 1,961,368 troops without incident or disorder between August and October 1945.[13]

The Japanese surrender delegation in Manila reported on 19 August that the strength of their naval personnel on 1 August was 1,024,255.[14] These forces were organized into the major commands of Naval Section of the Imperial General Headquarters, Fleet Headquarters, Southwestern Area Fleet, Southeastern Area Fleet, and combined Naval Force Headquarters, plus ten naval station units, five area fleets, three air fleets, and one combined command corps.[15] These naval units under direction of the Navy Ministry were responsible for demobilizing the once powerful Imperial Navy.

On the recommendation of the theater intelligence, the Japanese Imperial General Headquarters was abolished on 13 September, a decisive step toward Japan's demilitarization.[16] Responsibilities formerly held by the Imperial General Headquarters were transferred to the Japanese War and Navy Ministries.[17]

By mid-September approximately 55 percent of the total of 2,353,414 army strength had been demobilized.[18] By October some 83 percent of the original strength was out of the army; on 15 October, the tentative target date assigned by SCAP,[19] the remaining tactical units that had not been disbanded were attached to their original depot headquarters for demobilization. All military forces in Japan were demobilized by December.

The largest of the three major Japanese ground force units was the First General Army (Group). This Army of 852,060 men, stationed in the northern Honshu area, was over 90 percent demobilized by October. Transportation difficulties, aggravated by a heavy typhoon and floods which further disrupted an already badly damaged rail system, slowed up demobilization of the Second General Army (Group); of its total of 700,723 men, about 75 percent was discharged by October; in November, demobilization was nearly complete.

The strength of the Fifth Area Army was approximately 150,700 men; of this force 72,600 were located in the Kuriles and Kara-

---

12 SCAP Dir No. 2, 3 Sep 45. See Ch. II.

13 GHQ SCAP, Final Rpt, Progress of Demob of the Japanese Armed Forces, 31 Dec 46 (R), p. 12.

14 ATIS Translation, 21 Aug 45, "Documents Furnished to SCAP by the Japanese Mission to Negotiate Surrender," delivered at the pre-surrender conference in Manila on 18 August 1945. Data later corrected to show 1,178,750 personnel.

15 GHQ SCAP, Final Rpt, Progress of Demob of the Japanese Armed Forces, 31 Dec 46 (R), Incl 61.

16 SCAPIN 17, 10 Sep 45, sub: Abolition of the Japanese GHQ.

17 SCAPIN 25, 13 Sep 45, sub: Functions of Imp GHQ to be Executed by Respective Ministries.

18 This figure does not include those troops of the Fifth Area Army in the Kuriles and Karafuto occupied by Soviet troops.

19 SCAPIN 137, 10 Oct 45, sub: Demob, Japanese Armed Forces.

futo, under Soviet control. The demobilization rate was obviously dependent upon the progress of repatriation. The Soviets, however, did not begin returning prisoners until December 1946, and in December 1948 approximately 408,700 were still held in Soviet areas. In comparison, over half of the Fifth Area Army, stationed in Hokkaido, was 87 percent demobilized by 24 September 1945; by the end of November, all personnel under SCAP jurisdiction had been released.[20]

The Navy data presented by the surrender envoys at Manila was ultimately found to be inaccurate. Navy strength in Japan proper, stated to be 1,024,225, was later established at 1,178 750. However, naval demobilization proceeded at a more rapid rate than that of the Army. By 10 September approximately 82 percent of the total naval strength in Japan had been demobilized; by the end of November the only personnel on duty were those who had been discharged from the Navy and were employed by the Second Demobilization Ministry in a civilian status. They continued to work on essential naval tasks, such as mine-sweeping, operating disarmed vessels engaged in repatriation shipping, and maintaining Japanese war ships held for the Allied Powers. In addition to service personnel, the Japanese Navy at the end of the war employed approximately 739,000 civilians as workers and employees in naval arsenals, construction gangs, and other affiliated jobs; with the exception of those required in the demobilization program these civilians were promptly dismissed.

All personnel of both the Army and Navy Air Forces stationed in the four islands of Japan. (Plate No. 38) were reported at a strength of 262,000 Army and 291,537 Navy. Air Force personnel outside the Empire were discharged together with other forces and were not listed or handled separately. Ninety-five percent of the Air Force personnel in Japan was released by October; by the middle of December the Japanese Army and Navy Air Forces ceased to exist, and what was left of their installations and equipment was either destroyed by the Occupation forces, saved for reparations, or converted to civilian use.

Demobilization of Overseas Forces

At the same time that the home forces were being disbanded, the program for repatriating and demobilizing the Japanese forces overseas was also initiated. The overseas forces at the close of the war consisted of approximately 3,450,000 service personnel and over 3,000,000 civilians. The repatriation of these began promptly after surrender and progress was comparatively rapid in all areas except those controlled by the Soviet Government.[21] The speed with which troops were demobilized in Japan obviously could not be duplicated for those overseas; the time element in the mechanics of repatriation was the delaying factor.

Japanese military and naval commands in appropriate port areas initially processed returning repatriates (civilian and military) through the existent machinery previously used by the Japanese Army and Navy in the deployment of their forces. On 28 September SCAP directed the Japanese Government to establish repatriation reception centers at designated ports.[22]

---

20 In addition to troops assigned to the three major ground force units, there were some 460,546 personnel in units under direct control of the War Ministry not including air force personnel, in military schools and administrative offices; the largest unit was the Army Ordnance Administration Headquarters with 38,294 assigned personnel; 95 percent of this group was demobilized by November and the remainder by December 1945. (GHQ SCAP, Progress of Demob of the Japanese Armed Forces, 31 Jul 48, p. 12.)

21 Repatriation is fully covered in Ch. VI. Discussion here will be limited to its effect upon demobilization.

22 Otaru, Niigata, Tokyo, Kobe, Osaka, Maizuru, Hiroshima, Moji, Shimonoseki, and Hakata. (SCAPIN 70, 28 Sep 45, sub: Rad Designating Certain Ports and Their Facilities to be Prepared for Use in Repatriation of Japanese.)

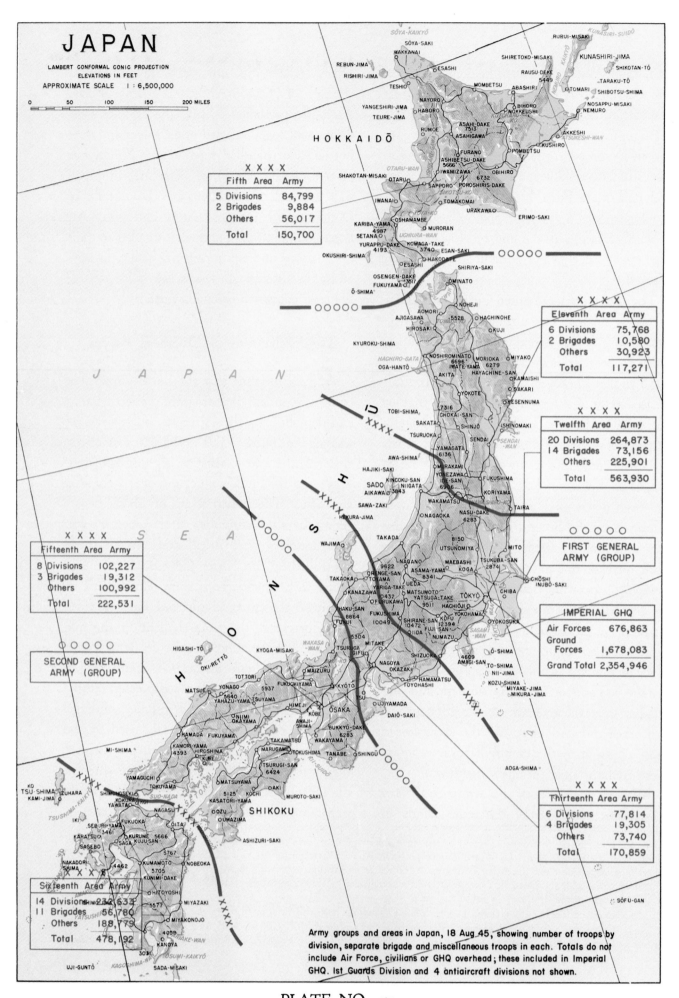

JAPAN

LAMBERT CONFORMAL CONIC PROJECTION
ELEVATIONS IN FEET
APPROXIMATE SCALE 1 : 6,500,000

0   50   100   150   200 MILES

XXXX

Fifth Area Army

5 Divisions	84,799
2 Brigades	9,884
Others	56,017
Total	150,700

XXXX

Eleventh Area Army

6 Divisions	75,768
2 Brigades	10,580
Others	30,923
Total	117,271

XXXX

Twelfth Area Army

20 Divisions	264,873
14 Brigades	73,156
Others	225,901
Total	563,930

XXXX

Fifteenth Area Army

8 Divisions	102,227
3 Brigades	19,312
Others	100,992
Total	222,531

FIRST GENERAL
ARMY (GROUP)

SECOND GENERAL
ARMY (GROUP)

IMPERIAL GHQ

Air Forces	676,863
Ground Forces	1,678,083
Grand Total	2,354,946

XXXX

Thirteenth Area Army

6 Divisions	77,814
4 Brigades	19,305
Others	73,740
Total	170,859

XXXX

Sixteenth Area Army

14 Divisions	232,633
11 Brigades	56,780
Others	188,779
Total	478,192

Army groups and areas in Japan, 18 Aug 45, showing number of troops by
division, separate brigade and miscellaneous troops in each. Totals do not
include Air Force, civilians or GHQ overhead; these included in Imperial
GHQ. 1st Guards Division and 4 antiaircraft divisions not shown.

PLATE NO. 37
Disposition of Japanese Army Ground Forces in the Homeland at the Time of Capitulation,
18 August 1945

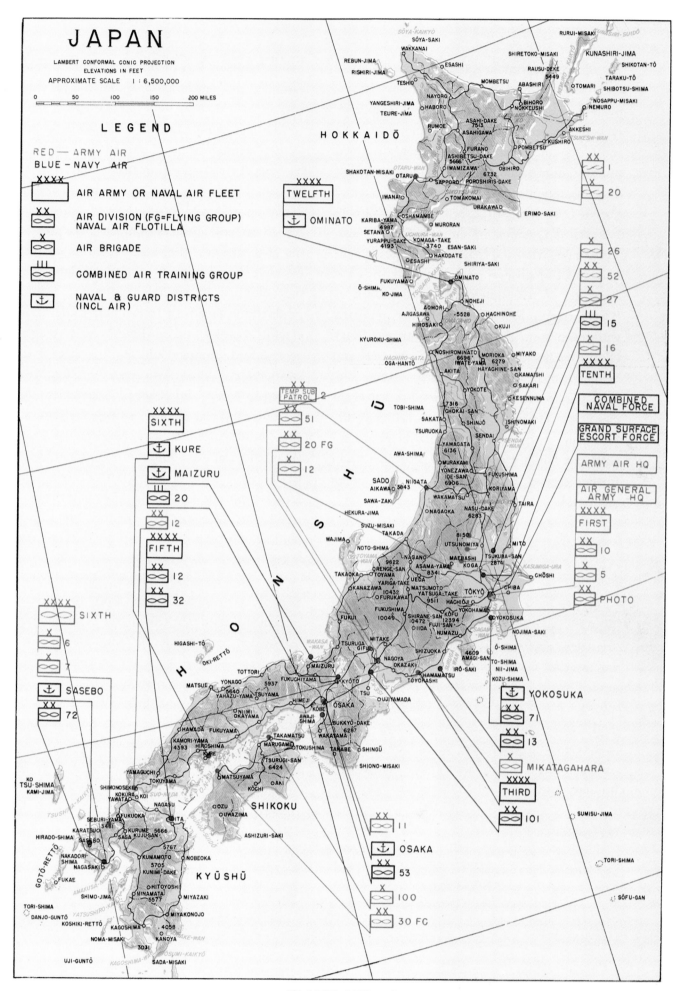

PLATE NO. 38
Japanese Army—Navy Air Dispositions, 15 August 1945

By 10 October under guidance of the War and Navy Ministries this had been accomplished. The centers were capable of temporarily housing, feeding, and extending emergency relief to all repatriates, whether disarmed military units or individuals. Following a later directive, reception centers were established and operated at Maizuru, Shimonoseki, Sasebo, Senzaki, Kagoshima, Kure, Hakata, Uraga, Yokohama, Moji and Hakodate.[23] Subsequently, control of all agencies concerned with the operation of reception centers and known as "Repatriation Relief Bureau" was gradually withdrawn from the Japanese War and Navy Ministries (including succeeding agencies) and assigned to the Welfare Ministry. (Plate No. 39) The former military demobilization agencies at the reception centers handled only the processing required to properly release repatriated military and naval personnel from further service and get them to their home stations.

Reorganization of the Demobilization Machinery

Under basic Japanese plans prepared with SCAP's approval, the War and Navy Ministries were abolished on 30 November,[24] inasmuch as all major components of the Japanese armed forces had been demobilized.[25] In their places a First Demobilization Ministry (Army) and Second Demobilization Ministry (Navy) were created. They were headed by a civilian minister and staffed partly by demobilized military and naval officers in a civil capacity.

Prime Minister Kijuro Shidehara concurrently assumed the portfolio of the two new ministries.

The regimental district headquarters at prefectural capitals were abolished and replaced by "Local Assistance Bureaus." Staffed partly by demobilized officers whose technical skill in demobilization administration was indispensable, those local agencies completed the processing of repatriates; they also served as contacts between unrepatriated servicemen and their next of kin. As the demobilization burden gradually lessened, the machinery came under careful scrutiny and in June 1946 was again reorganized, sharply reducing the size of the two Demobilization Ministries.[26] They were renamed First and Second Demobilization Bureaus, and placed under a single Demobilization Board, headed by a Minister of State. (Plate No. 40) Preceding this important change, the Local Assistance Bureaus had been transferred from the Demobilization Ministries to the Home Ministry as a preliminary step to shifting jurisdiction to the prefectural civil authorities.

In the reception centers, demobilization procedure included submission of personal statements, used in clarifying the fate of missing personnel, processing of ashes and personal effects of deceased personnel forwarded from overseas, preparation of demobilization and discharge reports, and final settlement of pay status. The centers were also burdened with furnishing initial aid to dependents.

All personnel who were employed by the demobilization agencies assumed civilian status

23 SCAPIN 142, 15 Oct 45, sub: Reception Centers in Japan for Processing Repatriates. (Superceded SCAPIN 70)

24 (1) Plans were submitted to the CofS GHQ SCAP by the Japanese Government on 2 October 1945. They consisted of draft programs for further demobilization of military and naval forces. (2) SCAPIN 137, 14 Oct 45, sub: Demob, Japanese Armed Forces.

25 There remained 14 members of the Air Force who were demobilized prior to 15 December 1945.

26 SCAPIN 993, 1 Jun 46, sub: Approval of Plans for Establishment of Demob Bd in Lieu of the Two Demob Ministries.

but continued to perform their duties until their phase of the job was completed,[27] key personnel included specialist crews for mine-sweeping.

The basic organization of the Demobilization Board remained unchanged until it was dissolved on 15 October 1947. By this time over half its task had been completed.[28] There had been a progressive and marked reduction in personnel of the Board, and repatriation centers at Uraga, Nagoya, Hiroshima, Hakata, and Senzaki were closed; the Second Demobilization Bureau's operation of repatriation shipping was discontinued in January 1947. Meanwhile, with the adoption of the new constitution and the Japanese Local Autonomy Bill on 3 May 1947,[29] the Local Assistance Bureaus, previously placed under Home Ministry jurisdiction, became sections of the Welfare Department, on the prefectural level.

As a transitional step, the First Demobilization Bureau and its local agencies were transferred intact to the Welfare Ministry which was already partly operating the repatriation centers; the Second Demobilization Bureau and its regional agencies were temporarily placed in the Prime Minister's office. The next step in the reduction of the demobilization machinery was the elimination of the Second Demobilization Bureau which was approved by SCAP on 10 January 1948.[30] Its former functions of mine-sweeping, ship maintenance, and related necessary activities were assumed by the Maritime Bureau of the Transportation Ministry and the remaining associated activities were charged to the First Demobilization Bureau which became simply the Demobilization Bureau. By 31 May 1948 the number of repatriation ports and demobilization centers had been reduced to three—Hakodate, Maizuru, and Sasebo. At that time, the last remnants of the Japanese demobilization machinery were eliminated as independent agencies[31] and their functions and responsibilities completely transferred to the Repatriation Relief Agency, Welfare Ministry.[32] Within one month after the completion of repatriation and therefore of physical demobilization, the Japanese Government planned to decrease the size of the Repatriation Relief Agency to a small Repatriation Liquidation Bureau. The latter, in turn, was scheduled to operate for just one year. Only when the last Japanese servicemen had been returned to Japan could the demobilization of the Japanese armed forces be considered completed, and the existence of a well-integrated and efficient demobilization system terminated.[33]

Progress of Demobilization

Due to a later start (December 1946), temporary delays, and low monthly rate of repatriation of Japanese from Soviet controlled

---

27 The employment of ex-service personnel declined rapidly from a total of 190 ex-generals and ex-admirals in January 1946 to 6 in July 1948. Total employment dropped from 80,474 demobilization employees (50,227 Navy; 30,247 Army) to 5,232 in July 1948 (1,364 Navy; 3,868 Army) or a total loss of 75,242 persons. (GHQ SCAP, Progress of Demob of the Japanese Armed Forces, 31 Jul 48, Plates 20, 21 and 22.)

28 SCAPIN 1791, 4 Oct 47, sub: Demob Machinery, Reorg of.

29 The establishment of local self government as provided in Chapter VIII of the new constitution.

30 SCAPIN 1843, 10 Jan 48, sub: Plan for Abolition of 2d Demob Bur.

31 SCAPIN 1791, 4 Oct 47, sub: Demob Machinery, Reorg of.

32 Ltr, Central Liaison and Coordination Office, Japanese Govt No. 1578 (2P), 4 May 48, sub: A New Plan for Reorg of Domob Machinery. (GHQ SCAP, Progress of Demob of the Japanese Armed Forces, 31 Jul 48, Incl 7.)

33 Apparently this policy is not followed by all nations. A rejected Soviet proposal suggested that a Japanese military unit be considered demobilized when disarmed and disbanded. (Tokyo, *Nippon Times*, 15 Feb 48, Kyodo-AP Rpt)

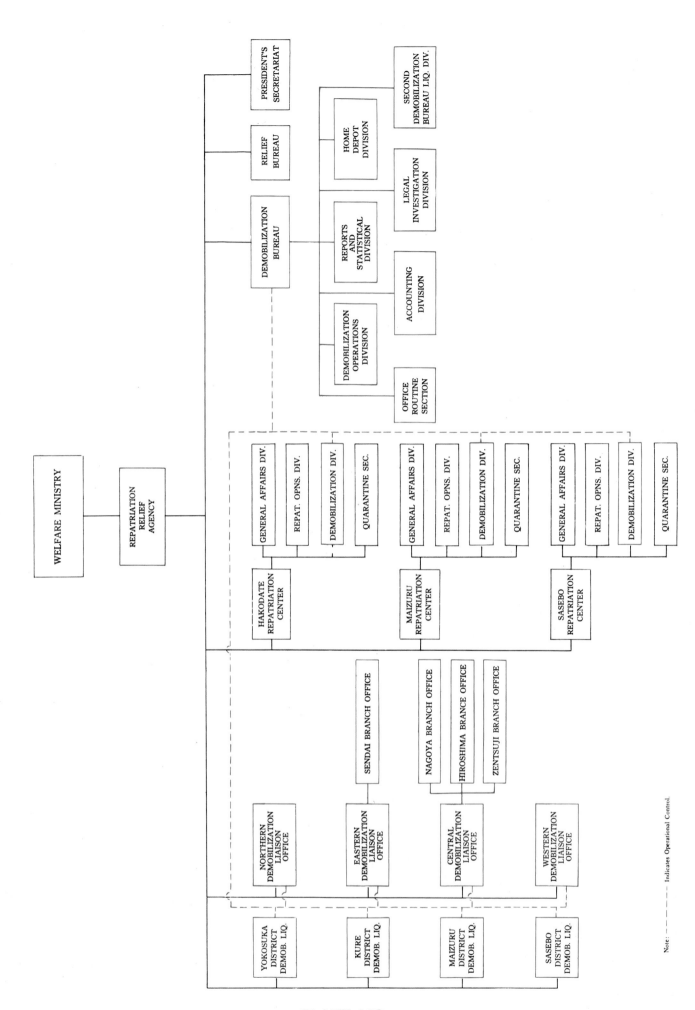

PLATE NO. 39
The Demobilization Organs of the Welfare Ministry, 1 June 1948

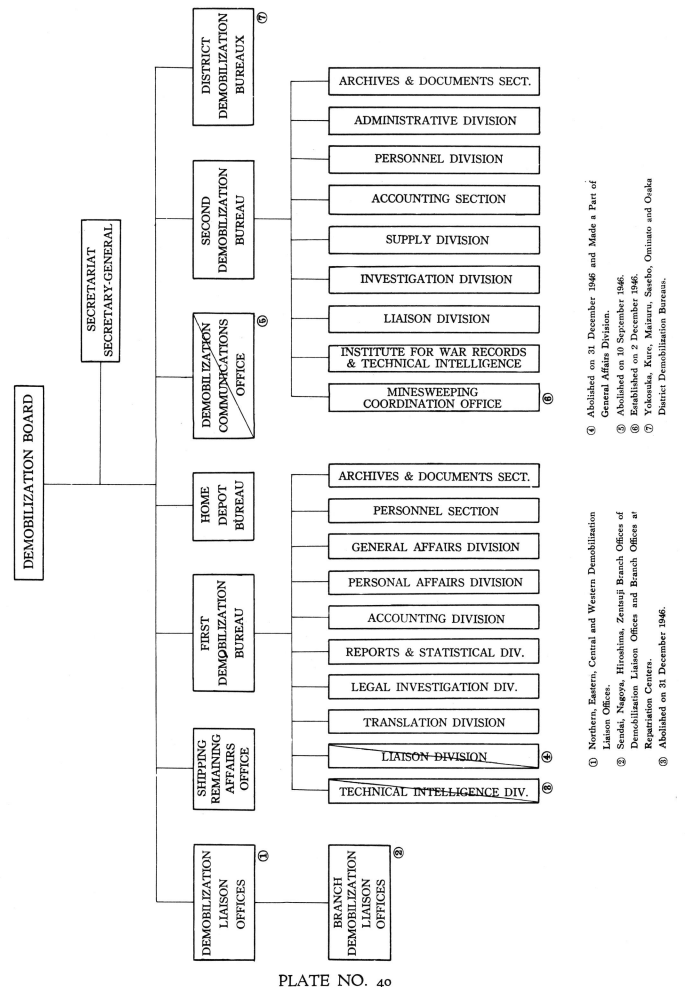

DEMOBILIZATION BOARD

SECRETARIAT
SECRETARY-GENERAL

DISTRICT DEMOBILIZATION BUREAUX ⑦

SECOND DEMOBILIZATION BUREAU

ARCHIVES & DOCUMENTS SECT.
ADMINISTRATIVE DIVISION
PERSONNEL DIVISION
ACCOUNTING SECTION
SUPPLY DIVISION
INVESTIGATION DIVISION
LIAISON DIVISION
INSTITUTE FOR WAR RECORDS & TECHNICAL INTELLIGENCE
MINESWEEPING COORDINATION OFFICE ⑥

DEMOBILIZATION COMMUNICATIONS OFFICE ⑤

HOME DEPOT BUREAU

FIRST DEMOBILIZATION BUREAU

ARCHIVES & DOCUMENTS SECT.
PERSONNEL SECTION
GENERAL AFFAIRS DIVISION
PERSONAL AFFAIRS DIVISION
ACCOUNTING DIVISION
REPORTS & STATISTICAL DIV.
LEGAL INVESTIGATION DIV.
TRANSLATION DIVISION
LIAISON DIVISION ④
TECHNICAL INTELLIGENCE DIV. ③

SHIPPING REMAINING AFFAIRS OFFICE

DEMOBILIZATION LIAISON OFFICES ①

BRANCH DEMOBILIZATION LIAISON OFFICES ②

① Northern, Eastern, Central and Western Demobilization Liaison Offices.

② Sendai, Nagoya, Hiroshima, Zentsuji Branch Offices of Demobilization Liaison Offices and Branch Offices at Repatriation Centers.

③ Abolished on 31 December 1946.

④ Abolished on 31 December 1946 and Made a Part of General Affairs Division.

⑤ Abolished on 10 September 1946.

⑥ Established on 2 December 1946.

⑦ Yokosuka, Kure, Maizuru, Sasebo, Ominato and Osaka District Demobilization Bureaus.

PLATE NO. 40
Organization of the Demobilization Board, June 1946—October 1947

areas and Communist-dominated districts of Manchuria, an estimated total of 499,000 Japanese army and 2,000 naval personnel still had not been returned to Japan in July 1948.[34]

Since repatriates included both civilians and servicemen, the totals of repatriation and demobilization do not coincide. All repatriates who were in Japanese military or naval service at the time of surrender were demobilized promptly and formally upon arrival at a Japanese repatriation port, although final processing was completed at the Local Assistance Section of the returnee's home prefecture.[35]

An aspect of demobilization which was of great importance to the Japanese although not of direct concern to the Occupation was the verification of the fate of the large number of personnel missing in overseas areas. The continuation of dependency allowances, the necessity for issuing valid death certificates for legal purposes, and humanitarian obligations of the Japanese Government to the next-of-kin of missing service personnel made such verification indispensable. The demobilization agency was charged with this increasingly difficult and time consuming task. The Home Depot Division, a subdivision of the Demobilization Bureau combined with the prefectural Local Assistance Sections, performed the bulk of the work.

The deaths of 1,402,153 servicemen who, prior to the surrender had not been reported dead or missing in action, were verified; and by August 1948 only 76,960 were carried as missing.[36] With a few exceptions, missing personnel were presumed to be dead.

---

34 GHQ SCAP, Progress of Demob of the Japanese Armed Forces, 31 Jul 48, p. 16. The Japanese servicemen had been completely repatriated and subsequently demobilized from all areas except those controlled by the Soviet Government and certain sectors of Manchuria. Since no information has been made available by Soviet authorities concerning the Japanese troops detained in Soviet controlled areas, it is not possible at this time (May 1949) to estimate the number dead or missing among the Japanese forces that surrendered to the Soviets and which were removed to Soviet territory or left in Communist dominated areas of Manchuria.

On 21 May 1949, an announcement was made through the official Soviet news agency Tass that " the remaining 95,000 Japanese PW's " would be repatriated between May and November 1949. The announcement made no mention of thousands of civilians which Japanese claim were in Soviet controlled areas. SCAP figures, based on those prepared by the Japanese Government, showed a total of 408,729 military and civilian prisoners still to be repatriated from Soviet controlled areas. See Ch. VI.

35 DEMOBILIZATION, Aug 45 to Jul 48:

	ARMY	NAVY	TOTAL
Demobilized in Japan proper	2,353,000	1,179,000	3,532,000
Demobilized in Repatriation	2,597,000	268,000	2,865,000
Total	4,950,000	1,447,000	6,397,000

36 JAPANESE ARMY AND NAVY PERSONNEL VERIFIED DEAD AND MISSING

TERRITORIES OCCUPIED AFTER SURRENDER	VERIFIED DEAD	MISSING
U. S. occupied territories	479,335	35,700
British and Dutch forces territories	207,626	4,500
Australian forces territories	199,205	1,800
French Indo-China	2,752	360
China (excl Manchuria)	202,907	1,800
Others (excl Manchuria & Soviet controlled areas, chiefly personnel lost enroute)	23,177	3,700
Total Army Personnel	1,115,002	47,860
Navy Sv pers (excl Soviet controlled areas)	151,072	2,600
Civilians attached to Navy (excl Soviet areas)	54,989	26,500
Total Navy Personnel	206,061	29,100
Known deaths awaiting repatriation (other than Soviet)	81,090	
Total	1,402,153	76,960
Total Dead and Missing		1,479,113

(GHQ SCAP, Progress of Demob of the Japanese Armed Forces, 31 Jul 48, p. 17.)

Since no information was made available by the Soviet authorities concerning the Japanese troops detained in Soviet-controlled areas, it was impossible to determine the number of missing men among the Japanese forces which surrendered to the Soviets. Of the 900,000 Japanese servicemen estimated to have surrendered to the Soviet forces, only 436,000 had been repatriated by 31 July 1948, and at the end of 1948 the fate of many of those under U.S.S.R. control had not yet been fully determined.[37]

General MacArthur, realizing the difficulties encountered in effecting complete demobilization of all Japanese armed forces, directed activities toward the speed-up of the demobilization program in Japan and in areas under SCAP or AFPAC jurisdiction on a geographical basis. It was obvious that American commanders could do little to accelerate demobilization of Japanese forces held by the U.S.S.R. until international disputes had been resolved and mutual agreements reached.

In a radio report to the American people on 15 October 1945, General MacArthur summarized the achievements of initial Occupation objectives:[38]

Today the Japanese Armed Forces throughout Japan completed their demobilization and ceased to exist as such. These forces are now completely abolished.

I know of no demobilization in history, either in war or in peace, by our own or by any other country, that has been accomplished so rapidly or so frictionlessly. Everything military, naval or air is forbidden in Japan.

This ends its military might and its military influence in international affairs. It no longer reckons as a world power either large or small. Its path in the future, if it is to survive, must be confined to the ways of peace.

Approximately seven million armed men, including those in the outlying theaters, have laid down their weapons. In the accomplishment of the extraordinarily difficult and dangerous surrender of Japan, unique in the annals of history, not a shot was necessary, not even a drop of Allied blood was shed. The vindication of the great decision of Potsdam is complete.

Nothing could exceed the abjectness, the humiliation and finality of this surrender. It is not only physically thorough, but has been equally destructive on Japanese spirit. From swagger and arrogance, the former Japanese military have passed to servility and fear. They are thoroughly beaten and cowed and tremble before the terrible retribution the surrender terms impose upon their country in punishment for its great sins.

Again, I wish to pay tribute to the magnificent conduct of our troops. With few exceptions, they could well be taken as a model for all time as a conquering army. Historians in later years, when passions cool, can arraign their conduct.

They could so easily—and understandably—have emulated the ruthlessness which their enemy have freely practiced when conditions were reversed, but their perfect balance between their implacable firmness of duty on the one hand and resolute restraint from cruelness and brutality on the other, has taught a lesson to the Japanese civil population that is startling in its impact.

Nothing has so tended to impress Japanese thought—not even the catastrophic fact of military defeat itself. They have for the first time seen the free man's way of life in actual action and it has stunned them into new thoughts and ideas.

The experience of an American lieutenant in an encounter with a Japanese armored column is typical of many similar events that occurred in the initial days of the Occupation. A jeep bearing a 43rd Division lieutenant was spinning along the road from Kazo to Kumagaya when an approaching cloud of dust resolved itself into a Japanese tank company moving to a

---

37 See Ch. VI, pp. 43–52.
38 GHQ USAFPAC Press Release, 15 Oct 45.

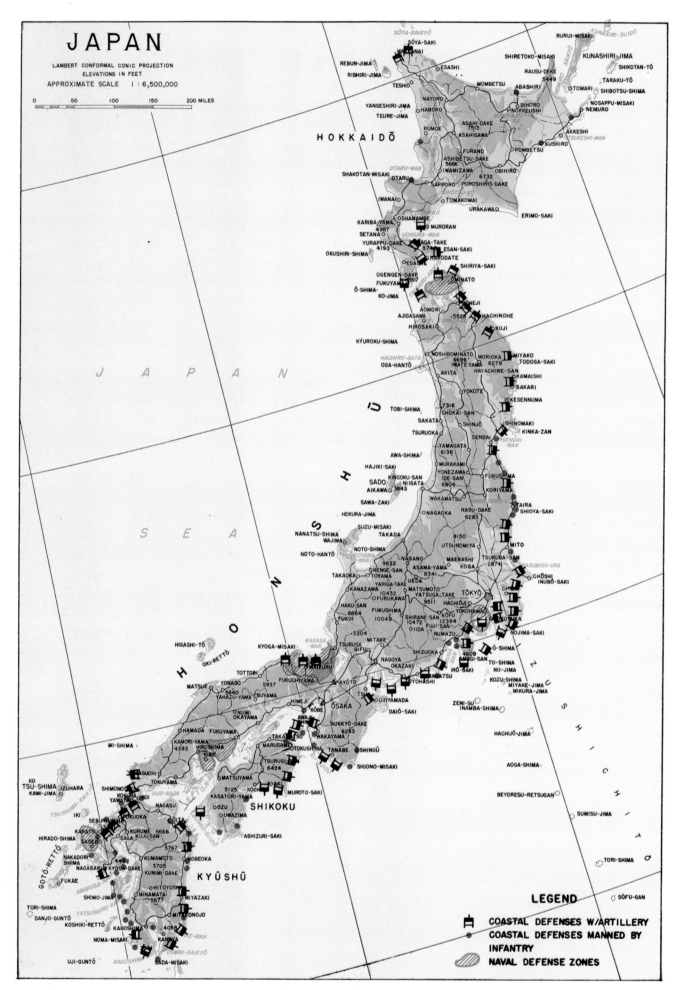

PLATE NO. 41
Japanese Coastal Defenses, 18 August 1945

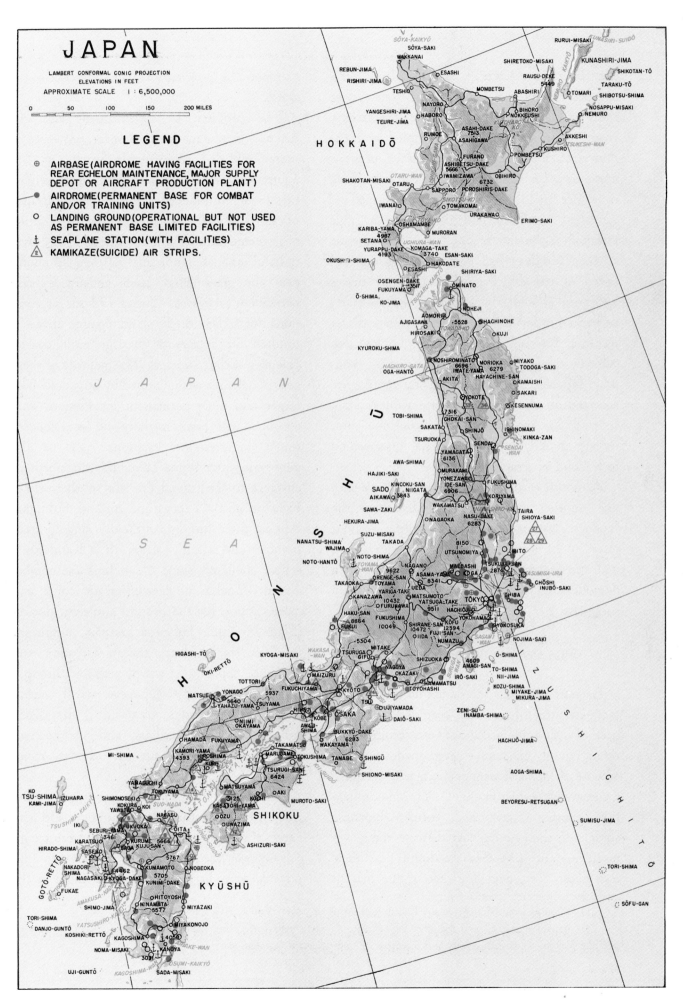

PLATE NO. 42
Japanese Airfields, 15 August 1945

demobilization center. As the lead tank stopped to permit passing, the jeep driver cautiously skirted it to the left on the narrow road. The soft shoulder crumbled and the American found himself tilted at a perilous angle with his vehicle mired in the soft muck of a rice paddy. Climbing out, the officer scratched his head and pointed to a cable attached to the side of one tank. Meanwhile a Japanese officer had come running up and asked in passable English if the tank driver had been at fault. Assured to the contrary, he barked orders to his men and the tank driver jockeyed his tank into position, hooked the cable on the jeep and pulled it back on the road. The Japanese captain bowed his apologies, accepted an American cigarette with thanks, ordered his tank column to continue and, waving amiably to the American, disappeared in a cloud of dust.

A month earlier these men would have shot one another on sight. Significantly, the Japanese armored unit was travelling without guard to be demobilized; the Americans and and the Japanese alike were integrated in a demobilization program which was evidently successful.[39]

The Process of Disarmament

As remarkable as the demobilization of the Japanese armed forces had been, it would have been of little value had it not been accompanied by an equally exhaustive program designed to dispose of Japanese weapons, armament, equipment, and other war materiel. The demobilization process transported former Japanese soldiers to their homes, left them to their own resources, and gave them freedom to lead their own lives. It provided an accounting system to report the progress of demobilization to the world.

The problem of disarmament and the disposal of war materiel, however, proved to be more difficult; considerable stocks of war equipment were dispersed amid the tangled masses of fire blackened girders, in thousands of caches located deep in the hills, in carefully constructed tunnels and warehouses, and over miles of Japanese landscape. Along the shores near the great ports, there remained many permanent fortresses. Japan's frantic preparations for a last ditch stand against invasion resulted in numerous hastily built coastal defenses. (Plate No. 41) The majority of these coastal defenses were manned by brigades. The larger and more permanent installations were equipped with heavy artillery and were concentrated in strategic locations such as the peninsula which forms Tokyo Bay, the northern entrance to the Inland Sea, the southern tip of Kyushu, and the coastline around Fukuoka. Almost three hundred airfields, ranging from bomber and supply strips to " Kamikaze " strips, sheltered some 6,000 Japanese combat aircraft capable of providing air cover and close support for the ground and naval forces. (Plate No. 42) Japanese arsenals, munitions factories, steel plants, aircraft factories, and ordnance depots were widely scattered throughout the country.[40] Japanese naval vessels consisting of carriers, battleships, destroyers, submarines, and auxiliary and maintenance craft were anchored in all of the major ports.

The initial disarmament procedures complied with the instrument of surrender and with early SCAP directives. The Japanese troops turned over their individual weapons to unit officers, who in turn assembled them in the

---

39   Occupational Monogr of the Eighth US Army in Japan, Vol. I, Aug 45—Jan 46 (C), p. 33.

40   Japanese arsenals and ordnance depots were located chiefly in Kyushu, and Kyoto—Osaka area, Nagoya area and the Tokyo—Yokohama area, and consisted of 108 principal installations.

supply rooms, warehouses, and depots formerly used by the Japanese Army. With the prompt disarmament and demobilization of the individual soldier the way was cleared for the disposal of more bulky war equipment.

As soon as the surrender arrangements were made, the four small islands protecting Tokyo Bay were vacated by the Japanese and the Allied Navy entered the Bay without a shot being fired. The Japanese had cleared the important naval installations of all personnel except for skeleton crews, demilitarized all coastal defense and antiaircraft installations, and had marked the latter with large white flags. When the initial landing parties came ashore, Japanese officers and guides led them to the facilities available at the Yokosuka naval base, thus setting a pattern for a peaceful occupation.

The burden of location and disposal of ammunition, explosives, military stores and any other property belonging to the Japanese forces was placed upon the Japanese; they were ordered to collect all war materiel and assemble it as directed by the local United States commanders.[41] Items which could not be readily transported were reported as such and processed later.

Spot inspections covering all of Japan, completed by 1 October 1945, attested to the full compliance with surrender terms by the Japanese Army and Navy Air Forces. Except for a few types which were preserved for technical air intelligence purposes, all aircraft were at that time grounded and were in the process of being destroyed. Initial destruction methods of enemy aircraft employed by the Occupation

forces are typified in the following account:[42]

With the XI Corps Artillery in Mito—Two of the white peace negotiation planes bearing green crosses were among the 1,500 Japanese aircraft destroyed during the past 12 days by men of the 637th Tank Destroyer Battalion which is located just northeast of Tokyo.

Moving in on 12 airfields, and covering a ground area of 800 square miles, these men have organized into what they call "Destruction Incorporated" crews. A crew consists of five men, a Japanese full track prime mover and a gas pump spray mounted on a Japanese truck.

The system for destruction is simple, but believed to be foolproof. Two men on the prime mover pull the planes to the selected burning area. One man searches the entire plane for bombs and ammunition. Another member punctures all gas tanks to prevent explosion. The remaining man stands by the gas pump spray and at the signal "all clear" sprays Japanese synthetic gas over the plane to be destroyed. It is then ignited and the crew moves on to the next aircraft.

Because of the large number of agencies involved in the destruction or scrapping of Japanese aircraft and because of the variations in nomenclature and other statistics, exact figures of planes destroyed were not available. However, the Occupation authorities made certain that there were no Japanese planes in operational existence in the four home islands. During the early days of the Occupation many of the planes were disabled with no intent to salvage materials. That procedure was later discarded in favor of an economical scrapping program. Dismantling naturally proceeded at a slower rate than burning or demolition, but the salvaged items were useful in aiding

41 Japanese armed forces were defined to include all Japanese-controlled land, sea, and air forces and military and para-military organizations, formations, or units and their auxiliaries and civilian volunteer corps, wherever situated. (Memo, SCAP for IJG, 24 Sep 45. In AG 402.5.)

42 GHQ SCAP, Press Release No. 1030, 13 Dec 45.

restoration of the war torn Japanese economy.[43]

Surrendered War Materiel : Disposition

Prior to the Occupation of Japan it was anticipated that the quantities of Japanese general war materiel would be enormous and tentative plans were made to dispose of it. Based on plans and directives from technical agencies and ample experiences in other theaters, the program for the disposition of this materiel was formulated on the premise that large numbers of Japanese service troops and adequate numbers of Japanese military vehicles would be available. However, in many areas of Japan the military forces had been completely demobilized prior to the Occupation. Vehicles were already lacking both in quantity and quality. Completion of the disarmament program was delayed as the personnel used in final disposition of the materiel consisted of Japanese laborers, a limited number of Japanese technicians, and specialist crews from United States forces. Tactical troops were often used initially in congested areas to perform the work of destroying the materiel as it was located or to oversee its transportation to waterfronts for loading and dumping. Army LCM's and Navy craft were used for this purpose. As fast as Japanese ships and crews could be substituted, the United States personnel were relieved. In the Sixth Army zone during the month of November 1945, at least ten ports were in operation, and approximately 4,500 tons of ammunition were disposed of daily.

One of the most interesting features of the disarmament program was the disclosure of the precarious condition of the Japanese defending forces in the home islands. After Allied victories of Iwo Jima, Okinawa, and the Philippines and the establishment of Allied naval blockade of China, only the troops in Japan were supplied by the homeland. On 31 August 1945 the Japanese reported on hand 1,369,063 rifles and light machine guns with limited ammunition of only 230 rounds per weapon. Records later indicated that actually some 2,468,665 rifles and carbines were received by the Occupation forces and later disposed of. The Japanese reported more artillery ammunition than small arms ammunition. Ammunition for the grenade launcher, often known as the " knee mortar," was also more plentiful ; some 51,000,000 rounds were reported, or an average of 1,794 rounds for each weapon.

As in the case of demobilization, the infantry regiment was also the chief instrument in the disarmament program, charged with seizing all Japanese military installations and disposing of all confiscated materiel. As inventory lists were received from the Japanese, reconnaissance patrols, consisting of an officer and a rifle squad, made the rounds in the regimental area to verify these inventories and to search for any unreported installations or caches of materiel. The infantry company became the working unit

| 43 | DISPOSAL OF JAPANESE AIRCRAFT (Progress Report, 31 Dec 46) : | | | | | |
DISPOSITION	PURSUIT	TRAINER	TRANSPORTS	MISC	GLIDERS	TOTALS
Total to be Disposed of	720	1,118	69	10,797	31	12,735
Destroyed	511	788	22	8,429	16	9,766
Scrapped	35	39	1	1,016	2	1,092
Allied Operations	9			179		188
Intelligence Research	27			73		100
Total Disposed	582	827	23	9,697	17	11,146
Total on Hand	138	291	46	1,100	14	1,589

(8,962 planes were located on Honshu, 2,637 on Kyushu, 631 on Shikoku, and the remainder on Hokkaido.) (GHQ SCAP, Progress of Demob of the Japanese Armed Forces, 31 Dec 46, pp. 69–70.)

Japanese laborers place gasoline drum under plane to be destroyed, Kyoto, Japan.

Japanese tanks are rendered impotent by use of dynamite prior to scrapping.

PLATE NO. 43
Scrapping of Japanese Equipment, October 1945

which performed supervision of disarmament and disposal of equipment. Among unreported installations was an extensive underground fighter aircraft engine plant, with a capacity of 100 per month, which was discovered by 1st Cavalry reconnaissance units in the Tokyo area. The entrances to tunnels, which had been in the process of being extended and expanded during the war, were cleverly concealed and in all probability could not have been detected from the air.

It was found that some discrepancies noted in the Japanese inventories were due to the difference in Japanese phraseology and nomenclature and errors in translations. For example, at Matsuyama Air Base on Shikoku Island, "20 Needles" were thought to refer to some sort of Japanese aerial weapons. Examination by troops of the 24th Infantry Division proved them to be packages of ordinary sewing needles.

Ammunition and weapons, particularly small arms, could have been hidden easily by rebellious individuals or groups, only to be brought out at some later time in revolt against the Occupation forces. Apparently there were more than a few abortive attempts in that direction, for although the Japanese military commanders appeared to be acting for the most part in good faith in surrendering their arms and equipment, every month of the Occupation disclosed new caches of military supplies. Though the caches usually were not heavily stocked, their very existence was enough to indicate that the chain of Japanese responsibility had broken down somewhere. Thorough reconnaissance and inspection by the Occupation forces brought to light many situations which were resolved before they could become serious problems.[44] For example, a check on the police stations in Aomori, Hirosaki, and Sambongi (all towns in Aomori Prefecture) produced some 1,880 rifles, 1,881 bayonets, 18 light machine guns, 505,260 rounds of rifle and machine gun ammunition, 46,980 rounds of blank ammunition, one case of TNT, and 150 military swords. Daily G-2 and CIC reports revealed many instances of smaller caches, sometimes in school compounds. Officials and teachers, when questioned, usually pleaded ignorance, and very often investigation did show that faulty dissemination of instructions had been the root of the trouble.[45]

The G-4 sections of the various commands were designated to supervise the disposition of war materiel and report on progress. Systems were established to indicate readily by means of maps and charts the type and class of supplies located in each dump, the status of disposition within each camp, the percentage of dumps recovered, and dumps returned to the Japanese. Continuous information was sent to all echelons regarding the locations of principal installations in their zones. All equipment, whether received by unit commanders or uncovered by patrols, was secured and labeled, the date and place of surrender or discovery indicated, a record made of the unit concerned, and a statement made to show that it had been acquired by the United States armed forces.[46]

---

44 (1) Tokyo, *Pacific Stars and Stripes*, December 5, 1945; (2) GHQ SCAP Press Releases, 21 Dec 45 & 19 Feb 46.
45 HQ Eighth US Army, G-2 Periodic Rpt No. 74, 10/11 Nov 45.

46 To the average US soldier in Japan one of the more interesting aspects of the demilitarization program was something that affected him personally : the distribution of war trophies. WD Cirs No. 155 and 267 (1945) authorized the issue of souvenirs to military and naval personnel who had served in the SWPA during World War II. On the basis of these circulars, each officer and enlisted man received one of the following articles : rifle, carbine, saber, bayonet, pistol, or pair of binoculars. Responsibility for collection of these items rested with corps commanders, who issued instructions for their distribution to field units under their respective commands. The War Trophy Depot, located in Yokohama, issued trophies to officers and men who were on orders to return to the US. A central issuing agency for fleet units within the Eighth Army area was established at Yokosuka Naval Base for distribution to naval personnel at sea. GHQ and FEAF personnel were supplied by Eighth Army facilities.

Japanese arms are inspected by an American soldier at the Katsuura School.

Ammunition is removed from storage cave at Takatsuki Dump, Osaka.

PLATE NO. 44
Disposal of Weapons and Ammunition, October 1945

Methods of Disposal

Policy directed that enemy equipment would be destroyed or otherwise disposed of at the location where the Japanese turned it over to the disposal units. In destroying equipment other than ammunition and explosives, units were granted authority to use any practical method to render the materiel useless. The most common methods employed were: smashing, cutting with acetylene torches, burning with thermite grenades, or salvaging and melting down in blast furnaces. The resulting scrap was turned over to the Japanese Home Ministry. Negotiations were opened with steel plants and blast furnaces and contracts were drawn for the disposition of Japanese ordnance items. Arrangements were made to transport all such equipment to industrial areas for disposition. Destruction and re-smelting were accomplished rapidly and the ingot metal turned over to custody of Home Ministry representatives. Unfused artillery ammunition, bombs, and other inert projectiles were transported to former munitions factories where they were broken down to save both the explosive (for conversion to peacetime use) and the scrap metal.

Because the work was hazardous, special instructions were issued to all units for the immediate disposal of explosives, chemicals, and poison gases. All Japanese ammunition, bulk explosives, and other loaded equipment (ordnance, chemical ammunition, and engineer explosives) were destroyed without delay, with the exception of items desired for technical intelligence purposes. The principal method utilized was dumping into the sea at a depth in excess of 300 feet (later 600 feet). In areas that prohibited transportation to port facilities both detonation and burning were used to dispose of large quantities of munitions.

The most persistent difficulty encountered during the destruction of Japanese ordnance material was the acute shortage of qualified technical personnel, both Japanese and American. Even under normal circumstances the disposal of large quantities of Japanese ammunition and explosives would have presented many risks. With the loss of skilled technicians due to the demobilization program in Japan and the readjustment program in the U. S. Army, the task became even more complicated. Most of the work had to be done by slow and unskilled Japanese laborers; their apparent disregard for personal safety, combined with the language barrier, made the job dangerous. In accordance with agreements between the commanders of the Sixth U. S. Army and Fifth U. S. Fleet, Sixth Army assumed responsibility for disposition of naval equipment and installations ashore in western Japan. Some of Japan's largest naval installations were located in this area and the quantity of naval equipment increased the disposition problem considerably. Mine and bomb disposal specialists were borrowed from units in the Occupation forces, both Army and Navy, and ordnance explosive technicians from all available sources were located and utilized. Efforts to locate skilled technicians through the Japanese Home Ministry met with indifferent success. The rapidity of the demobilization of the Japanese armed forces had scattered these persons to all parts of Japan.

Under the best conditions, there is a certain peril connected with handling ammunition stored without adequate safety precautions. Japanese supply dumps were located in caves, on small islands, in marshlands, and in forests. In many of these areas seepage led to deterioration of highly sensitive ingredients such as fuses, safety devices, and packaging materials. The lack of safety devices on much of the Japanese equipment often made it impossible

Weapons of the Japanese 58th Army are loaded aboard LSM for dumping at sea.

Japanese ammunition on its way to the bottom of the Pacific Ocean.

PLATE NO. 45
Disposal of Weapons and Ammunition, October 1945

to remove and detonate the munitions in accordance with the usual safety procedures. Wherever this situation existed, the contents of a cave or tunnel were detonated at the site; this method, to mention one example, had to be used in handling 100,000 pounds of picric acid and blasting powder stored in a cave on Eta Jima. Deterioration had progressed to a point where movement of the stores was impossible and detonation on the spot became the only solution.

Progress of the munitions disposal program was sporadic. While disarmament of the troops and demobilization of personnel were accomplished rather rapidly, materiel disarmament took much longer. The destruction of munitions was equally slow but by the end of 1946 the program was reported 80 percent complete.[47]

Return of Demilitarized Materiel to the Japanese

Throughout the process of disarmament, at no time was there any wanton destruction of materials and equipment; those stores which could be reasonably converted to civilian use were saved. There was urgent need for the return of salvaged materials to the economy of Japan. The country was impoverished. Many of its people were near starvation and generally in need of clothing. A large percentage of the nation's houses in the urban areas had been destroyed by heavy bombing. To alleviate these conditions in every possible way, the Occupation forces returned to the Japanese Government all Japanese military stores of food, extensive stocks of uniforms, rubber boots, garrison coats, medicines, and other items.[48]

47 (1) USAFPAC, Adm Hist of the Ord Sec, 24 Jun 45 to 13 Dec 46, p. 16. (2) GHQ SCAP, Progress of Demob of the Japanese Armed Forces, 21 Jul 48 p. 20, gives the following statistics on progress of munitions disposal as of that date:

ITEMS	QUANTITY CAPTURED AND SURRENDERED	DISPOSED OF: TROPHY, MUSEUM, TECHNICAL USE	DESTROYED	RETURNED TO JAPANESE (a)
Rifles and Carbines	2,468,665	1,226,146	1,242,519	None
Bayonets	1,568,254	713,832	854,422	None
Pistols and Revolvers	81,061	62,760	9,559	8,742
Swords and Sabers	661,621	372,609	289,012	None
Artillery	201,244	11,260	189,984	None
Automatic Weapons	186,680	3,203	183,377	None
Tanks and Tankettes (b)	2,970	435	2,535	None
Ammunition (all types) (c)	1,192,000 tons	—	1,192,000	None
Fire Control Equipment	90,700	—	90,700	None
Vehicles	14,494	—	—	14,494
Aircraft	12,725	—	8,000	None

(a) The only weapons returned to Japanese were a small number of pistols for use of civil police.

(b) USAFPAC, Adm Hist of the Ord Sec, 24 Jun 45 to 13 Dec 46, p. 16.

(c) 100,000 tons of chemical warfare supplies were also destroyed. (Corrected Verbatim Minutes of the 15th Meeting of the Allied Council for Japan, Tokyo, 18 Sep 46, Afternoon Session).

48 More than 21,000,000 pairs of socks, approximately 7,000,000 woolen blankets, and over 5,000,000 pairs of leather shoes were returned to the Japanese Government for distribution to Japanese citizens.

Further need for these supplies developed with the inception of the repatriation program. More than six million Japanese were repatriated, many of them returning without sufficient clothing.[49]

Engineering and automotive equipment, vital in rebuilding devastated areas, was specifically excluded from the list of materials to be destroyed and much of it was returned to the Japanese. Initial requirements of the Occupation forces in such articles as nails, ropes, cement, wire, and plywood were met but, in general, these and other construction items were redistributed for Japanese civilian use.

Disposal of Japanese Fleet Units

On 18 August 1945 the Japanese emissaries at Manila presented reports with detailed information concerning the Japanese Navy, names, condition, classification, and location of naval vessels, location of mined areas, shore installations, ammunition and fuel on hand; this information was incomplete due to lack of recent surveys and the fact that certain units were at sea.[50] Later documents were filed by the Japanese Government and accurate information was finally available in early September. (Plate No. 46) Following SCAP Directive Number 2, Japanese naval vessels were promptly rendered inoperative for war purposes.[51] As early as 12 September the Imperial Japanese General Headquarters reported that all war and merchant ships, both in home ports and at sea, had been demilitarized.[52]

By October, the majority of Japanese naval units were undergoing inspection and 114 vessels had been selected for use in the huge shipping program of repatriating Japanese from other countries.[53] In addition to the repatriation vessels, all mine-sweeping vessels were inspected and allocated to the urgent task of clearing necessary ports and sea lanes.

As soon as repatriation and mine-sweeping were under way, orders were issued, on 3 September 1945, that all Japanese naval vessels not required for transportation of personnel or for mine-sweeping were to be retained in Japanese waters, either in Tokyo Bay, or Sasebo. Suicide craft, midget submarines, and other surface craft so designated were to be retained at occupied naval stations in an inoperative condition; fleet commanders were to report all naval or merchant vessels of 100 tons or over.[54]

Unfavorable weather caused a delay in carrying out the first of these orders. Meanwhile, since there was a possibility of suicide craft being used by some fanatical group or individual, the second order was amended and all such craft were ordered immediately destroyed or delivered into custody of American personnel; actually only one attempt to use suicide craft during the postwar demilitarization of Japan occurred. On 31 August 1945 three suicide craft were seen moving from Picnic Bay, Hong Kong, after British naval units had made their entrance. One was sunk, one was turned back to the harbor and sunk, and the third

---

49   GHQ SCAP, Progress of Demob of the Japanese Armed Forces, 31 Jul 48, p. 20.

50   These documents were translated and published by GHQ USAFPAC, Office of the ACofS, G-2, ATIS, on 21 August 1945.

51   SCAP Dir No. 2, 3 Sep 45, par. 8e.

52   SCAP Dir No. 2, 3 Sep 45, Annex B established in GHQ USAFPAC, a Naval Liaison Group representing CINCPAC. The Japanese Senior Naval Commanders were ordered to adjust their boundaries to coincide with those of the Sixth and Eighth Armies and to report to the commanders of the Fifth and Seventh US Fleets for instructions in demobilization and disarmament.

53   See Ch. VI.

54   GHQ SCAP, Final Rpt, Progress of Demob, of the Japanese Armed Forces, 31 Dec 46 (R), p. 86.

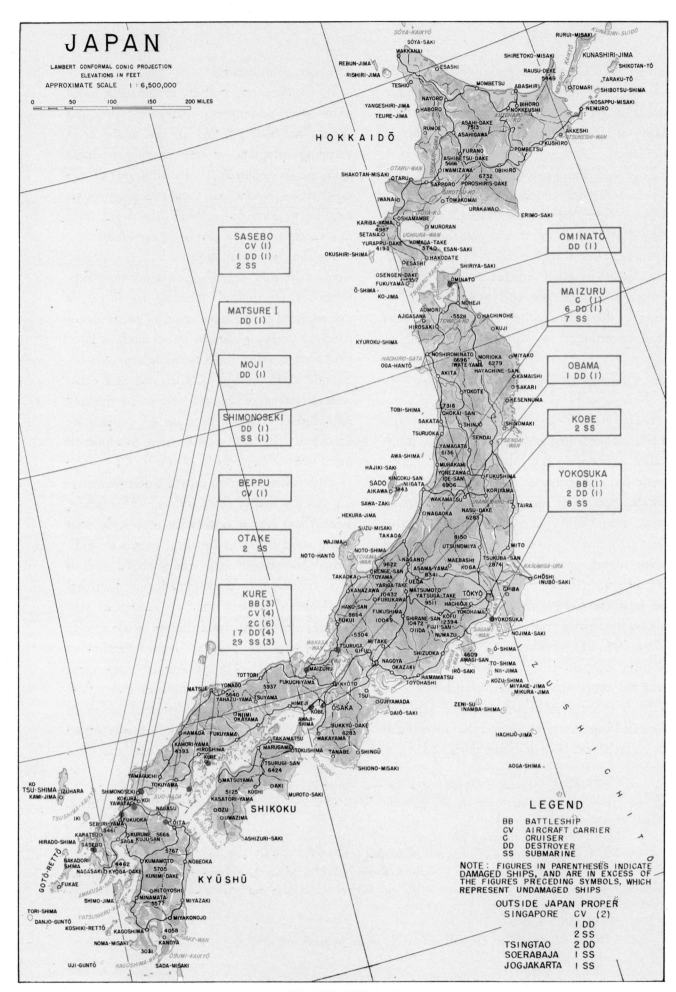

PLATE NO. 46

Disposition of Major Japanese Fleet Units, 1 September 1945

was beached and later destroyed.[55]

In Japan, various types of suicide craft were reported in twenty-four scattered port areas: 393 midget submarines, 177 human torpedoes, and 2,412 suicide surface craft.[56] By October over 90 percent of this fanatical arsenal was either destroyed or placed under immediate control of the Occupation forces. As the Occupation progressed, the remaining 10 percent, together with 141 additional midget submarines, was destroyed.

The general reports regarding all Japanese vessels, merchant and war, revealed 2,524 vessels of all kinds belonging to the Japanese Navy.[57] By February 1946 the Second Demobilization Ministry was using 408 vessels of the former Imperial Japanese Navy—138 for repatriation, 269 for mine-sweeping, and one for transportation of fuel. Many of the ships so used were former aircraft carriers, cruisers, escorts, submarine chasers, transports, and hospital ships.

By mid-October 1946 the number of vessels employed by the Second Demobilization Bureau had been progressively reduced to 250 vessels, 89 in repatriation service and 160 in mine-sweeping activities. In the first month of 1947 all of these craft were withdrawn from control of the Second Demobilization Bureau and were reassigned to the Civilian Merchant Marine Committee. On 1 January 1948 the Second Demobilization Bureau's functions of mine-sweeping and ship maintenance, were assumed by the General Maritime Bureau of the Transportation Ministry. The last transfer of functions relieved the remaining military or naval demobilization agencies completely of operating any ships.[58]

On 12 February 1948 the Far Eastern Commission belatedly ordered an early completion of the disarmament and demobilization of the Japanese Armed Forces and, in general, approved the steps already taken by General MacArthur toward the completion of this gigantic task.[59]

Combatant ships of destroyer tonnage and less were divided among the United States, United Kingdom, Soviet Russia, and China when no longer needed in the service of the Occupation. Deliveries of the several lots were based on four separate drawings held in Tokyo. During the remainder of 1947 a total of 135 former Japanese naval ships were allocated and delivered to the four major Allied Powers.[60]

Japanese crews, consisting of former naval personnel, sailed all ships to ports previously specified by the receiving nations. The vessels assigned to the U. S. S. R. were delivered to the port of Nakhodka; the Chinese lot to Shanghai and Tsingtao; the United States lot to Tsingtao, Yokohama, and Yokosuka; and the United Kingdom lot to Singapore and Kure. Three ships in the first lot, all of the ships in the second lot, and the bulk of the third lot received by the United States were held in Japan for scrapping. In the four drawings, the U. S. S. R., the United States,

---

55   *Ibid*, p. 84.
56   *Ibid*, p. 84.
57   *Ibid*, p. 86.
58   SCAPIN 1791, 4 Oct 47, sub: Demob Machinery, Reorg of.
59   JCS Dir No. 89, 17 Mar 48.
60   Ships Delivered to Allied Powers, 1947:

Destroyers	26	Sub-chasers	5
Destroyer Escorts	67	Torpedo Boats	1
Minelayers and Auxiliary Minelayers	11	Transports	8
Minesweepers and Auxiliary Minesweepers	14	Supply Ships	3
		Total	135

PLATE NO. 47

The Japanese Light Cruiser *Ibuki* in Drydock at Sasebo—64 percent Scrapped, 14 March 1947

and China received thirty-four vessels each, and the United Kingdom thirty-two vessels.[61] Smaller craft of one hundred tons or less were returned to the Japanese for use as fishing or cargo vessels, ferries, freight barges, and other peacetime purposes; those returned totaled some 200,000 displacement tons of shipping.

According to a plan prepared by COM-NAVJAP and approved by SCAP on 2 April 1946, all former Japanese Navy combatant ships larger than destroyer class were to be completely scrapped within one year of their release from the repatriation service. Wrecked and heavily damaged ships were to be sunk in deep water. By October 1946 all submarines (a total of 151) had thus been disposed of and the scheduled scrapping of other vessels was well under way. Eighteen Japanese scrapping companies were assigned to carry out the disposal of the major ships.[62]

The scrapping and salvage work on former Japanese warships was almost completed in the second half of 1948.[63] The 421 former warships in the scrapping program ranged in size from the *Ise*, a 40,000 ton battleship, to small torpedo boats of about twenty tons. Types of craft included aircraft carriers, destroyers, destroyer escorts, cruisers, submarines, and high speed transports. Most of these ships had suffered damage during the war but were still afloat. Steel and other metals obtained from salvage were turned over to the Japanese Government as returned enemy material to be used in peacetime industries.[64] Scrapping costs were high due to the high cost of carbide and the low market value of the scrap.

With the completion of the scrapping of the Japanese cruiser *Tone*, the last of the large remaining combat vessels above the 3,000 ton class was destroyed. On 15 January 1949 the U. S. Navy reported that the scrapping program and disarmament of the Japanese naval strength was complete: the Japanese Navy was extinct.[65]

---

61   GHQ SCAP, Progress of Demob of the Japanese Forces, 31 Jul 48, p. 23.
62   COMNAVJAP, Comd Narr, 21 Jan to 1 Oct 46 (C), p. 15.
63   COMNAVFE, Comd Narr, 1 Apr to 30 Sep 48 (C).
64   Tokyo, *Pacific Stars & Stripes*, September 17, 1948.
65   *Ibid*, June 5, 1949.

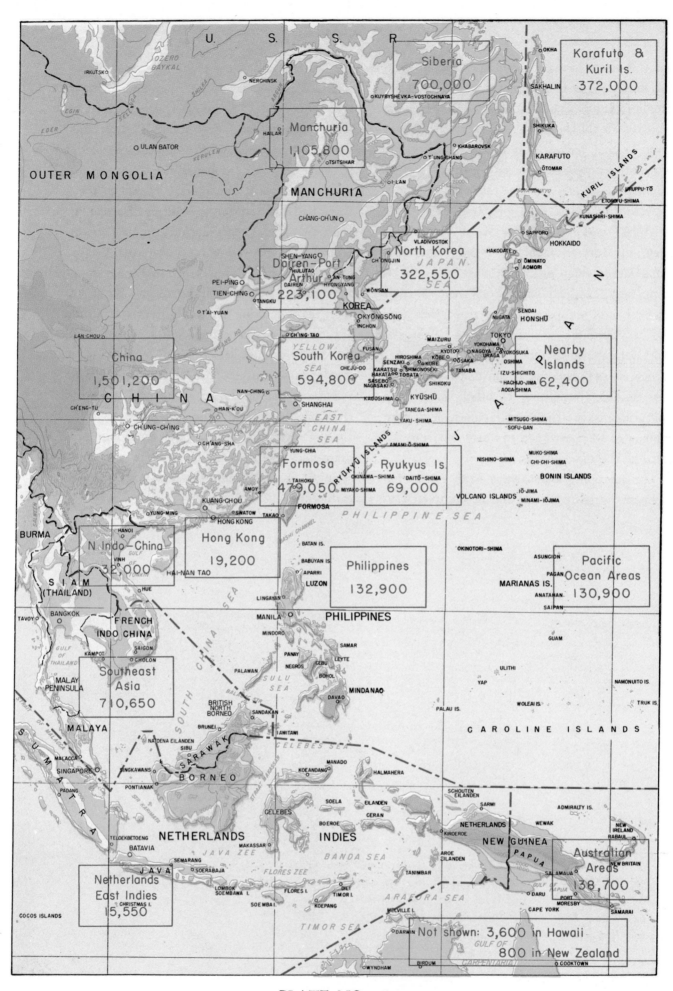

PLATE NO. 48

Japanese to be Repatriated: August 1945

CHAPTER VI
OVERSEAS REPATRIATION MOVEMENTS

At the end of the war over six million Japanese were scattered throughout the islands in the Western Pacific and on the Asiatic mainland. Their repatriation became one of the major problems confronting General MacArthur. Their early return to Japan was desirable for purely humanitarian reasons as well as for the purpose of easing the economic burden of the liberated countries. (Plate No. 48)

In addition, there were approximately 1,170,000 aliens in Japan, many of whom had been forcibly removed from their homelands. Early in September 1945 a large number of these displaced persons flocked to ports in southern Honshu and Kyushu, hoping thereby to obtain preferential treatment for their repatriation. This influx resulted in congestion and created health and sanitation problems which threatened public welfare in Japan. Recognizing this urgent problem, SCAP promptly initiated a program for mass repatriation, placing it under the staff supervision of G-3 in conjunction with the Naval High Command.

Mass repatriation can be divided into four phases. The first phase covered the initial period from 14 September 1945 to 28 February 1946. Throughout this period the only shipping available for repatriation was that which was recovered from the Japanese and such United States manned ships as could be utilized at this time. Evacuation from United States controlled areas in the Western Pacific was given priority.

During the second phase, 1 March to 15 July 1946, United States owned ships were made available to the Japanese to augment their own meager resources in shipping; repatriation from overseas areas was at its peak and reached a maximum rate of 193,000 persons per week. Throughout this period evacuation from Chinese and British controlled areas was emphasized. Approximately 1,600,000 Japanese were returned to Japan from these two areas alone.[1]

The third phase of mass repatriation covered the period from 16 July 1946 to 19 December 1946. It was marked by a decline in the numbers repatriated, owing to the diminishing numbers of repatriates delivered to embarkation ports from areas outside Japan.

Following 19 December 1946, the program was largely concerned with the repatriation of approximately 1,617,650 Japanese from Soviet controlled areas. Throughout the course of this fourth phase, however, approximately 100,000 Japanese were repatriated from British controlled Southeast Asia, a residual program substantially completed by October 1947.[2]

---

1   This chapter is based primarily on Draft Report, G-3 GHQ SCAP, " Report on Mass Repatriation in the Western Pacific," April 1947. Original strength statistics, however, have been adjusted using latest available figures as given in G-3 GHQ SCAP & FEC, Status of Repatriation Reports. Original strengths given in these reports have been revised to coincide with actual numbers repatriated. No allowance has been made for deaths of Japanese prior to repatriation, a highly controversial issue.

2   G-3 GHQ SCAP & FEC, Status of Repatriation Rpt, 1 Jul 49.

The general repatriation program was characterized by the large numbers moved, the fact that all repatriation had to be conducted over sea lanes, often over very great distances, and the amount of coordination which was necessary between SCAP and the various overseas area commanders.

This chapter covers only the details of mass repatriation of Orientals in the Western Pacific, defined as that portion of the Asiatic-Pacific Theater west of the 180th meridian; it excludes the repatriation of Occidentals, diplomats, and other special categories since these were handled on their individual merits. The narrative is not final because at the end of 1948 repatriation of Japanese from Soviet controlled areas was still not complete;[3] it does, nevertheless, cover the period during which a great mass of repatriates was moved and the agreements reached under which the remainder would be eventually returned home.

The Task

In arriving at a feasible solution to the problem of transporting more than seven and a half million persons over ocean areas, shipping not required to support the economy of Japan was made available from the remnants of Japan's once powerful navy and merchant marine. A variety of ship types were represented: aircraft carriers, cruisers, destroyers, three masted sailing ships, escorts, troop transports, hospital ships and merchantmen. It was necessary to demilitarize all naval ships before using them and the majority of vessels had to be converted to make them suitable for transporting personnel. All of the craft were in a very poor state of maintenance and repair, hence considerable work was necessary before they could be operated efficiently. The most suitable shipyards where this could be accomplished were located at Yokosuka, Kobe, Osaka, Kure, Sasebo, Maizuru and Ominato. While there was a lack of materials to be used in ship repair, many parts could be procured by stripping beached and sunken Japanese ships for spare parts and scrap metal. It was estimated that about 167 Japanese ships with a total passenger carrying capacity of 87,600 spaces could be operated 50 percent of the time. Sailors who had formerly manned ships in the merchant marine and navy were immediately available for assignment to repatriation ships. Operational control and supervision of maintenance was exercised by the U. S. naval representative of SCAP for merchant ships and by the commander of the U. S. Fifth Fleet for naval ships.

The necessary logistic support to the repatriation program was available from Japanese resources except for the supply of fuel oil for ships. In order to commence the program at an early date, oil used by repatriation ships was provided initially from United States sources.

Although rolling stock was somewhat limited, the rail system in Japan was relatively intact and could be utilized with little dislocation of normal functions for the transportation of personnel to and from ports. The ports and port areas, however, presented quite a different picture. Bombing by U. S. forces had caused widespread destruction of port facilities. Mines in the harbors, channels and inland waters precluded the use of many fine ports and made the operation of shipping in others extremely hazardous.

Since repatriation involved personnel in areas under various Allied commanders and

---

3 *Ibid*, 31 Dec 48.

was to be implemented by the Japanese, closely centralized control was necessary.[4] Under the concept of the Occupation, the machinery of the Imperial Japanese Government (IJG) was utilized for implementation of the repatriation program.

The threat of epidemics was realized, but this risk had to be accepted. Provisions for rigid quarantine procedures at points of entry in Japan were required; similarly, certain controls had to be established in Japan to prevent unauthorized traffic in goods, currency, financial instruments, and precious metals. To provide these controls, the flow of repatriates was channeled through designated focal points called "Reception Centers." Responsibility for their operation and maintenance was charged to the Japanese Ministry of Welfare, in conjunction with the demobilization machinery operated by residual military and naval personnel in a civil status.

Policies

SCAP evolved certain basic policies which with minor modifications governed the planned repatriation program throughout its implementation. The original policies were :[5]

a. *Maximum utilization will be made of Japanese naval and merchant shipping allocated for repatriation of Japanese nationals.*

b. *Japanese naval vessels and those Japanese merchant vessels designed primarily for the transport of personnel and not required for inter-island or coastal passenger service, will be utilized for the repatriation of Japanese nationals.*

c. *Personnel to be repatriated will be transported on cargo vessels only to the extent that the cargo*

carrying capacity of the vessel is not curtailed thereby.

d. *The Imperial Japanese Government will operate, man, victual and supply Japanese shipping used for repatriation to the maximum practicable extent.*

e. *First priority will be granted to the movement of Japanese military and naval personnel, and second priority to the movement of Japanese civilians.*

f. *All Japanese personnel will be disarmed prior to return to Japan proper.*

g. *In the evacuation of Japanese nationals from areas under the control of CINCAFPAC and CINCPAC, the former will prescribe the percentage of shipping allocated for repatriation purposes, to be employed in servicing the respective areas. Priorities for the evacuation of specific areas will be established as necessary. . . .*

h. *In the evacuation of Japanese nationals from areas under the control of the Generalissimo, Chinese Armies, SACSEA, GOCAMF and the Commander in Chief, Soviet Forces in the Far East, SCAP will make the necessary arrangements.*

The Plan

The plan, as finally conceived, provided for the division of responsibility as follows :

a. *SCAP*

1) Completed the necessary arrangements with coordinate and subordinate commanders for the evacuation of repatriates.

2) Assumed responsibility for repatriates after they were embarked on SCAP-controlled ships.

3) Retained control of the repatriation fleet to include the allocation of shipping to the several areas concerned.

4) Issued necessary directives to the Imperial Japanese Government for: the reception, care, demobilization (of military and naval personnel) and transport to their homes of returning Japanese

---

4   The following commanders participated in repatriation : Commander in Chief, Army Forces Pacific (CINCAFPAC); Commander in Chief, Pacific Fleet (CINCPAC); Supreme Allied Commander, Southeast Asia Command (SACSEA); Commanding General, United States Army Forces in Korea (CG USAFIK); Commanding General of the Soviet Forces in the Far East; Generalissimo, China; General Officer Commanding Australian Military Forces(GOCAMF); and commanding generals of the Occupation armies.

5   G-3 GHQ SCAP, Rpt on Mass Repatriation in the Western Pac, Apr 47, p. 4.

repatriates; transportation from their homes in Japan to the evacuation ports in the case of the repatriates from Japan.

5) Supervised the over-all execution of the program.

b. Responsibility for the operational control of repatriation shipping and the supervision of its maintenance was vested initially in Commander, U. S. Fifth Fleet, insofar as it concerned former Japanese naval ships, and in Fleet Liaison Officer, SCAP, (FLTLO-SCAP) for former merchant ships.

c. The Imperial Japanese Government was charged with the execution of the provisions of the repatriation directives published by SCAP. This included establishment, organization and operation of repatriation reception centers, transporting of repatriates to and from these centers, and providing of crews and supplies for repatriation ships. At the reception centers the IJG was required to subject each repatriate to physical examinations and quarantine procedure, as were necessary; inoculations against cholera and typhus, vaccination against smallpox, and disinfestation by DDT of person and baggage; screening for war criminals; inspection of baggage and persons to prevent unauthorized traffic in goods, financial instruments and precious metals. In addition, the following functions were performed at reception centers: rail and ship movements were coordinated; food and clothing, to be placed aboard repatriation ships or to be used at the centers, were assembled and distributed; returning Japanese soldiers and sailors were demobilized and furnished free rail transportation to their homes.[6]

First Phase: 17 September 1945— 28 February 1946

In order to save time, repatriation from United States controlled areas was set in motion concurrently with the preparation of the over-all program. Short range shipping was allocated to Korea and the Ryukyus, while long range shipping serviced more distant islands in the Pacific. Korea, the Ryukyus, and the Philippines were cleared expeditiously except for small remaining numbers of prisoners of war. For all practical purposes, mass repatriation from these areas was completed by January 1946. The rapid rate at which the U. S. Army Forces were redeployed to the Zone of Interior created an acute shortage of labor in the Ryukyus, Philippine Islands, and Pacific Ocean Area. To compensate for this shortage, authority was granted to retain temporarily prisoners of war and Japanese surrendered personnel in areas under control of U. S. Army Forces Western Pacific (AFWESPAC), U. S. Army Forces Middle Pacific (AFMIDPAC), and CINCPAC.

During this phase, arrangements were concluded with the Chinese Government, the General Officer Commanding Australian Military Forces and the Supreme Allied Commander, Southeast Asia Command, for repatriation of Japanese nationals under their control. These arrangements were relatively simple. It was agreed that the governments and commands evacuating Japanese nationals were to be responsible for delivering repatriates to designated ports of embarkation, processing them for communicable diseases, and inspecting for excesses in amount of authorized articles in their possession and for contraband. The overseas commanders were further charged with overseeing proper loading of ships prior to departure and furnishing necessary emergency supplies.

Allocation of shipping to the various areas was based on the original number of persons to be returned from each area and the geographical distance from Japan.

When reduced to passenger spaces, however, the Japanese shipping became completely in-

---

6 *Ibid*, pp. 6–7. Since the majority of repatriates were in the military or naval categories, the demobilization process, at reception centers, was a major operation. Staff supervision was exercised by G-2, in the development of demobilization plans and procedures, in conjunction with the Sixth and Eighth Armies.

Ashes of comrades are carried from Rabaul for delivery to families in Japan.

Japanese commanders receive Allied instructions on disarmament and repatriation.

PLATE NO. 49
Repatriation Begins

adequate. For this reason, representations were made to Soviet Russia, China, Southeast Asia Command, and Australia to utilize Japanese shipping then under their jurisdiction. This shipping was to be used under SCAP control to support a minimum economy of Japan and for repatriation. SACSEA responded by reporting fourteen ships with a total carrying capacity of 23,000. These ships eventually were operated for repatriation purposes under SCAP control. Repeated efforts to obtain shipping from China and the Union of Soviet Socialist Republics were unproductive. Australia reported that she had confiscated no shipping which was suitable for this purpose.

During this phase, the repatriation of non-Japanese from Japan was progressing satisfactorily. Of those desiring repatriation, 58 percent of the Koreans, 63 percent of the Formosans, 97 percent of the Chinese, and 12 percent of the Ryukyuans (Japanese) were returned to their respective homelands.[7]

The naval organization controlling repatriation shipping underwent considerable change during this period. A U. S. naval organization, known as the Shipping Control Authority for the Japanese Merchant Marine (SCAJAP), was established in Tokyo on 12 October 1945.[8] On 6 March 1946, when the office of Commander, Naval Activities, Japan (COMNAVJAP), was established, SCAJAP was integrated into that office as an important subdivision, but continued to perform the same functions. In dealings with the Japanese Government, SCAJAP worked through the Ministry of Transportation and the Ministry of Navy until the latter went out of existence on 31 December 1945; thereafter SCAJAP worked through successive agencies established under the Japanese naval demobilization program.[9]

Early in 1946 it became apparent that, statistically, repatriation in the Western Pacific would take several years unless the shipping resources of the Japanese were substantially augmented; action was accelerated to increase shipping assigned to repatriation. Following this policy, 100 U. S. Liberty type cargo ships, 100 LST's, and sufficient U. S. hospital shipping to move 25,000 patients before July 1946 were made available to SCAP for repatriation early in March 1946. These ships were operated under SCAJAP and were manned by Japanese crews.

In the first half of January 1946, operation procedures were incorporated in a single paper entitled: " Agreements Reached at Conference on Repatriation, January 15–17 1946, Tokyo, Japan." Similarly, all directives to the Japanese were combined in a single directive during March of the same year.

Under the broad concept of the Occupation, the Sixth and Eighth U. S. Armies established troop detachments at each of the reception centers so that close supervision over the Japanese could be exercised. When the Sixth Army was inactivated in January 1946, the Eighth Army became the sole local supervising agency.

As the first phase neared completion, the basic policies had been published and operational procedures had been established and tested. A good beginning had been made since approximately a million and a half Japanese had been returned to their homes and over 800,000 non-Japanese evacuated from Japan.

---

7 G-3 GHQ SCAP, Rpt on Mass Repatriation in the Western Pac, Apr 47.

8 SCAJAP took over duties formerly performed by FLTLOSCAP (US Pacific Fleet Liaison Group with SCAP) and the Commander, U. S. Fifth Fleet—direct control over all ships greater than 100 gross tons operated by the Japanese. SCAP effected coordination with SCAJAP in repatriation matters through the G-3 Repatriation Section.

9 See Ch. V.

SCAP was ready to speed up the program of repatriation.[10]

Second Phase: 1 March—15 July 1946

During the second phase of the repatriation program, emphasis was placed on evacuating over a million and one-half Japanese in China proper and Formosa, and the three quarters of a million in British areas in the Pacific.[11] The largest portion of the burden was borne by United States shipping, made available early in 1946.

Liberty ships from War Shipping Administration, vessels released in the Philippines, and Navy LST's released in the Marianas began arriving in February. They were turned over to the Imperial Japanese Government under an indemnity agreement; the Japanese were to be fully responsible for manning, supplying and repairing. Although the ships had been demilitarized prior to arrival in Japan, there was considerable refitting to be done to make them suitable for carrying passengers. Since the ships' crews were to consist of Japanese, all signs and instructions had to be changed rom English to Japanese. SCAJAP was responsible for training the crews and, in carrying out this task, did an outstanding job.

The ships were ready for use in early March and were initially assigned to shuttle between China (including Formosa) and Japan in accordance with the schedules agreed upon at a conference in Tokyo the preceding January. Except for minor departures, the original schedules were followed. Formosa was cleared for all practical purposes by 12 April and

China proper by 12 July 1946. Vast numbers were moved under oriental passenger standards —the carrying capacities of the Liberties and LST's were raised to 3,500 and 1,200 passengers respectively, an increase of 1,000 and 300 each over the maximum number established by the U. S. forces during the war for the same type ships.[12]

The problem of clearing the China Theater was complicated by a cholera epidemic which occurred among repatriates who were being returned from Haiphong, French Indo-China; Canton, China; and Kiirun, Formosa. This situation interfered considerably with the repatriation program since infected ships were quarantined and the passengers held aboard, examined, and treated until medical authorities were satisfied that they no longer constituted a hazard to the public health of Japan. Some of these ships were held in quarantine as long as thirty days. To indicate the magnitude of the problem, there were at one time twenty-two ships with a total of 76,000 repatriates in quarantine at Uraga, Japan. A total of 438 persons died of cholera before the epidemic was brought under control; only the determined efforts of the Public Health and Welfare Section of SCAP and port quarantine agencies prevented introduction of widespread epidemics into Japan.

During the peak of repatriation from China, great demands were made on the reception centers and rail system in Japan. In two successive weeks reception centers in Japan handled loads of more than 185,000 persons per week. Effective prior planning by reception centers and transportation units permitted the housing, welfare, and ultimate absorption into

---

10 G-3 GHQ SCAP, Rpt on Mass Repatriation in the Western Pac, Apr 47.

11 G-3 GHQ SCAP & FEC, Status of Repatriation Rpt, 4 Mar 49.

12 Normal carrying capacity of a liberty ship during combat was 1,500, and of an LST, 400; for emergency evacuation and short trips, up to 2,500 Americans can be carried on a liberty and 900 on an LST.

Troops pack their kits near Shanghai preparatory to the final voyage to Japan.

Homeward Bound: Yokosuka

PLATE NO. 50
Shanghai to Yokosuka

Japan of these large numbers without any major difficulties.[13]

When United States owned ships began operating in March, long range Japanese ships, previously on the China shuttle, were diverted to evacuate over three quarters of a million Japanese in Southeast Asia and Australia. In April, when the requirements for shipping from China decreased appreciably, authority was obtained from the U. S. Joint Chiefs of Staff to also utilize United States ships for repatriation from these areas. As a result, by August 1946, Australia and Southeast Asia were cleared of all Japanese, except for war criminals and those retained for labor.

In addition to returning Japanese from China, Australia, and Southeast Asia, repatriation shipping under the control of SCAP transported about 65,000 Koreans from Chinese controlled areas to Korea. Movement of these nationals was an extension of the United States policy of repatriation, as expressed in the Potsdam Declaration, and was executed under instructions from the U. S. War Department.

In February 1946, after the initial rush to be repatriated had subsided, there was a marked decrease in numbers who wished to be repatriated from Japan. This was particularly noticeable among Koreans. Most commonly advanced reasons for this change of heart were the poor economic and political conditions reported as existing in Korea, and the restrictions against removing goods and currency from Japan. In order to determine how many persons still desired to be returned to their homelands and to set a target date for the completion of SCAP's responsibilities to repatriate all non-Japanese, it was decided to register all Koreans, Formosan and Chinese nationals, and Ryukyuans (actually Japanese).

For those who indicated a desire to be repatriated, the privilege of review by United States authorities of legal proceedings as ruled by Japanese courts was continued. The Japanese Government was also held responsible for their continued welfare, transportation to reception centers, and ultimate embarkation on repatriation ships. For those who did not indicate a desire to go back to their home countries, these privileges were withdrawn. Thereafter, according to established policies, they were required to live on the indigenous resources of Japan. Furthermore, the decision to remain in Japan once made, was considered irrevocable and such persons were no longer entitled to the privilege of repatriation. This same policy was followed in respect to persons who were scheduled to be repatriated, but who failed to report where ordered. Exceptions were made only when such failures to report were due to unavoidable circumstances. In furtherance of this policy the mass return of Chinese nationals and Formosans was considered completed in May 1946. The repatriation of Koreans continued at a sluggish rate of about 6,000 per month during the period.

Efforts were again made to initiate repatriation from Soviet controlled areas on the local military level. In January 1946 the Commanding General, U. S. Army Forces in Korea, conferred at Seoul with the Commanding General of the Soviet Forces in the Far East, in order to effect repatriation from North Korea to Japan. These negotiations were unsuccessful due to certain demands made by the U. S. S. R., chiefly the furnishing of food and rail transportation through Korea for the repatriates. In Japan a plan for repatriation from North Korea was proposed to the Soviet member of the Allied Council for Japan. No agreement could be reached on matters

---

13 A distinction must be made between "repatriation" (G-3) i. e., overseas shipments and delivery to port centers and "demobilization" (G-2) i. e., inland movements from centers to home towns and villages.

concerning the supply of fuel oil for repatriation ships and the granting of preferential treatment to repatriates destined for North Korea.

Early in June it was realized that shipping available for repatriation far exceeded the number of repatriates that could be sent to evacuation ports. Mass repatriation had reached its peak and was then on the decline.

Third Phase: 16 July— 31 December 1946

With China proper cleared and Southeast Asia shipping requirements established, there was a lull in repatriation activities beginning in mid-July 1946. The number of repatriates to evacuation ports dropped to negligible figures except in the case of Hulutao, Manchuria, from which repatriates were being evacuated at a rate of 7,500 a day. Meanwhile, except for unproductive laborers, repatriation from United States controlled areas had been temporarily suspended. The British announced their intention to retain 113,500 PW's in their areas until some time in 1947. By this time South Korea had been cleared.

A review of repatriation shipping requirements was made and at this time it was decided that fifty-five U. S. Liberties could be sent back to the War Shipping Administration. These ships were returned to the United States by Japanese crews who later came back to Japan in other SCAP Liberties dispatched from Japan. The first of these ships sailed for the United States on 15 August 1946.

The lull was of short duration. For some time SCAP had been faced with the question of retaining Japanese nationals in United States controlled areas. Due to the rapid demobilization of our own forces and the difficulty of obtaining satisfactory labor, the major commanders were desperately in need of the services of Japanese PW's in order to perform the important task of terminating our wartime bases.

The issue was squarely met on 8 August 1946, when SCAP announced plans to return all Japanese PW's and displaced personnel in United States controlled areas by the end of the year. This affected some 45,000 in the Philippines, 5,000 in Hawaii, 7,000 in the Pacific Ocean Area, and 12,000 in Okinawa. These were duly evacuated in three equal increments from each of the above areas during the months of October, November, and December.

Return of Okinawans was authorized during the latter part of July after the transfer of military government from CINCPAC to CINCAFPAC was effected on 1 July 1946. The plan, involving the return of some 150,000 from Japan and Formosa during the period of 15 August to 31 December 1946, was organized and implemented without any major problems.

The flow of Japanese from Hulutao, Manchuria, increased progressively until by the end of September over 10,000 were being evacuated daily. Because of a cholera epidemic in Hulutao, it was difficult to supply shipping to maintain the above rate, as all ships from cholera ports were held in quarantine until cleared by public health officials. With the advent of cold weather, the threat of this disease diminished and the critical shipping situation eased. Manchuria was cleared by the end of October 1946, except for certain groups in areas controlled by Chinese Communist forces and a limited number of technicians retained by the Chinese Government. These were estimated to number about 68,000.[14]

14   G-3 GHQ SCAP & FEC, Status of Repatriation Rpt, 12 Nov 46.

It is interesting to note that while the Chinese Nationalist forces and Chinese Communist forces were conducting civil war, the truce teams under General Marshall were instrumental in obtaining an agreement from the Communists to repatriate the Japanese under their control. Because of this understanding, Japanese nationals in Communist held areas of Manchuria were sent home through Hulutao which was under control of the Nationalist forces (with exception of the 68,000 noted above).

During this period General MacArthur's Headquarters directed evacuation of some 89,000 Japanese nationals released from the British controlled areas in Southeast Asia. On various occasions, General MacArthur requested governmental action to induce the British to return all their Japanese nationals by 31 December 1946. These efforts failed and some 80,000 remained in Malaya and Burma at the year's end.

On 26 September the representative of the Soviet Government in Japan announced to General MacArthur that they were ready to repatriate Japanese PW's and other Japanese nationals; this was quite a conciliatory attitude on the part of the Soviets after ignoring (since January 1946) continuous SCAP attempts to start repatriation. Action was immediately taken to conclude an agreement governing this repatriation. The negotiations moved slowly and it was not until 19 December 1946 that full agreement was reached. Under its terms the Soviets guaranteed to return all Japanese surrendered personnel and all Japanese civilian personnel who desired to come back to Japan.

General MacArthur agreed to furnish the necessary shipping and to assume all responsibility for repatriates from time of embarkation. He accepted a rate of 50,000 per month although he had offered to evacuate up to 360,000 per month. A total of approximately 30,200 were returned from North Korea, Siberia, Dairen-Port Arthur, Sakhalin, and the Kuriles during December.[15]

Repatriation from Japan continued slowly. By the end of 1946 all non-Japanese and Ryukyuans who desired repatriation had either been repatriated or had forfeited their privilege to return. The only exceptions were those destined for northern Korea and a few others who could not move due to circumstances beyond their control. These latter cases were reviewed and decisions were made on their individual merits.[16]

Fourth Phase: 1 January 1947—31 December 1948

At the close of 1947 approximately 625,000 Japanese had been repatriated from Soviet controlled areas (Dairen, Siberia, North Korea, and Karafuto-Kuriles). In addition, some 294,000 Japanese had crossed from North into South Korea and had been repatriated from there, although this movement received no official sanction.[17]

The Occupation authorities estimated that some 751,000 Japanese remained to be repatriated from Soviet controlled areas as of 31 December 1947.[18] The Soviets were exceedingly secretive about the number of deaths among

---

15 *Ibid*, 10, 17, 24 and 31 Dec 46.

16 By 31 December 1946, the third phase of repatriation was completed. A total of 5,103,323 had been repatriated to Japan, 1,152,632 evacuated from Japan, and 187,600 repatriated directly from other areas in the Pacific. (G-3 GHQ SCAP & FEC, Status of Repatriation Rpt, 6 Jan 47.)

17 *Ibid*, 2 Jan 48.

18 *Ibid*. Japanese Demobilization Records and Status Reports in the Surrender Agenda supported this figure.

Processing Repatriates : Customs

Displaced civilians are processed at Hakata Reception Center, Kyushu.

PLATE NO. 51
Soldiers, Sailors and Displaced Civilians

internees so this figure was not necessarily accurate. To expedite repatriation from Soviet controlled areas the United States representative on the Allied Council for Japan, on 29 October 1947, offered enough shipping (including fuel) to increase the rate of repatriation immediately to 131,500 persons for the first designated month, and to 160,000 per month thereafter. No Soviet answer to this offer was received. On the other hand, allegedly because climatic conditions made the use of embarkation ports in Siberia and Karafuto in winter impossible, the Soviet authorities suspended all repatriation of Japanese from December 1947 until May 1948.[19]

From June 1948 on, the Soviets did not fulfill their 50,000 monthly quota as specified in the agreement of 19 December 1947, in spite of General MacArthur's repeated protests; they suspended repatriation for periods of several months without any apparent justification. The repatriation of Japanese nationals still detained in Soviet areas thus evolved into a perplexing situation, involving difficulties of an entirely different type than those encountered in repatriation from other areas. Heretofore, the problems of repatriation consisted of tremendous distances, limited shipping, epidemics inherent in mass movements under crowded conditions, and integration of millions of returnees into the economic and political life of Japan; repatriation from Soviet areas, however, posed a problem in the uncompromising attitude of the Soviets. Their repatriation policy was probably predicated on the prolonged use of inexpensive Japanese labor. Interrogation of repatriates also revealed calculated indoctrination in political camps.

The Soviets completely disregarded the individual rights of approximately 469,000 Japanese who, as of 31 December 1948, were still held by them under conditions of slave labor, and made no attempt to justify their actions in the eyes of the world. Their repatriation policies should have demonstrated to the peoples of the Far East what international communism really holds for them. The issue was squarely met in General MacArthur's response to a Soviet charge that SCAP was pursuing policies in violation of the Potsdam Declaration:[20]

There is a deep and natural resentment throughout Japan at what is generally regarded by all Japanese as a basic disregard of human and moral values in the retention in Russia after more than three years following surrender of half a million Japanese prisoners employed under shocking conditions of forced servitude in works designed to increase the Soviet war potential. This, despite solemn undertaking entered into by the Allied Powers in Clause 9 of the Potsdam Declaration offered as a condition to the Japanese surrender, which reads as follows: " The Japanese military forces, after being completely disarmed, shall be permitted to return to their homes with the opportunity to lead peaceful and productive lives."

Evacuation of Japanese from South Korea

In the early days of the Occupation, a high priority was given to the evacuation of Japanese nationals from Korea, south of 38° north latitude. In that part of Korea, there were some 600,000 Japanese nationals, the majority of whom were either military, former admin-

---

19 A total of 87,546 Japanese were repatriated from Soviet controlled areas during May and June 1948. As of 30 October 1948 a total of 877,015 Japanese had been repatriated from these areas during the whole program while some 446,670 were still awaiting repatriation. Also during this fourth phase over 80,000 Japanese were repatriated from Southeast Asia, the program from that British controlled area being substantially completed by the end of 1947. (G-3 GHQ SCAP & FEC, Status of Repatriation Rpts, 5 Nov & 2 Jan 48.)

20 GHQ SCAP Press Release, 18 Sep 48.

istrators, or technicians. In accordance with United States policy for a self-governing Korea, it was necessary to clear the way for a democratic government representative of the freely expressed will of the Korean people, by removing at the earliest date possible the influence exerted by the former Japanese officials, military and civilian.

Coincident with the surrender, the Japanese had resumed passenger ferry boat schedules between Korea and Japan. This shipping was promptly augmented by assigning short range Japanese vessels to assist in the repatriation of Japanese from Korea. By the end of September 1945 an average of 4,000 persons per day was being evacuated from South Korea. Additional shipping spaces were obtained by shuttling Japanese from Korea in LST's, which were under control of CINCPAC and were engaged in moving the U. S. XXIV Corps from Okinawa to Korea. A total of twenty LST's were employed for this purpose and returned approximately 20,000 Japanese to Japan between 12 and 16 October 1945. Similarly, 50,000 Japanese were evacuated in LST's from Saishu, a large island off the southern tip of Korea.

Because of the importance of this operation, the Japanese nationals were cleared from South Korea rapidly. All Japanese military and naval personnel, except some 2,650 retained for labor were evacuated by 21 November 1945. The sole purpose of holding a small group of Japanese was to have them aid in the repatriation of Japanese civilians, who, except for key technical advisors, were evacuated by the end of March 1946. The final contingent of the Japanese Army was returned home on 28 April 1946.

An additional repatriation burden was imposed upon the XXIV Corps[21] by Japanese nationals who crossed the 38° parallel into South Korea. While this border was technically closed, many Japanese seeking repatriation evaded the road blocks and drifted into the United States zone as early as September 1945. At first, the number of Japanese from North Korea was low. During the period from 15 September 1945 to 21 March 1946, only 42,500 were evacuated via South Korea. However, from 21 May to 30 June 1946, about 10,000 Japanese per week entered the United States zone from North Korea, Manchuria, and Siberia. This number was further increased to approximately 1,500 per day by the middle of August 1946. To protect the public health of Korea, collecting stations were established along all natural avenues of approach into South Korea from the north. All Japanese were rounded up and brought to these collection centers where they were examined medically, immunized against small-pox, typhus, and cholera and dusted with DDT to prevent the introduction of epidemic diseases into South Korea. They were then evacuated through reception centers to Japan.

The repatriation program from this area was handicapped by various incidents. In January 1946 all repatriation activities were suspended for a four-day period because of a threatened general strike. Flood conditions caused another halt of activities for six weeks, from 26 June to 10 August 1946. A railroad strike in Korea caused a further delay in repatriation from 26 September to 17 October, while a cholera epidemic made it necessary to place all repatriates in quarantine prior to their evacuation. This quarantine lasted from 10 August to mid-December 1946.

Prior to 10 August 1946, SCAP controlled shipping was placed on shuttle service to Korea; subsequent to that date, however, ships were dispatched on request of XXIV Corps as processed repatriates became ready for shipment.

The clearance of the Japanese from South

---

21   Later known as the U. S. Army Forces in Korea (USAFIK).

Japanese repatriates arrive at Beppu, Kyushu, for processing
prior to returning to their homes.

Japanese repatriates arrive at Uraga, one of the principal
reception centers in Japan.

PLATE NO. 52
Debarkation: Beppu and Uraga

Korea was accomplished more expeditiously and completely than from any other area. Approximately 592,000 were evacuated from the beginning of the program until 31 December 1946.[22]

Return of Koreans

In September 1945 the Japanese reported that approximately 1,356,400 Koreans were located in Japan. The policy concerning repatriation of Koreans provided that they should be treated as liberated people insofar as military security permitted. Those desirous of repatriation, who were not being held as war criminals or for security reasons, would be returned to their homeland as soon as practicable. However, since they had been Japanese subjects, they could, at SCAP's discretion, be treated as enemy nationals and, if circumstances so warranted, be forcibly repatriated. In essence, all Koreans in Japan were given the opportunity to be repatriated, provided they had not been in active support of the Fascist governments or guilty of distributing propaganda. Those in the latter category were repatriated regardless of their desires.

Initially, Koreans flocked to repatriation ports in southern Honshu and in Kyushu in uncontrolled movements, thereby causing a serious health menace and congestion in these port areas. Since regularly scheduled ships were repatriating Japanese from Korea at the outset of the Occupation, these ships were used to repatriate Koreans on the return voyage.[23]

The shipping assigned to repatriate Koreans could not evacuate them fast enough to alleviate the overcrowded conditions in reception centers. This situation was eased when United States and Japanese-manned LST's, used to repatriate Japanese from northern China, on their return trip were utilized to transport Koreans.

During the period from 6 January to 17 February 1946, the average daily rate of Koreans being transported dropped to 3,000, and the Japanese Government reported that its job of inducing Koreans to move to reception centers had become increasingly difficult. This slowing down of repatriation to South Korea was attributed to the confused political situation which existed in Korea, housing shortages, widespread unemployment, general lack of organized agencies in Korea to aid repatriates, and economic conditions which were reportedly much poorer in comparison with those in Japan. The limitation on the amount of money and baggage that could be taken out of Japan especially warranted serious consideration on the part of those Koreans who had been established in Japan for a long time.

In order to solve the problem so that the Occupation forces could discharge the implied obligation to repatriate Koreans from Japan within a reasonable period of time, it was necessary to determine the number of Koreans in Japan who were desirous of repatriation, establish a plan for their evacuation by a definite date, and impose a forfeiture feature upon those who would not move according to plan.

As a result of this plan, on 17 February 1946, the Japanese Government was directed to conduct a registration of all Koreans in Japan to determine their desires concerning repatriation.[24] The Koreans were told at the time of

---

22 G-3 GHQ SCAP & FEC, Status of Repatriation Rpt, 31 Dec 46.

23 During the period 15 September 1945 to 6 January 1946, approximately 630,600 Koreans were evacuated, averaging approximately 5,500 per day.

24 G-3 GHQ SCAP Rpt on Mass Repatriation in the Western Pac, Apr 47. This registration revealed that there remained approximately 508,100 Koreans in Japan, 9,200 of whom formerly lived in North Korea and 498,900 in South Korea.

registration that if they did not request repatriation, they forfeited this privilege until regular commercial facilities were available. At the same time, those who indicated they desired repatriation, but refused to move according to plan set up by the Japanese Government, also forfeited this privilege. A deadline date of 30 September 1946 was established for repatriation of Koreans from Japan. Application of this forfeiture proviso was not arbitrarily enforced, however; such cases were subject to review and when circumstances warranted, provision was made for later repatriation.

The initial policy for repatriation had been to return Koreans from north of 38° via South Korea. This became such a burden on the railroads and the economy of South Korea that it was decided to suspend movement of Koreans to North Korea until such time as they could be returned directly to their homes.

During June 1946 heavy rains and floods disrupted rail and highway communications from the major ports to the interior and damaged crops and buildings. By the end of the month the damage to communications was severe enough to cause repatriation activities to be discontinued. Although the Commanding General, USAFIK, requested that the temporary suspension remain in effect until 30 November, General MacArthur, considering the political repercussion that could result if Koreans were prohibited from returning to their homeland, lifted the suspension on 10 August 1946 and repatriation was resumed. As a result, the date for completing the program of returning Koreans to South Korea was set at 15 November 1946. Another stoppage of repatriation was due to a railway strike in Korea during the period 26 September to 17 October. This unexpected delay changed the estimated date for completion of the program to the end of December.

In September 1946, as an added incentive for Koreans in Japan to return to Korea, provision was made whereby each Korean family was allowed to ship home 500 pounds of household goods, and 4,000 pounds of tools and handicraft equipment. This allowance was in addition to personal belongings which they carried with them. Provision was also made for Koreans who had already been repatriated to have their tools and handicraft equipment left behind in Japan shipped to them.

During September 1945 illegal traffic between Korea and Japan began flourishing by means of small unregistered ships. Until May 1946 unauthorized persons smuggled by these ships (mostly Koreans) were no serious threat to the health or economy of either country. Late in the same month, however, South Korea suffered an epidemic of cholera. The entry into Japan of unauthorized persons consequently constituted a grave danger to public health, since the illegal entrants were not processed through any quarantine ports. To stop this traffic, vigorous patrol measures were undertaken by units of the U. S. and British Navies, the Allied Occupation forces, and the Japanese Government. Those illegal ships which were apprehended were impounded and the passengers and crews placed in quarantine. After this isolation terminated, the Koreans were returned to their country under guard.

From August to the end of December 1946, some 15,400 Koreans, trying to gain illegal entrance into Japan, were apprehended and returned to Korea.[25] The majority of those, it was discovered, were former repatriates who were returning to resume residence in Japan.

By the end of December 1946 a total of approximately 929,800 Koreans had been re-

---

25 G-3 GHQ SCAP & FEC, Status of Repatriation Rpt, 6 Jan 47.

patriated from Japan, excluding the illegal entrants.[26] There remained some 5,570 who were eligible for repatriation and whose return was scheduled during the early part of 1947. By May 1947 repatriation of Koreans was substantially completed.

Pacific Ocean Areas

Evacuation of the 171,000 Japanese and other nationals dispersed throughout the many islands of the Japanese defensive system in the Pacific[27] presented one of the more difficult problems of repatriation from United States controlled areas. Personnel and shipping shortages delayed the start of the operation, but within a month after V-J Day, movement of Japanese, Ryukyuans, Koreans, Formosans, and Chinese was well under way.[28] A few individuals had requested and obtained authority to remain because of past residence in these areas for over ten years.

By September 1945 Japanese shipping of a total passenger capacity of 18,000 was allocated to the clearance of these areas. This shipping was augmented by a number of small American manned ships which had been operating in the Pacific Ocean Area. In the second month of 1946 those United States ships that were designated for use as SCAJAP controlled, Japanese manned repatriation ships sailed for Japan with full loads.

During the period 15–17 January 1946, a conference was held in Tokyo by representatives of all commanders concerned with repatriation in order to establish standard operating procedures. It was agreed that repatriation of Japanese nationals would be suspended until July 1946, except for ineffectives; repatriation of remaining Formosans, Koreans and Chinese would be continued under existing arrangements; repatriation of other nationals (of Indonesia, Malaya, Manchuria and the Celebes) would be handled separately in each case. As a result of this conference, processing of repatriates was expedited, operation of shipping facilitated, and additional passenger comforts made possible. The areas where repatriates would be processed and refueling ports were decided upon. The commander of the Marianas area at Guam was made responsible for onward routing and supply of repatriation vessels while within the limits of the Pacific Ocean Area. During the winter months, repatriation ships were stocked from United States sources with blankets and warm clothing for the prospective passengers. This equipment, the cost of which was charged against reparations, was later collected at debarkation ports in Japan. The articles, after being dyed and marked, were further distributed by the Japanese Government for relief purposes. Eventually, customs processing procedures established at the conference were strictly applied when it was found that many PW's were returning from the Pacific Ocean Area to Japan with large quantities of newly-purchased luxury items of United States manufacture, wrist watches, fountain pens and silk stockings; all items in excess of amounts normally required by individuals were confiscated.

Though hampered by the low operational efficiency (about 50 percent) of the Japanese shipping and occasional supply shortages, repatriation schedules set in September were maintained with minor interruptions and negligible loss of life through mid-March 1946. Since by that time 163,000 had been repatriated

---

26   *Ibid.*

27   These were in general the Bonin, Volcano, Marianas, Caroline, Marshall and Gilbert Islands.

28   Numerically they consisted of approximately 131,000 Japanese, 26,000 Ryukyuans, 14,000 Koreans, 600 Formosans, and 100 Chinese.

Customs search for contraband and weapons.

Repatriate from Soviet territory returns to his family.

PLATE NO. 53
From Port to Home

and the remaining 7,000 were being utilized as labor, shipping schedules were curtailed except for evacuation of those no longer needed for labor.

On 8 August 1946 General MacArthur requested CINCPAC to return all remaining Japanese prisoners of war and surrendered personnel in three monthly increments starting in October 1946, so that the target date of 31 December 1946 for the completion of the over-all repatriation program could be met. CINCPAC agreed to the plan, and through its implementation, the task of repatriation from the Pacific Ocean Area was completed ahead of schedule when on 24 December 1949 the Japanese ex-destroyer *Sugi* with her last load of repatriates arrived at Uraga, Japan.[29]

When Phase Three of the repatriation program ended, a total of approximately 130,800 persons had been returned to Japan and 40,700 returned directly to Formosa, the Ryukyus, China and Korea.[30]

Philippine Islands

Extensive United States base installations which existed in the Philippine Islands facilitated control and evacuation of the 152,400 repatriates.[31] Principal concentrations were on Luzon, Mindanao, and Leyte. The initial proportional share of Japanese repatriation shipping allotted to the Philippine Islands amounted to only 12,000 spaces but was augmented by routing supply ships returning empty to the United States from the Philippine Islands via Japan. On 7 October 1945 the first Japanese ships, modified to transport repatriates, arrived in the Philippine Islands.

Both United States and Japanese ships were supplied with additional life-saving equipment, overside latrines, and food and water stores. During cold weather, blankets and warm clothing, furnished by the United States, were placed upon all ships engaged in repatriation; the passengers were allowed to keep the clothing issued to them.

Until February 1946, with slight modifications, evacuation of Japanese proceeded according to plan. On 24 December 1945 General MacArthur directed the Commanding General, AFWESPAC, to route shipping on the Japan shuttle via Takao, Formosa, to permit return of approximately 12,000 Formosans from the Philippines and subsequent transport of Japanese in Formosa to Japan. On the same date movement of approximately 1,400 Koreans and 53,000 Chinese direct to their respective homelands was also authorized.

Suspension of repatriation in January affected approximately 43,600 Japanese PW's who were required for maintenance and repair of essential installations in the Philippine Islands. Evacuation of sick and other ineffectives from this group in American cargo ships continued until May 1946. At this time, authority to utilize United States shipping was withdrawn and limited SCAJAP Japanese shipping was substituted.

When General MacArthur decided that all United States controlled areas were to be cleared by the end of 1946, a plan was set up to clear the remaining Japanese from the Philippine Islands. Shipping was prepared to remove the Japanese from camps located near Tacloban, San Fernando, and Manila. Approximately equal monthly increments were

---

29 Concurrent with incoming shipments to Japan, some 160 pre-war residents of the Bonin, Caroline, and Marianas Islands were transported to their homes.

30 G-3 GHQ SCAP, Rpt on Mass Repatriation in the Western Pac, Apr 47, p. 29.

31 This total includes approximately 1,400 Koreans, 6,000 Chinese and 12,000 Formosans who were returned direct to their respective homelands.

evacuated during October, November, and December 1946. By the end of the year only 665 Japanese remained in the Philippine Islands. They were detained there either as witnesses or as suspected criminals for the war crimes trials. There was also an undetermined but fast dwindling number, probably not exceeding 500, hiding in the mountains.

Ryukyu Islands

Although the Ryukyus, because of their proximity to Japan, should have presented an easy repatriation problem, such was not the case. The Ryukyus, especially Okinawa Island, had been ravaged by invasion and rehabilitation proceeded slowly. As late as the spring of 1946 there ware still 130,000 residents homeless on Okinawa itself. Never self-supporting, the food situation on Okinawa was further aggravated by the loss of many acres of arable land taken over for base installations.

Initially, military government in the Ryukyus south of 30° north latitude was exercised by CINCPAC. As such, that headquarters was responsible for the return of some 69,200 Japanese military personnel.[32] A ferry service was established to the Ryukyus in October 1945 to transport only the Japanese military. This was supplemented almost immediately by the assignment of short range Japanese shipping, and further augmented by empty United States cargo ships returning home via Japan.

Japanese military were returned to Japan by the beginning of 1946, with the exception of 14,000 whose return was temporarily suspended until the last quarter of the year. During this period their services were utilized to repair war damaged facilities and to assist the native population to return to their former homes.

The return of displaced Ryukyuans was not so easily achieved. There were approximately 160,000 Ryukyuans in Japan who had been hurriedly evacuated from their homes just prior to the invasion by the United States forces. They had been permitted to carry with them little in the way of baggage, clothing or funds. Their situation in Japan rapidly became worse from a social and economic standpoint. It was therefore to the interest of General MacArthur's headquarters to return them to their former homes.

Early agreements with CINCPAC were reached under which repatriates from Japan destined for localities in the Ryukyus other than Okinawa would be accepted. Consequently, Ryukyuans were loaded on shuttle ships which were returning Japanese. The program for the return of Okinawans moved slowly. Repeated representations to CINCPAC to initiate this program were unproductive. CINCPAC, with considerable justification, refused to accept the Okinawans on the grounds that food and shelter were not available locally to support the added increase in population. When the responsibility for military government of the Ryukyus was transferred from the Navy to the Army on 1 July 1946, the matter was reconsidered. General MacArthur was most anxious to evacuate the Ryukyuans because they were a serious relief problem in Japan. It was for this reason he directed that they be repatriated without further delay and that necessary food and shelter be provided for them from Japanese and United States resources. A conference was called in Tokyo on 22 July, at which time the representatives of AFWESPAC and SCAP agreed upon a plan for the repatriation of all Ryukyuans in Japan who were willing to return home.

This plan, published late in July, was quite complicated because of conditions in the Ryukyus. It provided that repatriation would begin on 5 August 1946; repatriates would be

---

32   G-3 GHQ SCAP & FEC, Status of Repatriation Rpt, 1 Jul 49.

segregated in Japan and loaded on ships according to destination;[33] further distribution in the Ryukyus would be made by small boats; and all repatriates would undergo a six-day quarantine period before departing. The rate of repatriation to Okinawa was established at 4,000 per week until 26 September, after that at 8,000 per week until the program was completed. Incorporated in the plan were provisions for the return of approximately 140,400 Ryukyuans from Japan.[34] Careful supervision smoothed out the complicated mechanics of the entire operation.

The military government authorities in the Ryukyus were faced not only with the task of receiving the repatriates but of transporting them to their homes and providing shelter and food for them. Inter-island transportation was provided by small native and United States craft, including six LST's made available by SCAP. Overland transportation was furnished from the meager resources of the military government authorities in the Ryukyus.

Houses for the incoming repatriates were built of lumber, with cement and nails furnished by SCAP. Over 17,000 simple dwellings were constructed; the frames were of wood while the roofs and walls were of thatch. Almost 10,000 pyramidal tents were used to provide for immediate needs.[35]

All remaining Japanese prisoners of war and surrendered personnel retained in the Ryukyus for labor were returned to Japan in three monthly increments starting in October 1946. The program was completed by the end of the year.

China Theater

Because of the large numbers involved, repatriation of over 3,000,000 Japanese and other nationals from China and adjoining areas became another of the more difficult and pressing tasks on V-J Day. On that date, this mass of humanity, consisting of approximately equal numbers of military and civilian personnel, was reported to be geographically situated as follows:[36]

Area	Numbers
China	1,501,200
Manchuria	1,105,850
Formosa	479,050
North Indo-China	32,000
Hong Kong	19,200

Two factors made necessary the assignment of a high priority to repatriation from China and adjoining areas. First, it was United States policy to assist in the establishment of a sound central government in China. This objective could not be accomplished as long as the security of China was threatened by the presence of large numbers of Japanese troops. Second, large numbers of Japanese were located in areas of conflicting interests of the French Government, Viet Nam, Chinese Nationalists, and Chinese Communists, making early evacuation of these groups imperative to prevent their being used as pawns in the various political disputes. These factors combined with extremely poor interior transportation and communication facilities in war-ravaged China made even the concentration of repatriates at evacuation ports a formidable task.

---

33   These were Okinawa, Amami Oshima, Miyako, and Ishigaki.

34   G-3 GHQ SCAP & FEC, Status of Repatriation Rpt, 6 Aug 46.

35   During the period 1 July to 31 December 1946, over 545,000 pounds of food were furnished repatriates from US resources.

36   G-3 GHQ SCAP & FEC, Status of Repatriation Rpt, 1 Jul 49.

Japanese repatriates aboard ship.

Repatriates are admitted to the Matsuasa Restaurant at Omori.

PLATE NO. 54
Flotsam of War: Displaced Civilians

Full appreciation of the repatriation problem in Chinese areas is possible only through knowledge of the role played by the U.S. forces stationed in China. Upon the cessation of hostilities with Japan, the U.S. Joint Chiefs of Staff assigned the task of advising and assisting the Chinese in repatriation of Japanese to the U.S. Army Forces, China Theater, (later redesignated as the U.S. Army Forces, China). When this headquarters was discontinued, its duties were transferred to the Peiping Headquarters Group, acting mainly in an advisory capacity to the Chinese Government, General MacArthur, and the U.S. Navy in China. Of the coordination tasks assigned to the various U.S. Army forces in China, the maintenance of effective liaison with the Chinese authorities was the most difficult. Successful liaison was accomplished only through patient, persistent efforts.

No time was lost in getting the program under way. Under an interim plan implemented early in October 1945, the first shipping was used in evacuating Japanese situated near Shanghai and Tangku. Concurrently, a more complete organization for repatriation was developed by SCAP through a series of conferences, in which the Chinese and United States ground and naval commanders in China were integrated into the SCAP repatriation system. As in the case of other areas, many of the ships and direction of the program came from the United States. The Chinese Govern-ment was made responsible for the delivery of repatriates to the ports, their medical and other processing and their correct loading aboard the SCAP controlled ships according to the monthly quotas scheduled; however, supervision of this loading and processing was also made a responsibility of the United States forces in China. This was accomplished by sending American liaison teams, which included communications and medical personnel, to the main evacuation ports in China. These teams solved the communication problem and greatly reduced the amount of epidemic diseases carried to Japan.

After two previous conferences (representatives came from General MacArthur's headquarters, Navy Command in the Pacific, and United States Forces in China) had resulted in establishment of general policies regarding ships, shipping routes, and embarkation rates,[37] a third one was called for 15–17 January 1946 in Tokyo. At this time, all United States commands in the Pacific and Far East (except AFMIDPAC) were integrated into a theater-wide organization for repatriation. Operational procedures and schedules were developed with emphasis on the plan for evacuation of China. The results of this conference were published as "Agreements Reached at Conference on Repatriation 15–17 January 1946, Tokyo, Japan." This document governed repatriation procedures from that time on.

At the conference, daily evacuation rates

---

37 Agreements on general policies included: utilization of US naval ships, when available, to augment Japanese shipping removing Japanese from areas occupied by forces in China; vessels to be back-loaded with Chinese, Formosans or Koreans and Japanese civilians from Japan; US cargo ships to be used for repatriation when space was available; embarkation rates aggregating 154,000 monthly for Japanese were established for the Tientsin, Tsingtao, and Shanghai areas; monthly rates of reception of Chinese from Japan were set at 10,000 for the Tientsin area and 2,000 for the Shanghai area.

Upon receipt of an offer from Washington of 100 Liberties and LST's as needed, for use in repatriation, a second conference was held at Tokyo on 7 December 1945, as a result of which it was recommended that 100 Liberties, 100 LST's and 7 hospital ships be made available to SCAP for repatriation. The ships were to be converted in Japan to carry repatriates and were to be crewed by the Japanese. (G-3 GHQ SCAP, Rpt on Mass Repatriation in the Western Pac, Apr 47, p. 39.)

were set as follows: North China, 4,000; Central China and Formosa, 16,000; South China and North French Indo-China, 15,000; an aggregate of 1,050,000 per month. These rates were based upon use of United States shipping for Chinese repatriation.[38]

Within two months of the 17 January conference, repatriation from Chinese areas was limited only by the numbers made available at evacuation ports. With the exception of stragglers, war criminals, and 28,000 civilian technicians retained by the Chinese Nationalist Government, the greater part of China was cleared by June 1946.[39]

South China was cleared by 25 April 1946, repatriates being removed through the principal ports of Canton, Amoy, and Swatow. Hainan Island was cleared without incident in March. Also included in South China repatriation was that part of French Indo-China north of 16° north latitude. Although operational control of this area was being transferred from the Chinese Nationalists to the French Government concurrently with evacuation of Japanese, the area was cleared during May 1946 without difficulty other than a major dislocation of shipping due to a cholera epidemic.

The Hong Kong area of South China, under British control, was cleared early in May through combined use of Japanese manned United States repatriation ships and British cargo vessels. The British, however, retained about 1,300 Japanese for labor until December 1946, when this number was reduced to 268. These were subsequently repatriated.

Central China evacuation schedules were interrupted by an outbreak of smallpox in Shanghai in April, a typhus epidemic in May, and cholera in June. On the Shanghai-Sasebo shuttle, the only major shipping accident of the entire repatriation program occurred on 22 January 1946 when the *Enoshima Maru*, carrying 4,300 Japanese civilians, struck a free mine and sank slowly, fifty miles out of Shanghai; through the assistance of another repatriation vessel, all but seventy-seven of the passengers and crew were saved. Except for stragglers, Central China was cleared in July 1946.

Repatriation from Formosa was delayed until early December 1945, when the Chinese Government landed troops and took control of the island. The northern half of Formosa was cleared through Kiirun and the southern portion through Takao. The Japanese located in a comparatively inaccessible strip on the east coast were removed through Karenko by small draft vessels loaded by lighters. Cholera once again slowed the program. However, except for some 24,000 technicians required for operation of essential public facilities, Formosa was cleared by 15 April 1946. By the end of 1946 those retained by the Chinese had been reduced to 11,000 through use of both Chinese and SCAJAP shipping.

---

38 Of the shipping requested, 106 Liberties and 100 LST's were received, but only 85 of the LST's were retained for repatriation, the remaining 15 LST's being utilized to support the economy of Korea. Upon arrival in Japan, under direction of SCAJAP these ships were modified to carry passengers, provided with trained Japanese crews, and placed in service at a rate of 25 a week. Six of the Liberties were converted into hospital ships of about 1,200 beds each. Since total available passenger capacity of these SCAJAP vessels was approximately 400,000 by the end of March 1946, all Seventh Fleet shipping was released from repatriation. Over 50 percent of the total Japanese repatriation fleet, with a capacity of 100,000 spaces supplemented US shipping. Consequently by 1 March, it became apparent that the flow of passengers from the interior could not fill available shipping to capacity.

39 Concurrently with the main repatriation program of Japanese in China, a total of approximately 31,200 Chinese and 32,000 Formosans were repatriated from Japan while 7,500 Chinese and 36,300 Formosans were repatriated from other areas in the Pacific. Also some 52,650 Koreans were repatriated from Chinese areas. The British assumed responsibility for return of 287 Koreans in Hong Kong.

North China repatriation, though affected by the Chinese Communist and Nationalist military operations which occasionally blocked the ports of Tangku and Tsingtao, was completed late in May 1946. During periods of internal Chinese strife and strained relations in North China, repatriation was expedited through efforts of the U. S. Marines.

By comparison with the rest of China, repatriation from Manchuria proved the most difficult. Though the Chinese Communists had agreed upon the desirability of repatriation of Japanese, few efforts were made by them to cooperate until the fall of 1946. Though never definitely ascertained, it was estimated that 612,000 Japanese were concentrated in the Mukden-Hulutao area, 387,000 near Changchun in central Manchuria, 310,000 in the vicinity of Harbin in north Manchuria, and 250,000 in the Dairen-Port Arthur area.[40]

After the Nationalist forces had advanced well beyond Mukden, repatriation began in April through the port of Hulutao. The initial evacuation rate of 3,000 daily was increased to 7,500 daily by July. Peak loads were transported to Japan during the summer months except for minor interruptions because of a flood in the interior and another delay of three weeks during August because of cholera. During this period every effort was made to push repatriation in order to complete the program in Manchuria before the port of Hulutao was frozen in. Out of the 1,300,000 believed to be in the area, only 469,000 Japanese, mostly civilians, had been repatriated by mid-August 1946.

During the summer repeated attempts were made to secure evacuation of Japanese from central and north Manchuria under Chinese Communist control. Early in September evacuation from Chinese Communist areas was at last made possible; the outflow from Hulutao increased to 10,000–15,000 daily during the next two months. By the end of October all Japanese had been evacuated from Manchuria except the 250,000 under Soviet control and some 68,000 unaccounted for in the interior.[41]

A straggler program was set up in September 1946 to accomplish repatriation of scattered groups of Japanese at Canton, Hainan, Shanghai, and Formosa. Included in this program were the 24,000 Japanese technicians and their dependents held in Formosa. They were initially expected to be transported to Japan by Chinese ships. Of this group SCAP actually provided transportation for all but 3,000 of the 13,000 repatriated by the end of 1946.[42] When in December 1946 repatriation shipping facilities were further reduced, SCAP established a policy to provide transportation for only those straggler groups of more than 200 persons.

Repatriation of Koreans from China to Korea was started late in January because of military expediency, medical considerations, and availability of surplus repatriation shipping from China shuttles. Because of the limited port facilities in Korea, the traffic was divided between the ports of Inchon and Fusan.

By mid-March 1946 the situation of remaining Koreans in north and central China awaiting repatriation had so deteriorated that their early repatriation was imperative. Consequently, schedules were advanced and this repatriation was completed in June 1946.

During the repatriation program from China, cholera, typhus, and smallpox epidemics origi-

---

40 G-3 GHQ SCAP, Rpt on Mass Repatriation in the Western Pac, Apr 47. These figures are based on information obtained from the Japanese Government. Although there is no absolute proof of their accuracy, Japanese Government figures proved to be quite accurate in repatriation from other areas.

41 It is believed that retained technicians and labor and inaccurate initial estimates partially explain the discrepancy.

42 G-3 GHQ SCAP, Rpt on Mass Repatriation in the Western Pac, Apr 47.

Orderly embarkation under U. S. Navy.

Aboard an LST at Tsingtao, China.

PLATE NO. 55
Repatriates from China and Manchuria.

nating there during the spring and summer of 1946 had a tremendous effect on reception facilities in Japan. Shipping and passengers tied up in the quarantine ports of Uraga, Hakata, and Sasebo at times totalled over eighty vessels with more than 150,000 repatriates aboard. Control of quarantine ports and maintenance of nearly normal evacuation rates from all areas during the spring and summer of 1946 required a high degree of rapid and effective coordination of all United States and Japanese agencies; with the institution of adequate measures to limit the return of unauthorized Koreans to Japan in small craft, even minor outbreaks of these diseases in Japan were eliminated.

Mass repatriation from Chinese areas was completed by the end of December 1946, with some 3,101,700 Japanese returned home.[43]

The problem of repatriating Japanese stragglers in Manchuria still existed, however; in a G-3 report of 29 April 1949 it was estimated that there were slightly more than 60,000 Japanese still in the Chinese Communist controlled areas of Manchuria.[44] Their repatriation could be accomplished only if they were able to infiltrate into Nationalist areas and then be transported to ports on the coast. General MacArthur was prepared to send shipping whenever there were sufficient number of Japanese available for repatriation. (Plate No. 56)

Southeast Asia

In September 1945 approximately 710,670 Japanese awaited repatriation from areas under control of SACSEA.[45] The immediate problem involved disarming the Japanese and assembling them in areas near appropriate ports of embarkation. According to British policies regarding Japanese civilians, those who entered British or other Allied areas after the outbreak of the war were to be repatriated. Those individuals, nevertheless, who had either resided in such areas prior to the outbreak of war or were not objected to by territorial authorities, did not have to be returned to Japan.

It was agreed between SACSEA and SCAP that useable Japanese shipping recovered in Southeast Asia areas[46] would be utilized, under United States control, in transporting repatriates from Southeast Asia ports directly to Japan. In addition, such other Japanese shipping as could be made available would also be allocated to Southeast Asia repatriation.

Because of the limited number of ships and the distance involved only 34,300 Japanese had been repatriated from SACSEA by 21 April 1946.[47] Early in 1946 it was realized that four or five years would be required to complete the Southeast Asia repatriation program with shipping then available. This situation was unacceptable to both British and United States authorities, and various sources for procurement of additional shipping were investigated. Previously, some 106 Liberties and 85 LST's had been made available to SCAP from United States resources to accelerate repatriation from China. By the end of March 1946 it was foreseen that some of these ships would be in excess of the repatriation requirements of China

---

43 *Ibid.*

44 G-3 GHQ SCAP, Status of Repatriation Rpt, 29 Apr 49.

45 It developed that initially about 14,000 passenger spaces in SEA recovered shipping were available, plus an additional 9,000 spaces from SCAP controlled shipping, making a total of 23,000 spaces allocated to service these areas. The first repatriation ship departed Singapore on 22 November 1945.

46 G-3 GHQ SCAP & FEC, Status of Repatriation Rpt, 1 Jul 49.

47 *Ibid*, 23 Apr 46.

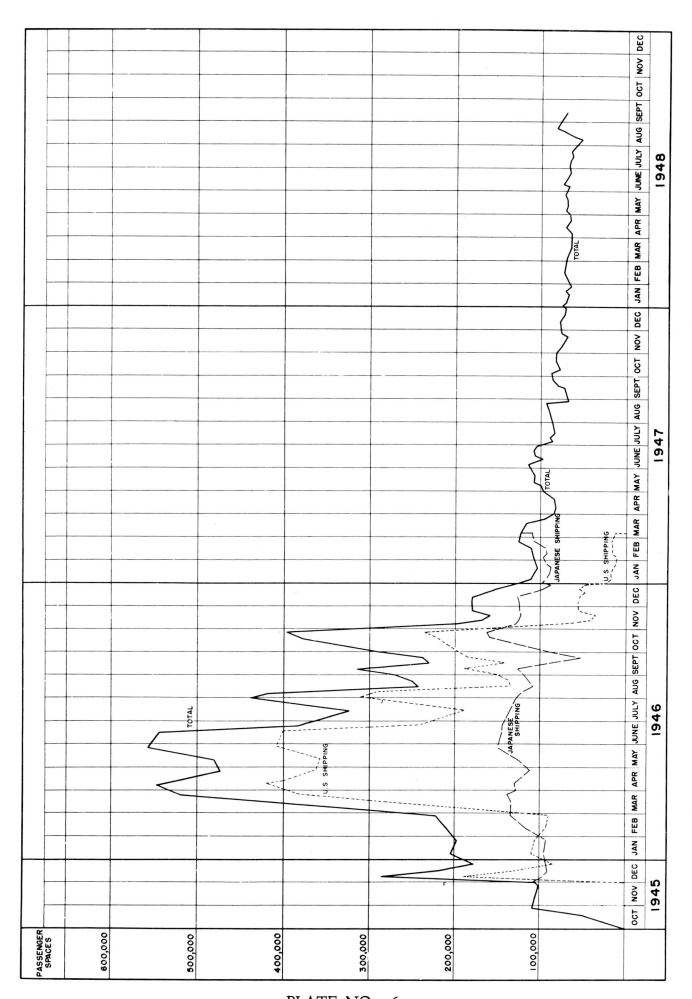

PLATE NO. 56

Repatriation Shipping: October 1945—September 1948

and could be used profitably in the evacuation of Japanese from Southeast Asia. Authority was therefore obtained from the U. S. Joint Chiefs of Staff early in April to employ United States owned shipping in this manner on a charter free basis until 30 June 1946. The British agreed to make available operating supplies such as fuel, emergency victuals and stores in kind, that were required for SCAP shipping used in repatriation service from SEA areas. After 30 June 1946 the British were obliged to pay charter hire for United States owned ships used in repatriation from their areas.[48]

SACSEA established priorities for clearing areas in the following order: North Borneo, south French Indo-China, outer Netherlands East Indies, Siam, Malaya, Java, Sumatra and the inner Netherlands East Indies, and Burma. A plan for repatriating Formosans and Koreans directly to their home lands was integrated into the program. Similarly, provisions were also made for the movement of sick evacuees by SCAP controlled hospital shipping. Two British hospital ships, the *Gerusalemme* and the *Amapoora*, assisted by returning one shipment each of invalid Japanese.

In July 1946 SCAP set 31 December 1946 as the target date for the completion of the repatriation program. The British, however, contemplated retaining some 90,000 Japanese prisoners of war and surrendered personnel for labor during 1947.

Representatives of SCAP and SACSEA conferred at Tokyo from 11 to 17 June 1946, consummating agreements which covered immediate shipping requirements, disposition of shipping recovered in Southeast Asia, and details of fuel supply and charter hire. In short,

it was agreed that SCAP would supply the necessary ships to repatriate such Japanese as the British would agree to release through August 1946, but would make no commitments of repatriation shipping after that time. The British on their part agreed to fuel all repatriation ships on a round trip basis and to pay charter hire for the use of United States owned ships utilized. Further agreements were reached whereby three Japanese warships would be placed at the disposal of SCAP on their last repatriation trip to Japan, and that Japanese ships other than warships recovered in Southeast Asia would be returned to SACSEA upon completion of the program. These agreements were approved by SCAP and SACSEA. By the middle of August provisions had been made for the return of virtually all repatriates from Southeast Asia areas, except those retained for labor.

General MacArthur did not agree to the postponement of repatriation and made statements to this effect to the U. S. War Department and to SACSEA. The British continued to retain 82,000 Japanese in areas under their control and in addition turned over 13,500 to the Netherlands East Indies (NEI) Government.

In November 1946 SCAP made a final offer to SACSEA to evacuate all Japanese repatriates from Southeast Asia to Japan, and in a separate action endeavored to dispose of the ships in accordance with the June agreement. The British did not accept the offer and, in addition, expressed a desire to retain all Japanese ships and their crews seized in Southeast Asia. The last Japanese repatriates were evacuated from that area in October 1947, except for those retained for war crimes trials.[49]

---

48 On 16 April 1946, the first of 48 Liberties and 4 LST's, in addition to 22 Japanese ships, departed Japan destined for SEA ports. In late May, 40 Liberties, 4 LST's and 15 Japanese ships comprised the second major lift to SEA areas.

49 G-3 GHQ SCAP & FEC, Status of Repatriation Rpt, 31 Oct 47.

In December 1946 the Netherlands Government agreed to return the 13,500 Japanese held under their control. Repatriation from the Netherlands East Indies was completed in May 1947, but for those Japanese who were held as witnesses or defendants for war crimes trials.[50]

Australian Areas

Following Japan's surrender, the respective areas of responsibility of Australian Military Forces (AMF) and SACSEA were not clearly delineated. During autumn 1945 and prior to the actual inauguration of repatriation from AMF areas, successive phasing resulted in the establishment of AMF control of the Australian mainland, New Guinea east of 142° east longitude, and the Admiralty, Bismarck (New Britain, New Ireland), and Solomon Islands. Approximately 138,700 Japanese awaited repatriation in these areas.[51]

By agreement between AMF and SCAP, some Japanese shipping (including warships) capable of making the long voyage, was dispatched in late 1945. Because many evacuees in AMF areas were sick or disabled, a large amount of hospital shipping was provided by SCAP. By the first of March 1946 some 31,900 Japanese had been repatriated.[52]

Early in April authority was obtained to utilize Japanese manned United States Liberty ships to augment the seventeen Japanese ships then engaged in repatriation from AMF areas. The Australian Government agreed to make available operating supplies in kind as required for SCAP shipping when used in such repatriation service. Consequently, eight Liberties were assigned to the clearance of AMF areas.

This number was eventually increased to sixteen. By early April, the Australian mainland had been cleared of Japanese. Only a few were held in connection with war crimes activities.

In April and May the program was nearing completion. Shipping was kept flowing into Rabaul to the limit of the port's ability to process and load repatriates. By 13 June 1946 all areas controlled by AMF had been cleared of Japanese, Korean and Formosan repatriates. Eight hundred Japanese held for war crimes or judicial investigation were returned to Japan in November, leaving a balance of 816 as of 31 December 1946.[53] The area was completely cleared during the following year.

Soviet Controlled Areas

Incomplete reports available indicated that there were approximately 1,617,650 Japanese in areas controlled by the U.S.S.R. at the conclusion of hostilities.[54]

Following instructions from the U. S. Joint Chiefs of Staff, appropriate representations were made in October 1945 to the Soviet Government requesting that it turn over to SCAP ships recovered in areas under Soviet control to be used for repatriation and to support a minimum economy in Japan. No replies to this or other radios of a similar nature were received until 12 April 1946. It was only then that the U.S.S.R. Member of the Allied Council for Japan reported the amount of shipping recovered from the Japanese by the Soviet Government but stated that none was suitable for repatriation purposes.

On a local level, the respective military

---

50   *Ibid*, 20 May 47.
51   *Ibid*, 1 Jul 49.
52   *Ibid*, 6 Mar 46.
53   *Ibid*, 31 Dec 46.
54   *Ibid*, 1 Jul 49.

Japanese repatriate children aboard ship.

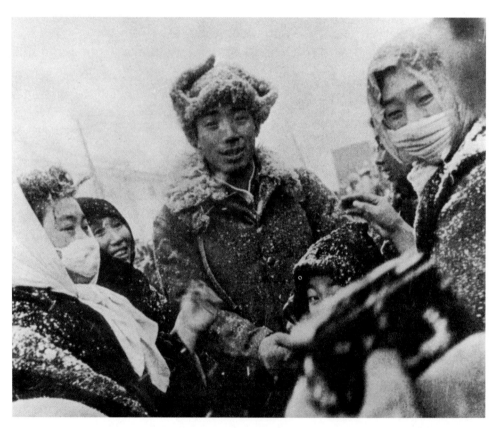

Repatriate from Soviet territory is met by his family.

PLATE NO. 57
Repatriates from Soviet Territory

commanders exercising authority in North and South Korea conferred in January 1946, on the question of repatriating Japanese nationals located in North Korea to Japan via South Korea. The main difficulty involved was the supply of fuel for rail transportation, but repatriation of Japanese from North Korea actually adjusted itself while these and later conferences were in progress. Although there was no legal repatriation traffic across the 38° border in Korea, a total of some 292,800 Japanese filtered through and were repatriated to Japan through South Korea. When negotiations were finally consummated it was found that there were less than 15,000 Japanese to be repatriated from North Korea.[55]

During the period between October 1945 and April 1946, sporadic attempts to effect repatriation of isolated groups from restricted areas under Soviet control were made without success. In April 1946 SCAP forwarded proposals for mutual repatriation between Japan and North Korea to the Soviet authorities. The proposals contained in this document were patterned on the existing agreements made by SCAP with other Allied governments and commands. In May the Soviet Government returned the document suggesting certain changes to the proposed agreements. As a result of this communication, a conference was held in Tokyo the following month. No agreement was reached inasmuch as the Soviet Government requested preferential treatment be given to Koreans in Japan who were to be returned to North Korea, but was not willing to furnish any fuel or other supplies for repatriation ships.

A further conference between representatives of SCAP and the Soviet Government was held in Tokyo in July 1946. SCAP proposed that agreements be reached regarding repatriation of Japanese from northern Korea and the Dairen-Port Arthur area, Manchuria. Since the Soviet representative was not authorized to discuss the return of Japanese prisoners of war and surrendered personnel from those areas, the conference was adjourned. To support SCAP's position, the basic authority contained in the Potsdam Declaration was used, wherein the Allied Powers announced their intention to permit the Japanese military to return to Japan; hence the repatriation of civilians was secondary, being conducted primarily for humanitarian reasons. The entire matter of repatriation from Soviet controlled areas was then presented to the War Department, requesting that arrangements be conducted on a governmental level.[56]

In the latter part of September 1946 Soviet authorities advised SCAP of their willingness to undertake the repatriation of Japanese PW's and civilians from the U.S.S.R. and territories under its control; repatriation could begin the following month. By 3 October 1946 SCAP had forwarded proposals for repatriation of Japanese nationals from the Soviet and Soviet controlled areas. The proposals were similar to those sent to the Soviet authorities in April. In an attempt to overcome points of difference encountered in the June conference, the plan contemplated the use of Japanese coal burning ships. Japanese oil burning ships and United States owned ships were to be used for repatriation only when payment for fuel and charter hire by U.S.S.R. had been arranged on a governmental level.

From 14 October until mid-December 1946, a series of thirteen conferences were held in an attempt to reconcile points of difference: the

---

55 *Ibid*, 31 Dec 46.

56 On 22 August 1946 a radio was received from Washington which contained proposals, essentially the same as those proposed by SCAP at the Tokyo Conference, to be presented to the Soviet Government by the United States. As the situation later developed, this action was not undertaken by the US Government.

Home.

And a new life.

PLATE NO. 58
Return to Home and a New Life

rate of repatriation, the payment of fuel oil for repatriation ships, and the furnishing of emergency supplies and services in the Soviet controlled ports. Impatient to complete the repatriation program, SCAP conceded all the major points and agreed to accept responsibility for the return of all Japanese nationals from Soviet ports up to 360,000 per month. Sole responsibility of the Soviet Government was to deliver them to the evacuation ports. The Soviets finally accepted but established the rate at 50,000 per month.[57] In this same agreement, signed on 19 December 1946, the Soviet Government consented to receive 10,000 Korean repatriates from Japan.[58]

While the over-all agreement was being negotiated, a conference was held at the request of the Soviet authorities on 18 November 1946. They proposed an interim agreement to repatriate 25,000 Japanese from Soviet areas[59] before the end of November; this agreement was to be based on portions of the over-all accord which had been confirmed. SCAP agreed to the proposal at once, but final approval was not received from Moscow until late November 1946.

Under the interim agreement, ships were dispatched to Soviet ports and a total of approximately 28,400 Japanese were repatriated. Of the 10,000 Koreans estimated for return from Japan to North Korea, only 233 accepted repatriation; the remainder forfeited their privilege to be returned.[60]

In the first five months of 1947 the Soviets did repatriate Japanese at a rate of better than 50,000 a month, but thereafter the rate fell below that figure.[61] Consequently, the Representative for the Supreme Commander and Chairman of the Allied Council, Mr. W. J. Sebald, raised the issue at a meeting of the Council on 29 October 1947. He stated that SCAP could and would supply ships to repatriate as many as 160,000 Japanese per month, and within five months SCAP was prepared to return to Japan every Japanese then in Soviet controlled areas.

The Acting Soviet Member replied to Mr. Sebald's statement by saying that he considered the subject of repatriation outside the purview of the Allied Council for Japan. He contended that the failure to repatriate 50,000 monthly since June 1947 should not be commented upon, as the average over the entire period since December 1946 was slightly in excess of the 50,000 rate.[62]

Approximately one month after SCAP's offer to accelerate repatriation, the Soviet Member stated in a letter to SCAP (2 December 1947) that repatriation would be suspended due to climatic and icing conditions from December 1947 until the opening of navigation in April 1948.

SCAP replied to this action of the Soviets on 10 December 1947, by offering icebreakers to clear Soviet ports and stating that SCAP controlled shipping could be dispatched to any other ports where "the difficult icing and climatic conditions would not be encountered."

In contradiction to their first letter, the Soviet authorities' reply to SCAP's offer on

57   See pp. 16–17.

58   The first request for shipping, received shortly after the agreement was signed, was for 86,000 spaces during the month of January. The first ships to make this lift were enroute prior to 31 December 1946.

59   5,000 each from Karafuto, Siberia and Dairen, and 10,000 from North Korea.

60   5,600 from Karafuto, 5,000 from Siberia, 6,100 from Dairen, and 11,700 from North Korea. (G-3 GHQ SCAP & FEC, Rpt on Mass Repatriation in the Western Pac, Apr 47.)

61   G-3 GHQ SCAP, Status of Repatriation Rpt, 17 Sep 48.

62   As of November 1948 this average stood at 38,574 repatriates monthly.

24 December stated that the offer was unacceptable because of difficulties in assembling Japanese at the repatriation ports and the overloaded condition of the Soviet rail transportation system. It was stated that the decision to suspend repatriation would remain unchanged. No reply was made to SCAP's offer to send shipping to other Soviet ports. The letter also stated that the monthly average as of that time approximated the 50,000 quota of the agreement.

In response to previous inquiries, the Soviet Member informed SCAP on 5 April 1948 that Japanese repatriation from Soviet controlled areas would be resumed in May instead of April as had been indicated initially by the Soviets. He stated that due to unfavorable climatic conditions this year and also taking into consideration transportation and technical facilities, the repatriation would be resumed in May of this year.[63]

A SCAP press release of 8 September 1948 stated:

Notwithstanding constant and persistent efforts on the part of SCAP to expedite the repatriation of Japanese from Soviet and Soviet-controlled areas, all efforts to date have been unavailing and without result, a SCAP spokesman said today. This continued SCAP concern over the failure of the Soviet authorities to repatriate Japanese from Soviet-controlled areas on schedule and in accordance with the repatriation agreement of 19 December 1946, was indicated in a sharply worded letter dated 3 September 1948, sent on behalf of SCAP to Lt. Gen. Kusma N. Derevyanko, Soviet Member, Allied Council for Japan.

The letter indicated that not since May 1947, have repatriates released from Soviet and Soviet-controlled areas reached the 50,000 monthly rate, and that August 1948, marks the fifteenth consecutive month that the Soviet repatriation authorities have failed to meet the agreed upon rate. It was further stated in

the letter that "the Supreme Commander for the Allied Powers has complied explicitly with all provisions" of the agreement of 19 December 1946 " and expects the other signatory to said agreement to do likewise."

The SCAP spokesman recalled that the problem of repatriation from Soviet-controlled areas was thoroughly aired and discussed in the 44th meeting of the Allied Council for Japan and that additional reliable information available to the Supreme Commander indicates that conditions approaching slave labor continue to apply to the estimated more than 500,000 Japanese still held by the Soviets. He further referred to the mounting concern of the Supreme Commander over this unprecedented situation and to the circumstance that this near-slave labor is being utilized in Soviet and Soviet-controlled areas, under appalling conditions of servitude, to increase the military potential of Soviet Russia. It is reported that these men are used in munitions plants and airfield construction as well as in the mines.

The spokesman further said that the offer made by SCAP almost a year ago to repatriate Japanese held by the Soviets at the rate of 160,000 per month still stands, but that this offer remains unanswered and ignored by the Soviet Representative in Japan.

The spokesman said that the Soviet attitude on the question of repatriation is in marked contrast with the fulfilment of the relevant provision of the Potsdam Declaration by the Governments of Australia, China, France, the Netherlands, New Zealand, the Philippine Republic, the United Kingdom, and the United States which have offered prompt and full cooperation in the implementation of the repatriation program. Additionally, he stressed that "the Soviet authorities have callously refused to provide SCAP with statistics of any kind relating to Japanese held in Soviet and Soviet-controlled areas, and that to date SCAP is completely without official information concerning the health, living conditions, numbers, names, or whereabouts of a single Japanese held by the Soviet authorities."

---

63 During May, June, and July 1948, approximately 45,000 Japanese were repatriated from Soviet controlled areas each month. In August the number fell to approximately 40,000. (G-3 GHQ SCAP, Status of Repatriation Rpt, 17 Sep 48.)

Confusion at the Railroad Station.

Repatriates form cordon and challenge police.

PLATE NO. 59
Repatriates from Soviet PW Camps. 1949

Since the resumption of repatriation on 1 May 1948—after complete cessation of the program since early in December 1947, the Soviet authorities have again failed month after month to meet the agreed upon monthly rate of 50,000 repatriates. The latest SCAP letter told the Soviet Member that " at the beginning of the fourth year of the occupation of Japan, it is hoped that an increased effort on the part of the Government of the USSR to meet the agreed repatriation rate may bring the Japanese repatriation program to a conclusion without further delay.

At the end of the year an estimated 408,743 Japanese remained in Soviet controlled territory.[64] A few repatriates arrived from Siberia in the early part of 1949 bringing the estimated total still to be repatriated to 408,729 as of April 1949.

Information of vital importance to the Japanese regarding death, disappearance or illness of Japanese prisoners of war was again requested of the Soviet Government by Mr. Sebald, chief of SCAP's Diplomatic Section, in April. His letter stated: " . . . there has at no time been any report whatsoever from Soviet authorities concerning Japanese prisoners of war held in the Soviet Union nor is it apparent from information available to the Supreme Commander that any effort is being made by Soviet Authorities to furnish such information. . . ." The letter went on to state that " . . . more than a dozen Japanese-operated ships under SCAP control are standing by awaiting word from Russia to renew the repatriation of war prisoners which was halted during the winter. More than 400,000 Japa-

nese are still held in Siberia or territory under Russian control, almost four years after the war's end."[65]

A startling Tass press release in Moscow on 20 May announced that only 95,000 former Japanese troops remained to be repatriated. This figure was at complete variance with the official compilations by the Demobilization Bureau of the Japanese Government and GHQ G-2 and G-3 Demobilization Repatriation Record Sections. Their records listed a total of 469,041 personnel still to be repatriated from Soviet controlled areas.

Repeated efforts by SCAP to obtain precise information from Soviet authorities on general prisoner of war totals or on deaths of Japanese internees were fruitless. Soviet repatriation authorities not only refused to allow repatriates to carry ashes of their dead back to their homeland, an old Japanese tradition, but did not even permit the transmittal of rosters of deceased internees. Japanese authorities were required to complete death lists through exhaustive and time-consuming interviews of returnees. Under this system prisoners were not officially listed as dead until the exact date, place, and cause of death were substantiated by at least two witnesses. It was believed that failure of the Soviets to report deaths among prisoners held for over three years in Siberian camps could possibly account for the wide differences between repatriation figures released by the U.S.S.R. and the Japanese Government.[66]

---

64   G-3 GHQ SCAP & FEC, Status of Repatriation Rpt, 31 Dec 48.

65   Tokyo, *Pacific Stars & Stripes*, April 26, 1949.

66   According to the Japanese Government, the surrender of the Japanese Army in 1945 placed under Soviet responsibility 2,723,492 Japanese (civilian and military) approximately 700,000 of whom were transported from Manchuria and Korea into Soviet territory for internment. As of May 1949, the repatriation account showed 469,041 military and civilians still to be repatriated and chargeable to the Soviet prisoner of war authorities. These Soviet authorities were consequently accountable for 374,041 persons after crediting them with 95,000 to be repatriated by the end of 1949 by their own announcement. The Japanese Government estimated 153,509 possibly alive, based on the receipt of postal

Soviet Indoctrination of PW's [67]

In 1946 when repatriation to Japan was opened for the first time the Soviets chose the weak, infirm and aged for return. The reason for this choice was obvious: they could not work and would contribute nothing to the internal economy of Russia. It was hardly worth-while to indoctrinate them; the weak and infirm would probably die under hardships still ahead, while the aged possessed rigid thought patterns less easily subverted. Almost without exception these first returnees were extremely bitter toward their captors.

The next step taken by the Soviets was designed to sift and classify prisoner groups. Older, high-ranking officers were sent to segregated camps; medium rank officers, too, were separated. The remainder (company grade officers and enlisted men) consisted mainly of younger, politically inexperienced, naive men, whose minds had not hardened into thought patterns and could not adjudge the proffered ideology in the light of firmly rooted beliefs and opinions.

Under the impact of a cleverly calculated barrage of propaganda, buttressed by the Soviet directed propaganda newspaper, *Nippon Shimbun*,[68] a formalized indoctrination program was launched. It included a closely interwoven network of schools, lectures, study groups, cultural societies, and Communist cells; former Communists and sympathizers, and other dissident elements were trained to lead in embracing and propagating communism's disruptive principles. With this firm core of protagonists, the Soviets found it relatively easy to expand their program so as to enlist at least half-hearted support of great numbers of individuals who originally had been neither pro- nor anti-Communist.

The remainder, who opposed the Communist ideology, usually came to heel, ostensibly at least, when they realized that the rapidity of their repatriation would depend greatly on how thoroughly they convinced their more aggressive comrades and their Soviet keepers that they subscribed to the Communist doctrines.

Consequently, except for the diehards who refused to weaken, Japanese PW's accepted the propaganda to a greater or lesser extent. As time went on, and especially during the latter part of 1947, the prisoners saw conditions around them steadily improve. Food became more abundant and more palatable. Living quarters, bathing, recreational, and medical facilities were improved, and many internees

---

66 (contd.) cards by relatives in 1947 and 1948; this was by no means conclusive, and exceeded, under any criterion, the official Soviet admission:

	Soviet Areas	Manchuria	Total	
Unrepatriated	408.729	60,312	469,041	
Soviet admission	95,000		95,000	
Verified dead	39,937	17,418		57,355
Verified alive (Mil)	129,871			129,871
Verified alive (Civ)	23,638			23,638
Status unknown	215,283	42,498		258,177
Total accountable	313,729	60,312	374,041	469,041

67 (1) GHQ FEC MIS GS, CIS Periodical Sum, 15 Feb and 15 Mar 49 (S); (2) GHQ FEC MIS GS, Plans and Est Br & CIS Sp Int, Internal Factors as Security Problems for the Occupation Forces (Rev), 1 Jan 49 (S).

68 日本新聞 (Nippon Shimbun) was published in Khabarovsk, Siberia, under the direction of political and propaganda specialists of the USSR Intelligence Section. It sparked the class hatreds between officers and enlisted men; it was the basic textbook in all phases of the political re-education of prisoners; it supported all changes ordered by Moscow. The influence of the Nippon Shimbun was tremendous as it was virtually the only source of " news " to the vast majority of internees.

Family struggles to keep repatriate from joining Communist demonstration.

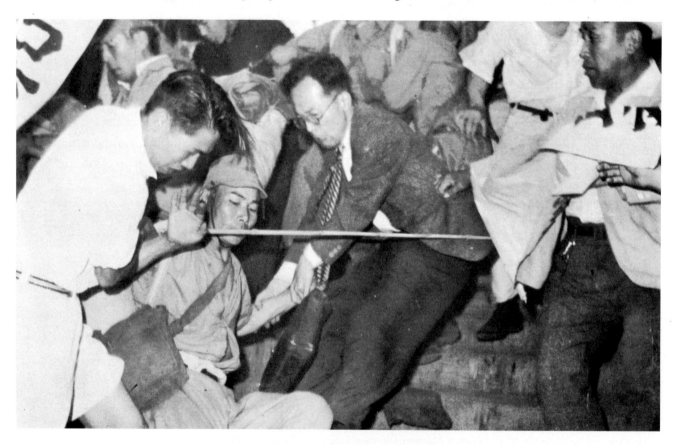

Communist-led disorders at railroad station.

PLATE NO. 60
Repatriates from Soviet PW Camps, 1949

began to work an eight-hour day for which they were paid a fairly reasonable wage, expendable for small luxuries. At the same time, Soviet citizens, who heretofore had wallowed publicly in misery comparable to that suffered by the internees, also began edging upward in their planes of living. Thus the prisoners had visual evidence that the Soviet system was producing results which appeared favorable.

The repatriates of 1947 were more thoroughly subverted than those of 1946. Those who returned in the latter part of 1948 were indoctrinated to a much higher degree and appeared to be much better organized. The first instance of mass refusal of repatriates to cooperate with the Occupation authorities occurred when the *Eiho Maru* docked at Maizuru on 20 November 1948. Immediately after the ship anchored, an unusual loud burst of singing of Communist songs and dancing startled the U. S. officers who had boarded earlier. Although repatriate leaders stopped the demonstration when so ordered, many defamatory remarks were heard, obviously meant for Occupation personnel and the troop commander.

Shortly afterward, when processing cards were distributed to all repatriates, they refused to fill them out until their leaders authorized it. Several communistic speeches were made during processing, and statements such as " being in enemy territory " and " don't weaken now " were heard. After leaving the repatriation center, Communist agitators again took charge and led the group in mass singing of communistic songs, which continued until the train pulled out of Maizuru station. This shipload of repatriates was different from other groups only in that they were better organized. Indoctrination in the U.S.S.R. had built up an actually hostile feeling in repatriates against the United States and the Japanese Government.[69]

Several days prior to the arrival of this shipload of repatriates there was a sizeable altercation among members of an earlier arrived group in which Communists and non-Communists came to blows. This fight stopped as soon as Occupation forces appeared. Such fights have occurred in the past; they became more frequent and the number involved appeared to be on the increase.[70] (Plate No. 61)

[69] GHQ SCAP MIS GS, Spot Int Rpt, 3 Dec 48, sub: First Instance of Non-cooperation of Japanese Repatriates with Occupation Authorities. In MIS 014. 33—1948.

[70] When repatriation from Soviet controlled areas was resumed in June 1949, these disturbances continued. One of the most serious occurred on 4 July 1949 when a large group of members of the Communist Party and the League of Koreans Residing in Japan staged a demonstration at the Kyoto Railway Station. When the first trainload of repatriates debarked, the Communists tried to persuade them to join the demonstration. When police interfered, the Communists resorted to violence. Two of the Communist leaders were arrested. Repatriates who witnessed the arrests refused to board the train unless the two Communists were released. Officials finally persuaded them to board, but they got off again, singing the " Internationale ", when asked by the Communists to remain and stage a joint struggle for the release of the two Communist leaders.

The second and third trains arrived several hours later and repatriates aboard were persuaded to join the struggle in front of the Kyoto station, making a total of approximately 1800 repatriates and 1000 Communists in the demonstration. The majority of the repatriates did not dare enter the special train in fear of their leaders. However, when eighty-seven who were returning to the Osaka district marched to the platform to board, members of the Communist Party attempted to stop them. Again, when the police interfered, violence ensued.

The Kyoto station authorities announced that two special trains would depart at approximately 1030. The repatriates refused to board. Shortly after midnight, however, the repatriates began to voluntarily move to the platform; by 0300 all of them were aboard and the trains had departed. The people on the platform had already returned to their homes by the time the repatriates boarded.

It was observed that the repatriates greatly feared their leaders and did not resort to " individual action ". It was further noticed that they seemed to be shrinking from the Communist Party line. Some repatriates told the police that " succeeding units are outwardly the same as we. The police must go into action with determination. It is only that all of us are fearful of the leader." (CIC Sum of Info, 15 Jul 49, sub: Repatriate Incident at Kyoto Sta.)

Nippon Times

Published by
The Nippon Times, Ltd.
KIYOSHI TOGASAKI, President

TOKYO OFFICE:
1, Ichome Uchisaiwai-cho, Chiyoda-ku Central P.O. Box 144, 352, 356 Telephone: Ginza (57) 303, 463, 5857, 5858, 5859, 7003.
Telegraphic Address: "Times Tokyo-yubin".

OSAKA: Dojima Bldg. Tel.: Horikawa (35) 177.

SUBSCRIPTION RATE:
¥2.945 per copy ¥0.055 charges incidental to sales tax. Thursday issue with supplement ¥4.905 ¥0.098 charges incidental to sales tax One month ¥89.00. ¥165 charges incidental to sales tax Obtainable directly from all newspaper agents in Japan. By mail ¥104.5 per month, ¥1.79 charges incidental to sales tax. For foreign countries postage ¥150.00 per month extra

TOKYO, FRIDAY, AUG. 5, 1949

Men or Beasts?

Are these men or beasts the Soviets are sending back to Japan from their prison camps? It is no wonder that an anguished mother welcoming her long-absent son should cry out, "What have they done to my son?" That cry has been echoed and re-echoed many times since the begining of this year's repatriation program.

These questions are asked because the repatriates have shown time and again that they apparently lack the basic sentiments and feelings which differentiate human from beasts. For almost a week with their native land in sight and with loved ones waiting, a shipload of repatriates have sullenly refused to land. Others have snarled and snaped at the warm words of welcome and the kind hands extended in heartfelt sympathy. Still others have stonily brushed aside their families, who have been impatiently waiting these many years to have them back under their family roof, to stay with the pack. Moving as animal herds, they move and act at the direction of the pack leaders whatever the action or course may be.

Where is their individuality? Where is their feeling for family and home? Where is their sentiment for their native land? Where is their respect for law and order?

Perhaps the repatriates themselves should not be judged too severely for they are the products of Communist training. They are the ones so well indoctrinated that the Soviets allowed their return. They are Communists.

It is small wonder that the families of the repatriates should ask, "What have they done . . . ?" The Japanese know now, if they did not know before, what communism does to men. What sensible, freedom-loving people would take in an ideology which robs men of their individuality and their sensibility as human beings?

Excerpts from Japanese newspapers of the same period verify the opinion expressed in the above editorial:

東京日日新聞（七月三日）‥‥引揚達者もほとんど全員が都や知友の出迎えを黙殺赤旗組の熱狂的な歓迎にインターナショナルの歌をうたい、赤旗を打ち振つてこの歓迎にこたえるなど、これまでの引揚列車に見られぬ異風景を展開した。

朝日新聞（七月六日）‥‥ホームにあふれる家族たちの拍手と隣接ホームにならんだ共産党員のインターナショナルに迎えられて四十三名が下車、家族に囲まれて泣き出すもの、すがりつく家族に"同志が行く、離せ"と叫んでふり拂おりとするもの——

時事新報（七月廿一日）マイズル発——‥‥両船とも乗つている引揚者はこれまでにない拒否的な態度、沈黙戦術に出て関係方面を当惑させた。故國の山河になんの感動もないのだろうか、聞けば大郁丸引揚者 千名はナホトカ出港以来、完全沈黙を守り復員カードなどの復員業務を拒否し——

讀賣新聞（八月三日）マイズル発——‥‥入港後もこの要求貫徹までは下船しないと引揚業務を拒否しこのため入院患者は上陸完了まで約八時間入院不能に陥り重症患者は闘病のうちに"上陸させてくれ"と呼び続けるという状態となつた。一看護婦の話『重症患者達は病室で"早く下船させてくれ"と悲痛な声で叫び船医や看護婦が容体を見ようとして近づくと入口や重症患者の側に付添うリーダー格の引揚者が往診を拒否するため満足な手当もできない』

Tokyo Nichi Nichi Shimbun, 3 Jul—...Most of the repatriates completely ignored the salutes of the Tokyo Governor and metropolitan officials. Instead they sang the "Internationale" and waved red flags in answer to the enthusiastic receptions by red-flag welcomers. This was an aspect unlike any observed repatriate trains in the past....

Asahi Shimbun, 6 Jul—...Forty-three repatriates alighted from the train amidst a burst of cheers by waiting families and the singing of the "Internationale" by Communists. Some, surrounded by family members, burst into tears, while others tried to tear themselves away from their families, crying, "Let me go with my comrades."...

Jiji Shimpo, 21 Jul (Maizuru Dispatch)—...The repatriates on board these two ships displayed the greatest defiance and silence yet seen, perplexing the authorities concerned....they appeared emotionless on viewing their native country. It is said that the 2,000 repatriates on board the Daiiku Maru maintained a strict silence ever since the ship left Nahodka and that they refused to cooperate in the execution of repatriation business. .

Yomiuri Shimbun, 3 Aug (Maizuru Dispatch)—...The repatriates refused to fill out repatriation papers and as a result stretcher cases had to wait eight hours before they could be landed to be hospitalized....When doctors or nurses tried to approach the patients to give them treatment, the leaders of the repatriates and attendants of the patients turned them back....

PLATE NO. 61

Japanese Press Expresses Opinion on Soviet Indoctrination of Repatriates, 1949

Communist indoctrination and propagandizing of Japanese prisoners progressed with steadily increasing success, especially after autumn of 1947. To a considerably greater extent than had been observed earlier, a number of later repatriates in the 20–30 year age group exhibited a belligerent attachment to Communist ideology which often amounted to fanatical zeal. Many declared their determination to become active adherents of the Japan Communist Party; others showed undisguised hostility to Japan's social and governmental system and violent antagonism to the United States and its occupation policies. These zealots had a firm conviction that capitalism must disappear, not as the result of a gradual evolutionary process, but by the violent efforts of the "people", who must overthrow it and usher in the "ideal" Communist social order.

It is important to note that the degree of the U.S.S.R.'s success in indoctrinating prisoners of war in communism was in direct proportion to the length of time prisoners had been kept in the U. S. S. R.

Summary: 1945–1948

In the relatively short period from 1 October 1945 to 31 December 1946, mass repatriation in the Pacific as a major operation was completed. A total of approximately 5,103,300 Japanese were returned to their homeland. The bulk of Japanese nationals remaining to be repatriated, estimated at 1,316,000, were under the control of the U.S.S.R. A smaller group of about 80,940 were retained for labor by the United Kingdom in Southeast Asia but were finally repatriated by October 1947, while the Netherlands East Indies Government held 13,500 until May 1947. The Chinese Government kept in China, Formosa, and Manchuria, a total of 70,000, the majority of whom were technicians and their dependents who had elected to remain. In all areas a few individuals were detained as war criminals or as witnesses for the trial of war criminals.[71]

A total of approximately 1,152,650 Koreans, Chinese, Chinese-Formosans, Ryukyuans and natives of POA were returned to their respective homelands from Japan in repatriation shipping.[72] All who desired to be moved under the repatriation program were evacuated. The few remaining were those who had forfeited their privilege to repatriation; Koreans destined for Korea north of 38° north latitude, and some few who could not move due to circumstances beyond their control.

Koreans, Chinese, Chinese-Formosans, and Ryukyuans were found in every area. Rather than transport these individuals to their respective homelands through Japan, it was more expeditious to repatriate large groups directly. About 187,650 were repatriated from areas in the Western Pacific directly to their former homes.[73]

At the peak of the repatriation program 188 Japanese ships with a carrying capacity of 200,000, and 191 United States owned ships with a carrying capacity of 334,000, were available for repatriation. These ships, however, could not be operated at all times.

During the period of mass repatriation, principal reception centers in Japan were in operation at Hakata, Hakodate, Kagoshima, Kure area, Maizuru, Nagoya, Sasebo, Senzaki, Tanabe, and Uraga. (Plate No. 62) At the end of 1948 reception centers were still in operation at Hakodate, Maizuru, and Sasebo.

71 (1) G-3 GHQ SCAP & FEC, Status of Repatriation Rpt, 6 Jan 47; (2) G-3 GHQ SCAP, Rpt on Mass Repatriation in the Western Pac, Apr 47.

72 G-3 GHQ SCAP & FEC, Status of Repatriation Rpt, 6 Jan 47.

73 Ibid.

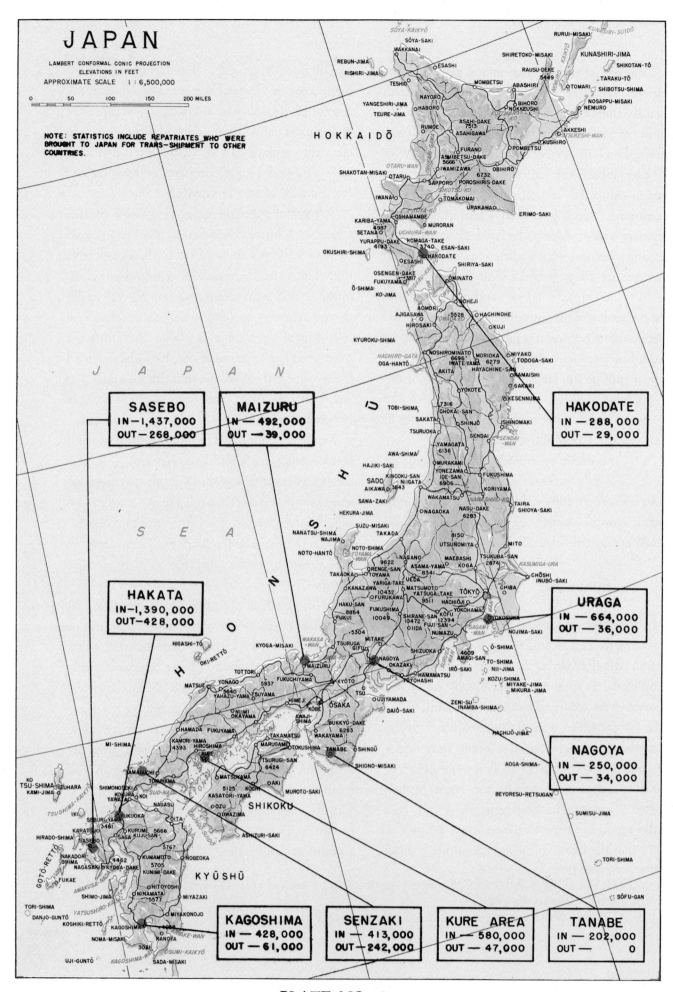

PLATE NO. 62
Principal Reception Centers and Repatriates Processed:
30 September 1945 to 31 December 1948

All incoming and outgoing repatriates were processed through these centers, and their efficient operation was a vital factor in the successful accomplishment of the program. At one time when cholera broke out among over 80,000 repatriates from South China at the reception center of Uraga, they were held in quarantine aboard ships in the harbor while infected individuals were examined and treated. At the peak of the program in May 1946, the centers arranged rail transportation for 550,000 repatriates returned from China during a three week period.[74]

The mass repatriation effected in the Western Pacific was a waterborne migration in scope without parallel in history. The smoothness of an operation transporting over six and one-half million orientals from areas as far south as Melbourne, as far east as Hawaii, and as far west as Burma could only have been the result of a high degree of cooperation among responsible authorities. Careful staff planning and brilliant execution were reflected in the vast numbers moved, and the attendant negligible loss of life was caused by accident or disease and not by shipwrecks. This rapid and successful accomplishment was a major factor in raising the morale of the Korean and Japanese peoples and contributed materially to the success attained by the Occupation forces. The only exception to this outstanding record of one of the major missions of the Occupation was the uncompleted repatriation from the Soviet areas.[75]

---

74   G-3 GHQ SCAP, Rpt on Mass Repatriation in Western Pacific, Apr 47.
75   As of May 1949.

CHAPTER VII

THE EIGHTH ARMY MILITARY GOVERNMENT SYSTEM

Concept of Military Government

The present-day connotation of "military government", developed following the close of World War II, is an outgrowth of control measures under the Potsdam Declaration initiated by the Occupation forces of Germany and Japan. The Occupation of Japan differed widely in its manner of operating from that of Germany.[1]

In Germany, with the collapse of the Nazi regime, all government agencies disintegrated, or had to be purged, leaving the four occupying powers no alternative but to create a new government system for the whole country. The Occupation of Japan presented a different picture. The abrupt termination of hostilities, permitting an unopposed landing in Japan, was not designed to disrupt an integrated, responsible government and it continued to function almost intact.

A decision of the Joint Chiefs of Staff, implemented by appropriate SCAP action, to utilize the Japanese governmental agencies for the execution of Allied policies made the task of Occupation in Japan much easier than in Europe. By preserving the Emperor system, the Allies continued an acknowledged head of the Japanese people, whose traditional influence permitted immediate governmental control. Although stripped of his former power, the Emperor still commanded the respect of the Japanese masses who obeyed implicitly his order to cooperate with the Occupation forces.[2] These factors determined the method under which Military Government was to operate in Japan.[3]

Since the Japanese civil government was capable of operating, Occupation authorities were relieved from directly administering a "conquered" country; instead, they were charged with seeing that the Japanese Government complied with SCAP's di-

---

1 Unless otherwise noted, information contained in this chapter is based on original manuscript prepared by the 10th Information and Historical Service, HQ Eighth US Army, Eighth Army Military Government System in Japan, 1945–48 (R).

2 This factor was carefully evaluated by G-2 in the surrender negotiations in Manila, when the personal treatment of the Japanese emissaries, civil and military, and the phraseology of documents were handled with extraordinary attention to psychological effect against a background of Japanese cultural traditions.

3 Although Military Government had been planned and organized prior to the end of the war, it was not in effective operation during 1945 and the best part of 1946. Only one-third of GHQ was in Tokyo during the critical early phases of the Occupation (September 1945—March 1946). Troops and staffs were concerned with establishing their garrisons and military areas. Neither the Civil Sections, SCAP, nor their executive offshoots, were in a position to exercise "military government"; policies and detailed instructions were in continuous process of realistic formulation. The principal priority objective during this period was the disarmament and demobilization of the armed forces of Imperial Japan. Plans and policies for this delicate and risky undertaking were made by GHQ, Tokyo, in a coordinated effort that involved the General Staff sections primarily; the demobilization ports and camps were run by the Japanese.

rectives.[4] Military Government was also to advise Japanese officials on matters in which they had no previous experience under a totalitarian regime. In effect, there was no " military government " in Japan in the literal sense of the word. It was simply a SCAP superstructure over already existing government machinery, designed to observe and assist the Japanese along the new democratic channels of administration.

General MacArthur exercised governmental authority through instructions issued directly to the Japanese Government by the Central Liaison Committee.[5] The Central Liaison Committee routed these instructions to the proper Japanese ministry which, through Japanese governmental channels, notified prefectural governors of the action required by SCAP. Neither the Occupation authorities, civil and military, nor any subordinate agency ever displaced any element of the Japanese Government. The operational directives which were used to implement the SCAP policies were designed to carry out the ultimate Allied objectives, as stated in the United States Initial Post Surrender Policy for Japan:[6]

The ultimate objectives of the United States in regard to Japan to which policies in the initial period must conform are to insure that Japan will not again become a menace to the United States or to the peace and security of the world, and to bring about the eventual establishment of a peaceful and responsible government which will respect the rights of other states and will support the objectives of the United States as reflected in the ideals and principles of the charter of the United Nations. The United States desires that this government should conform as closely as may be to principles of democratic self government but it is not the responsibility of the Allied Powers to impose upon Japan any form of government not supported by the freely expressed will of the people.

Military Government, while supervising the economic, political, social, and cultural structure of Japan, was to intervene as little as possible in Japanese governmental matters. The governmental reins remained in the hands of Japanese officials, and intervention was limited to cases of inadvertent or deliberate abuse of this privilege. The Japanese were constantly being prompted to take the initiative in bringing about prescribed reforms.

Military Government operated on two levels: the policy and plans level, a General Headquarters function, and the operating level, in the Sixth and Eighth U. S. Armies. General MacArthur established seven staff sections,[7] which were primarily concerned with the non-military, civil affairs, and governmental aspects of the Occupation, for planning and policy direction.

On the operational level. the commanding generals of the Sixth[8] and Eighth Armies were

---

4 The Civil Sections, SCAP, particularly the Natural Resources Section and the Economic and Scientific Section became the great policy-making agencies of the Occupation, employing specialists in every field from the United States to set into motion great reform movements for every major subdivision of the Japanese Government and the economy of Japan.

5 All contacts between SCAP sections and Japanese governmental organs were made through the Central Liaison Committee composed of Japanese officials appointed by the Prime Minister, and American officers, assigned by GHQ, SCAP. This Committee maintained a liaison group in GHQ, under operational control of G-2.

6 GHQ USAFPAC PRO Release No. 227, 23 Sep 45, sub: US Initial Post Surr Policy for Japan.

7 They were: Government Section (GS); Economic and Scientific Section (ESS); Natural Resources Section (NRS); Public Health and Welfare Section (PH&W); Civil Intelligence Section (CIS), including Public Safety Division (PSD) which supervised the Japanese Police, Fire Department, Maritime and Customs Police Services; Legal Section (LS); and Civil Information and Education Section (CI&E).

8 For the first four months of Occupation Sixth Army was in control of the southern half of Honshu and the islands of Kyushu and Shikoku, with headquarters in Kyoto.

The Emperor, renouncing a tradition of divinity, steps from behind the bamboo screen to meet the people.

The people, free for the first time to express convictions, meet to protest against an unpopular government policy.

PLATE NO. 63
Japan's Emperor and the New Democracy

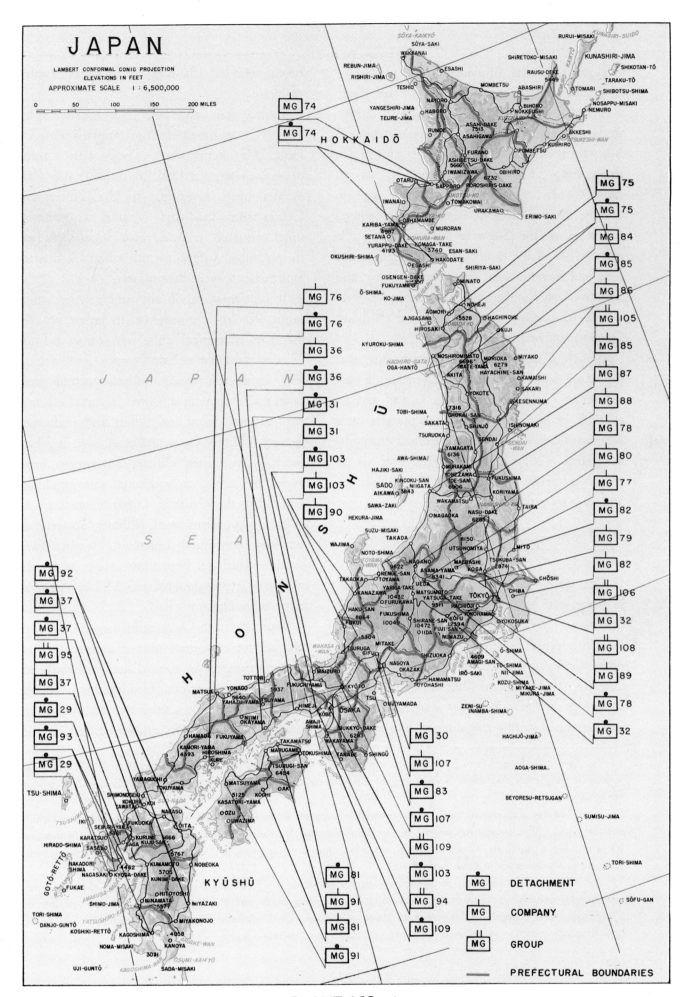

PLATE NO. 64
Disposition of Military Government Units, January 1946

charged with the implementation of SCAP directives. After inactivation of the Sixth Army in January 1946, the Eighth Army, under General Eichelberger, assumed responsibility for the organization, activities, and proper functioning of Military Government in all Japan.[9] His mission on this level was to oversee the Japanese in executing the general directives of the Supreme Commander. To accomplish this, local operational directives designed to implement the policies, plans, and directives of the Supreme Commander were issued to tactical units as well as Military Government teams.

Eighth Army Military Government was organized with three principal agencies: a staff section at Army Headquarters, a staff section at each of the two corps headquarters, and Military Government units stationed throughout Japan. Eighth Army served both as an enforcing agency, implementing SCAP policies, and as a reporting agency.

Formative Period

The development of Military Government in Japan can be traced in certain background activities. While Eighth Army was still in the Philippines, Military Government was set up as Civil Affairs Section under G-1.[10] Anticipating the problems that could arise with an abrupt termination of the war, this section was expanded during the summer of 1945 and began detailed planning for eventual control of Japan.

Immediately after the surrender, GHQ, AFPAC, authorized the organization of four MG companies. These were formed of specialists provided by GHQ and Civil Affairs units operating in the Philippines. Officer specialists and Military Government units activated in the United States were held in readiness, subject to call when Occupation requirements were determined.

In anticipation of any emergencies which might develop upon arrival in Japan, selected members of tactical units were organized into Military Government staff sections at divisional and regimental levels. These sections conducted necessary liaison with Japanese officials, requisitioned labor and billets and performed general Military Government duties. In October 1945, as trained Military Government units began to arrive, tactical units were gradually relieved of their Military Government responsibilities. On Army level, Military Government activities continued under the Civil Affairs Section until 21 September 1945, when the section was redesignated the Military Government Subsection of G-1.[11]

Soon after the Occupation began, duties of this section assumed greater proportions; it was reorganized as the Military Government Special Staff Section, Headquarters, Eighth Army. The newly established section was to make appropriate recommendations to the

---

9 Gen Eichelberger, who brilliantly led Eighth Army during three years of active service in the Pacific and served with equal distinction the Allied cause during the first three years of Occupation, returned to the ZI on 4 August 1948 for retirement.

10 The initial concept of "military government" was apparently heavily influenced by its known application in Italy and Germany. This concept was inapplicable in the Philippines, a sovereign, associated country, and basically unsound for Japan since a legitimate, amenable government was in operative existence, and it was decided a priori to maintain the Japanese Government and operate through it.

11 This must be considered an ineffective change of phraseology. Psychologically, the term "military government" was bound to undercut the position of Japanese functionaries, who had to carry a substantial load. Four years later, on 1 July 1949, SCAP changed the designation of Military Government to Civil Affairs Section; this change was accompanied by a thorough cut in personnel strengths which eliminated the prefectural teams.

commanding general concerning economic, political, and sociological matters pertaining to the civil population; prepare and disseminate local orders and directives necessary to carry out SCAP orders; coordinate and control the procurement of supplies, labor and other facilities from the Japanese Government; and maintain liaison on matters of Military Government with the other general and special staff sections, the Navy, and separate commands of the United States and the Allied Powers stationed in the Eighth Army area.[12]

Military Government units had been formed into groups and subordinate companies.[13] Both contained specialists in engineering, legal matters, medicine, public safety, natural resources, industry, supply, translator service, labor supervision and control, salvage operations, and transportation.

By mid-November 1945 seven groups and eighteen companies had been assigned to the Eighth Army. Three groups and two companies were placed directly under the Army; the others were attached to the corps under Eighth Army and the U. S. Army Service Command-C (USASCOM-C),[14] which operated at corps level in the Kanagawa Prefecture. A special detachment was set up to administer Military Government in Tokyo.

Eighth Army planned to have Military Government administration uniform throughout Japan. Military Government groups and companies were slated for use as integral teams and were not to be assigned other duties. The scheme had groups attached to corps for the purpose of administering the functions of Military Government on a geographical, regional level and companies attached to subordinate units within the corps to perform identical duties in one or more prefectures.[15]

After all Occupation duties were assumed by Eighth Army on 1 January 1946, the Military Government units throughout Japan were reorganized to make up six groups, twenty-four companies, and twenty-eight detachments.[16] (Plate No. 64)

The first six months of 1946 was a period of exceptionally heavy readjustment and tactical redeployment of troops. Redeployment in the number of tactical units brought about a series of administrative changes and consolidations among Military Government units; however, no major policy changes were involved. In the BCOF zone and in the Tokyo and Kanagawa Prefectures, the work went on directly under the Eighth Army staff section; elsewhere the activities continued under Military Government groups or special staff sections under the corps.

Since there were not enough Military Government units for each of the prefectures, it became necessary to break up some of the organizations into detachments. As the administrative procedures became more complex and it appeared that qualified specialists were not being employed to the best advantage, a new type unit known as a "team" replaced

---

12 HQ Eighth US Army, 10th Info and Hist Sv, Eighth Army MG System in Japan, 1945–48 (R), p. 4.

13 The former consisted of 13 officers, 1 warrant officer, and 26 enlisted men, the latter of 12 officers and 6 enlisted men.

14 See Ch. II.

15 At the end of the war, Japan was administratively divided into nine regions and further sub-divided into 42 prefectures, one territorial administration (for Hokkaido), and three city or municipal prefectures. Several purely administrative changes subsequently took place, and by 1948 all these major subdivisions were considered as prefectures. For purposes of MG administration, two of the nine regions (Tokai and Hokuriku) were combined, and Hokkaido was considered as a district. (One unit combined functions of both district headquarters and prefectural team.)

16 HQ Eighth US Army, 10th Info and Hist Sv, Eighth Army MG System in Japan, 1945–48 (R), p. 5.

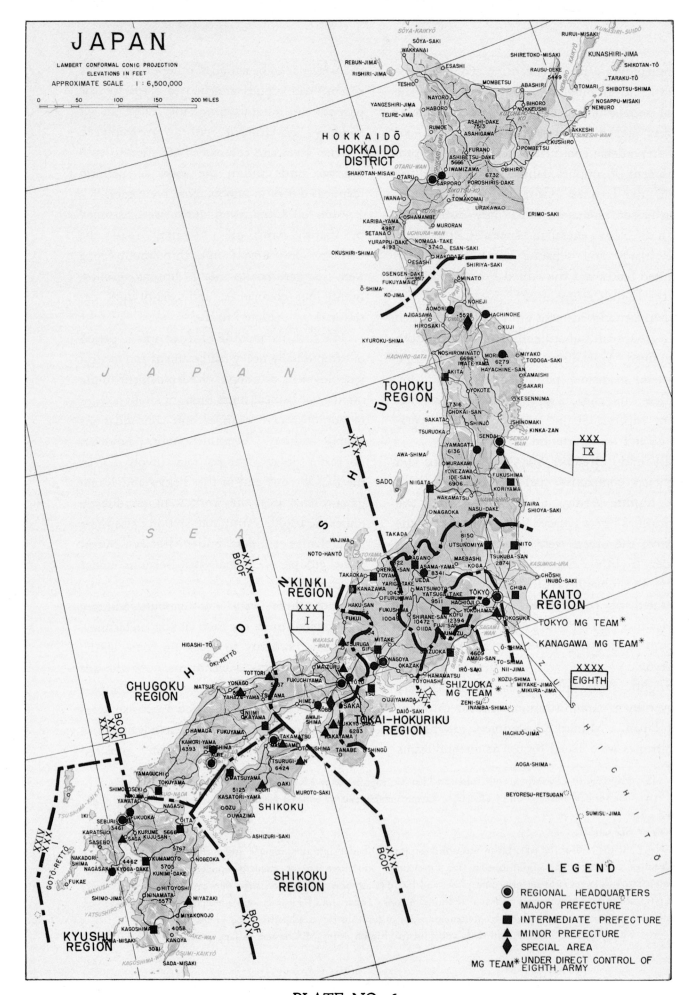

PLATE NO. 65

Organization of Military Government in Japan, July 1948

the detachment. The new team paralleled Japanese governmental organization, so that Military Government groups, companies, and detachments transformed into teams were identified with the name of the prefecture to which they were assigned.[17] For the purpose of administration and control, prefectural teams were grouped under seven regional Military Government teams. (Plate No. 65) Economy in the use of critical personnel was achieved by creating three types of prefectural teams— major, intermediate, minor—and two special teams, each in accordance with the relative importance of the area to which assigned and the nature of the requirements.[18]

Evolution of Organization: 1946-1948

Military Government organization, as evolved in Japan, (Plate No. 66) consisted of a staff section at Eighth Army Headquarters, two corps headquarters, I and IX Corps, each of which had a Military Government staff section, and fifty-three Military Government teams—one team for each of the forty-six prefectures and one for each of the seven administrative and geographical regions. Hokkaido was considered a " district " in which one unit combined the functions of both the district headquarters and the prefectural team. With the exception of the Tokyo, Kanagawa, and Shizuoka prefectural teams, the regional and prefectural teams within each corps area were attached to the corps and operated under the direct supervision of the corps commander.[19] The three excepted teams and all regional and prefectural teams in the BCOF area operated under the direct supervision of the Eighth Army Commander. Although no Military Government responsibilities were delegated to the BCOF Commander, a number of Australian officers and enlisted men did serve in each of the eleven MG teams in the BCOF zone of occupation.[20]

The duties of the Military Government staff sections consisted mainly of administration, investigation, and the preparation of numerous reports. The sections were also charged with inspections of field teams, training of subordinate units, and supervision of the adminis-

17 This was an essential point. The prefecture is an executive and functional unit in the Japanese Government as well as an administrative or liaison unit. It was placed under the general purview of Military Government, hence affiliation with the prefecture was essential. As a matter of fact, the MG teams or units progressively conformed to and became accustomed to working in the provincial boundaries of the prefecture.

18 With the change of organization and the attending economy of personnel, the field strength dropped from 2,800 to 2,288. With the Army undergoing its readjustment program, it had become increasingly difficult to secure military personnel with which to fill positions in the numerous specialized fields, and early in the year Eighth Army had been authorized to employ civil service personnel in a wide variety of positions. (HQ Eighth US Army, 10th Info and Hist Sv, Eighth Army MG System in Japan, 1945-48 [R], p. 6.) Some civilians, trained and experienced in such specialized fields as economics, sociology, and government, were procured. Despite all efforts to adjust the MG organization to meet the needs of the Occupation with available personnel, shortages continued. In August 1948, there were 396 civilians against an authorized 529, and the military strength had dropped to 1,772 against an authorized strength of 1,911. (HQ Eighth US Army, 10th Info and Hist Sv, Eighth Army MG System in Japan, 1945-48 [R], p. 7.)

19 In each corps, one of the regional teams served as the corps headquarters, MG staff section.

20 After June 1947, one officer and two enlisted men were assigned to each MG team operating in the BCOF area: 76th MG Co (Hiroshima, Yamaguchi and Shimane Prefectures); 91st MG Co (Kagawa and Ehime Prefectures), 81st MG Co (Kochi and Tokushima Prefectures), 36th MG Co (Okayama and Tottori Prefectures). These personnel were under the supervision of the team commander and assigned to tasks in the same manner as US Army personnel. The operation of these groups as part of the US teams was most successful.

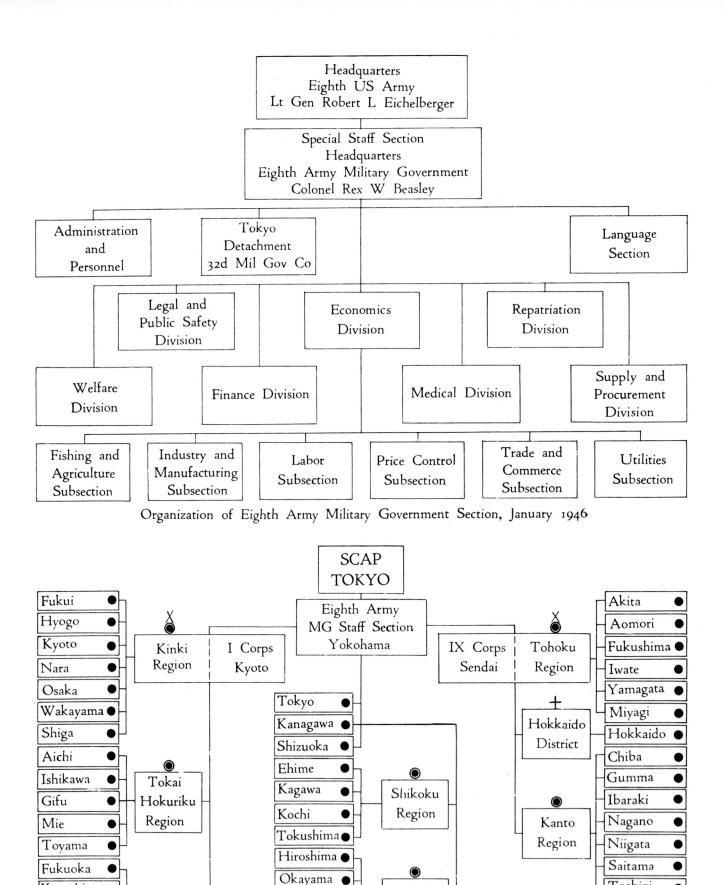

Organization of Eighth Army Military Government Section, January 1946

PLATE NO. 66

Military Government in Japan, January 1946—July 1948

tration and supply activities of the regional prefectural teams.[21]

The prefectural teams were the "front line units" of Military Government in the field. The personnel of these teams came in frequent contact with the local Japanese and could observe conditions and activities at first hand. They advised the Japanese authorities as to missions and objectives of the Occupation and kept them informed of directives and the initiation of programs designed to promote the welfare and education of the people in the community. (Plate No. 67) The reports in matters of compliance with SCAP policies came from these teams. Suggestions were offered for the correction of observed errors in the execution of directives. Despite these manifold activities, team commanders were in no sense military governors.[22] The direct issuance of an order or the taking over of any Japanese governmental agency was to be undertaken only in grave emergencies or when specifically authorized by the Army commander.

Social Affairs Division

Those phases of the Military Government mission which required the most direct approach to the Japanese people as individuals were handled through a Social Affairs Division, consisting of five sub-sections devoted to Civil Education, Civil Information, Public Health, Public Welfare, and Repatriation. All of these sub-branches dealt with social, as distinguished from financial or economic, responsibilities of the Japanese Government.

On the basis of reports and recommendations submitted by Military Government units in the field, the MG staff section forwarded consolidated reports and recommendations to GHQ, SCAP, designed to keep policy-making officials fully informed regarding the impact of the Occupation upon Japanese social and economic conditions.[23]

At corps level, MG functioned through a staff section with intermediate control over the execution of operational directives, applying them to corps zone conditions, facilities, and available personnel. The regional MG offices, at the next lower level, provided a working relationship with the Japanese Government's regional bureaus and a channel to the teams and tactical units in the region. In operating at team level, MG, particularly through the activities directed by the Social Affairs Division, worked closely with the Japanese people through individuals and groups representing the Japanese Government and civilian organizations in prefectures, cities, towns, and villages.

The prefectural team, SCAP, approached the Japanese people through a variety of channels; these included newspapers, motion pictures, street shows (*kamishibai*), radio programs, courses of instruction, demonstrations, exhibits, conferences, interviews, inspections, mass meetings, and special meetings of pro-

---

21 The strength of the section in August 1948, was 52 officers, 57 enlisted men, and 73 Department of the Army civilians. Approximately 70 foreign nationals and Japanese were employed as clerks, typists and interpreters, and for allied duties. In August 1948 the teams varied in strength from 6 officers and 19 to 26 enlisted men in the minor prefectural teams to 12 officers and 71 enlisted men in the largest of the teams. (HQ Eighth US Army, 10th Info and Hist Sv, Eighth Army MG System in Japan, 1945–48 [R], p. 8.)

22 The functioning of the typical MG teams is shown on Plate No. 67.

23 SCAP had other means of keeping informed. The Counter Intelligence Service maintained field stations in every prefecture, paralleling MG field stations but concentrating on ultra-nationalist movements, subversion, sabotage, espionage, operations of Japanese or foreign agents, social unrest and agitation, the development of Communism, etc. Public opinion was thoroughly covered in the "Daily Press Translations" of ATIS, embracing metropolitan as well as provincial newspapers.

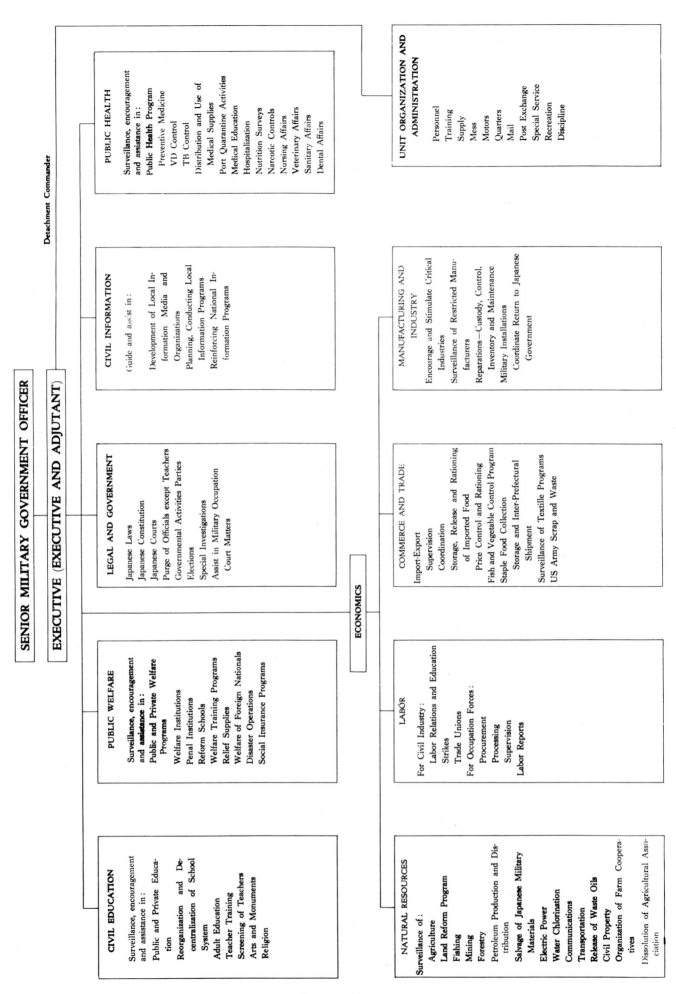

PLATE NO. 67

Functions of Military Government Units in Japan, July 1948

fessional and non-professional groups (teachers, farmers, parents, students, doctors, editors, unionists and others). Through these channels the team collected first-hand information on current and anticipated conditions, lent advice and assistance in the solution of immediate problems, and submitted reports and recommendations.[24]

Civil Education: The Potsdam Declaration directed the Japanese Government to establish " freedom of speech, of religion, and of thought." The United States Initial Post-Surrender Policy for Japan declared that "ultra-nationalistic and militaristic organizations and movements will not be permitted to hide behind the cloak of religion."

Prior to the surrender, the Japanese school system was highly centralized and was administered by a hierarchy of officials headed by the Minister of Education; all officials and teachers were appointed by the government, and all courses and teaching methods were prescribed by the Ministry. The strictly controlled education program was heavily influenced by ultra-nationalism, militarism, and " State Shintoism".[25] There was no real freedom of speech, thought, learning, or religion.

By the time the war ended, the educational system had been disrupted and paralyzed. Over 3,000 of the nation's 40,000 school buildings had been destroyed; thirty-one of the country's forty-nine universities were partially demolished; approximately 16,000,000 students were idle; and only a small percentage of the necessary equipment, textbooks, and other supplies was available. The need for a complete reorganization was obvious and acute. Before Occupation forces landed, the Japanese Ministry of Education had ordered the schools reopened, directed the closing of military and naval academies, abolished military training in the schools, issued a statement of new educational principles, specified methods of modifying and adapting text books, and removed militarists from teaching positions. In outlining the basic policy for education reform, SCAP directed that dissemination of militaristic and ultra-nationalistic ideology and all military education and drill be discontinued. Inculcation of concepts and establishment of practices in harmony with representative government, international peace, dignity of the individual as well as such fundamental rights as freedom of assembly, speech, and religion were encouraged. Following the new education policy, existing curricula, text books, and teachers' manuals were examined and replaced as soon as new instruction materials could be prepared. Personnel of all educational institutions were investigated, approved or removed, reinstated or appointed, and reorientated and supervised in accordance with the new policy. Religious activities were separated from governmental control, banning " State Shintoism " from the educational system.[26]

Under the policy guidance of the Civil In-

---

24 It should be noted here that the practical control of newspapers, motion pictures, theaters, etc., was exercised by the Civil Censorship Division (CCD), an operating agency of the Civil Intelligence Section, SCAP ; CCD maintained stations in the field, especially in communications centers. See Ch. VIII.

25 As a quasi-religious ideology, the " State Shinto " had been used by militarists and ultra-nationalists in Japan to foster, through school and home education, a military spirit among the people to support a war of expansion.

26 (1) SCAPIN 178, 22 Oct 45, sub : Administration of the Educational System of Japan. (2) SCAPIN 212, 30 Oct 45, sub : Investigation, Screening, and Certification of Teachers and Educational Officials. (3) SCAPIN 448, 15 Dec 45, sub : Abolition of Governmental Sponsorship, Support, Perpetuation, Control, and Dissemination of State Shinto (*Kokka* Shinto, *Jinja* Shinto). It should be noted that all details of the educational reform movements were planned and directed by Civil Information and Education Section (CI&E), one of the many SCAP sections created to initiate governmental reforms ; MG became one of several agencies of execution.

formation and Education Section (SCAP) in the reform and rehabilitation of the nation-wide school system, civil education officers of MG teams were required to give special attention to surveillance activities, personnel investigations, school inspections; assistance in school management, budgeting, and administrative matters; guidance in teacher training and placement; and encouragement of local leadership and responsibility.

Although the screening of school officials and teachers was directed in October 1945, it was May 1946 before the Japanese Government submitted a plan for screening, through special committees established in each prefecture, which was acceptable to SCAP. In November 1946 a Military Government survey of prefectural committees indicated that twenty-one of the forty-six were unsatisfactory and should be reorganized; in April 1947 screening committees' tabulations showed that approximately 22 percent of the nation's school officials and teachers had resigned or were removed by the screening committees. By June 1948 approximately 700,000 individuals had been screened, of whom less than 3,000 had been found unfit to continue in the educational service.[27]

The program to eliminate objectionable courses, practices, and textbooks from the schools became a matter of continuing concern to Military Government. SCAP had directed the Japanese Government to reform the school program, specifically eliminating the teaching of Japanese history, morals, and geography until all traces of the old nationalism and militarism had been erased from these subjects.[28]

The Ministry of Education issued instructions for bringing textbooks and the subject matter of courses into line with the new program. Corps commands were directed to inspect five schools in each prefecture of their commands every month to assure that schools and teachers complied with the instructions of the Ministry; eventually the responsibility for these inspections was delegated to the civil education officers of the MG teams.

Many of the reforms recommended by the U.S. Education Mission which visited Japan in March 1946 were inititated.[29] Among these were the plans for decentralizing the school system and the introduction of compulsory teaching of "Romaji", a simplified system of writing Japanese in Roman characters. Efforts toward developing a modern system of free education continued.

Civil Information: Constituted as a subsection of the Social Affairs Division, the Civil Information Branch was responsible for observing and reporting on all similar Japanese activities. This necessitated the indoctrination of press and radio representatives in the privileges and responsibilities attached to their positions in conjunction with other SCAP agencies.[30] The civil information program was planned, controlled, and implemented at the SCAP level through the Japanese Government and the utilization of the Japanese press, radio, and motion picture industries on a nationwide basis. At the lower levels the information program was a part of the civil education mission, and a large measure of the progress made

27 HQ Eighth Army, 10th Info & Hist Sv, Eighth Army MG System in Japan, 1945–48 (R), p. 14.

28 SCAPIN 519, 31 Dec 45, sub: Suspension of Courses in Morals (*Shushin*), Japanese History and Geography.

29 A group of distinguished American educators visited Japan to make a study of the education system. They advised SCAP and the Japanese Minister of Education on technical matters. (SCAPIN 571, 9 Jan 46, sub: Committee of Japanese Educators.)

30 Civil Censorship, in prefectural field stations, operated an efficient surveillance system in all public information fields to enforce a standard Press and Publications Code.

An American Education Mission studies the school system.   Many of the suggestions of this mission have been incorporated in the Japanese educational program.

Self-instruction material for adults is provided by Civil Information and Education Libraries located in the major cities of Japan.

PLATE NO. 68
Modernized Civil Education, March 1946

in education reforms was due to the information projects for reorientation of the Japanese people. It became particularly helpful in connection with matters of public health and welfare, crop collections, price control and rationing, land reform, conservation and utilization of natural resources, tax collections, labor relations, and all forms of education.

Civil Information programs, on the SCAP level, were evolved with Japanese Government agencies.[31] Upon the basis of national planning, the Civil Information Subsection, in cooperation with other staff section elements, prepared detailed information plans and distributed these to the units in the field. Corps and regional offices processed the plans through other elements on their levels and forwarded the program to the prefectural teams.

The approach to the Japanese at the local level, was through Japanese newspapers, radio stations, and receivers which were outlets for the Broadcasting Corporation of Japan;[32] all public speaking systems; motion picture projectors and theaters; citizen's public halls; magazine, book and pamphlet publishers; public libraries and reading rooms (except school libraries and SCAP libraries); dramatic and theater groups; and English-speaking societies. Primary responsibility for MG activities in connection with other Japanese agencies (such as farm organizations, public welfare institutions, and professional societies) rested in each case with the team officer whose special work was related to that particular agency.

Censorship as such was not a responsibility of civil information officers. Materials which came to their attention and seemed to violate censorship policy were reported to the nearest Civil Censorship Detachment (CCD) or to G-2, GHQ, SCAP. Neither was the suppression of obscene books, pictures, and films a function of Military Government; complaints or observations in matters of this kind, however, were called to the attention of the proper SCAP civil section and certain Japanese law and enforcement agencies.[33]

Public Health: In the occupation of a devasted and impoverished country where health and sanitation were at best sub-standard and resistance to disease was dangerously low, the initiation of an adequate public health program became an immediate public problem and development of the program was a major objective. MG officers, in conjunction with the Public Health and Welfare Section, SCAP, began at once to exercise close supervision over all Japanese health agencies and facilities and gave assistance wherever needed. Their efforts during the first three years of the Occupation had an important bearing upon the reduction in dysentery cases and other intestinal maladies traceable to unsanitary conditions and practices. Through their vigilant surveillance and reporting, they forced the Japanese Government and its agencies to take positive action against venereal diseases, illegal use of narcotics, disease-bearing insects and rodents, impure foods, and other threats to national health.

As in other phases of military government, the burden of work was in the field. Policies and national programs were developed by the Ministry of Welfare with SCAP-level direction, advice and assistance, but the success of the plans depended directly upon prefectural and local agencies. The prefectural health depart-

31 Policy responsibility: CI&E Section, one of the major operative civil sections of SCAP.

32 Policy responsibility and field supervision by joint action of CCD and CI&E.

33 In the early part of the Occupation, the policy-making civil sections were largely situated in Tokyo, as staff agencies of SCAP; field operations, surveillance, and enforcement devolved on agencies in the field; in this category only three had practical effect: MG, CCD and CID.

ment, the city health offices and clinics, and the district health centers were the agencies through which the MG team public health officer and his staff worked.[34]

An example of the operations of Military Government surveillance in public health was the abolition of neighborhood health associations at the end of August 1948. The SCAP directive was based on field reports indicating that "racketeers" had obtained control of health associations and were selling vaccines, drugs, and insecticides initially issued by Japanese health authorities to local governments for free distribution. Counterintelligence reports also showed that political bosses were beginning to control the health associations as substitutes for the SCAP prohibited *Tonari Gumi* (Neighborhood Associations) through which the Ministry of Interior used to exercise complete political control over the people.[35]

Public Welfare: Public welfare was one of the first concerns of Military Government in Japan, a country in which the government had previously acknowledged relatively little responsibility for the care of its people, in need of food, clothing, shelter, or medical attention. It was estimated that at least one-ninth of the population needed employment or public assistance. Occupation authorities initiated and supervised nationwide surveys of relief needs, assisted in the organization of emergency relief programs, exercised surveillance over Japanese agencies responsible for the disposal of former army and navy supplies, and checked on the distribution of commodities through ration channels. When the SCAP-inspired "Daily

Life Security Law," the first comprehensive welfare legislation ever enacted in Japan, was passed by the Diet, MG teams were required to see that the prefectural and municipal officials understood the law and complied with its provisions. This act placed the burden of responsibility for public welfare on local government agencies and provided for assistance to the destitute, care of the homeless, distribution of free food and clothing in necessitous cases, care of foreign nationals, inspection of institutions, and disaster relief planning. In view of the impoverished condition of the country, the lethargy of public officials, and the lack of trained social workers, the position of the public welfare officer in Military Government was difficult.

Typical of the many matters confronting welfare officers were the grievances of foreign nationals, the illegal disposal of food and clothing formerly the property of the Japanese Army and Navy, falsification of relief claims, and the problem of caring for vagrants and homeless children. Foreign nationals complained about unfair distribution of ration tickets, high prices, and the unsanitary conditions in the stores designated by the Japanese Government to handle the supplemental food rations.

Early in 1946 MG units verified the Japanese inventories of former army and navy food supply and clothing stocks held by prefectural governments and kept surveillance over the disposition of these supplies and over the relief program for unemployed. Despite all efforts, unreported or diverted stocks of food and clothing continued to be a source of illegitimate

---

34 Some of the means used to advertise the health program were hygiene courses, physical examinations, demonstrations and exhibits, radio programs, newspapers, magazines, slides, film strips, charts, posters, street shows and health clubs.

35 One of the main objects in creating the *Tonari Gumi* in pre-surrender Japan was to facilitate police supervision over the thoughts and loyaly of the people by encouraging inter-community spying on the same pattern as was used by the Nazi Gestapo. This is still a favorite method of the special police branch of the people's Commissariat of Interior (NKVD) in the USSR.

Large stocks of Japanese Army and Navy medical supplies, uncovered by Military Government officials, are distributed to Japanese medical and relief agencies.

Excess American Army food is distributed to the needy to augment the depleted Japanese stocks.

PLATE NO. 69
Control of Medical Supplies and Distribution of Army Rations

income for unscrupulous blackmarket profiteers. Welfare Ministry investigating teams, acting under Military Government surveillance, discovered vast stores of unreported goods in various prefectures. As a result of their findings, seven prefectural governors were removed, five reassigned, and others severely reprimanded for their lax administration of relief.[36]

In mid-summer of 1946 a field study of the child welfare situation revealed that the larger cities were overrun with homeless children, without visible means of support. A survey was conducted to determine the number of orphanages available, the types of educational facilities provided in them, the source of their funds and rations, and the number of waifs at large. At Military Government urging, Japanese authorities were required to enforce control, conduct more frequent " pick-up " campaigns, and make maximum use of the established relief stations for vagrants. The Military Government representatives developed and maintained a close working relationship with national, prefectural, and local Japanese public and private welfare agencies. The primary objectives of the over-all program were : to establish and maintain a program which would provide for the welfare of the civil population to the extent necessary to prevent unrest, to provide for a system of administering public assistance and welfare services on the basis of individual need, and to improve the care of

inmates in welfare institutions. For operational purposes, the field of public welfare was divided into eight major projects : public assistance, child welfare, disaster relief, penal and welfare institutions, in-service training of welfare personnel, community organization, foreign nationals' rations, and information.

Repatriation: The subject of repatriation of millions of Japanese nationals to Japan, and foreign nationals (mainly Chinese, Koreans, Formosans, and Ryukyuans) from Japan, has been covered in all its aspects in Chapter VI. The very complicated governmental machinery designed to operate this project was planned by G-2 and G-3, GHQ, in conjunction with the former Japanese military and naval authorities. The work of manning and operating ships, providing supplies, operating medical, sanitary, and customs inspections was done by the Japanese Welfare Ministry.

The part played by Military Government in the repatriation program was limited to supervision over standards prescribed by SCAP, quarantine controls, maintenance of records, inquiries regarding disposition of exceptional cases, and forwarding recommendations for improved service. MG representatives maintained surveillance of port operations, investigated charges of discrimination lodged against Japanese officers by outgoing repatriates, checked into shipments of repatriates' baggage, uncovered contraband, assisted Japanese officials in the

---

36 Under the emergency relief program, unlawful relief claims were prevalent. Public welfare officials expected to reveal 100,000 "ghosts" on the Tokyo relief rolls alone through a census recheck. It was known that many families were drawing rations for deceased relatives, that the names on many ration cards were fictitious, and that rations were being drawn for persons, particularly Koreans and Chinese, who had left the country early in the repatriation program.

In Hyogo Prefecture, CCD intercepts indicated the existence of a sizeable "ghost" population on the critical foods ration lists. Acting on these leads, the ration records were examined on an exhaustive scale and in this one prefecture alone it was discovered that during a three months' period 2,571,028 days' rations had been drawn by "ghosts". In the course of this investigation, 33,000 bushels of food, principally rice, were confiscated, 17,336 "ghosts" laid to rest and 611 cases prepared for prosecution. As a result of the startling developments in this incident practically every prefecture in Japan undertook similar investigations, the result of which contributed immeasurably to the equitable disposition of critical foods, thereby lessening the amount of food required to be imported from America and elsewhere. (Memo, CCD for G-2 GHQ FEC, 14 Jun 49, sub : Mo Rpt of Activ)

diagnosis and disposition of communicable diseases found among repatriates, and through strict quarantine and other control measures helped to localize outbreak of disease in port areas. They were also responsible for sanitary inspection of all repatriation ships. Thus, although Military Government was not directly responsible for any phase of repatriation, its representatives contributed to the success of the program which caused more than seven and one-half million persons to move into or out of Japan in less than three years.

Economic Division

The primary duty of the Economic Division was described in an Occupation report: " Through surveillance, supervision, investigation, surveys, inventories, studies, and reports, Military Government kept thousands of sensitive fingers on the economic pulse of the patient, and by advice and assistance, encouragement and insistence, injected stimulants into the economic bloodstream."[37]

This Division, from the earliest days of the Occupation, operated through field sub-sections responsible for particular phases of Japanese economy. Some of the original sub-sections were dropped, others added. In August 1948 there were four: Natural Resources, Manufacturing and Industry, Labor, and Trade and Commerce. Their individual importance varied with the changing political and economic situation.[38]

During the war much of Japan's productive capacity had been crippled by aerial bombardment, food production had declined steadily as manpower was drained from the farms, and consumer goods had been depleted because of the complete conversion of the Japanese industry to the war effort. The cessation of hostilities brought this disrupted economy to a virtual halt. ESS and NRS, the major civil sections, SCAP, influenced the Japanese recovery to an important degree, utilizing Military Government and Technical Intelligence teams for the field supervision of such programs as land reform, development of natural resources, education and organization of an alert labor force, and maintenance of agriculture experimental stations.

Natural Resources : When the war ended, the natural resources of the nation were in a depleted state. This was particularly noticeable in the fields of agriculture, fishing, electric power, and mining. It was immediately apparent that production would have to be increased tremendously to meet the needs of the populace, and that the feudal agricultural system would have to be revamped if the farmers were to increase the yield. It was necessary to increase fertilizer stocks and the supply of farm implements in order to augment food supplies. Since it was obvious that actual starvation would result if food production were not supplemented by outside stocks, the Occupation authorities recommended and supervised a rationing system. Stocks of American food were added whenever the domestic stocks fell below the subsistence level.

With only one-fifth of the land in Japan arable, it was important that all tillable land be cultivated. The many Japanese airstrips which were no longer needed were released for farming. Later, a program was initiated in the urban communities to place under cultivation much of the land laid waste by Allied bombing.

---

37   HQ Eighth Army, 10th Info & Hist Sv, Eighth Army MG System in Japan 1945–48 (R), p. 26.

38   Policy direction and major economic rehabilitation measures were under the Economic & Scientific Section. one of the major operative civil sections, SCAP ; the able chief of this section was one of MacArthur's pre-war staff officers in the Philippine period, Maj Gen W. E. Marquat.

212

One of the principal problems facing Military Government was keeping farm products in the authorized channels. The farmers, who mistrusted government promises of fertilizer and farm implements, withheld large quantities of their products from the legitimate distribution channels and diverted them into the black-market. The first attempted solution of the problem was the establishment of patriotic farmers' unions which encouraged full deliveries of the rice quotas set by the government. Concurrently, the pressure for land reform legislation was increased until acceptable laws were passed in late 1946.

By the end of the year resentment of farmers over the failure of the government to provide fertilizer and implements which had been promised resulted in a movement to hold up rice deliveries until the incentive goods were received.[39] Actually, only 45 percent of the 1946 rice quotas were filled by the end of the year, and if it had not been for the efforts of the Military Government teams which kept the collection agencies under close surveillance and did all in their power to encourage farmer compliance, collections would have been even less.

During 1947, under the Land Reform Program, the government purchased over two million acres of land for redistribution. By May 1948 the first prefecture, Yamagata, reported that it had completed the resale of government purchased land to tenant farmers. Constant liaison with the regional bureaus of finance and agriculture, education of the farmers concerning their rights, and supervision of the

actual transactions did much to expedite this program.

Of immediate importance to the economic recovery of the country was the rehabilitation of the coal mining industry. When the Occupation forces first entered Japan, the mines were in need of drilling equipment, were hampered by other shortages caused by rail breakdown, and were operated by slave labor which was immediately eliminated. Stockpiles of coal had dropped to less than two million tons by the end of 1945. Following the SCAP instructions to repatriate the Korean coal miners, the shortage became so serious that the mining industry was placed under special study. One of the big problems was the labor unrest and the many work stoppages, especially prevalent in Hokkaido. The Natural Resources Sub-section worked in cooperation with the Labor Sub-section and, through development of unions, higher wage rates, use of special food rations for the miners, and release of incentive goods such as American cigarettes and clothing, coal production was gradually increased.[40] At the same time, special attention was given to the rehabilitation of the rock drill manufacturing companies.[41]

The third major project of the Natural Resources Sub-section was the rehabilitation of the fishing industry. Initially, the greatest need was for boats. Another serious shortage was in twines and nets, but with the partial rehabilitation of the spinning industry and the importation of hemp from the Philippines, this shortage was overcome. Fuel remained

39 G-2 GHQ FEC had in its possession definite proof that Communist agitation was largely responsible for this condition. See GHQ SCAP, Int Ser, Vol. IX, *Operations of the Civil Intelligence Section, GHQ, SCAP* (S).

40 The production for 1946 was approximately 22,000,000 tons. The production quota for 1947 was set at 30,000,000. Actual production, however, did not exceed 27,500,000 tons, 90.6 percent of the last established quota. ESS, SCAP, established a production quota of 36,000,000 tons for 1948 (the minimum necessary for Japanese economic independence). Actual production was 34,791,300 tons, 96.6 percent of the quota.

41 This program was so successful that rock drills became an item of export in 1948.

a critical item, but the amount of fish available for distribution increased steadily from the beginning of the Occupation and, with increased fuel allotments, this trend continued.

Electrical output was inadequate in the early days of the Occupation, and during the severe drought of 1947 a national educational program to conserve electricity was fostered and publicized. The production of hydroelectric and thermoelectric power became more satisfactory in 1948.

Manufacturing and Industry: During the early phases of the Occupation the basic mission of the Manufacturing and Industry Sub-section was to initiate procedures for the early resumption of production and distribution of commodities and services necessary to meet Occupation needs and a subsistence requirement for the Japanese, and to make an inventory of the industrial machinery earmarked for reparations to the Allied nations. The physical problem in inventorying all the potential reparations plants entailed so much labor that it became necessary to draw personnel from tactical units. These units were also utilized to furnish guards for the plants listed for reparations until the armed strength had been so depleted through the redeployment program that Military Government was forced to utilize Japanese guards to protect the plants.[42]

Loss of rolling stock imposed an almost insurmountable transportation bottleneck. The big industrialists would not operate for fear that their plants would be seized as war booty;

labor was scarce and lethargic; and electric power and coal were lacking for those industries still capable of operation.

The first step taken by ESS, SCAP, was to initiate a licensing system under which the manufacturers could receive permits to operate with some guarantee that their plants would not be touched for reparations. This step, administered through the Manufacturing and Industry Sub-section, MG, resulted in a noticeable increase in production.[43]

With the removal of some plants from the reparation lists, the lessening of governmental restrictions, and the encouragement of the Economic Division, producers began to retool for production; but they continued to be hampered by the lack of raw materials. Coal production was the key to the industrial situation and the greatest emphasis on the MG teams during this phase was the rehabilitation of those plants most needed to produce the tools required for the full operation of coal mines.

In November 1946 GHQ, SCAP, issued instructions relieving Eighth Army Military Government of the responsibility of processing the Japanese Government requests to utilize plants slated for reparations.[44] This function was taken over directly by SCAP. Shipment of reparations equipment began on 16 January 1948 when a load of machinery was dispatchad to China. Crating and shipping of reparations machinery continued under the supervision of the Military Government teams. Concurrently with this program, the Manufactur-

---

42 Policy direction and major economic movements were directly handled by ESS, SCAP. Technical Intelligence, a war-time operating agency of G-2, assisted in the field inspection of laboratories, factories and raw materials.

43 A committee, appointed in 1946 by the President to investigate Japan's ability to make reparations, suggested that all industrial rehabilitation should be subordinated to reparations and that the finest Japanese industrial equipment should be reserved for dismantling and removal. These recommendations adversely influenced the economic recovery, and it was not until more favorable recommendations were made by later committees that Japanese manufacturers gained confidence and production took a more positive upswing.

44 SCAPIN 1355, 22 Nov 46, sub: Permits for Conversion and Reconversion of Industrial Plants (ESS).

Indicative of progress in rehabilitation of industry is the launching of a train-ferry boat, second ship completed by Mitsubishi Shipbuilding, Ltd., after the end of the war.

The first shipment of silk from occupied Japan is loaded on the *Marine Falcon*, 18 March 1946.

PLATE NO. 70
Rehabilitation of Industry

ing and Industry Sub-section carried out a program for the destruction of machinery capable of producing armaments and continued the high priority inventory of critical materials.

Labor: When the Labor Sub-section, MG, was first established, it faced the conflicting problems of meeting the labor requirements of the Occupation forces and of sponsoring an organized, informed, and independent labor force. The first mission of the Sub-section was the detailed study of the over-all wage picture for presentation to the Economic and Scientific Section of GHQ, SCAP, which had the final responsibility of promulgating a wage scale that would be equitable and applicable to the entire country.

The first labor unrest became evident about three months after the beginning of the Occupation. At that time workers began to assert themselves and test their newly granted rights. The Labor Sub-section kept in close touch with the situation and watched the effect of the new policy on the wage picture.

A difficult problem was the control and eventual elimination of the *gumi*, or contractors' gangs, which were rigidly controlled by labor bosses (*oyabun*), who exercised complete control over pools of unskilled labor. Following a completely feudalistic pattern, the bosses accepted contracts for these groups, collecting the rations and pay and giving the laborers only as much as they thought suitable. In an effort to combat this vicious system, employment agencies were established where all workers could register and become available for employment on Occupation projects. Bids by at least three labor organizations were required for any major project, and wages and rations were paid directly to the workers. The bosses were required to register and to submit the financial reports required of other employers.

Another practice which became an issue early in the Occupation was the employment of prison labor by private industry. This labor was allotted to employers at rates ranging from one-third to one-half of the prevailing wage scale. The prisoners were allowed to retain one-tenth of their pay, the remainder being kept by the authorities for the upkeep of prisons. Thus, prison labor not only provided unfair competition against free labor but also gave employers a cost advantage over their competitors. This practice was discontinued during the prison reform movement, initiated by the Public Safety Division, SCAP.

By early spring 1946, labor unions had enrolled 2,700,000 members—over six times more members than had ever been enrolled in prewar Japan. Labor then had the numbers to carry out successful programs but lacked the discipline and knowledge necessary to develop workable ones. Consequently, the working men frequently ran into difficulties because of undisciplined actions and impossible demands.

Throughout 1946 the unionization movement was evident in mass parades and labor demonstrations, all of which were closely observed by Occupation authorities. Evidence of communistic agitation was uncovered, although in general the parades were orderly and well handled. Many of the banners, while publicizing the specific objectives of the groups which paraded, thanked the Americans for having given them a true freedom. Typical demands of the parading groups included petitions for complete purge of war criminals, supervision of food rationing by the people, protection for working women, and closer regulation of prices.

By the end of 1946 the Japanese themselves realized the complexity of their labor problem and established a Labor Ministry during the first Diet session after the adoption of the new constitution.

Following the many evidences of ignorance in the newly organized labor groups the Occupation officials responsible for labor relations placed major emphasis on education of the laboring man. The educational program was carried out through the encouragement of union educational committees and discussion groups, the establishment of libraries, the dissemination of literature on the labor movement, and the advocacy of " recourse to law " for the meeting of many union objectives. Second in importance to the educational program was the constant surveillance of factories to see that the newly adopted labor policies were enforced, and of the Japanese Labor Standards Office to see that it performed its functions whenever violations of the labor laws were discovered. Other major concerns of the Labor Sub-section included continued efforts to maintain employment at the highest possible level, to require labor bosses to comply with the new labor laws, and to check prefectural governments' records to guarantee that the legally liable employers filed reports and paid the premiums required by the unemployment compensation provisions of the new laws.

Trade and Commerce : Prices skyrocketed after the surrender, and it was essential that some of the wartime controls be continued to prevent the complete collapse of the Japanese financial system. This was the mission of the Price Control Sub-section which was later to be merged with the Trade and Commerce Sub-section. To prevent the defrauding of U.S. Army personnel, street peddling was abolished and supervised bazaars were established. A tax exemption certificate relieved Occupation personnel of paying the high tax on luxury items. Prices in laundry and dry cleaning establishments were fixed and the Japanese police were prodded into forcing Japanese merchants to observe the official price scale. Bringing the prices throughout Japan

under control was not simple, for the blackmarket had become part of the national scene. The acute food shortage, the insufficient official prices paid to producers for rationed food, the breakdown of the collection system, and the despair and loss of morale of a defeated people were all contributing factors to wideopen blackmarket practices.

Although price control, as it concerned domestic prices, was left to the Japanese, the MG sub-sections did aid in reducing prices by offering incentive goods to the food producers who delivered their output to the official agencies. They also worked with the Economic and Scientific Section, SCAP, in the rehabilitation of those industries which were necessary to supply needs for food, clothing, fuel, and building materials.

The MG Trade and Commerce Sub-section began an immediate inventory of Japanese goods suitable for export. Of these, the most important single item was raw silk. Although nothing was done immediately to open foreign trade, early in 1946 GHQ, SCAP, authorized the organization of *Boeki Cho* (the Japanese Government Board of Trade).

The Price Control Sub-section was absorbed by the Trade and Commerce Sub-section in 1946. The duties of the expanded Sub-section included the supervision and coordination of imports and exports ; storage, release and return of imported goods ; price control and rationing ; crop collection ; storage and interprefecture shipmen of rice allotments ; surveillance of textile projects and the pearl industry ; control and disposition of Japanese Army-Navy supplies ; and disposition of U.S. Army scrap and waste materials.

The major emphasis was on imports and exports, crop collection, price control, and rationing. Imports fell into three categories : those considered essential to prevent disease and unrest, those required to accomplish the

Japanese accused of blackmarket activities await trial by military provost court.

Silver ingots, uncovered by Military Government teams, are loaded on trucks for transfer to the Bank of Japan vaults in Tokyo.

PLATE NO. 71

Blackmarket and Precious Metals

Occupation mission, and those needed to sustain a minimum economy under policy directives of ESS. All imports in the first year of Occupation were included in the first two categories. All of the initial import-export business was carried on by a system tantamount to barter ; contracts for export items were not approved until they were covered by contracts for imports of equal value. Trading was carried on by only one Government agency, *Boeki Cho*, which was required to route all of its contracts through GHQ, SCAP, for final approval. As the demand for Japanese products began to increase, more products were made available for export, and contracts were permitted which called for payment in dollars or sterling, or on open accounts when such agreements existed. Because one government agency handled foreign trade for the entire nation and thus prevented the desired expansion in trading volume, individual traders and exporters were permitted to carry on negotiations among themselves by mid-August. They were required to procure export licenses issued by *Boeki Cho*, however, and their sales contracts required both *Boeki Cho* approval and SCAP validation.

Control of inflation was a problem from the earliest days of the Occupation. Military Government personnel worked with all echelons of the Japanese Government in an effort to prevent runaway inflation and economic chaos. Japanese reports in the field of economics were found to be unreliable and misleading, making close supervision over this phase of the problem essential.

Legal and Government Division

All aspects of an occupation depend directly upon the functioning of government. In Japan, because the existing governmental machinery was used to execute SCAP directives, the functions and operation of the MG Legal and Government Division (initially the Legal Divison) were limited.[45] The mission of the Legal and Government Division was to expedite the establishment of an efficient, democratic, and decentralized Japanese Government, with effective law enforcement agencies working for public interest, and a fair and efficient court system upholding individual rights. To accomplish this, Legal and Government personnel exercised surveillance, made studies and investigations, and filed reports with the Government Section, SCAP. They observed elections, interpreted Japanese law for military authorities, served as liaison in legal matters with Japanese agencies, and gave legal advice and assistance to all echelons ; they offered instruction and guidance to Japanese officials, and served as advisers and reporters on all matters related to Japanese law, courts, the new constitution, the purge of officials, governmental and political activities, elections, and public safety. The Division was also responsible for the surveillance of certain customs and immigration matters and served as an advisory agency on these subjects to the MG teams in the field.[46]

45 Although initially separate, the Legal Division and the Public Safety Division were consolidated in January 1946 under the title " Legal and Public Safety Division." Three months later it was redesignated as the " Legal and Government Division ". In July 1948 the Local Government Division of the Government Section, GHQ, SCAP, was transferred to the Legal and Government Division, Military Government Section, Eighth Army.

The Government Section, SCAP, was one of the major policy-making civil sections of SCAP. Its chief, Brig Gen Courtney Whitney, was one of the small staff group which had been serving under General MacArthur for many years.

46 The interlocking, interdependent character of the Occupation control must be constantly kept in mind ; the line of demarcation between SCAP and Eighth Army MG agencies was not rigid. Several SCAP agencies maintained field stations throughout Japan, covering each prefecture. Public safety, as a form of police control, fell into the purview of the PSD, SCAP, an operating agency of G-2, charged with the organization of police reform on the American pattern.

Surveillance of the Administration of Justice: Legal and Government representatives personally dealt with Japanese officials and institutions in carrying out their mission of observation and close supervision; the officers frequently visited summary and district courts and local procurators' offices to show Japanese officials that the Occupation forces were interested in the operations of the courts. They encouraged and assisted Japanese officials to administer justice in accordance with the new constitution, the new criminal code, changes in court practices, and other new legislation. It must be pointed out, however, that Military Government did not give orders to nor interpret Japanese laws for Japanese courts. In the discussions, emphasis was placed on the civil liberties provisions of the constitution. An attempt was made to develop the dignity of the judicial system, to eliminate favoritism toward influential persons, and to reduce the backlog of untried cases.[47] Interpretations placed upon instructions and new laws by the local Japanese authorities were checked against SCAP and Eighth Army directives; bureaucrats, as well as elected individuals, were warned that they were serving the people.

Legal and Government Division officers worked closely with individual Japanese officials, and were familiar with police organization in their prefectures, though policy direction was charged to PSD, SCAP. Recommendations were made by Military Government concerning removal of undesirable officials for acts detrimental to the Occupation, for improper activities, and for inefficiency.

Surveillance of Political Parties and Elections: Conferences were held with party leaders and members of local assemblies to determine their programs and platform. The strength of parties and their activities were subjects of monthly reports. Observation of elections was one of the periodic tasks of the MG Legal and Government Division. When the number of polling places was so large that Military Government could not provide enough teams to insure adequate supervision, tactical troop personnel furnished assistance.

Civil Liberties, Inspections of Jails and Police Methods: Prior to the Occupation the Japanese police were notorious for mistreating suspects, confining prisoners for long periods without trial, and denying them counsel. The new constitution and the new criminal code forbade these and other abridgements of civil rights. Jails, police stations, and other places of confinement were visited, and by personal observation and questioning of inmates, MG representatives determined whether individual rights had been violated. Violations were reported to the proper Japanese authority, and a report was sent to higher headquarters.[48] When Japanese individuals were deprived of civil rights by the Occupation forces, Military Government took corrective action by contacting the military unit concerned.

Surveillance of the Administration of the Purge: The administration of the purge program became ultimately a Japanese responsibility, and Military Government did not attempt to interpret purge laws for screening committees.[49] However, when MG officers

---

47 Policy direction was under the Legal Section, SCAP. Prison surveillance and reform, on the policy level, was part of the mission of PSD or CIS.

48 Prison reform and the corollary functions of inspection, were charged to the Public Safety Division, an operating agency of G-2, which employed American experts in its police and prison reform program.

49 SCAPIN 93, 4 Oct 45, sub: Removal of Restrictions on Political, Civil and Religious Liberties. Several SCAP Sections were heavily involved: the MG Section and CIS checked the war-time, ultra-nationalistic records of many individuals. Immediately on landing, G-2 secured invaluable police and administrative personnel records.

Women, permitted for the first time to take part in the elective and administrative functions of the government, cast their ballots in an election of Diet members.

The Women Diet Members' Club meets to discuss current affairs.

PLATE NO. 72
Women's Franchise : Milestone of Politics, April 1946

suspected a violation or when violations were reported by the Japanese, the information was forwarded to SCAP. The actual purge list was practically completed by the end of 1947. Thereafter, emphasis was placed on injunctions prohibiting these persons from holding public office, engaging in politics, or exercising influence in public life or over persons holding public office. SCAP directed local investigations of reported violations.

Legal and Government Division was also responsible for making investigations, forwarding claims, and maintaining liaison with other Occupation officials and with appropriate Japanese authorities. Another important function of this Division was the surveillance of customs, quarantine, and immigration.

Investigations were made when required by higher headquarters or upon receipt of information from other sources. Japanese police, procurators, and agencies were utilized. The police were encouraged and supported in their efforts to control large scale blackmarketing.

Military Government did not operate a claims service, but Japanese and other nationals often requested information and submitted claims to the teams. These were forwarded through channels to the Judge Advocate Section, Headquarters, Eighth Army, or to SCAP for appropriate action.

The Legal and Government Division officer maintained close liaison with Civil Intelligence Section and tactical troops on legal, government, and police affairs, and with appropriate Japanese authorities concerning government admission, laws, courts, procurators, legislative bodies, political parties, fire departments, and penal institutions.[50] Civil

Information officers were assisted in publicizing elections and new legislation.

The Legal and Government Division was concerned with the entry and exit of personnel and personal property, the import and export of commercial cargo, and the surveillance of Japanese customs. Although these functions were the duties of Military Government customs units at the designated ports, vessels occasionally stopped at other than specified ports of entry. For this reason all Military Government teams were required to be familiar with directives and regulations pertaining to customs, quarantine, and immigration.

The arrival or departure of all non-military personnel, personal baggage, and cargo was checked at designated ports in accordance with SCAP directives. Observation of the Japanese in customs inspection and examination of international parcel post was another duty of Military Government. Surveillance generally consisted of semi-monthly inspections. When the regulations established by SCAP for weight or content of packages were violated, the excessive or prohibited articles were confiscated and given to Military Government for disposition through established relief agencies.

Finance and Civil Property Division

The initial concern of the Finance (later redesignated the Finance and Civil Property) Division of Military Government was to assure Japanese compliance with SCAP instructions as they pertained to the closing of stock exchanges, and to the closing and liquidation of wartime banks, development companies, and other financial institutions which were

---

50   The full account of CIS activities may be found in GHQ SCAP, Int Ser, Vol. IX, *Operations of the Civil Intelligence Section,* GHQ, SCAP (S). The Public Safety Division (PSD), a branch of CIS, was responsible for organization and surveillance of activities of Japanese police, prisons, jails, fire departments and other institutions concerning public safety. CIS was under the control of G-2, GHQ, SCAP, and was primarily a security surveillance unit.

organized to finance the Japanese war effort or to aid in the exploitation of occupied countries.[51] From these strictly fiscal activities, the Division's field of responsibility was broadened to include the custody and control of Axis property, precious metals and stones belonging to the Japanese Government, and valuables belonging to designated individuals, institutions, and organizations scheduled by SCAP for restriction or dissolution.

The Bank of Tokyo was designated as the liquidating agency for certain banks. The Division maintained close supervision of the personnel engaged in this work to prevent removal, defacement, or destruction of books, records, or other property. It submitted weekly reports on the progress of liquidation and matters of special financial interest. One of the spectacular tasks of the Occupation dealt with collecting and putting under guard the great hoards of gold, silver, precious stones, foreign postage stamps, engraving plates, and all currency not legal in Japan. Even though the bulk of this wealth was collected and placed under United States military custody by Japanese officials, undeclared caches of these treasures were known to exist. Consequently, the task of investigating, uncovering, inventorying, and safeguarding all property in this category was a continuing and increasing responsibility.[52] The precious metals were stored in the United States vaults of the Bank of Japan at Tokyo and in the Imperial Mint at Osaka. Eighth Army furnished custodial staffs for both depositories. The Osaka vaults were initially used for the storage of all types of seized property but in May 1946 the Bank of Japan was designated

as the sole depository for precious stones.

In April 1946 Eighth Army was relieved of supervising bank liquidations and its responsibilities were limited to the guarding of buildings, records, and physical assets. The functions of the Division thereafter were mainly: inspection and supervision of Japanese tax collection and administration; rehabilitation of postal savings branch offices; supervision of matters pertaining to the seizure and custody of civil property; and preservation and protection of United Nations nationals' property (not yet restored to its owners), Axis property, and looted property (which included packing, crating, and delivery to owners). Civil Property Custodian personnel (SCAP) attached to Military Government teams handled civil property affairs in areas not covered by regional custodian service teams.

Tax Collections: During the fiscal year beginning with April 1947, Japanese tax collections lagged to a serious extent. In January 1948 Military Government was directed to expedite national tax collections. Surveillance was begun immediately by the seven regional bureaus located at Sapporo, Tokyo, Nagoya, Osaka, Hiroshima, Takamatsu, and Kumamoto. Teams from tactical units began detailed supervision of the 450 local tax offices in February. Fifty-five teams were initially used on this project, which enabled semimonthly inspections at each local tax office. Initial difficulties were: the public's general noncompliance with tax laws, particularly payment in advance of the self-assessed income tax, and the opposition and slowdown tactics of tax collectors' unions. However, improvement in tax payments was immediately notice-

---

51 A SCAP civil section, as usual, controlled this particular field, utilizing field agencies for local implication; fiscal and banking controls, including assets and alien properties, were handled by ESS and the Civil Property Custodian.

52 All Occupation agencies were engaged in this search; the counterintelligence, including field agencies, were enormously productive: between 30/40,000 carats of diamonds were recovered, war loot from South East Asia.

able when the program started, and supervision was extended for an indefinite period.

Occupation personnel did not attempt to interpret tax laws to Japanese officials. They first ascertained the tax goals set for each financial bureau and the allocation of quotas to local tax offices, then determined the progress made in the collections. Following that, they encouraged publicity of the program and exerted their influence to promote efficiency. Action was taken to alleviate the general shortage of competent personnel in the Japanese tax structure. Surveillance discouraged corrupt practices, and much was accomplished through the prosecution of dishonest tax officials and tax evaders, although relatively few of them were brought to trial.

Financial Restrictions: The *Zaibatsu*[53] and the many affiliates and subsidiaries which controlled the Japanese industry prior to the Occupation were reorganized by SCAP to eliminate monopolistic practices. These restricted firms were not permitted to perform financial transactions, except normal operating collections and payments, without specific SCAP approval. SCAP approval was necessary for: loan transactions, property transfers, stock transactions, construction contracts, and donations.[54] Military Government personnel did not maintain surveillance over these firms but did report monopolistic practices and illegal transactions by such concerns whenever reliable information indicated such violations.

The Japanese financial institutions which were created to finance and exploit Japanese conquests outside the home islands were closed early in the Occupation period. The " Closed Institutions Liquidating Commission " (Japanese) accomplished the detailed work of liquidation.

Rehabilitation of Postal Savings Branch Offices: The progress of rehabilitation in fourteen of the twenty-eight Postal Savings Branch offices in Japan was subject to surveillance and report by Military Government. Japanese made deposits in local post offices, but permanent records were kept in branch offices. During the war many of the branch offices were damaged and records were destroyed. Originally, reports on all twenty-eight branches were required, but with improved conditions, supervision and reports for fourteen of the branches were discontinued by April 1948.[55]

Civil Property Custodian Regional Service Teams: The Civil Property Custodian Section (CPC) was established by SCAP on 8 March 1946. It developed general policies and established procedures for control or custody of the various properties and assets over which SCAP exercised authority. The seizure and custody functions became the responsibility of both MG field teams and tactical units; in view of manpower limitations and the technical nature of some of the property, it was found necessary to attach CPC (SCAP) personnel to Military Government units for this type of work.

Regional service teams of the Property Service Branch, Comptroller Division (CPC) were attached to Military Government teams in areas which could not be conveniently covered from Tokyo. The teams, composed of civilian personnel and augmented by Japanese hired locally, varied in strength and composition. Members had the same status

---

53 *Zaibatsu,* big financial trusts, six of which (Mitsui, Mitsubishi, Yasuda, Sumitomo, Kawasaki, Fuji), together with their affiliates and subsidiaries, controlled practically all financial, commercial, and industrial life of pre-surrender Japan.

54 HQ Eighth Army, 10th Info & Hist Sv, Eighth Army MG System in Japan (R), p. 45.

55 *Ibid,* p. 46.

Study of synthesis of nylon is carried on in the Organic Chemistry
Laboratory, Noguchi Research Institute, Tokyo.

Study of Van de Graeff Generator is made in the Physical Chemistry Laboratory,
Tokyo University.

PLATE NO. 73
Field Inspection of Laboratories by Technical Intelligence
Detachment, G-2, GHQ, FEC

as members of the Military Government teams to which they were attached except that work assignments were made by CPC.

Seizure and Custody of Government Property: Eighth Army was directed to seize and maintain custody of precious metals and diamond stockpiles owned or controlled by the Japanese or Axis governments in Japan during the war. Eighth Army agencies were also authorized to confiscate and deposit precious metals and gems in the United States vaults in Tokyo or Osaka whenever such items were to be found in violation of SCAP directives. The program, as it pertained to known stocks, was practically complete by August 1948. Hoarded precious metals and industrial diamonds, found from time to time by field units, were taken into custody,[56] and many offenders were prosecuted in provost courts.

Eighth Army was directed to take custody of excess movable property of Axis repatriates and movable property of Axis business firms which had ceased operating. Property to be taken in custody was specified for each repatriation operation of Axis nationals and for each seizure from Axis individuals or concerns. Seizure was accomplished by tactical troops on orders from Eighth Army. This property was then stored in three CPC warehouses which were operated by Eighth Army agencies in Tokyo, Kurihama, and Osaka respectively. The local accounting system in each CPC warehouse was prescribed by Eighth Army. Under the direct supervision of the CPC, property subject to deterioration was sold; it was auctioned off to the Occupation forces for dollars, while property unsuitable for sale to Occupation forces was sold to the Japanese Government for yen.[57]

United Nations and Axis Property: The preservation and protection of United Nations property confiscated by the war-time Japanese Government became a concern of Military Government teams. The Japanese prefectural governments were required to furnish prefectural MG teams lists of wrongfully transferred items; checks were then made to determine whether there was proper maintenance and protection of such property. The Japanese Government was charged with preventing deterioration but was not required to rehabilitate war damage. It was further required to impound and maintain Axis property, and periodic inspections were made by Military Government teams to ensure compliance.

Restitution: Surveillance was maintained over the restoration of United Nations nationals' property. Most of it was American, British, or Dutch property which was taken over or disposed of by the Japanese Enemy Property Custodian during the war.

Copies of the applicable SCAPIN were given to the owner and to the Military Government team in the area where the restitution was to be made. A Military Government officer was present at the meeting between the owner and the Japanese Government representative in charge of the restitution to guarantee that SCAP directives had been obeyed and the owner received just compensation.

Some property ordered restored to United Nations owners had been utilized under procurement demand by the Occupation forces. In these cases the title transaction was completed by the military forces who continued to occupy the property until the necessity for its

---

56 Personnel operating the US vaults in Tokyo Bank of Japan were assigned to the MG Section, HQ Eighth Army, and those at the Osaka Mint to the Kinki MG regional team. The operating staffs were attached for administration to the Tokyo MG team and the Osaka MG team, respectively. The accounting system used in the depositories was prescribed by SCAP.

57 SCAPIN 5358-A, 6 Mar 48, sub: Disposal of Certain German Property.

continued use no longer existed.

Looted Property: All property suspected as having been seized in areas occupied by the Japanese armed forces was classified as looted property unless definite legal ownership could be established. In general, it was handled directly by SCAP through the Japanese Government. Military Government personnel reported illegal transactions, prevented unauthorized transfers or movements, and maintained general surveillance over such property. Plundered property included occasionally in reparation plans was ordered removed from reparations inventory. In such cases, the property (usually machinery) was left in place and given a Civil Property Custodian number.

The Japanese Government was directed to maintain a " watch list " of looted vehicles. In August 1948 it was directed that all property which had been taken from or produced in areas occupied by Japanese armed forces during the war be impounded and reported. The Japanese Government was required to pack, safeguard, and deliver pillaged items to ports of shipment. Close observation and spot checks were conducted to ensure compliance.

Procurement Demand

The Occupation forces in Japan were self-sustaining in food, clothing, ammunition, and other essential supplies. It was necessary, however, to procure billeting and office space, certain communication facilities, construction supplies, and labor.

A General Procurement Board was established in September 1945, and authority was delegated to the commanding generals of the Sixth and Eighth Armies for the normal overall procurement of indigenous supplies. The Japanese Government created a Central Liaison Office in September 1945 which established branch offices in each of the prefectural governments to expedite all requests submitted by the Occupation forces. Initial operations were carried out by the Supply Division (later redesignated Procurement Division) of Military Government, which was instrumental in determining policy and procured all supplies and services needed by military units under Sixth and Eighth Army control. In January 1946 Eighth Army assumed control of all Occupation troops in Japan, and by March 1946 every Military Government unit included in its organization a procurement officer who was responsible for processing demands made by the various units located within his area. In order to expedite the procurement of various items and services, the commanding general of Eighth Army, in March 1946, delegated approving authority to the commanders of I and IX Corps, base commanders, and senior commanders of Air, Navy and BCOF forces.

To minimize Occupation demands upon the exhausted Japanese economy, special lists were prepared enumerating the items which could not be procured without specific approval from the controlling headquarters involved. These lists included such items as medical and dental supplies, nearly all types of food, petroleum products, certain categories of commercial vehicles and communications equipment, and numerous other indigenous products. Certain classes of real property which could not be procured without direct approval from Headquarters, Eighth Army, included religious institutions, any property occupied by members of the royal family, educational institutions, hospitals, and facilities designated for the distribution of food, clothing and shelter.

The procurement of communications and transportation was a Military Government responsibility at the beginning of the Occupation, but by the end of November 1946 procurement of communications supplies and

Check on Japanese machinery marked for reparations. This machine, destined for Great Britain, is inspected for proper crating.

Military Government representatives check scrapping of "special purpose" machines which cannot be converted to any peaceful use.

PLATE NO. 74
Military Government Team in Action, February 1948

services became a direct responsibility of Eighth Army Signal Section. In January 1947 the Third Military Railway Service assumed control of the procurement of all necessary rail service, right-of-way, and related facilities.

Early in the Occupation hand receipts were required where immediate procurement was necessary, but numerous reports showed that unauthorized appropriation was common practice throughout Japan. Many of these local appropriations were justified; in view of this fact SCAP ruled that all hand receipts in the possession of Japanese nationals dated prior to April 1946 would be honored on a confirming procurement demand.[58]

Under the procurement plan all supply requests were submitted to the Military Government teams in the area of the approving headquarters. Necessary papers were prepared by the local procurement officers and submitted to the Japanese liaison official. The Japanese Government was responsible for locating manufacturers and raw materials and allocating the latter. By late 1946 certain changes in Occupation missions and the institution of long range planning made central procurement necessary. Team procurement offices were closed and, in July 1947, Eighth Army announced that all items and services would be obtained thereafter by central procurement on a forecast basis. The Procurement Division set up four district offices at Sapporo, Sendai, Yokohama, and Kyoto. The main islands were divided into four administrative districts, but because of the large area under the Kyoto district, four branch officers were established at Osaka, Kure, Kobe (later at Nagoya), and Kokura. In addition, because of heavy needs, a Tokyo branch of the Yokohama Office became responsible for procurement for GHQ and other units in that area.

Before a request for an article could be submitted, the design and other physical aspects of the required item were ascertained. Following final approval, the necessary papers were submitted by the Procurement Division to the Japanese Government which placed the contract. Working against specific delivery deadlines, the manufacturer was required to submit samples to the requesting agency for testing. The Procurement Division maintained a testing laboratory available to all interested parties.

Whenever an adequate supply of raw materials was not immediately available, the expediting officers of the Procurement Division attempted to locate the needed materials, even though this was a Japanese responsibility. Upon final delivery, each shipment was accepted on a procurement receipt which indicated completion of the contract and enabled the supplier to collect payment from the Japanese Government. The expediters were not in control of fuel and power allocations but assisted in obtaining increased allotments for manufacturers of items on procurement demand.

In August 1947, by direction of SCAP, a Special Procurement Board (SPB) was established as an agency of the Japanese Government to replace the agencies previously utilized for procurement purposes. The detailed operational procedures of the SPB became the responsibility of the Eighth Army Commander, who in turn delegated the authority to the Procurement Division. The Division implemented SCAP procurement policy and fulfilled requirements by methods based on practices in the Zone of Interior. The Tokyo branch of the Yokohama District Office supervised the over-all operation of the Special Procurement Board. The agency and its field repre-

58   HQ Eighth Army, 10th Info & Hist Sv, Eighth Army MG System in Japan, 1945–48 (R), p. 50.

sentatives were authorized to receive and settle procurement receipts and to make payments to suppliers, thus expediting both delivery and payments.

Real estate and local construction projects also came within the province of the Procurement Division. Large amounts of real estate were placed on demand early in the Occupation. Many pieces of property, however, had been Japanese military or naval holdings and, as such, were confiscated as surrendered enemy equipment and installations.[59]

From the beginning, the over-all effort was primarily a vast planning program. Producers and contractors were instructed in modern production methods and standardization of specifications and design. By centralized procurement and large scale contracts, the Procurement Division substantially reduced production time and materially increased production. In April 1948, to meet the demands of its mission, the Procurement Division was established as a special staff section of Headquarters, Eighth Army.

General Conclusion

The functions of Military Government in Japan were limited to inspecting the activities of the government whose officials continued to perform the duties of actual administration of the country. All officers in the Japanese Government were appointed or dismissed by the Japanese themselves, subject only to the SCAP purge directives. All of them were directly responsible to Japanese authorities. The Military Government agencies could report on and recommend the removal of any Japanese government official found corrupt, inefficient, or uncooperative.

The smoothness with which the complicated machinery of the Occupation worked in Japan surprised competent observers all over the world. Its success must be credited to four main factors: the foresight of Allied high level planning in utilizing the existing Japanese Government and the authority of the Emperor institution; the wisdom of the Supreme Commander in solving the complex problems arising from a program designed to transform a totalitarian country into a democracy, by tolerant and humane treatment of a vanquished foe, rather than by punitive measures for past crimes; the patience and tact with which Occupation agencies handled a humiliated and defeated people whose national psychology differed radically from that of any western peoples; and the unexpected cooperation of Japanese officials and population, in response to tolerant and intelligent guidance.

---

59 Prior to July 1947 all procurement requests were audited on an account basis of relative values, which were stated in units rather than in dollars or yen. The total number of unit values expended were converted into dollar equivalents by use of a predetermined conversion factor.

CHAPTER VIII

OCCUPATION SECURITY AND INTELLIGENCE MEASURES

Assignment of Responsibilities

Parallel with the establishment and slow growth of Military Government, the operations of certain civil and counter intelligence units and agencies entered into play as an indispensable factor in the tranquil development of the Occupation. As the Occupation progressed, the duties of combating and controlling diverse elements, subversive or inimical to the objectives of the Occupation, which were envisioned in the basic plan for Operation " Blacklist,"[1] were expanded immeasurably to cover every facet of the intelligence problem.

Developed before Japan's capitulation[2] the Intelligence Annex to " Blacklist " was originally designed to serve only during the initial phase of the Occupation; however, it already contained the essentials later appearing in the second basic document relating to the general intelligence information mission, "Basic Directive for Post-Surrender Military Government in Japan Proper."[3]

" Blacklist " recognized the " joint character of operational and counter intelligence "[4] and further envisaged that:

The surrender of Japan . . . will alter the general mission of Counter Intelligence operations. In addi-

tion to insuring military security by denying information to the enemy, Counter Intelligence personnel will be confronted with the problem of suppression of organizations, individuals and movements whose existence and continued activities are considered an impediment to the lasting peaceful reconstruction of Japan.[5]

This paragraph of " Blacklist " clearly characterized the operation of CIS from the beginning of the Occupation to the end.

"Blacklist" specifically identified in a general "wanted list" some of Japan's most dangerous elements, naming particularly the *Kempei Tai* (Military Police), *Tokumu Kikan* (Secret Intelligence Service), *Kokuryu Kai* (Black Dragon Society), *Dai Nippon Seijikai* (Political Association of Greater Japan), *Koku Sui-to* (Extreme Nationalist Party), and other extremist organizations, as well as lists of top personnel in the general staff and government.[6] It arranged for coordination in the field between counter and operational intelligence staffs in their work of apprehending and interrogating persons on the " wanted lists," and for a central card file on all persons arrested; this coordination also covered the seizure and safeguarding of valuable documents and the interrogation of prisoners and suspects.[7]

In addition to these specific tasks, the nor-

---

1 Military blueprint to cover Occupation of Japan and Korea under non-invasion conditions (3d ed), 8 Aug 45.
2 On the basis of a Joint Chiefs of Staff (JCS) Directive.
3 JCS Dir 1380/15 (TS), 3 Nov 45.
4 GHQ USAFPAC, Basic Outline Plan for " Blacklist " Opns (TS) (3d ed), 8 Aug 45, Sec. I, par. 5.
5 *Ibid*, Sec. X.
6 *Ibid*, Sec. I, 4.
7 *Ibid*, Secs. V and VI.

mal responsibilities of counter intelligence regarding enemy espionage, sabotage, and subversive activities continued in force, and intensive security education programs to alert troops in vigilance (especially necessary in enemy territory) were instituted.[8]

The civil censorship responsibilities outlined in " Blacklist " called for centralization of the technical direction and control at theater level. This control was to be exercised with the primary objective of promoting military security and the peaceful future of the country, for action by appropriate agencies and regulation of communications and information media.[9]

A general SCAP memorandum[10] defined certain responsibilities: criminal and police agencies were to be purged of undesirable elements; prisoners held solely under abrogated laws were to be released; certain Japanese political associations and all military and civilian ultra-nationalistic, terroristic, and secret patriotic associations and their affiliates or agencies were ordered dissolved; military training was banned; foreign nationals were required to identify themselves and be registered. CIS was instructed to place under protective custody diplomatic and consular officials of countries, except Japan, which had been at war with any of the United Nations, as well as to hold those civilians from neutral countries or United Nations nationals (resident or interned in Japan) who had participated in the war against the United Nations. The instructions also contained provisions to intern certain categories of Japanese who had played active and domi-nant roles in the formation of Japan's program of aggression and to hold suspected war criminals incommunicado without distinction as to rank or position; Japanese and Korean collaborators were to be removed from positions of responsibility as rapidly as possible. CIS was further directed to establish censorship of civil communications and to preserve certain governmental and civil records.

Basic Plan for Civil Censorship

The Basic Plan for Civil Censorship as formulated before Japan's surrender called for censorship control of Japan under military invasion conditions.[11] This outline was subsequently modified by " Blacklist " which delineated the primary objectives of civil censorship under " conditions of peaceful occupation."[12] A third plan, the one eventually followed, was adjusted to meet the favorable conditions actually encountered in the first days of the Occupation.[13] Under this modification, Civil Censorship in Japan developed into a medium of information on the Japanese military, economic, social, and political activities through control of Japanese communications. It became apparent early that the extent of compliance with terms of the surrender, and the trend of acceptance by the Japanese of Occupation directives could be determined. The Press Section of Civil Censorship was to assist also in the enforcement of the free and factual dissemination of news based upon United Nations standards. Through intelligent eval-

---

8   *Ibid*, Sec. X.

9   *Ibid*, Sec. XI.

10   The implementation of JCS Dir 1380/15 was by SCAP Memo No. 6 (TS), 28 Nov 45, which also assigned to various staff sections the execution of the provisions of JCS Dir 1512, 13 Sep 45, and State, War, Navy Coordinating Committee, Dir 176/9, 13 Oct 45.

11   GHQ USAFPAC, Basic Plan for Civil Censorship in Japan, 10 Jul 45.

12   GHQ USAFPAC, Basic Outline Plan for "Blacklist" Opns (TS) (3d ed), 8 Aug 45, Sec. XI.

13   GHQ USAFPAC, Basic Plan for Civil Censorship in Japan, 30 Sep 45 (Rev).

uation of intercept information, Civil Censorship would assist in prevention of secret rearmament, the apprehension and conviction of suspected war criminals, the prevention of disorders, the location of Japanese overseas assets, and the recovery of property seized during the war. By control of communications, military security would be maintained as leads developed to expose the existence and activities of underground or other subversive elements and of blackmarket operators.

Evolution of Civil (Occupation) Intelligence

The original CIC mission was defined in orders of long standing:

> ...to assist in maintaining security by detecting and taking countermeasures to nullify enemy intelligence operations, to investigate matters pertaining to espionage, sabotage, treason, sedition, disaffection, and subversive activities occurring within the military establishment, and to make security surveys and assist in the security instruction of military personnel....[14]

Upon arrival in Japan, the basic mission was expanded to include detecting conditions inimical to the general objectives of the Occupation, with special emphasis on subversive activities, in addition to current responsibilities of CIC within the military establishment.[15]

By September 1945 plans for the organization of the Allied Forces which would occupy Japan were completed.

The evolution of *civil intelligence*, a term adopted in counterdistinction to purely military *strategic theater intelligence*, was gradual. The objectives of the Occupation, in its civil aspects, predominated in all missions: gradually, all counter intelligence activities were directed toward that end as surveillance and security operations.

The *Civil Intelligence Section* played a dual role in the Occupation, as a SCAP Staff Section (CIS) and as an operating agency (Counter Intelligence Division); with its various components, distributed throughout Japan, this agency became a sort of F.B.I. for the Occupation in its special field of security surveillance.[17] It functioned in four major components: Operations Branch, the 441st Counter Intelligence Corps, the Civil Censorship Detachment, and the Public Safety Division.[18] (Plate No. 75)

The *Operations Branch* acted as a coordinating staff: evalution of information gathered from the field by CIC and CCD and the initiating of staff action pertaining thereto were its primary interests. From "research for future operations," the mission of its wartime predecessor, the scope of the division abruptly broadened to one of coordination and action on all aspects of counter intelligence activities.

In the fall of 1945, the apprehension of Japanese war criminal suspects became an immediate and urgent mission. Allied public opinion exerted heavy pressure on Occupation authorities to take prompt action against the war criminals. The responsibility of selecting the priority or "Class A" group, who would be tried before the International Military

---

14   Ltr, WD to CG's Concerned, 31 Oct 44, sub: CIC. In AG 322 (CIC).

15   Ltr, GHQ USAFPAC to CG, Eighth A, 22 Mar 46, sub: Employment of CIC Pers. In AG 322 (CI).

16   SCAP GO No. 2, 2 Oct 45. On 2 October Maj Gen C. A. Willoughby was appointed Assistant Chief of Staff, G-2 and Brig Gen E. R. Thorpe, Chief, Civil Intelligence Section; concurrently, Gen Thorpe remained Chief Counter Intelligence Officer, GHQ, AFPAC.

17   In the period of 1947/1948, new conditions and problems facing the Occupation caused a revision of administrative and operational procedures. By order of G-2, a number of changes were made in the organization of CIS, including its name which became Occupation (Civil) Intelligence.

18   SCAP GO No. 13, 2 Oct 45.

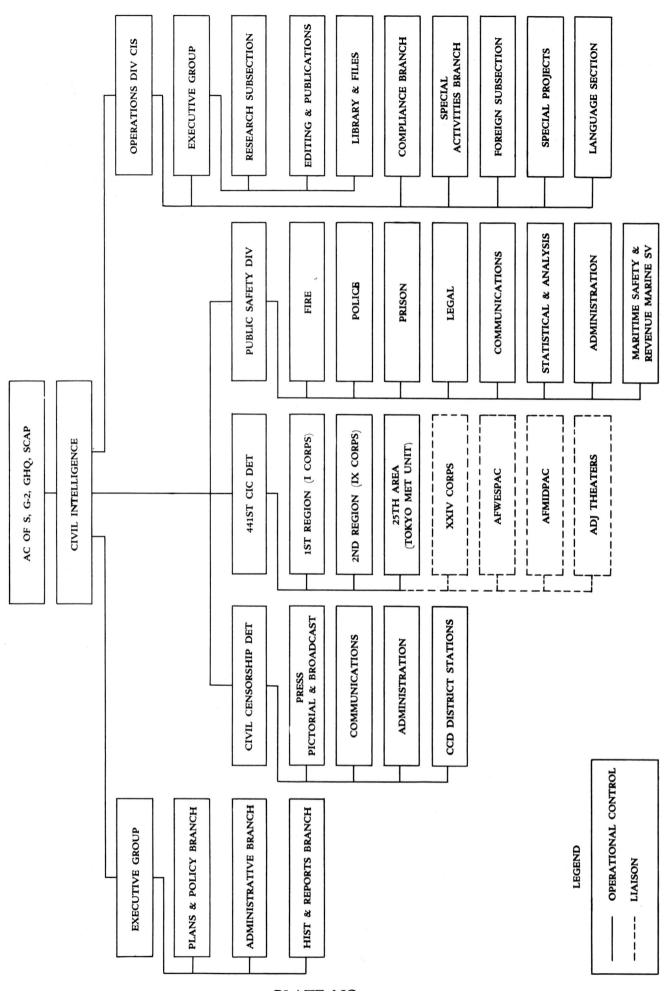

PLATE NO. 75
Organization of Civil (Occupation) Intelligence Division, 15 October 1946

Tribunal, was a heavy one. Utilizing information developed by intelligence agencies in the Philippines, War Department instructions and new data obtained in Japan, the first list of such persons was compiled on 11 September 1945.[19] It was headed by General Hideki Tojo, the premier who led Japan into war, and listed forty men charged with directing the Japanese war effort. The 441st Counter Intelligence Corps was assigned the initial task of apprehending these war criminal suspects; on 13 September 1945, however, the Japanese Government was ordered to turn over to Occupation authorities all of those on the " wanted list." In February 1946 the investigation of war criminals was undertaken by Legal Section, GHQ, SCAP, which became responsible for their prosecution.[20] This relieved CIS of further responsibility for Japanese war criminals, although it retained the task of arresting " neutral nationals who actively participated at war against any one of the United Nations." Nevertheless, CIS continued to be interested in those war criminal suspects who were interned through its efforts; their cases were studied and recommendations made for release of those suspects whose arrest was not justified.

An early accomplishment of CIS was the issuance of two important directives which made possible the modification of police laws and agencies through which absolute control over the Japanese people had been maintained.[21] Under a series of regulations which were gradually strengthened over the years, especially during the war, the Japanese police exercised virtually unlimited power; their control extended into the fields of economics, drama,

press, politics, and religion. Many enforcement groups operated secretly and extreme influence was wielded by the Special Higher Police. There were also the " Thought Police " who, under the " Protection and Surveillance Law for Thought Offense " and partially through use of the " neighborhood associations," attempted to control, supervise and regulate the trends of people's thought and opinion. Their methods were often brutal; they could hold persons for long periods without charges and, by using third degree tactics, they could force confessions to false charges from those who had incurred their disfavor.

SCAP Directives issued 4 and 10 October ordered the elimination of laws permitting such actions and of police agencies which carried them out. They further directed the immediate release of political prisoners and required the removal from office of numerous top police officials, including the chiefs of the metropolitan police departments and of each prefectural police department in Japan; also relieved from office were the Minister of Home Affairs who directed police policy, and the Chief of the Home Ministry Bureau of Police. All these mandates were designed to pave the way for the emergence of a democratic Japan.

One of the first important investigations initiated by CIS in the Occupation concerned the *Kempei Tai* and *Tokumu Kikan*, the particular adversaries of counterintelligence agencies during the war. On 4 November the Japanese Government was ordered to submit complete information about these organizations, including lists of all members, organizational charts, descriptions of functions and operations,

---

19 Ltr, GHQ USAFPAC, to CG Eighth A, 11 Sep 45, sub: Apprehension and Detention of Certain Individuals. In AG 383.7 (CI).

20 SCAP GO No. 21, 9 Dec 45.

21 (1) SCAPIN 93, 4 Oct 45, sub: Removal of Restrictions on Political, Civil, and Religious Liberties; (2) SCAPIN 115, 10 Oct 45, sub: Answer to Pro Memoria Conc the Memo of SCAP on Removal of Restrictions on Liberties, dated 4 Oct 45.

and the policies and laws under which they acted. This was the beginning of comprehensive studies on the two groups, which had been abolished at the beginning of the Occupation concurrently with the demobilization of Japanese armed forces.

From the outset Operations Branch maintained special channels of information which were in direct contact with Japanese sources, and thus often made possible more rapid acquisition of specific data needed for immediate action. Initially, CIS also collected Japanese documents and source material on ultra-nationalistic individuals and organizations which were to be purged; later this activity was extended to include left-wing extremists as well. Dossiers and files were prepared on all foreign nationals resident in Japan, as well as a monthly chart showing the distribution of these persons within the country. Based on these valuable records, recommendations regarding the repatriation of foreign nationals, especially the German groups, became a CIS function, as was the apprehension of non-Japanese who assisted in the Japanese war effort, including both neutrals and non-neutrals. Seventy-two persons (among them two Americans) were apprehended in the early days of the Occupation; all were eventually returned to their own countries; some were prosecuted as war criminals.

Approximately 2,000 enemy nationals, whose records were verified by CIS, were removed from Japan in two mass repatriation movements; the majority of these were Germans —former diplomats, interned military and naval personnel, and members of the Nazi party. Their elimination from Japan under Washington policies strengthened the Occupation by reducing security risks.

Civil Censorship Detachment (CCD): Although less sensational in nature, the administration of censorship over Japanese media of public expression offered no less responsibility and no fewer problems than the investigation of war criminals. It was soon evident that close scrutiny of every newspaper, radio script, movie scenario, dramatic production, book, magazine, and pamphlet in Japan would be necessary. The job required inspection not only of the current production of material, but also of that prepared in the years during and before the war. The immediate need, however, was to introduce a code of ethical practice for disseminating organs.[22]

To establish a permanent criterion, press and radio codes were devised, based on ethical practices in the United States. These were passed on to the Japanese Government in the form of memoranda: the " Press Code for Japan,"[23] and the " Radio Code for Japan."[24] Each followed the directions set forth in the " Freedom of Speech and Press " directive, but also elaborated on several points. One salient stipulation was included in the Press Code: " There shall be no destructive criticism of the Allied Forces of Occupation and nothing which might invite mistrust or resentment of those troops." During the early months of the Occupation this and the public tranquility clause were the most frequently violated press rules.

22   Ltr, CCD to Ch CI USAFPAC, 15 Sep 45, sub: Periodic Rpt of CCD. In 319.1. Radio and press censorship was instituted on 10 September when the Japanese Government was officially notified that thereafter there would be no dissemination of news " through newspapers, radio broadcasts, or other media of publication which fails to adhere to the truth or which disturbs public tranquility." (SCAPIN 16, 10 Sep 45, known as the " Freedom of Speech and Press " directive) The directive pointed out, however, that " freedom of discussion of matters affecting the future of Japan is encouraged by the Allied Powers, unless such discussion is harmful to the efforts of Japan to emerge from defeat as a new nation entitled to a place among the peace-loving nations of the world."

23   SCAPIN 33, 18 Sep 45.

24   SCAPIN 43, 22 Sep 45.

Japanese censor reviews film in Motion Picture Department of
Press, Pictorial, Broadcast Division of CCD, Osaka.

After being read by Japanese nationals, material of interest is referred to the
senior translator who passes on the matter and translates it into English.

PLATE NO. 76
Censorship, July 1947

As early as 18 September the first case of public reprimand of a newspaper occurred when the *Asahi Shimbun* was suspended for two days for violating the press code.[25] The following day the *Nippon Times*, Tokyo English language paper, was also suspended for twenty-four hours.[26] These suspensions, which were accompanied by explanations of pertinent policy, brought home sharply the standards required by SCAP.

The next step in the direction of establishing free speech and free press in Japan was made by removing government controls from the agencies of public expression. *Domei News Agency* exercised a monopoly of the news dissemination field, operating under strict censorship of the Board of Information. The *Mainichi-Asahi-Yomiuri* newspaper combines, also under careful government control, similarly monopolized the newspaper publishing field. A directive of 24 September, prepared by CIS, ordered that :[27]

> *In order further to encourage liberal tendencies in Japan and establish free access to the news sources of the world, steps will be taken by the Japanese Government forthwith to eliminate government-created barriers to dissemination of news and to remove itself from direct or indirect control of newspapers and news agencies....*

This memorandum further provided that no preferential treatment be accorded to any news distributor. Foreign news agencies were thus permitted to serve the Japanese press. Communications facilities were also made available to newcomers in the field. Aside from that, the existing system of distribution of news in Japan was tolerated under strict censorship "until such time as private enterprise creates acceptable substitutes for the present monopoly." Soon afterward the *Domei News Agency* was voluntarily abolished.

Another memorandum, "Clarification of Censorship Directive,"[28] covered radio news broadcasts, which were restricted to Radio Tokyo. Regulations for the Japanese press handling news regarding the Occupation forces were also stipulated : news items would be usable only if they had been cleared through the GHQ Public Relations Office.

Censorship Advance Detachments were authorized to impound international mail found during their initial surveys and on 13 September the postal division of CCD took over the Japanese postal system, to place communications in every prefecture under Occupation scrutiny.[29]

Shortly thereafter pre-publication censorship of all major Tokyo newspapers and magazines and Japanese news agency dispatches was initiated ; censorship detachments in the field began surveys of post offices, mail channels, press, drama, and radio organizations, and control was placed over telecommunication outlets from Japan. Four district censorship stations had been installed by the end of 1945.[30]

Examination of internal communications became immediately one of the most direct and reliable "intelligence" sources. Through this medium, leads were developed in practically all cases against major blackmarket operations. In the pictorial field there were sporadic attempts by foreign nations to distribute motion pictures that were likely to stir

---

25 SCAPIN 34, 18 Sep 45, sub : Suspension of Tokyo Newspaper, *Asahi Shimbun.*

26 SCAPIN 37, 19 Sep 45, sub : Suspension of Tokyo Newspaper, *Nippon Times.*

27 SCAPIN 51, 24 Sep 45, sub : Disassociation of Press from Govt.

28 SCAPIN 52, 24 Sep 45.

29 Memo, Ch Postal Div for OCCO CCD, sub : Activation of Postal Censorship, Tokyo, 13 Sep 45.

30 Dist I, Tokyo ; Dist II, Osaka ; Dist III, Fukuoka ; Dist IV (XXIV Corps), Seoul and Pusan, Korea.

up public unrest. In the broadcast or relay of certain foreign news services, there was a positive field of publicizing racial hatreds, foreign ideologies, and anti-American, anti-Occupation attacks which required constant supervision. The enormous volume of internal mail and telegrams checked by CCD constituted a strong security measure;[31] for example, intercepts of foreign subversive propaganda being mailed into Japan from Hong Kong ran as high as 295 pounds in one week.

Examples of security coverage can be found in a continuous flow of information in the form of " spot intelligence reports " on public rallies, formations, plans and programs of organizations bent on disturbing the public peace : the May-Day celebrations ; the Korean riots in the Kobe-Osaka area ; and inflammatory rallies, usually instigated by Communist agitators, involving as high as 50,000 participants.

It was a general policy of SCAP to relax all restrictions progressively, as the Japanese recovered their pace and reform movements became practicable. Under this policy and because of the marked decrease in violations and a concurrent upswing in the number of publications submitted for pre-censorship, press

censorship was modified on 6 June 1947.[32] Another relaxation of censorship control—the first major one— occurred on 1 August when all Japanese broadcasting stations were transferred to post-censorship, though they were required to submit for precensorship questionable material concerning the Allied Powers, and the Occupation or its objectives.[33] During the following month a close check on broadcasts revealed that radio stations had taken great pains to conform to the radio code. Only two tenths of 1 percent of the broadcasts were disapproved during the period.[34]

The second major reduction of censorship took place on 15 October, with the transfer to post-censorship of all book publishers excepting fourteen who specialized in ultra-right and ultra-left material. These continued to be on the pre-censorship list.[35]

On 15 December came the third relinquishing of censorship control, when 97 percent of all magazines edited, published, and distributed in Japan were placed on post-censorship.[36] Again ultra-right and ultra-left publications and those which, because of circulation, subject matter, censorship record, or influence, required closer surveillance were kept on pre-censorship. There were twenty-eight

---

31   Civil Censorship Detachment Communication Division Activity for October 1948 (HQ CCD Mo Opnl Rpt, 1–31 Oct 48):

Mail flashed	22,754,985
External mail examined	184,659
Internal mail examined	3,779,003
External telegraph and cables examined	14,788
Internal telegrams examined	3,537,375
Telephone calls monitored	25,889
Reportable intercepts	67,876
Comment sheets allocated to user agencies	33,991
Valuable intercepts processed	23,751

32   Memo, CofS to G-2, 6 Jun 47, App "L", sub: Modification of Censorship Controls in the Occupied Area, FEC.

33   *Ibid.*

34   Memo, G-2 to CofS, 10 Sep 47, sub: Post-Censorship of Broadcasts.

35   CCD Mo Opnl Rpt, Oct 47.

36   CCD Mo Opnl Rpts, Nov, Dec 47.

magazines in this category.

The fourth major relaxation of censorship control over informational media was effected on 26 July 1948, when all pre-censored newspapers and news services were transferred to post-censorship.[37] The pre-censored, indigenous press was transferred to a post-censorship status in four separate increments during the period 15 through 25 July 1948.[38]

In each of the three major publications fields, some publications were on post-censorship even before these major transfers. In each field, however, the existence of partial pre-censorship controls was an indirect but effective restraint on the post-censored publishers as well. The possibility of being returned to pre-censorship status was sufficient incentive to keep most post-censored publishers in line with the Press Code. When this indirect restraint was largely removed by the major transfers to post-censorship, the effect on the volume of Press Code violations was graphic: the monthly violation rate in news-

papers was five times as great, in books, twenty times as great, and in magazines, twice as great as before transfer. The upsurge in magazine violations was less pronounced than in newspapers and books because of the fact that twenty-eight extremist magazines were kept on pre-censorship, whereas 100 percent of the newspapers and books were post-censored.[39]

On 15 October 1947 twelve publishing firms had been placed on post-censorship with but one proviso: that all books dealing with the Allied Powers, the Occupation or its objectives were still to be pre-censored. On that same date fourteen others had been retained on the complete pre-censorship list. By 30 August 1948, however, these companies were notified that thenceforth all of their publications would be post-censored.[40]

At the end of the year, magazines, books, prefectural newspapers, broadcasts, and motion pictures were being post-censored. This release from pre-censorship control over the major portion of the Japanese publishing field

---

37 Censorship control had been gradually relaxed as reflected in the volume of work handled by Press, Pictorial & Broadcast Division in the month preceding complete transfer to post-censorship, June 1948: (PPB CCD, Mo Stat Rpt, 30 Jun 48. In CCD 319.1.)

	Pre-censored	Post-censored
News items	140,854	
Newspaper issues		14,796
Magazines	26	3,515
Books	15	1,943
Bulletins		3,698
Periodicals		593
Pamphlets		106
Sheet music		50
Catalogues		41
Motion pictures	148	
Lantern slides	686	
Theatrical scripts	1,702	
Theatrical productions reviewed		374
Kami-shibai chapters	3,656	
Broadcast scripts	464	20,987
Recordings		198

38 *Ibid*, Jul 48.

39 Memo, G-2, 19 Jul 49, sub: Relaxation and Elimination of Censorship: PPB.

40 PPB CCD, Mo Stat Rpt, Aug 48. In CCD 319.1.

permitted CCD's Press, Pictorial, and Broadcast Division to expand its mission as an intelligence and analysis agency.[41]

As the facilities and communications surveillance techniques for obtaining information of subversive activities developed, this phase of CCD operations increased in importance until it dominated Communications Division reporting. Surveillance of telephone, telegraph and postal channels yielded a continual flow of " action leads " information to user agencies. Such reporting was concerned with violence, strikes, Communist activities or any other developments which were of a subversive or possible subversive nature. In addition to intelligence of this type, CCD often obtained, chiefly through the monitoring of telephone conversations, valuable advance information on plans for strikes, demonstrations and other activities. These spot reports were forwarded immediately to CIC and other action agencies in time for them to take precautionary measures. Individuals and organizations believed to be of a subversive nature were watch listed by CCD and communications to or from them were carefully studied by personnel trained to detect subversion and clandestine correspondence methods.

In January 1948 communications surveillance reporting of public reaction based on four million intercepts per month was instituted, providing all SCAP agencies with an unbiased, accurate picture of public reaction to the government, to SCAP policies, and to other controversial issues.

Information obtained through censorship was forwarded to SCAP sections or other user agencies in the form of so-called " comment sheets " that were, in fact, substantiated bases for corrective action. An enormous volume of information otherwise unobtainable by user agencies, since they did not maintain field surveillance themselves, was furnished through these comment sheets. (Plate No. 77)

The effect of this type of information was recognized as a direct contribution to the economy of Japan. Many SCAP civil sections benefited from this service and acknowledged its direct monetary or economic values. In a single month, CCD " leads " furnished to ESS disclosed thirty-eight large scale economic violations, leading in turn to the indictment of ninety-three companies and two hundred seventeen persons with a recovery of materials aggregating a value of 101,071,017 yen.[42]

CCD " watchlist " reports of over a year enabled ESS to recover critical items in illegal market operations to an aggregate amount of 431 million yen; blackmarket value of these goods was estimated at five billion yen.[43] Through investigation of one CCD intercept, the Civilian Property Custodian located 16,000 carats of industrial diamonds. Further searching disclosed the location of sufficient diamonds to make the final total 30,000 carats. As a result of only one intercept 52.5 pounds of hoarded platinum, with an official value of 53,679,377 yen, was recovered.[44]

The 441st Counter Intelligence Corps:
The 441st Counter Intelligence Corps (CIC)

---

41   Memo, G-2 to CofS GHQ FEC, 18 Jan 48, sub : Post-Censorship of Newspapers.

42   Rpt, CCD to G-2 GHQ FEC, 14 Jan 49, sub : Contributions to the Occupation.

43   *Ibid.*

44   *Ibid.* In consonance with the CinC's general policy of relaxation of all forms of restrictive measures vis-a-vis the Japanese people, all categories of Civil Censorship operations were discontinued on 31 October 1949. This policy decision was one more decisive step toward liberalization of the Occupation and enlarged freedom of action and responsibilities on the part of the Japanese Government.

Civil Censorship, an operating agency of G-2, was instituted under JCS Directive in 1945 primarily as a preventive and security operation. It was designed to implement the broad features of the Potsdam Declaration with a view to

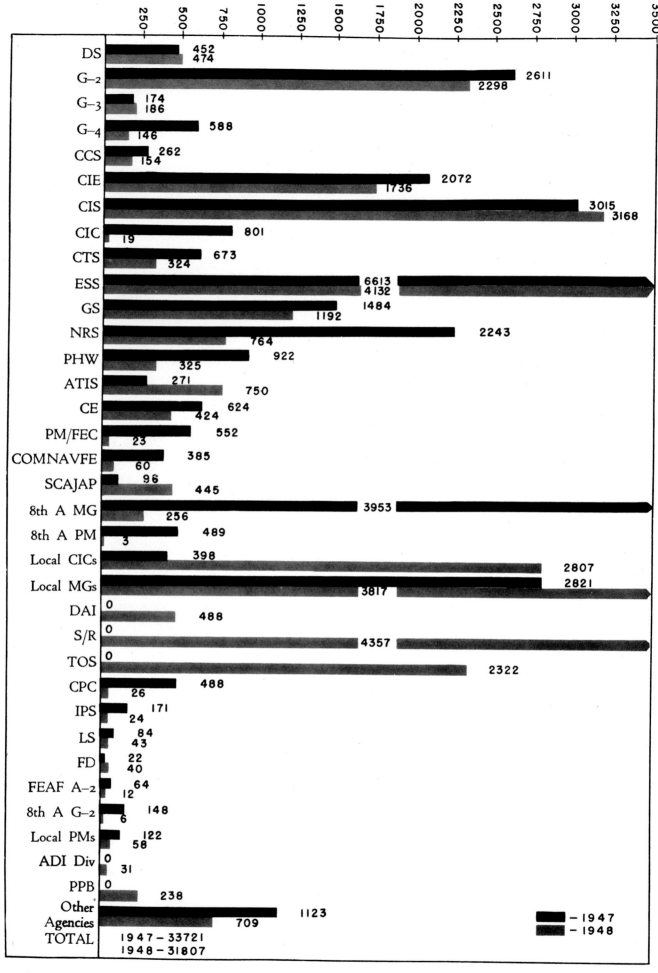

PLATE NO. 77
Comment Sheets Disseminated by CCD to User Agencies:
Comparison between June 1947 and June 1948

and the 319th Military Intelligence Company (MIS linguist unit) constituted the major investigating agencies in the field pertaining to foreign espionage, sabotage, treason, sedition, subversive activities, security violations or other acts inimical to Occupation objectives. In the field of counter intelligence the surveillance coverage of Japan was uniform through national distribution of field detachments. (Plate No. 78)

Fifty-eight separate Counter Intelligence Corps field detachments were established in localities corresponding to the political, prefectural division of Japan. The 441st CIC was closely coordinated with the Occupation troops : the First CIC region corresponded to the I Corps Area ; the Second CIC region, to that of the IX Corps. Six CIC districts coincided with areas assigned to United States divisions and British units. Fifty field units, with seven additional sub-detachments were distributed to cover every important political subdivision of Japan, i. e., the prefecture, the hub of provincial administration.

Reports on activities of field detachments in investigating potentially subversive or other undesirable individuals and organizations were sent to the 441st Headquarters in Tokyo.

Initially the check on enforcement of SCAPIN's was the responsibility of the agency initiating them or the one whose functions were most closely related to their

purposes ; however, in early 1946 SCAPIN's were developing faster than surveillance agencies could be organized to cope with them. It was during this period that two of the most important SCAPIN's were issued : they ordered the abolition of certain ultra-nationalistic organizations and the removal of those office holders whose wartime policies and activities indicated they were unfit to lead Japan along democratic lines.[45]

Under these "purge directives" CIS, in conjunction with the Government Section, furnished advisory opinion concerning the eligibility of persons to hold public office or a position of responsibility and influence in public or important private enterprise. CIC field teams were soon taking definite action in relation to these SCAPIN's. When informed that a person considered unfit was still holding office, CIC took immediate steps to determine the validity of the allegation, and, if proved, to remove the man from his position.[46]

On other occasions the activities of certain organizations indicated to CIC agents evidence of doctrines propagated by officially banned groups. Members of a purged organization sometimes joined or created new groups under different names and seemingly different constitutions but with the same old militaristic or supra-nationalistic tendency.[47] CIS' connection with the purge directives terminated in

---

44 (contd.) eliminating and controlling ultra-nationalistic, militaristic, and subversive influences. The record of censorship in Japan was one of patience and liberal interpretation and steady, progressive relaxations in each successive year : authorization of locally originated radio broadcasts in February 1946, removal of pre-censorship of radio in August 1947, of books in October 1947, of magazines in December 1947, and of newspapers in July 1948.

What minor restraints then remained consisted chiefly of post-facto, sensible precautions against attempts by extremist minorities to abuse the civil liberties granted the Japanese people under a tolerant Occupation. In October 1949 even these barriers of rational protection were lifted, and the Japanese public information and communication media were on their own.

45 (1) SCAPIN 548, 4 Jan 46, sub : Abolition of Certain Political Parties, Assns, Societies and Other Organizations; (2) SCAPIN 550, 4 Jan 46, sub : Removal and Exclusion of Undesirable Pers from Pub Office.

46 441st CIC Det, Mo Info Rpt of Activ, Mar 46.

47 Such was the Japan Science and Culture Association, which claimed as members 90 percent of the SCAP banned Japan Aerial Academic Association.

early 1948. Elsewhere, CIC continued to investigate non-compliance with SCAPIN's but essentially only in the role of a fact-gathering agency.[48] To CIC, well deployed in every prefecture in Japan, went the additional and informal responsibility of enforcing the directives of other SCAP agencies until they were ready to function in the field.

Another SCAPIN which absorbed much of CIC's attention in the early days of the Occupation concerned the surrender of arms by the Japanese people.[49] This responsibility continued throughout the Occupation in conjunction with troop patrols, and small caches of arms or ammunition were uncovered at irregular intervals.

Following the completion of apprehension of the majority of " Class A " war criminals, the tasks of CIC shifted largely to detection and reporting of subversive activity.[50]

The CIC Training School, which opened in the Brisbane area in 1943, provided special training in investigative procedures for officers and agents and replaced its " combat courses " with classes pertaining to Japanese social, political, and economic life. Lectures were given by native authorities on political changes in Japan during the war; Japanese court and newspaper systems and methods used by civil and military intelligence, police and secret agencies were studied. An effort was made to concentrate on the practical aspects of CIC activities; great emphasis was laid on the Japanese prefectural and national government structure and means by which CIC could best utilize Japanese investigative facilities.[51]

Public Safety Division: The organization of a public safety regulatory body was another

---

48   Ltr, HQ 441st CIC Det to all CIC Units in Japan, 5 Aug 46, sub : Direct Action on Removal from Office Taken by Local CIC Det.

49   SCAPIN 181, 23 Oct 45, sub : Instns Conc the Surr of Arms by the Civ Pop of Japan. Also see Ch. V.

50   This trend is illustrated by comparison of the following figures :

	June 1947		June 1948	
	Closed	Pending	Closed	Pending
Sabotage	5	12	5	3
Espionage	7	14	8	28
Treason	0	0	0	0
Sedition	0	0	0	0
Subversive Activities	260	432	195	736
Disaffection	0	1	0	1
Violations of AR 380–5	0	2	0	0
Security Risks	1	0	2	10
Security Investigations	56	66	99	108
Security Surveys	0	1	0	3
Miscellaneous	43	45	32	100

The increase in the number of cases of subversive activity can be largely attributed to the activities of the Japan Communist Party that were inimical to the policies of the Occupation. The number of espionage cases increased with the rise in the number of repatriates returned to Japan from Soviet occupied areas. With the beginning of the repatriation program of Japanese prisoners from Soviet occupied territories, CIC organized Port Interrogation Teams to screen repatriates as they arrived at ports of entry in Japan who were believed to be of interest to CIC. Following the return of these people to their homes, a surveillance in their local prefectures resulted in the detection of espionage agents among some of such returnees.

51   441st CIC, Mo Info Rpts of Activ, Dec 45–Apr 46. Extensive courses in report writing, the jurisdiction and limitations of CIC operations, and investigative procedures were offered, along with briefings on the organization of CIS G-2, AFPAC, and SCAP. As had been the case since the first CICTS class, outside experts on all subjects related to the counter intelligence mission came as guest speakers to give the agents a thorough indoctrination.

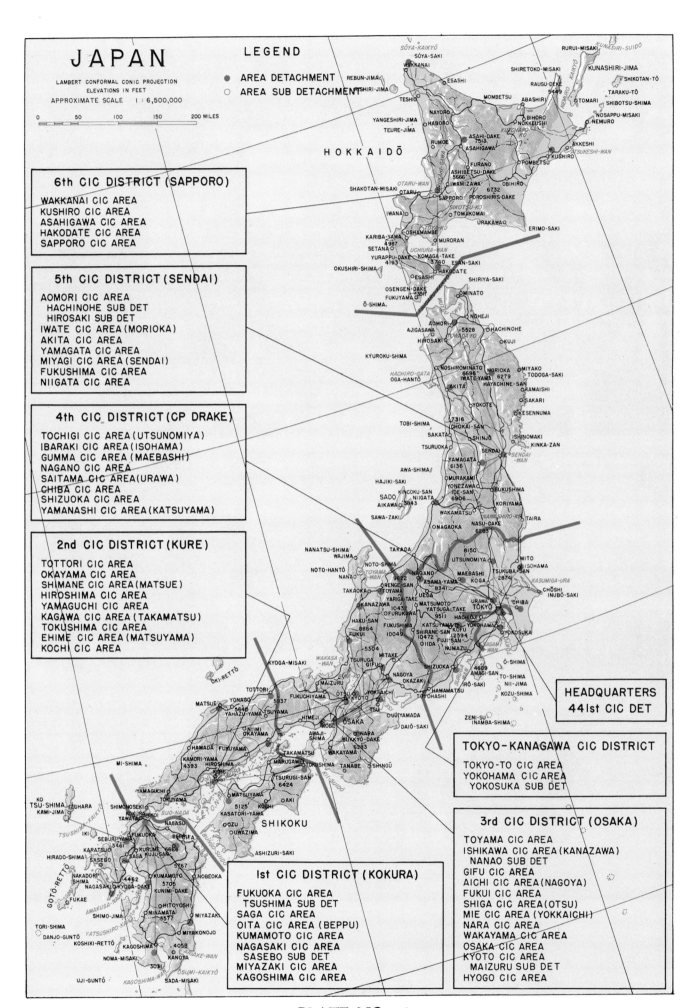

JAPAN

LAMBERT CONFORMAL CONIC PROJECTION
ELEVATIONS IN FEET
APPROXIMATE SCALE 1 : 6,500,000

0   50   100   150   200 MILES

LEGEND
● AREA DETACHMENT
○ AREA SUB DETACHMENT

6th CIC DISTRICT (SAPPORO)

WAKKANAI CIC AREA
KUSHIRO CIC AREA
ASAHIGAWA CIC AREA
HAKODATE CIC AREA
SAPPORO CIC AREA

5th CIC DISTRICT (SENDAI)

AOMORI CIC AREA
 HACHINOHE SUB DET
 HIROSAKI SUB DET
IWATE CIC AREA (MORIOKA)
AKITA CIC AREA
YAMAGATA CIC AREA
MIYAGI CIC AREA (SENDAI)
FUKUSHIMA CIC AREA
NIIGATA CIC AREA

4th CIC DISTRICT (CP DRAKE)

TOCHIGI CIC AREA (UTSUNOMIYA)
IBARAKI CIC AREA (ISOHAMA)
GUMMA CIC AREA (MAEBASHI)
NAGANO CIC AREA
SAITAMA CIC AREA (URAWA)
CHIBA CIC AREA
SHIZUOKA CIC AREA
YAMANASHI CIC AREA (KATSUYAMA)

2nd CIC DISTRICT (KURE)

TOTTORI CIC AREA
OKAYAMA CIC AREA
SHIMANE CIC AREA (MATSUE)
HIROSHIMA CIC AREA
YAMAGUCHI CIC AREA
KAGAWA CIC AREA (TAKAMATSU)
TOKUSHIMA CIC AREA
EHIME CIC AREA (MATSUYAMA)
KOCHI CIC AREA

**HEADQUARTERS
441st CIC DET**

TOKYO-KANAGAWA CIC DISTRICT

TOKYO-TO CIC AREA
YOKOHAMA CIC AREA
 YOKOSUKA SUB DET

3rd CIC DISTRICT (OSAKA)

TOYAMA CIC AREA
ISHIKAWA CIC AREA (KANAZAWA)
 NANAO SUB DET
GIFU CIC AREA
AICHI CIC AREA (NAGOYA)
FUKUI CIC AREA
SHIGA CIC AREA (OTSU)
MIE CIC AREA (YOKKAICHI)
NARA CIC AREA
WAKAYAMA CIC AREA
OSAKA CIC AREA
KYOTO CIC AREA
 MAIZURU SUB DET
HYOGO CIC AREA

1st CIC DISTRICT (KOKURA)

FUKUOKA CIC AREA
 TSUSHIMA SUB DET
SAGA CIC AREA
OITA CIC AREA (BEPPU)
KUMAMOTO CIC AREA
NAGASAKI CIC AREA
 SASEBO SUB DET
MIYAZAKI CIC AREA
KAGOSHIMA CIC AREA

PLATE NO. 78
441st CIC Districts and Field Detachments, 4 October 1948

Police trainees at National Rural Police College in Tokyo
attended lectures on variety of subjects.

Entire motorcycle force of Tokyo lined up prior to parade
terminating " Traffic Safety Week ".

PLATE NO. 79
Police Training Program, 1948

task in the field of Occupation control and reform. Japan's pre-Occupation public safety services, developed under purely militaristic control, required new policies and re-education. Since the public safety organs were the only stabilizing forces which would remain in Japan upon the eventual withdrawal of the Occupation forces, the early reorganization and training of these agencies along democratic lines became a prime objective of SCAP. The Japanese pre-war police had been a national organization, directed from Tokyo, with wide powers of surveillance, arrest, and other forms of " protective custody." They were to be stripped of all illegal powers and their procedures were to be consonant with those of police in a democratic state. In order to cover activities which had been under the police, such as fire defense and fire prevention, wholly new organizations would have to be developed. The prison field, regarded chiefly as a money making organization, was to be brought into line with western standards and given a reform emphasis. The Japanese people, defeated in war, with their cities burned, their factories demolished, their economy bursting out of control, were in a difficult position. They lacked food, clothing and shelter, the basic necessities of life. National unrest developed quickly due in part to uncertainty as to Occupation attitudes and activities, but more to the disruptive activities of the discordant elements, including many recently released political prisoners.

Since the field of public safety was unexplored and not too closely related to previous assignments of CIS, it was necessary to build a Public Safety Division from the ground up. A skeleton staff was immediately appointed within the CIS administrative office, but the Public Safety Division (PSD) did not begin operating until early 1946.[52]

At that time CIS introduced experts in the public safety field from the United States to advise on the reform of corresponding Japanese organizations. Under the guidance of these specialists, the Public Safety Division supervised the reorganization of the Japanese police, fire fighting, and prison systems. In attempting to establish modern democratic organizations in these fields, it was necessary that the status of Japan's shattered economy be kept in mind while adequate measures were being provided to permit future realization of ultimate objectives as the level of Japan's economy was raised.[53]

On the basis of numerous suggestions by Police Branch, PSD, the Japanese Government submitted a master plan of police reform. All municipalities of 5,000 or more population were to have autonomous police departments. These were to be directed by municipally elected Public Safety Commissions. A few more than 1,600 cities fell in this population group, and 95,000 municipal policemen would serve. It was planned to police the non-urban areas of Japan with a national rural police force of 30,000. A National Public Safety Commission, appointed by the Prime Minister, would be charged with establishing policies and plans for the national force. This plan, ap-

---

52   For more complete coverage of PSD, see GHQ SCAP, Int Ser, Vol. IX, *Operations of the Civil Intelligence Section, GHQ, SCAP*, Part II (S). The mission of PSD is delineated in SCAP-FEC GO No. 13, 1945, and in SCAP-FEC Staff Memo No. 7, 1949, which required PSD to advise, guide, coordinate, inform SCAP and effectuate democratic practices and procedures in police, fire, prison and coast guard services of the Japanese Government.

53   GHQ FEC MIS GS, Rpt (S) sub: Org and Functions, G-2 SCAP & FEC, 1 Apr 48. The scientific character of Occupation reforms was evident in the high caliber of its consultants. PSD employed the services of Mr. L. J. Valentine, former Police Commissioner of New York and Mr. O. G. Olander, Superintendent of the Michigan State Constabulary.

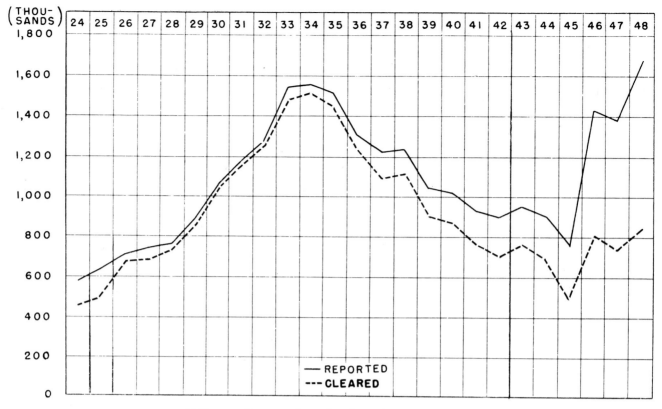

Offenses Reported and Cleared: 1924–1948

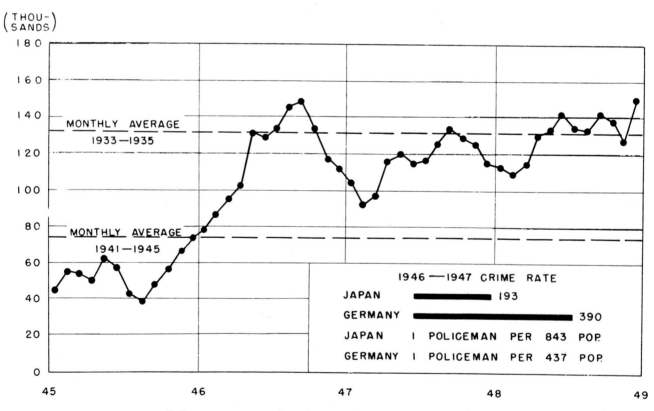

Offenses against the Criminal Code: 1945–1948

PLATE NO. 80
Crime Statistics and Police Effectiveness: 1924–1948

proved in principle by SCAP, was passed by the Diet in December 1947.

Now no longer under police control, the fire prevention agencies were necessarily re-grouped. Japan's fire losses, Fire Branch discovered, were largely due to the combination of closely spaced houses along narrow streets, the constant use of open fires and carelessness in handling them, and meager equipment for fire-fighting coupled with a lack of "know-how" among the thousands of volunteer fire fighters. Whenever conditions indicated that municipalities had ability to support a paid fire department, they were authorized to have them. These, like the local police, were under the local Public Safety Commissions; while on the national level the Fire Research Institute was under the national commission. Within one year of the opening of the first police school nearly 80,000 recruits had been given basic training in American methods as adapted to Japanese needs.[54] A series of schools followed: they continued to train the police in the powers, limitations, and responsibilities of law enforcement, oriented newly created prefectural and municipal Public Safety Commissions in their functions, and taught the Japanese people to consider the police as a safeguard of liberties and civil rights.[55]

Japan had never had a really excessive crime rate, although the middle thirties saw Japan's highest pre-war rate with an average of 130,000 offenses per month. The effectiveness of the wartime police reduced crime to the lowest recorded in police history: the 1941–45 average showed only 75,000 offenses per month. With the end of the war, the inherent unrest of a defeated people, the lack of adequate food, clothing and housing, and the return of millions of demobilized personnel, crime took an upward swing until it exceeded the high figure of the thirties. (Plate No. 80) This increase in crime required constant surveillance by the Public Safety Division.

Studies were made of police communications systems, police training, metropolitan police, and rural police. Along with its research work, the Division conducted numerous widespread investigations throughout Japan.[56] Inspections and surveys of public safety organizations

---

54 Months of inspection, evaluation and comparison went into development of a single PSD recommendation with approval having far reaching effect on Japanese life and welfare as well as the economic stability of their government.

55 84,000 police were trained and retrained during 1948 and early 1949. It was expected that 102,000 would be trained in 1949–1950. Modern texts and curricula were developed and revised. The National Public Safety Commission, with 46 prefectural and 1598 municipal commissions, became increasingly important in internal security, and required guidance. 125,000 police required effective arms and training in their use.

56 Continued assistance was essential since crimes, fires, illegal entrants and prison population necessitating PSD help showed no decline. PSD experts guided the Japanese Government in submitting and obtaining ample budgets on a sound basis. Amounts originally requested (subsequently reduced through PSD guidance), proposed by Finance Ministry (F/M), and recommended and obtained by PSD are shown below. Fifty-one billion yen was saved the Japanese Government without appreciable loss in effectiveness. (Figures in millions of yen)

	Requested	F/M Proposed	PSD Recommendation
Police	33,750	4,400	9,090
Coast Guard	8,370	2,800	3,500
Fire (Nat'l Budget)	480	30	80
Prison	29,000	5,000	7,300
Total	71,400	12,230	19,970

Cell blocks made spotlessly
clean and kept sanitary.

Kitchen made sanitary and food
improved in amount and quality.

Prison industries revitalized
and expanded.

All prisoners made to learn
and do useful work.

PLATE NO. 81
Fuchu Prison, Tokyo: Improvements Made, 1945–1947

were constant.[57] Many corrections were made on the spot, merely by supplying helpful suggestions. Almost all the police detention cells in Tokyo were rebuilt and modernized in this manner. Police brutality and corruption were curtailed and Japanese police inspectors were trained to continue the new program on their own initiative.

By thoroughly investigating the Japanese prison and reformatory systems, experts in penology were able to gain first-hand information of every important penal institution. The Ministry of Justice was abolished and the Attorney General took over the approved duties, but the change carried little of new import for the prisons. There was no change from national to local control but something far more difficult—a change in the prison and reformatory functions without a corresponding change in basic authority. Japanese prisons had been interested in making as much money as possible, thus keeping operating expenses at a minimum. Under the direct guidance and supervision of former American prison wardens, Fuchu and Yokohama Prisons became pilot plants to demonstrate American principles of operation. Again, it was possible to make many corrections on the spot with follow-up investigations to insure that suggestions were carried out. Several special projects were based on information thus obtained: guard training schools, prison industries, paroles and pro-

bation practices, and prisoner classification. After establishment of the Public Safety Division, the prisoner mortality rate in Japan declined sharply.[58]

Studies of Japanese public safety laws and regulations made by the Legal Branch, resulted in recommendations for changes in criminal and juvenile codes, jury laws, rules of evidence, criminal defense and prosecution procedures, and other legal aspects of public safety.

Equally effective work was accomplished in the other branches of the Division. The Fire Branch extended its investigations into every major city of Japan. A system of local autonomous fire departments was set up. Local units were gradually reorganized along functional lines, using the modernized Tokyo Fire Department as a model. A Fire Research Institute was established. Other problems encountered by this Branch included training in fire defense and in fire prevention, development of plans for disaster control, and long-range municipal planning to minimize damage from catastrophes.[59]

Great effort was made to improve the working conditions of the firemen, to remove them from the control of the police bureaucracy, and give them the basic fire fighting equipment. Detailed city grading studies were begun, based on the standard American fire underwriter's procedures. Deficiencies were brought to light in this way, and insurance rates were equalized.

57 During 1947–1948 PSD completed 216 major projects which involved 90 field trips, broken down as follows:

Unit	Conferences	Inspections
Police	529	1,462
Prison	493	155
Fire	575	105
Maritime Service	35	35

58 Field inspections revealed that 100,000 persons were incarcerated in 65,000 capacity space. Legislation for a relatively good prison and parole system was enacted but required supervisory implementation to be effective. Technical knowledge was lacking among Japanese Government officials.

59 Fire-fighting equipment remained a prime factor. The enormity of fire losses, although reduced, required continued technical aid due to the impact on national economy.

Japan's Fire Research Institute, April 1948, formerly the Japanese
Central Aeronautics Research Institute.

Ichikawa Fire Department is inspected by PSD Fire Branch, March 1947.

PLATE NO. 82
Fire Prevention

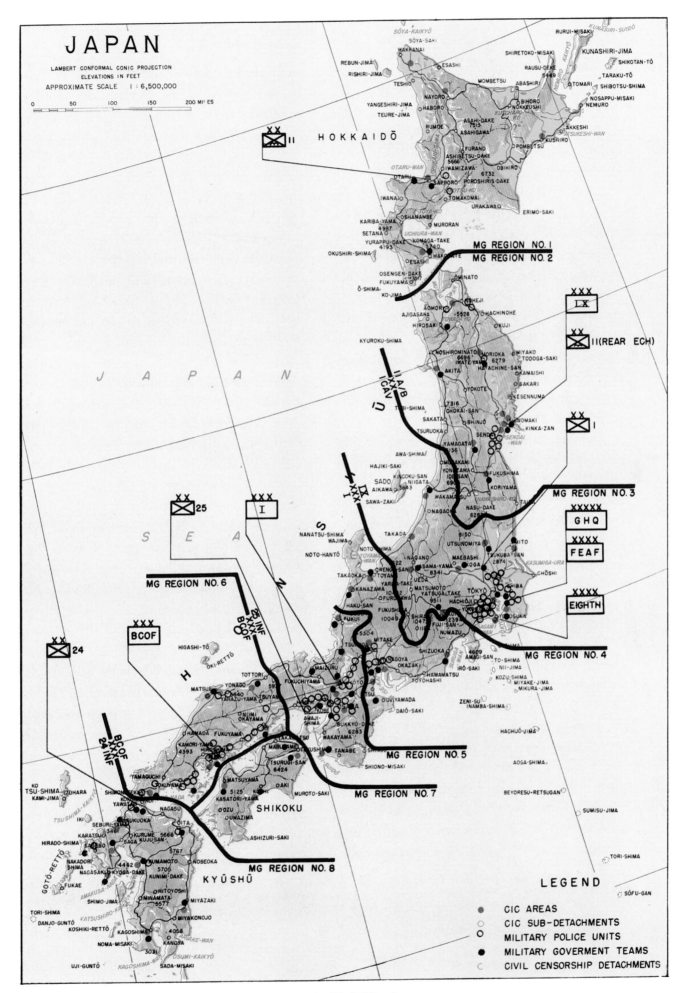

PLATE NO. 83

Relationship of Counter Intelligence, Civil Censorship, Military Police and
Military Government Detachments, 15 December 1948

By means of an elaborate publicity campaign during Japan's first "Fire Prevention Week" a great deal of cooperation was obtained from prominent citizens; neighborhood fire protection associations which gave valuable service in eliminating local fire hazards were formed.

Japan's geographical condition as a group of islands pointed to yet another phase of public safety, the maritime. Here the national control was weaker and jurisdiction over harbors was largely of a local character. Guided by PSD suggestions, the Japanese set up a Maritime Safety Board with functions similar to the American Coast Guard Service. A Maritime Training Institute was planned to supplement the seamen's training and the reconstruction of the nation's war-wrecked navigational aids system was given high priority.

The Maritime Safety Branch was primarily interested in the establishment of a Japanese Maritime Safety Service (Coast Guard) and made recommendations relative to navigational aids, sea-rescue, hazards to navigation, and prevention of illegal entry and smuggling.[60]

Security Surveillance and Law Enforcement

The initial and continuous tranquility of Japan, compared with other world areas, has perhaps been the outstanding success of the Occupation. This was primarily due to accurate counter intelligence information on every shade of public unrest—in the field of labor, in communist infiltration, and in movements of disillusioned, repatriated military personnel.

Certain law enforcement and surveillance agencies in the field maintained potential observation posts in affected areas, although their employment, missions and duties differed. From an intelligence point of view, the political, administrative and economic reporting of Military Government teams served to supplement and confirm CIC field reports and gave GHQ a factual picture of current activities. Both agencies continued to be deeply concerned with the maintenance of local law and order.

There was also inferential relationship between the Counter Intelligence Corps and the Criminal Investigation Division (CID) of the Provost Marshal (PM). Important leads for the PM/CID investigation of blackmarket movements, for example, came from CCD and CIC. The primary mission of the Provost Marshal however, continued to be that of troop control, while CIC was principally concerned with subversive acts by Japanese or foreigners inimical to the Occupation forces or the policies of SCAP. The Military Police and CID (PM) handled police cases as they related to the U. S. Army personnel: vehicle traffic, off-duty discipline, theft, and miscellaneous criminal charges. Counter Intelligence concern with United States troops and civilians was largely limited to questions of security, i. e., disaffection, disloyalty, and subversion. CID however, inevitably overlapped CIC investigative processes.

In a survey of the relative density and distribution of surveillance agencies (Plate No. 83) the concentration of Military police and Criminal Investigation Division strength naturally coincided with major troop distribution, the Tokyo, Yokohama and Osaka areas being heavily covered. As regards relative density, Military Police and CID maintained twenty-five units in only twenty-four prefectures, while the 441st CIC manned sixty posts in forty-six prefectures, a complete national coverage[61]

---

60   Twenty-three coast guard bases utilizing 46 patrol craft were established protecting 9,369 miles of coastline. Training for 10,000 personnel was inaugurated using new texts, curricula and methods. The coast guard agency was new to the Japanese Government which was utterly devoid of skilled technicians or know-how. Illicit traffic was declining.

61   As of April 1949. (Rpt, CIS to G-2 FEC, 28 Apr 49, sub: Rel Status, CIC, PM, CID [S].)

The Military Government teams more nearly approximated the prefectural distribution of the 441st CIC throughout. Their purposes and capacities were closely related to CIC surveillance in the same areas. Although "Blacklist" anticipated "combined operations" of these two agencies, they were never officially effected, but in practice CIC and MG units in the field cooperated closely.[62]

A major turning point in the development of the section occurred in May 1946 when it was placed under direct control of the theater G-2, thus eliminating the artificial staff division between counterintelligence and operational theater intelligence which had been considered a wartime weakness.[63]

Since the Government Section had final authority over questions regarding compliance with terms of the purge directives, the selective check had assumed such proportions as to make proper enforcement impossible for so small a unit as G/A Branch; this responsibility was transferred from CIS to Government Section on 11 January 1947.[64] Except for the continued filing of questionnaires in CIS for intelligence purposes, CIS was no longer concerned with enforcement of the purge directives.

A new element made itself felt in this period : loyalty checks on personnel working for or with the Occupation. The Loyalty Desk was established in June 1947 at a time when Washington, apprehensive of Communist infiltration into Government offices, required a thorough security investigation of all Army employees.[65] Two other special categories of security checks covered persons traveling in the FEC and certain aliens wishing to marry American Occupation personnel. The primary purpose of investigation in both cases was counterespionage.

The Loyalty Desk served other staff sections in numerous ways. It made record checks of proposed entrants for Civil Information and Education Section, appointees holding power of attorney for the Civil Property Custodian, and Japanese witnesses and lawyers required by the Legal Section to participate in war crimes trials held outside Japan. At G-1's request, checks were initiated on individual Japanese who desired to return home, and various other staff sections turned

---

62   Relative Coverage by 441st CIC, Military Police and Military Government :

	441st CIC			MILITARY POLICE			MILITARY GOVT.		
YEAR	STR.	STA.	COV.	STR.	STA.	COV.	STR.	STA.	COV.
1946	1076	61	100%	6709	19	30%	2251	47	79%
1947	1276	61	100%	6440	34	56%	2391	47	79%
1948	1221	60	100%	3804	34	57%	2313	54	98%

It should be noted that this coverage was accomplished with one-third the strength of the MP's. In terms of realistic percentage, CIC executed 100 percent security coverage as compared with 57 percent Military Police coverage, but on the numerical basis of approximately 30 percent relative strength.

63   See FM-101-5, Sec. II, par. 15 (b). A modification of functions for civil intelligence missions and development of new Occupation problems resulted in a reorganization of CIS Operations Branch into four main sub-units : Special Activities Branch (S/A) which dealt with left-wing subversion ; General Activities Branch (G/A) which was concerned with right-wing activity, ultra-nationalism, foreign nationals in Japan, checking on conformance with SCAP directives, and screening persons subject to the purge ; Compilations Branch, which gathered background information on personalities and organizations of counterintelligence interest ; and the Executive Group under which was placed the Publications and Files Section as well as a classification and control section which disseminated intelligence gathered by field agencies, collated and processed by the other branches.

64   SCAP Staff Memo No. 13, 11 Jan 47, sub : Removal and Exclusion of Undesirable Japanese Pers from Governmental and Influential Private Positions.

65   (1) Bull No. 4, 10 Apr 47, Sec II, Exec Order 9835, sub : Prescribing Procedures for the Adm of an Employees Loyalty Program in the Exec Br of the Govt ; (2) DA Cir 338, 28 Oct 48, sub : Organizations Considered by the AG to Have Interests in Conflict with Those of the U S.

to CIS for clearances of foreign nationals to handle classified information.[66]

Internal Subversion

The forces working against democracy were not all of foreign extraction. The pattern of Communist thinking was obvious enough, but the job of detecting it in individual cases was difficult. To establish enough positive evidence to take action against disaffected Americans in the Far East Command called for skillful and painstaking investigations.

The Domestic Subversion Desk was a control group which followed up G-2's interest in the arrest, transfer and/or release of war criminals, and in addition handled many types of cases (other than leftist) involving willful activity to undermine the interests of the United States. Illustrative is the following list of typical cases acted upon by the Subversion Desk during 1947: alleged American traitors; impersonation of CIC agents by Japanese and foreign nationals; Japanese underground movements; German intelligence activities in the Far East; requests for information from Allied Missions; information about "Tokyo Rose"; possible arson of Occupation forces installations; information on Japanese war criminals; investigation of hidden arms and ammunition; ultranationalistic, anti-Occupation activities; Army postal violations; information on hidden goods; information for trial of alleged war criminals in the United States; and military script conversion violations.[67]

The Compilations Branch included the Organizations, Personalities, Foreign, and Microfile Sections. Its role was that of a specialized information collection agency, with access to original Japanese documents, direct contact with innumerable Japanese persons, and a highly developed dissemination system geared to furnish operational information to other branches of Operations Division. Through continued liaison with CIC and the Document Section of ATIS, and through cultivation of

---

66 In 1947 when Washington authorities became seriously concerned with the problem of internal subversion and certain organizations and publications were publicly designated by the Attorney General of the United States as Communist, subversive or Fascist, CIS was given the responsibility of implementing the loyalty check on personnel in the FEC. In applying the loyalty criteria concerning communism, three categories had been set up: (standards prescribed in D/A Cir No. 17, par 2, 18 Jan 47) membership in the Communist Party, close affiliation with the Party, and close association with known members of the Party. In the FEC, association with Japan Communist Party members and organizations was also included. Membership or sympathetic association with any of the Attorney General's list of organizations was not taken as the sole criterion of disloyalty, however, but rather as a warning to the various CIS components to be on the alert, in their mission as "watchdog of the Occupation."

67 The Japanese political situation was of continuing interest to the Domestic Subversion Desk. The information compiled by political analysts in connection with the arrest of war criminals and the conduct of the purge proved invaluable in following the complicated course of mushrooming political parties, organizations, and individuals. The Political Subsection maintained current, detailed rosters of political parties within the Diet and a large miscellaneous file on activities within the political organizations which had potentialities of being antagonistic to the Occupation. Even after the staff reponsibility for the administration of the SCAPIN regarding undesirable personnel in public office was completely taken over by Government Section, the Political Desk continued to collate, evaluate, and report information on political trends for the special purposes of civil and counter intelligence.

Each repatriate to Japan was required to provide personal information: his name, destination, permanent address, registered address, branch of military service, military rank or civilian occupation, unit, place of internment, education and, if interrogated code indicating type of information supplied. One copy of each card bearing such information was forwarded to the ATIS Central Interrogation Center in Tokyo, and the duplicate was used to establish in G/A Branch a central repatriate file providing locator cards on adult Japanese repatriates and a supplementary file of all military men, organized by internment camps in which they spent the longest period. The purposes of the file were wide and varied. It offered to G-2 user agencies the possibility of locating uninterrogated repatriates after their processing at the port had been completed. It helped ATIS Central Interrogation Center locate subjects for re-interrogation, and aided CIC in checking addresses of repatriates of counter intelligence interest whose whereabouts were uncertain.

independent Japanese sources not generally or easily available to other less specialized groups, Compilations Branch built up a Japanese National Reference Library which was recognized as an authoritative source for original Japanese documentary material. Among its materials were thousands of personality and organization dossiers, an extensive microfilm index of Special Higher Police cards, and a large card file of higher Japanese Civil Service officials.

The Microfile Section recorded thousands of documents for other sections of CIS as well as for the Japanese National Reference Library. It included among its files the records of all cases pertaining to violations of the Peace Preservation and the Military Security Laws, the Saionji-Harada Memoirs (some 3,000 typewritten pages), the Marquis Kido Diary, and innumerable documents of counter intelligence interest.

Publications Section, as its name implies, was concerned primarily with the preparation of CIS' contribution to various G-2 publications. Its chief project, the "Periodical Summary," developed from the weekly "Situation Report—Japan" which was first published on 4 November 1945, and which after three issues became "Occupational Trends—Japan and Korea." Designed as "a compilation of Japanese trends in political, educational, psychological, and religious spheres, as gathered from reports submitted by counter intelligence agencies," the publication presented to theater commanders and to the War Department a full picture of the civil side of occupation intelligence.

In addition to the "Periodical Summary"

the Publications Section compiled the counter intelligence part of the G-2 Daily Intelligence Summary and contributed to the operations report for the War Department.

Special Projects Section was under direct control of the commanding officer of 441st CIC Detachment. To meet the international aspect of counter intelligence, Special Projects sub-sections were established in every CIC area in Japan.[68] The Section headquarters concentrated on cases concerning espionage, foreign inspired sabotage, and radical or foreign inspired subversion.

Organized labor, a force which, due to the machinations of left-wing leaders, at times threatened to defeat the liberal Occupation directives that had brought it into existence in Japan, was observed by the Labor Branch of Special Projects Section. This unit furnished considerable information to the Labor Division of SCAP's Economic and Scientific Section, as illustrated by the timely and continuous reports provided prior to the incipient but dangerous general labor strike in February 1947 and a similar disturbance planned by subversive elements in October of that year.[69] It was also responsible for notifying CIC field units of expected developments in the labor arena. It received reports from the field teams in case of strikes, important labor gatherings, the reaction of local labor organizations to speeches by prominent Communists, and other similar events.

Under the new freedoms granted to them by SCAP, the Japanese people rushed to organize in the political and labor fields to a degree that was bewildering to Western observers. With a hereditary talent for banding

---

68 441st CIC Det, Mo Info Rpts of Activ, Dec 46 and Dec 47. Cases of this nature processed through Special Projects Section increased from 453 for the month of December 1946 to 1,575 during December 1947, although a case load chart could not adequately indicate the labor involved. During December 1947, for example, of 139 cases completed in headquarters on JCP activities, 357 investigations were run in field units.

69 CIS Periodical Sum No. 11, 1 Feb 47.

together, Japanese from all walks of life took advantage of their freedom from the militaristic state domination which had guided them for centuries and the number of societies, parties, clubs, and leagues representing every shade of opinion grew without check. They held meetings, parades, and demonstrations to give vent to their feelings, whether on political matters or for the purpose of winning public support for higher wages. This development in the early months of 1946 was widespread and rapid; it soon became apparent that unless some method of keeping track of such events was established, there would be frequent opportunities for local troublemakers to circumvent the objectives of the Occupation. It was at this time, too, that under Communist prompting, organized labor was beginning its first major wave of strikes. To offset this situation, the use of "spot reports" was initiated to cover all unusual occurrences throughout Japan.[70]

Such incidents were defined to include any event which showed indications of actual or potential sabotage, treason, or other matters of CIC interest; fires, explosions, epidemics, earthquakes, or other accidents which might affect the Occupation effort; strikes, mass demonstrations, or misconduct of Occupation or Japanese personnel; and miscellaneous events such as attempts at assassination, attacks on the Japanese Government, and incidents precipitated by or indicating foreign interests. All such happenings were promptly reported to the 441st Headquarters.[71] For outlying areas the telephone presented the fastest mode of communication but, for incidents which occurred in the proximity of

GHQ, mobile radio equipment was often used by CIC.

Early in 1947 arrangements were made to utilize the Eighth Army teletype network for CIC spot reports on a twenty-four hour basis. By 15 March spot reports were flowing into 441st Headquarters via teletype, radio, and telephone in a steady stream. In that month alone, 113 CIC spot reports were sent to CIS to be forwarded to the AC of S, G-2.[72]

Repatriation

Both operational and counter intelligence agencies were interested in the interrogation of returning PW's.[73] In November 1946 the counter intelligence coverage of this field was begun. Although certain ports were designated as repatriation centers through which all internees entered Japan, the varied destinations of repatriates in Japan necessitated coordination of all CIC field units in handling this problem.[74]

In the 441st CIC Headquarters, a special Repatriate Branch was established within the Special Projects Section to coordinate the operations of the field units. The over-all plan entailed a three-step system of screening incoming repatriates. In the initial phase, all returnees, while still aboard ship, completed forms concerning their original address in Japan, full name, age, place of confinement, and intended place of residence following the completion of repatriation. The forms also asked for information concerning activities in the Japanese Army and later within the prison camp, indicating political affiliations, social activities, and indoctrination. By screening

---

70   Ltr, HQ, 441st CIC Det to all CIC units in Japan, 2 Aug 46, sub: Spot Int Rpts.

71   *Ibid.*

72   441st CIC Det, Mo Info Rpt of Activ, Mar 47.

73   For details of repatriation movement, see Ch. VI.

74   Ltr, Hq 441st CIC Det, 21 Nov 46, sub: Repatriates from Russian Occupied Areas.

Interrogation officers check passenger list with captain of the
Tokuga Maru.

Repatriates are given instructions on how to fill out repatriation forms.

PLATE NO. 84
Repatriation Interrogations, August 1948

these forms, it was possible to establish which repatriates were of immediate counterintelligence interest. These were interrogated at the port in coordination with Eighth Army intelligence officers, constituting the second phase in the plan. Japanese nationals were used to carry on much of the interrogation and routine work not involving classified information. CIC coverage of port customs check stations was maintained. The third phase included intensive interrogation by Allied Translator and Interpreter Section(ATIS) in Tokyo of those suspected of possessing sensitive information.[75]

Data from the personal history forms was transcribed on cards in English. A card file of repatriates was set up with master file by CIS Operations Division while files pertaining to repatriates in each CIC area were established in the CIC area office concerned.

As the number of repatriates continued to grow, a priority system for classifying them was adopted, to show those who merited intense interrogation without delay, those of counterintelligence importance who did not require immediate questioning, and those who were given a routine check within a designated time. Complete statistical data was kept on them and submitted monthly to 441st Headquarters, CIS, and G-2.[76]

In an effort to lighten the work load of personnel in the field, CIC operations at the repatriation ports were expanded and improved. More efficient interrogations were accomplished before the repatriates had a chance to begin their trek home.[77]

The Korean Minority Problem

One of CIS' problems in Japan centered in the Korean minority.[78] If they chose to remain in the country, they were expected to conform to Japanese laws and to receive equal treatment with Japanese citizens. The Koreans, however, in a surge of revulsion against their former oppressors, interpreted their liberation as meaning complete freedom from Japanese-imposed restraints of any kind. This at-

---

75 ATIS furnished translation, interrogation, and interpreter service to key civil and military sections in SCAP and GHQ, as well as to subordinate units, and procured and processed documents for evacuation to Washington. The large volume of work handled is indicated by the following figures:

	1946	1947	1948
Documents scanned	55,923	224,883	94,609
Documents translated	1,171	2,326	2,338
Periodicals translated	5,330	32,492	53,619
Documents processed	336,666	28,698	24,754
Documents evacuated to Washington .	417,497	14,193	8,391

During 1947 and 1948, ATIS translated monthly an average of 17,117 pages from issues of 450 different newspapers and magazines. An average of 13,234 communications per month from the Japanese to the CinC and the Allied Council was translated and analyzed to sample public opinion trends among the Japanese people. Those requiring action were forwarded to the responsible Occupation agency. (G-2 GHQ FEC, ATIS Hist Rpt, 1947–48)

76 Ltr, Hq 441st CIC Det to all CIC units in Japan, 28 Feb 47, sub: Subsequent Screening of Japanese Repatriates from Russian Occupied Areas.

77 The volume of work done by CIC in connection with the repatriation program can be illustrated by the following figures taken from two example months, one in 1947 and one in 1948:

	Interrogated by CIC Port Teams	Investigated, closely watched or checked by field units in local prefectures
September 1947	1356	39,825
September 1948	2428	34,965

78 Sp Rpt, Compilations Br, 9 Apr 47, sub: Koreans in Japan.

Japanese shipmaster of vessel returning repatriates to Japan, is
interrogated regarding number of passengers aboard.

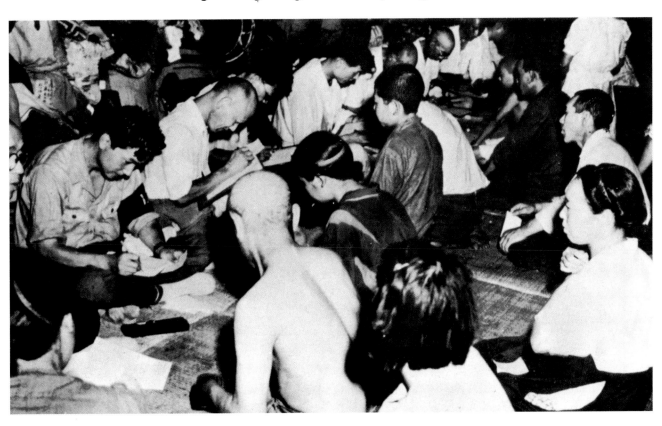

Repatriates are interrogated by members of the Home Ministry aboard
the *Tokugu Maru* at Hakodate, the initial processing phase.

PLATE NO. 85
Repatriation Interrogations, August 1948

titude of defiance led to recurring conflicts with Japanese authorities and in 1947 the rate of crime for Koreans was almost three times that for Japanese.[79]

Under a voluntary repatriation program initiated in March 1946,[80] more than 1,100,000 Koreans were repatriated. In March 1947 there were 542,139 registered Koreans remaining in Japan, constituting the largest minority group in the country.[81] Korean groups became increasingly restive and their numbers expanded through illegal entries.[82]

Although police apprehended 21,000 illegal entrants between April 1946 and January 1947, it was believed that those who evaded the patrols and successfully entered Japan greatly outnumbered those who were caught. Between March 1947 and March 1948 the registered Korean population actually increased by 10 percent.[83]

The most serious effect of unlawful entry aside from possible infiltration of agents or agitators into Japan was severe social and economic disruption. Most Koreans returned illegally had no assurance of a livelihood. Local Korean communities managed to circumvent the police by absorbing them speedily and by undertaking illicit activities to prevent their detection. To obtain the necessities of life, the illegal entrants procured unauthorized ration cards.[84] Living under assumed names and continually changing residence, this group constituted a prominent factor in disorder and lawlessness in Japan.

The pronounced nationalism developed by the long-oppressed Koreans made them over-zealous of anything Korean: their national language, their culture, and their temples were to be preserved by any possible means. Thus, when the Education Ministry issued a series of directives designed to attain uniform educational standards, the Koreans refused to admit that their schools which were not government subsidized should be affected.[85] The

---

79 GHQ SCAP, Mo Summation of Non Mil Activ, Jan–Dec 47.

80 SCAPIN 746, 17 Feb 46, sub: Registration of Koreans, Chinese, Ryukuans, and Formosans.

81 One third of this number was concentrated in the Kansai area (mainly in Kyoto, Hyogo and Osaka Prefectures), the remainder being scattered throughout Japan, with fairly heavy concentrations in Tokyo, Kanagawa, Yamaguchi, Hiroshima, Fukuoka, Aichi, Okayama and Shiga Prefectures.

82 CIS Periodical Sum No. 17, 15 Jun 47. While not concerned normally with smuggling activities either of persons or materials, CIC unit commanders were instructed to maintain close observation and report immediately all possibilities of subversive activities connected with illegal entrants (e. g. the smuggling into Japan of Communist literature). Cases which indicated no activity of counterintelligence jurisdiction were turned over to the local Military Government or tactical unit for disposition. (Ltr, HQ 441st CIC Det, 26 Aug 47, sub: Handling of Illegal Repatriates.)

83 G-2 GHQ FEC, Daily Int Sum No. 2009, 20 Jan 48. See also S/I, CIC Area 37, 12 Nov 47, sub: Illegal Repatriation of Korean Nat'ls at Hakodate.

84 (1) Sp Rpt, Compilations Br, 15 Dec 47, sub: Korean Smuggling Activities. (2) In Nagano Prefecture the Chief of Police reported that the majority of Koreans had no regular occupation and 60 to 80 percent were alleged blackmarketeers or bootleggers. (CCD Intercept JP/TOK/60053, 14 Oct 47) (3) In an attempt to obtain rationed goods for illegal sale, Koreans frequently resorted to the simple expedient of exaggerating the number of persons in a family or continuing to draw rations for individuals who had left the community. This "ghost population" was a problem in almost every Korean settlement. In one instance, four Koreans succeeded in obtaining ration books for 838 persons, with bogus official documents. By forging "Removal of Residence" certificates and pretending to reside in several villages simultaneously, they were able to amass approximately 300 bales of rice in a few weeks. (S/I, CIC Area 28, 4 Aug 47, sub: Arrest of Koreans.)

85 S/I, CIC Area 6, 8 Jan 48, sub: Meeting of Fight Committee of Ehime-ken HQ of League of Koreans Residing in Japan.

resultant demand for " racial autonomy " in education (i.e., approval of the use of Korean as the spoken language in the schools, continuance of the use of Korean textbooks, and placing of the schools under Korean management and supervision) precipitated one of the most serious outbreaks of violence during the Occupation.[86]

More than ninety Korean organizations came into existence following the surrender of Japan. The major organization, " League of Koreans Residing in Japan," ostensibly represented a consolidation of the aims of the many former groups to form a strong lobbying bloc to further interests of Korean residents in Japan ; the leftist nature of the League, however, was manifest almost from the first. When, through intrigue and intimidation, the minority communist faction gained control, a rightist group broke away from the League and formed the " Youth Organization for the Reconstruction of Korea " (*Kensei*).

In February 1946 the adult members in the *Kensei* formed a separate organization known, after a series of mergers and name changes, as the " Union of Great Korean Republics Residing in Japan " (better known under a former name, " Korean Residents' Union " or the *Mindan*). With a few exceptions the two rightist groups worked together in their pursuit of a mutual goal—foundation and recognition of a rightist government in Korea. Despite their efforts the rightist elements never reached the strength and power of the leftist groups in Japan. Meanwhile, leaders of the Japan Communist Party took note of the leftist trend of the League and promptly took steps to bring it into the communist sphere of influence.

The close relationship of the leftist Korean groups in Japan with the Japan Communist Party is well illustrated by the fact that some of the top leaders held positions in both. In joint movements, these groups were mutually supporting, each supplying certain essential elements for protest movements. The Koreans furnished enthusiastic mobs, pickets, and strong propaganda.

Subsequent to the termination of the war, Korean education was chiefly concerned with the teaching of the Korean language. Since the prospect of their remaining in Japan assumed a semi-permanent aspect and since their schools might be suppressed if nothing else was taught, formal revisions were made in the education policy to include subjects normally taught in Japanese schools.

Seventy-two Korean news agencies, newspapers and magazines disseminated news and information to the Korean people in Japan. In addition, the leftist Koreans utilized other media of propaganda, from the *Kami-Shibai*

---

86 Interpreting the demand for " racial autonomy " as a refusal to comply with the law, the Education Bureau ordered Korean schools closed and, when they continued to operate in defiance of the ban, undertook to close them. Demonstrations, petitions, and a spectacular series of disturbances featuring sitdown strikes, imprisonment, and intimidation of local officials and various other types of agitation extended over several weeks.

From 23 to 26 April 1948 Koreans in Kobe defied all authority, rioted, wrecked the governor's office, and forcibly detained prefectural officials until they signed, under duress, statements rescinding the order to close Korean schools and directing the release of all Koreans held in connection with the disturbance. (S/I, CIC Area 8, 25 Apr 48, sub : Korean Educational Strife.) In Osaka, 7,000 Koreans stormed and wrecked the prefectural governor's office following the arrest of 100 agitators and resorted to violence when police attempted to eject them. (S/I, CIC Area 9, 28 Apr 48, sub : Koreans Hold Mass Meetings and Demonstrations in Osaka City.) Rioting continued in both cities even after police had taken the ringleaders into custody. Both Japanese and Occupation Military Police reinforcements were called into action. Subsequently, the education issue was settled when Korean leaders agreed to comply with the original Education Ministry order. (G-2 GHQ FEC, Daily Int Sum No. 2096, 3 May 48.)

(picture stories for children) to nationwide poster campaigns. One of the most powerful and economical propaganda vehicles was rumor spreading, in which the Korean leaders excelled and to which the average Korean was extremely susceptible.

The Japan Communist Party

The greatest single political group as a medium of potential trouble for the Occupation was the Japan Communist Party (JCP), with its varied and persistent attempts to discredit and nullify the program of democratization. From the outset, it was recognized that this group's activities and methods made it less a political party and more a fifth column introducing alien ideologies into Japan. This factor became a prime concern of Counter Intelligence.[87]

Early in the Occupation, it was realized that the release of all political prisoners, a completely laudable political gesture, was also opening the doors to a group of well-trained, fully indoctrinated obstructionists. The Communists were quick to reorganize their Party and to start its program of anti-democratic activities, which sometimes found unexpected support from disorganized sections of the post surrender population.

As in every other non-Communist country, the Party in Japan proved to be a menace to all duly constituted authority. Its members, imbued with the philosophy that any means are justifiable as long as they promote the Party's aims, continually resorted to illegal, subversive, and undercover methods to attain their ends.

The JCP devoted its well-correlated energies to interfering with the vital food production, shipbuilding, merchant shipping, democratic organization of labor, and the collection of taxes—to name a few of the methods by which it maneuvered stumbling blocks in the path of Japan's democratization. It sponsored or took over many " front " organizations and put on a comprehensive propaganda program designed to create spiritual confusion among the populace and to promote an alien ideology.

In spite of the essentially conservative character of the Japanese people, the JCP achieved a relative degree of success in penetrating the higher echelons of organized labor during the first two and one-half years of the Occupation. Capitalizing on the confusion and readjustment which characterized the first postwar months, the Communist Party, repeating its tried methods of operation, infiltrated the countless labor unions which were springing up all over Japan as a part of the new democratization program.

The radical complexion of the National Congress of Industrial Unions (NCIU) and its wide control of the workers in Japan's key industries made it a major target for CIS as its activities became more and more openly threatening to the Occupation's goals. Communist infiltration had reached such proportions by August 1946 that the Party's Central Committee was able to instruct the Communist Party faction in the NCIU to incite the member unions to plan a general strike on 15 September 1946, coordinated with a threatened twenty-four hour strike of government railway workers.[88]

CIS, alerted by CIC and CCD reports,

---

87 (1) Ltr, MID, WD 350.09, pars. 3 (1), 4c (2), 9 Oct 45, sub: Far East Int Requirements; (2) SCAP GO 13, Functions of CIS, 2 Oct 45; (3) JCS Dir 1538, 5 Oct 45, sub: Provisions for the Coordinated Exploitation of Japanese Int Targets of Inter-departmental and International Concern; (4) SCAP GO 15, 9 Nov 45, sub: Japanese Civilian Int Targets.

88 S/A Br, CIS Sp Rpt, 12 Sep 46, sub: Threatened Gen Strike for 15 Sep 46.

watched this activity closely. Enough information had been correlated and forwarded by CIS' Special Activities Branch preceding the intended date of the strike to enable GHQ to know exactly what to expect and to plan accordingly.[89]

Following labor's futile attempt at a general strike in the fall of 1946, the Communist Party files in CIS expanded by leaps and bounds. Data continued to flow in from networks of informants. The NCIU by now was definitely established as being the instrument through which the JCP attempted strikes.[90] Through extensive G-2 reports, ESS and other staff sections were apprised of the fact that the NCIU contained many labor unions in a large number of vital industries, (e.g., coal, steel, communications, newspaper and radio, publishing and printing, and electric power) as well as such local unions as the Tokyo Area Government Railway Workers Union, which was thoroughly impregnated with Communists.[91]

The Civil Intelligence Section kept day by day progress studies of the NCIU and its Communist-dominated organizations. "Spot" reports were a valuable source of current information, often being forwarded to General Headquarters within a few hours after facts were uncovered by CIC investigators.

The Party's influence was tested in the fall and winter of 1947 when the Japanese Government, recognizing a tendency of farmers to withhold their crops from regular rationing channels for high blackmarket prices, set rice quotas for all prefectures to fill. The Communists, in attacking this form of regulation, hoped to bring discredit upon the methods as well as the personnel of the Japanese Government, meanwhile furthering the Party's

cause among farmers. In essence, the program took the form of encouraging farmers to hold back as much of their required rice production quota as possible. At the same time, in metropolitan areas, Communists pointed out that the Government was unable effectively to carry out its rice ration distribution program despite the constant threat of hunger to city workers.[92] In addition to obstructing the delivery of rice, the JCP also advocated that the farmers refuse to buy land from the Japanese Government, while at the same time in Tokyo they were agitating that the government sale of land to farmers had been a complete failure.

While not of threatening proportions, the Communist Party and its operations brought into sharp relief the security problem of the Occupation. The docility of the Japanese since war's end was encouraging, but the infiltration of foreign ideologies could not be discounted. As long as Occupation troops were available, the relative weakness of the new governmental structure was not apparent, nor would it be seriously tested. There was no question that the process of democratization was well under way, but there were certain factors that could not be ignored: the deterioration in national economy, the rising spiral of inflation, the increasing importance of the labor movement, the unrest in disaffected groups, and Communist penetration.

Communist Infiltration of Repatriates

The decrease of Occupation troops in Japan represented a steadily mounting internal security risk. As of the end of 1948 the total strength was set at 117,580 of which only 68 percent were combat troops available for emer-

---

89 S/A Br, CIS Sp Rpt, 2 Oct 46, sub: Sum of Strike Sit.
90 CIS, Sp Rpt, sub: Soviet and Communist Strategy in Japanese Labor Disputes.
91 *Ibid.*
92 CIS Periodical Sum No. 23, 15 Dec 47.

MILITARY OCCUPATION FORCES

PREFECTURE	POPULATION	NO. DEMOBILIZED ARMY & NAVY PERSONNEL	JAPANESE POLICE NUMBER OF POLICEMEN	NUMBER OF PEOPLE TO ONE POLICEMAN	M.P.	C.I.C.	M.G.	TROOPS (2)	NUMBER OF PEOPLE TO ONE OCCUPATION SOLDIER
HOKKAIDO (1)	3,852,821	291,947	4,619	834		93	78	5,110	754
AOMORI	1,180,245	88,209	1,216	971		17	50	4,327	273
IWATE	1,262,743	97,927	1,036	1,219		14	49	258	4,894
MIYAGI	1,566,831	133,007	1,818	862	195	56	46	5,831	269
AKITA	1,257,398	107,602	1,193	1,054		12	50	62	20,281
YAMAGATA	1,335,653	116,814	1,307	1,022		11	49	2,582	517
FUKUSHIMA	1,992,460	162,213	1,817	1,097		10	51	61	32,663
IBARAKI	2,013,735	136,594	1,527	1,319		11	50	61	33,012
TOCHIGI	1,534,311	155,814	1,541	996		13	50	63	24,354
GUMMA	1,572,787	103,364	1,561	1,008		12	50	1,977	796
SAITAMA	2,100,453	154,933	1,916	1,096		10	50	2,783	755
CHIBA	2,112,917	172,777	2,162	977		17	50	1,707	1,238
TOKYO	5,000,777	512,102	26,683	187	1,598	445	73	20,926	239
KANAGAWA	2,218,120	148,916	5,681	390	860	61	106	19,951	111
NIIGATA	2,418,271	196,672	2,233	1,083		14	50	61	37,785
TOYAMA	979,229	89,300	1,142	857		4	37	127	7,710
ISHIKAWA	927,743	196,050	1,089	852	86	15	37	52	17,841
FUKUI	726,264	185,244	794	915		4	37	41	17,714
YAMANASHI	807,251	103,806	792	1,019		12	50	62	13,020
NAGANO	2,060,010	97,367	1,918	1,074		13	52	65	31,692
GIFU	1,493,644	57,018	1,463	1,021		6	46	4,054	368
SHIZUOKA	2,353,005	123,890	2,209	1,065		13	56	99	34,101
AICHI	3,122,902	220,719	6,289	497		14	50	1,709	1,827
MIE	1,416,494	104,009	1,483	955		12	50	62	22,846
SHIGA	858,367	83,880	884	971		7	43	2,599	330
KYOTO	1,739,084	165,176	4,383	397	85	48	47	2,447	711
OSAKA	3,334,659	264,862	11,111	300	255	52	65	7,715	432
HYOGO	3,057,444	226,649	5,594	547	269	21	58	4,454	686
NARA	779,935	67,158	817	955		5	43	2,095	372
WAKAYAMA	959,999	79,743	1,117	859		5	37	42	22,857
TOTTORI	587,606	49,494	669	878		7	37	50	11,752
SHIMANE	894,267	98,611	925	967		6	37	228	3,922
OKAYAMA	1,619,622	124,799	1,632	994		11	50	47	21,887
HIROSHIMA	2,011,498	168,504	2,324	866		37	42	4,767	422
YAMAGUCHI	1,479,244	133,579	2,018	733		01	52	1,914	733
TOKUSHIMA	854,811	76,807	890	960		6	37	47	18,188
KAGAWA	917,673	73,315	944	972		9	37	56	16,387
EHIME	1,435,887	115,885	1,427	1,018		6	50	64	22,717
KOCHI	848,337	84,090	878	966		7	37	48	17,673
FUKUOKA	3,178,134	253,578	4,514	704	106	43	69	8,807	361
SAGA	917,797	70,232	934	983		5	49	54	16,996
NAGASAKI	1,531,674	103,374	2,118	723		14	65	3,598	426
KUMAMOTO	1,765,726	174,691	1,811	975		10	48	3,235	546
OITA	1,233,651	107,589	1,122	1,100		6	46	3,178	388
MIYAZAKI	1,025,689	74,583	1,165	881		7	37	44	23,311
KAGOSHIMA	1,746,305	132,781	1,767	988		10	50	60	29,105
TOTAL:	78,627,000	6,465,435	122,673		3,454	1,221	2,313	117,580	

(1) All Prefectures in Hokkaido consolidated under this one entry.
(2) Military Strength figures secured from G-2 source and are T/O strengths of various units considered available for the purposes of this study. The following type units were considered: Organic Divisional Troops of all Branches; Military Government Units including military personnel only; AAA, AGF, Chemical and Armored; Corps MP Platoons; Non-Divisional MP Personnel; BulkOverhead MP Personnel; FEAF; U.S. Navy; BCOF.

PLATE NO. 86
Analysis of Population, Military and Police Strength by Prefecture 15 December 1948

gencies. This force, plus a poorly equipped Japanese police force of 122,673 men, constituted the control force for almost 80 million people. (Plate No. 86)

Military Police and Counter Intelligence units were scattered so thoroughly throughout Japan that their numbers in any given area would have been insignificant in an emergency. However, they were in a position to furnish first warning of impending disturbance and to supply information to tactical troops dispatched to the areas.

Each prefecture in Japan contained a Military Government team. These units could have provided guidance and liaison, but would have been of no value tactically.

The British Commonwealth Occupation Force controlled nine prefectures on Shikoku and southern Honshu. BCOF was supplemented in its area by the Military Government teams, and counterintelligence functions were implemented by U. S. personnel. During 1948 the strength of BCOF troops had been reduced by about 70 percent, leaving some 4,600 officers and men of the Royal Australian Army to handle the principal Occupation activities in Hiroshima Prefecture. There were also 850 representatives of the Royal Australian Air Force, 200 of the Royal New Zealand Air Force, and 140 of the Royal New Zealand Army based in Yamaguchi Prefecture.[9]

By placing density of population figures against Occupation strengths, the ratio of repatriates to troops and police becomes significant.

Repatriates had become a target for the Communist Party. While there had been no incidents, no action of defiance in the past, the general demobilization and the progressive return of millions of jobless soldiers introduced a potential security problem.

There were five areas in Japan in which there were particularly heavy concentrations of repatriates and which were therefore critical areas from a security standpoint. Note the ratio of demobilized personnel to population density. Osaka, typical of this general situation, as of 31 December 1948 had:

Returned navy personnel *83,423*
Returned army personnel *181,439*
Total prefectural population *3,334,659*
Japanese police *11,111*
FEC troops *7,715*

The significance of these over-all statistics is in the ratio of police and the population density: one Japanese police to 300 population, and one Occupation soldier to 1,000 population. It is obvious that this insignificant ratio of Occupation personnel of one to 432 immediately available FEC troops in a critical area could hardly prevail against a restless population of over 3,000,000 with a highly trained 10 percent nucleus of military repatriates to furnish organized leadership.

On a national basis, at the end of 1948, similar ratios existed:

1 U.S. soldier per   *670 population*
1 Japanese policeman per   *640 population*
1 Military Police per   *22,800 population*
1 CIC operator per   *64,400 population*

These ratios were insufficient to counter a serious public disturbance or an aggressive fifth column.

---

93 GHQ FEC MIS GS, P&E Br & CIS Sp Int, *Internal Factors as Security Problems for the Occupation Forces*, 1 Jan 49 (S).

CHAPTER IX

AIR AND NAVY COMPONENTS

Part I—Far East Air Forces: Initial Operations

While the world's chancelleries deliberated the fate of the Japanese Empire, the Fifth and Seventh U. S. Air Forces continued to bomb Japan's lines of communication, industrial areas, shipping, aircraft, and various other military installations. After the Japanese Government notified the Allies of its acceptance of the peace terms, activity of these Air Forces was limited to reconnaissance, surveillance, and photographic missions. Meanwhile, during the interim which existed while arrangements were made for the formal capitulation, there were numerous interceptions of U. S. reconnaissance aircraft, indicating that the *Kamikaze* indoctrination had some effect. For this reason, American air activity over Japanese territory had to be temporarily suspended.[1]

From 19 August, when the Japanese Surrender Delegation flew from Atsugi to Ie-shima and was then escorted to Manila by American aircraft, until 30 August when General MacArthur landed at Atsugi, increased armed surveillance missions were flown over Japan by B-29's to insure that the surrender terms would be kept. This tremendous display of air power throughout Japan left no doubt of defeat in the minds of the Japanese.[2]

As rapidly as the advance party of the Far East Air Forces (FEAF) completed reconnaissance of the Tokyo airfields, established communications facilities, and set up an air traffic control center, the Fifth Air Force brought in its tactical units.

By the end of August FEAF air units were concentrated on Okinawa, preparing to deploy to the mainland of Japan. A mass shuttle to Atsugi airfield enabled the 11th Airborne Division to complete a speedy occupation of the Yokohama area on 30/31 August. All available troop carrier transport of FEAF was utilized as well as "Skytrains" and "Skymasters" of the Air Transport Command (ATC). Advance headquarters of GHQ, USAFPAC, Eighth Army, and FEAF were airlifted to Japan. Repatriated Allied prisoners of war and civilian internees in need of hospitalization were evacuated on the return flights of these planes to Okinawa and the Philippines.

To provide staging and servicing facilities for transport and transient aircraft, a small task force composed of service personnel and equipment was established in September in the Kanoya area, Kyushu. Considerable air traffic was staged through that area due to the relatively great distances from Okinawa and the Philippines to Japan. Subsequently, Fifth Air Force combat units with appropriate service elements occupied objective locations

---

1 GHQ SCAP & USAFPAC, Mo Sum of Opns, Aug 45 (S), Air Sum.

2 Unless otherwise noted the following account of FEAF activities in the Occupation of Japan is based on a report, HQ FEAF to G-2 GHQ FEC Hist Div, Nov 48, sub: FEAF Activ in the Occupation of Japan.

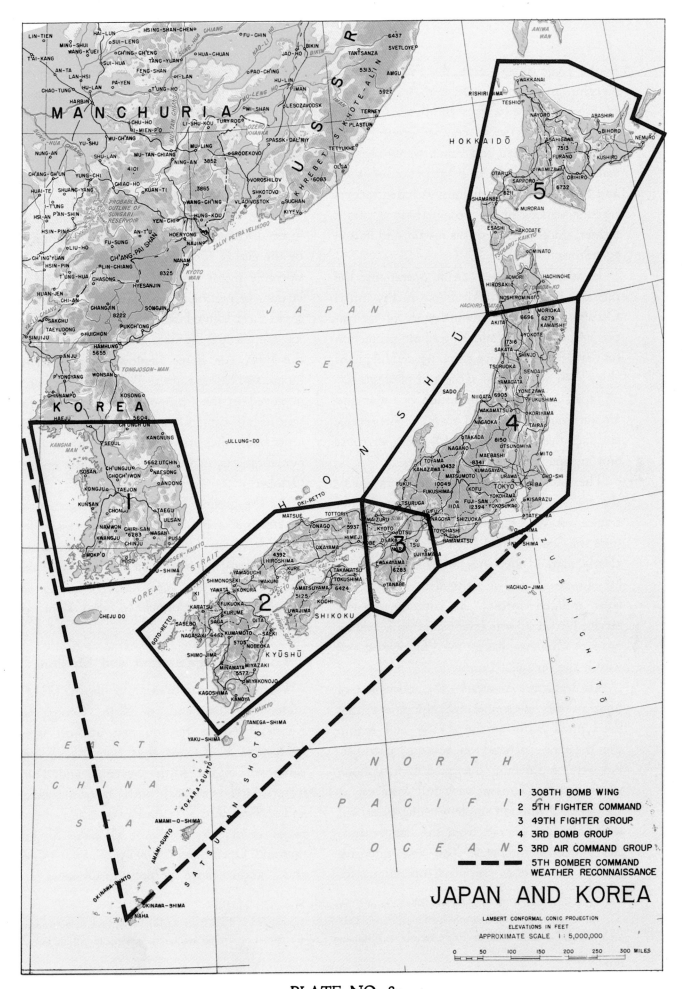

PLATE NO. 87
Fifth U. S. Air Force Zones of Responsibility, 1945–1947

in the Keijo area, Korea, the Fukuoka area, Kyushu, and in the Osaka and Aomori areas, Honshu. (Plate No. 87) In all, the Fifth Air Force provided twelve combat groups, both fighter and bomber, and about twenty separate squadrons for the initial Occupation of Japan and Korea. These echelons included tactical reconnaissance, photo reconnaissance, night fighter, troop carrier, air-sea rescue, and liaison squadrons.

In addition to these airlift operations, the missions of the Fifth Air Force in the initial Occupation included maintenance of air supremacy over Japan and Korea; air protection for naval forces, convoys, shipping, and lifeguard ships; aerial reconnaissance and photography of Japan and Korea; operation of radar and air warning services; and air-sea rescue service and facilities on the Tokyo-Okinawa air route and in Japanese and Korean waters.

The Fifth Air Force assumed operation of the former Japanese Government air courier service on 10 October 1945. Prior to that time the Japanese had been permitted to use clearly marked airplanes in scheduled flights for dissemination of surrender directives to their isolated forces; in addition, courier service for GHQ was established on a routine basis to Okinawa, Korea, the Philippines, and within the Japanese Empire.

Air transport missions—the movement of high priority personnel and equipment from the United States to the theater and within the theater—operated on routine schedules, but were considerably disrupted by a typhoon which struck Okinawa with full force on 11 October. Although ample warning permitted withdrawal of aircraft from the danger area, the added maintenance load and extensive damage to facilities hampered operations for

the remainder of the month. The Army Air Force Weather Control at Okinawa was completely demolished. When the storm delayed supplies and destroyed equipment in the Okinawa area, B-29's had to fly relief missions comparable to their prisoner of war supply drops during September.[3]

As on the ground and sea, the air situation in the Occupation plan had become stabilized by the end of October 1945. Although considerable repair and construction remained to be done before the former Japanese air facilities could meet United States standards, the areas for air occupation had been settled. With the Fifth Air Force deployed in Okinawa, Japan, and Korea and the Thirteenth Air Force deployed in the Philippines, preparations for routine air control were complete. All air units had either arrived, were en route to their new locations, or were loading by the end of October.

As the ground forces began occupation of all strategic areas in Japan, the necessity for air observation lessened. FEAF turned its efforts toward deploying air units to Japan for Occupation duties, meanwhile returning its "high-point" personnel to the Zone of Interior.

FEAF: Organization and Missions

Prior to the capitulation of Japan, FEAF, under the command of Gen. George C. Kenney, had its headquarters at Fort Wm. McKinley, P. I. At that time FEAF was composed of the Fifth, Seventh, and Thirteenth Air Forces, each with its own combat and service units. It had been assigned two major tasks: to coordinate air plans for the invasion Operations "Olympic" and "Coronet," and to move its forces to Okinawa.[4]

---

3 GHQ SCAP & USAFPAC, Mo Sum of Opns, Air Sum, Oct 45 (S).

4 See Ch. I. The Seventh Air Force, Pacific Ocean Area, assigned to FEAF on 14 July 1945, was to be responsible for air defense and air traffic control on Okinawa and for operating the air-sea rescue control for all air forces.

With the surrender came the task of redirecting this powerful offensive force along completely different lines.[5] Practically overnight the plans and missions had to be changed, even though the organizations remained intact until it was determined that the Occupation was to be a peaceful one. Reorganization and redesignation took place on 25 December 1945, at which time the Pacific Air Command, U. S. Army, (PACUSA) was activated.[6] The U. S. Army Strategic Air Force was discontinued. Its Headquarters and Headquarters Squadron, all its units, allotments, and personnel were released and assigned to PACUSA. (Plate No. 88) Under the command of General Kenney, PACUSA was assigned to U. S. Army Forces, Pacific, with its initial station at Fort Wm. McKinley and advance headquarters in Tokyo. Lt. Gen. Ennis C. Whitehead officially assumed command of PACUSA on 30 December 1945.[7]

Throughout the three year period following the cessation of hostilities the organization of PACUSA did not change materially. A few smaller units were activated, deactivated, or transferred in order to balance the Air Forces and keep them organized in a manner consistent with their missions. One exception was the reorganization of the supply and logistics agencies of PACUSA. At the close of the war active supply depots were operating under Far East Air Service Command(FEASC) at Townsville, Finschhafen, Biak, Leyte, Nichols Field, Guam, and Okinawa. Nichols Field, already a large depot and situated near a ready labor market, was built up rapidly and received the bulk of supplies from Townsville, Finschhafen, Biak, and Leyte. Manpower shortage made the closing of the Okinawa depot necessary in October 1946, and the Philippine Islands Treaty granted Nichols Field to the Philippine Government in mid-1947.

The designation of FEASC was changed to Pacific Air Service Command on 26 February 1946, and again on 1 January 1947 when it became Far East Air Materiel Command (FEAMCOM). On 21 January 1947 FEAMCOM moved from Fort McKinley to Fuchu, Japan.[8] Two depots were under the technical control of FEAMCOM: Marianas Air Materiel Area located at Guam, and Japan Air Materiel Area located at Tachikawa, Honshu, Japan. These depots, in addition to their normal functions of supply and maintenance, had the overwhelming task of locating, identifying, classifying, inventorying, and warehousing the tremendous amount of materiel left over from the war.

Headquarters, PACUSA (Administration), arrived in Japan on 16 May 1946 from Fort McKinley, occupying joint offices with the advance echelon in downtown Tokyo.[9]

---

4 (contd.) The Seventh was also responsible for the Army and Marine fighter units under its control, the radar warning system, and antiaircraft artillery units. The Fifth Air Force, commanded by Lt Gen Ennis C. Whitehead, was to move to Okinawa to carry the major load of the pre-invasion strikes. Part of the Thirteenth Air Force, commanded by Maj Gen Paul Wurtsmith, was to establish bases in southern Kyushu and supervise the air strikes for Operation "Coronet," while the Fifth was to be established on the Kanto Plain air bases.

5 See Ch. I.

6 HQ PACUSA, GO No. 1, 25 Dec 45. In HQ FEAF.

7 Gen Kenney left the Pacific in June 1945 for reassignment to the ZI, and was succeeded by Lt Gen Whitehead who was Deputy Commander at that time. Official transfer of command was made 30 December. Gen Kenney was the first CG of the Strategic Air Command which was activated in March 1946 as the US' long-range bombardment air striking force.

8 HQ FEAF, GO No. 3, 10 Jan 47, effective 1 Jan 47. In HQ FEAF.

9 On 7 June 1946 Headquarters, First Air Division was established at Kadena, Okinawa, and at the same time, Headquarters Eighth Air Force was reassigned to the Strategic Air Command, Washington, D. C., except for personnel and equipment which was transferred and/or reassigned to the First Air Division. Missions assigned to the Eighth Air Force remained the responsibility of the First Air Division.

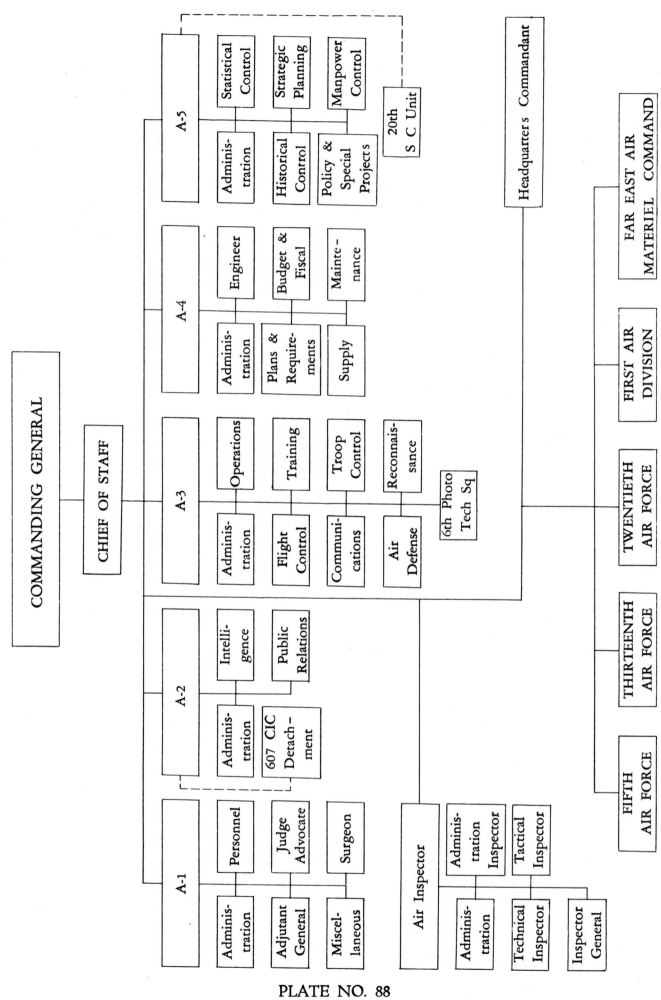

PLATE NO. 88

Organization of FEAF Command and Headquarters Staff, 1947

PACUSA lost one of its major air forces on 1 January 1947 when the Seventh Air Force was reassigned to CINCPAC.[10] At the same time several new units were assigned to PACUSA: the Pacific Divison of the Air Transport Command, the 43rd Weather Wing, and the 7th Airways and Air Communications Service Wing. All had parent units in Washington but were placed under the operational control of the Commander in Chief, Far East, who in turn delegated control to the Commanding General, PACUSA. All of these were service units vital to the proper functioning of balanced air forces, giving logistical and technical support to the tactical and administrative units of FEAF.

The title of Air Force Headquarters was again changed. On 1 January 1947 PACUSA became Far East Air Forces, U. S. Army, but with no change in assignment or organization. The final title change came in November 1947 when, as a result of the integration program of the Armed Forces, Far East Air Forces, U. S. Army, became Far East Air Forces, U. S. Air Force. FEAF remained under CINCFE, but on a parity of command with the other services. For the accomplishment of its missions, FEAF was allotted a substantial portion of the U. S. Air Force; in its designated areas of responsibility, FEAF operated and maintained a total of thirty-nine air bases and related installations involving some twenty-four airfields and airstrips.[11]

Maintenance of the Air Force in Japan

On V-J Day there were 300,000 Air Force officers and airmen in the Pacific Theater. Four months later 215,000 of these had departed for the United States and demobilization, leaving only 85,000 in the theater as of January 1946.[12]

The rapid demobilization of troops affected the essential team character of the Air Force combat units which thereafter operated at reduced strength until the flow of replacements exceeded the flow of departures for a sufficient period. On-the-job training was immediately established in all units, combining individual training with unit training; this plan had the advantage of maintaining organizational structure. In order to raise the level of technical knowledge in units, some civilian technicians were recruited from the United States. In September 1947 a FEAF-wide technical training program was established, offering over thirty courses, for the most part in specialties not then available through replacements; during the first year approximately 4,800 students were graduated. This program filled the gaps in individual training and developed unit training to a state of combat readiness unexcelled in the entire U. S. Air Force.[13]

---

10   HQ PACUSA, GO No. 160, 31 Dec 46.

11   Rpt, HQ FEAF to G-2 GHQ FEC Hist Div, Nov 48, sub: FEAF Activ in the Occupation of Japan. In the discharge of the general functions assigned, FEAF was committed to maintain an air power potential in the Far East Command area adequate to accomplish its missions, including: (a) maintenance of a balanced Air Force in the occupied areas of the theater; (b) provision of air defense of military and naval installations throughout the Far East Command; (c) provision of search and rescue operations in coordination with the Navy; (d) provision of aerial photography in support of the Army's post-hostilities mapping program in the Pacific; (e) assistance in operations to alleviate human suffering and preserve order in the event of disaster, and to quell disorders, riots, or other disturbances requiring use of the US armed forces; (f) establishment and control of military air routes, and operation of an internal air transport service in the Far East Command area.

12   Rpt, HQ FEAF to G-2 GHQ FEC Hist Div, Nov 48, sub: FEAF Activ in the Occupation of Japan.

13   *Ibid.*

PF-80 flies over rice fields near Tokyo on photographic reconnaissance mission.

Life boat descends by parachute in air-sea rescue operations.

PLATE NO. 89
Occupation Missions—FEAF

Aerial Mapping and Other Activities

FEAF's aerial mapping program developed into an important post-war activity. Mapping squadrons flew over 100,000 miles during which they mapped or charted thousands of square miles of previously uncharted territories in the Far East. The photographic negatives resulting from aerial photography were delivered to topographic units of the Corps of Engineers, and to the Aeronautical Chart Service of the U.S. Air Force. The Engineers were responsible for technical ground control and for the actual production of maps, while the latter was responsible for the production of aeronautical charts.

Additional miscellaneous activities of FEAF included the disposal of extensive stocks of war surplus property, maintenance of base facilities, provision for maintenance and protection of aviation ammunition stores, preparation of plans for Air Force bases involved in the permanent base construction program, and establishment of a civilian manpower control to insure the efficient allocation of civilian personnel employed by FEAF.

Troop Carrier Aviation and International Air Traffic

Both during and after the war, increased dependence was placed on Troop Carrier Aviation for the support of the armed forces. Unique logistical and administrative problems developed within the Far East Command which covered vast water areas, mountainous terrain, and small isolated islands, with climates ranging from tropical to sub-arctic. This area, extending from Hokkaido on the north to the Admiralty Islands on the south, required

a fast and reliable means of communication. Suitable port facilities and sufficient shipping were not available nor, except to a limited degree in Japan, did adequate railroad and highway facilities exist.

Measured by any standards, troop carrier operations in support of the Occupation of Japan were extensive. During a single representative month approximately four and one-half million passenger miles were flown, and over one and one-quarter million ton miles of cargo were distributed to various points within the Far East Command.[14] In addition, troop carrier missions included emergency movements of personnel, aerial food drops to posts isolated by floods, training with ground forces, airlifting units, and air evacuation of patients. To maintain this air traffic, a military airways system, under the control of FEAF, was established. (Plate No. 90) This airways system, as modern as any in the world, was complete with airways traffic service, control centers, radio aids to air navigation, instrument landing facilities, search and rescue facilities, and weather service. It contained 20,000 miles of controlled routes linking all points in the Pacific and Far East areas.

Shortly after termination of hostilities in the Pacific Theater, use of FEAF military airways system was extended to authorized civil air carriers operating over international air routes to, from, and within the Far East Command area. This resulted in a rapid and economical re-establishment of civil air commerce to war-torn countries of the Orient and contributed materially to economic rehabilitation.

FEAF—Present and Future

The Air Forces of FEAF consisted of balanced elements comprising modern conven-

---

14 *Ibid.*

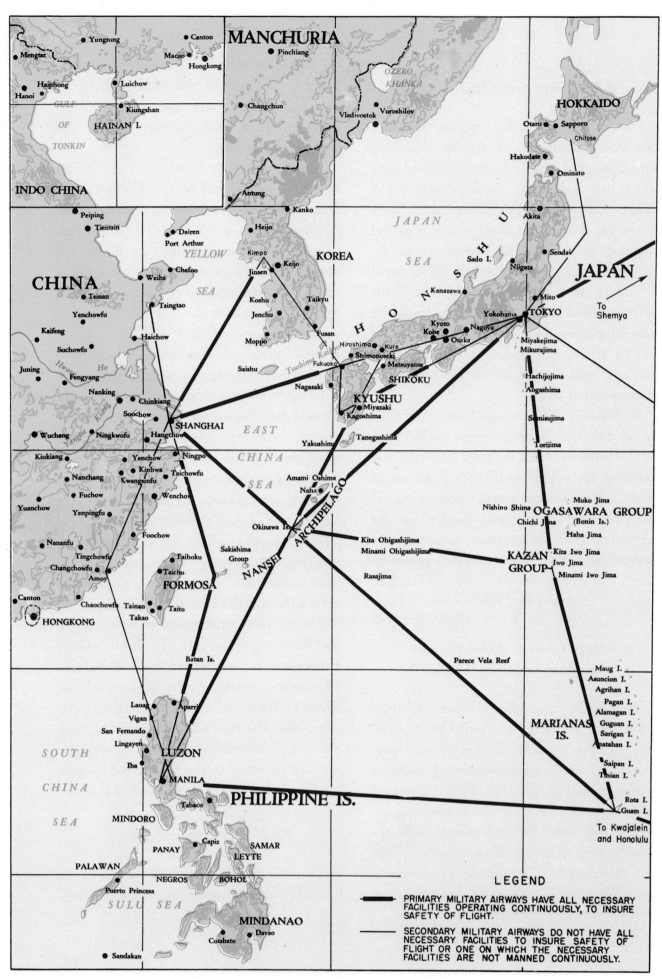

PLATE NO. 90
Pacific Military Airways, November 1948

tional and jet-type fighters, fast light-bombers, troop carriers, and, in addition, specially trained and equipped search and rescue units, which enhanced the safety of both military and civil air transport operations. Vigorous training of these units continued and was periodically tested through the conduct of exercises and maneuvers, including joint training operations with army and navy forces.

FEAF continued to cooperate with U. S. Army and U. S. Navy Forces in the discharging of responsibilities of the U. S. Government in the Occupation of Japan.

Part II—U.S. Naval Command in the Far East: Initial Operations

With the capitulation of Japan, the U.S. Pacific Fleet, consisting of the Third, Fifth, and Seventh Fleets and the North Pacific Force, occupied strategic naval areas of Japan and Korea and enforced the surrender terms imposed on the Empire.

In order to carry out preliminary missions for the Occupation, the U.S. Pacific Fleet Liaison Group with the Supreme Commander for the Allied Powers (FLTLOSCAP) was formed in late August 1945 under the command of Rear Adm. J. J. Ballentine, USN.[15] Offices were set up in Yokohama with the major section of GHQ, and communications with Commander in Chief, Pacific, (CINCPAC) were established through the USS *Teton*. FLTLOSCAP was to control disarmament, demobilization, and repatriation,

as these operations concerned the Navy; to advise GHQ on all naval matters; and to control Japanese Merchant Marine shipping until a special section was established with that particular responsibility.[16]

Naval zones of responsibility were defined to include the allocation of geographical areas to Third, Fifth, and Seventh U.S. Fleets, and to the North Pacific Force.[17] The Third U.S. Fleet, under the command of Admiral Halsey, occupied Tokyo Bay and established minor naval and naval air facilities ashore in support of the Eighth U.S. Army. The Fifth U.S. Fleet, commanded by Admiral Spruance occupied and patrolled the sea approaches and coastal waters of Japan west of 135° east.

Elements of the Sixth U.S. Army were landed and firmly established in Kyushu, Shikoku, and western Honshu, while the clearance of mine fields in the Tsushima Strait-Inland Sea area was initiated by the Fifth Fleet. The Seventh U.S. Fleet, under the command of Admiral Kinkaid, assisted in staging, training and transport of troops in support of operations of the U.S. Forces in China and Korea. The North Pacific Force, commanded by Vice Adm. Frank J. Fletcher, guarded the lines of sea communications from the Aleutians to Russia and initiated clearance of the mine fields in the Tsugaru Strait between Honshu and Hokkaido.[18]

Initial occupation tasks of the Navy were mine-sweeping channels and transporting occupation troops to Japan. During the early part of October mine-sweeping operations were

---

15   Rad (TS), SCAP to COM3rdFLT, 26 Aug 45.

16   FLTLOSCAP, Confidential Rpt of Activ, 1 Oct 45.

17   See Ch. II.

18   *Ibid.* Third US Fleet consisted of 6 battleships (BB), 4 heavy cruisers (CA), 3 light cruisers (CL), and 18 destroyers (DD). Two battleships, 2 light cruisers, and 2 destroyers of the British Fleet augmented this force. Fifth US Fleet consisted of 6 battleships, 4 aircraft carriers, escort (ACE), 2 heavy cruisers, 8 light cruisers, 2 large cruisers (CB), 44 destroyers, and 83 mine sweepers (AM). Seventh US Fleet consisted of 4 heavy cruisers, 2 light cruisers, 2 aircraft carriers, escort, and 17 destroyers. North Pacific Force was made up of 3 heavy cruisers, 2 light cruisers, 6 aircraft carriers, escort, and 24 destroyers. (GHQ SCAP & USAFPAC, Mo Sum of Opns, Sep 45 [S], Naval Sum.)

limited to these areas essential for conducting the Occupation : Tokyo and Sagami Bays, Tsugaru Strait between Hokkaido and Honshu, and areas off Kochi in Shikoku, Sasebo in Kyushu, and Sendai in northern Honshu. Later in the month, mine-sweeping operations began in Bungo Suido between Kyushu and Shikoku, Iyo Nada between Honshu and Shikoku, and Hiro Bay off Kure.

Amphibious forces of the Third, Fifth, and Seventh Fleets immediately began to bring in the troops assigned for Occupation duty and to evacuate prisoners of war from Japan on the return trips. These operations were completed by the end of October.[19] The Navy also became primarily responsible for transporting two million servicemen who were due to return to the United States. Escort carriers and attack transports were temporarily converted to augment shipping normally allotted for troop transport, and Operation " Magic Carpet " was successfully executed.[20]

COMNAVJAP : Organization and Missions [21]

As logistic conditions improved and the situation in Japan became stabilized, the functions and responsibilities of FLTLOSCAP changed. Shipping Control Authority for Japanese Merchant Marine (SCAJAP) was established under the command of Rear Adm. D. W. Beary on 12 October 1945 ; [22] this organization assumed control of all ships over 100 gross tons operated by the Japanese. SCAP retained operational control over SCAJAP in repatriation shipping and related activities through the G-3 Repatriation Section. In dealings with the Imperial Japanese Government, SCAJAP worked through the Ministry of Transportation and the Ministry of Navy until the latter was deactivated on 31 December 1945. Thereafter, SCAJAP worked through successive civil offices established under the Japanese naval demobilization program. The Commander of the Fifth Fleet, Admiral Spruance, was the senior U. S. Naval officer in the Japan area and all naval activities ashore were under his operational control.

On 28 January 1946 FLTLOSCAP was dissolved and a naval command known as Naval Activities, Japan (COMNAVJAP) was established under the command of Vice Adm. R. M. Griffin, who retained this command until 9 July 1948 when he was relieved by Vice Adm. Russell M. Berkey.[23] (Plate No. 91)

When the Far East Comand was estab-

---

19   See Chs. II and IV.

20   See Ch. II.

21   Unless otherwise noted, the following account is based on reports summarizing the Naval operations in Japan during the Occupation : FLTLOSCAP, Confidential Rpts of Activ, Sep, Oct, Nov 45, and COMNAVFE, Comd Narrs, 21 Jan–1 Oct 46, 1 Oct 46–31 Mar 47, 1 Apr–30 Jun 47, 1 Jul–30 Sep 47, 1 Oct 47–31 Mar 48, 1 Apr–30 Sep 48, 1 Oct 48–31 Mar 49.

22   Later Rear Adm. C.B. Momsen.

23   Incident to an oral request from SCAP the establishment of COMNAVJAP was authorized by CNO in a dispatch to CINCPAC/POA on 30 December 1945. The original plan contemplated the continuance of FLTLOSCAP but on 22 January, in a second dispatch to CINCPAC/POA, this was modified and FLTLOSCAP was ordered dissolved upon the establishment of COMNAVJAP. Pursuant to the above, COMNAVJAP was ordered established by COM5thFLT on 19 January 1946. COMNAVJAP included all naval activities ashore which at that time consisted of Fleet Activities, Yokosuka, FLTLOSCAP, SCAJAP, Naval Technical Mission to Japan (NAVTECHJAP), and Port Directors at Yokosuka, Tokyo, Nagoya, Wakayama, Kure, Matsuyama, Kagoshima, Nagasaki, Fukuoka, and Sasebo. On 4 February, Fleet Activities, Sasebo, was established under COMNAVJAP, the latter reporting to SCAP for operational control, although still under administrative control of CINCPAC. (COMNAVJAP, Comd Narr, 21 Jan–1 Oct 46.)

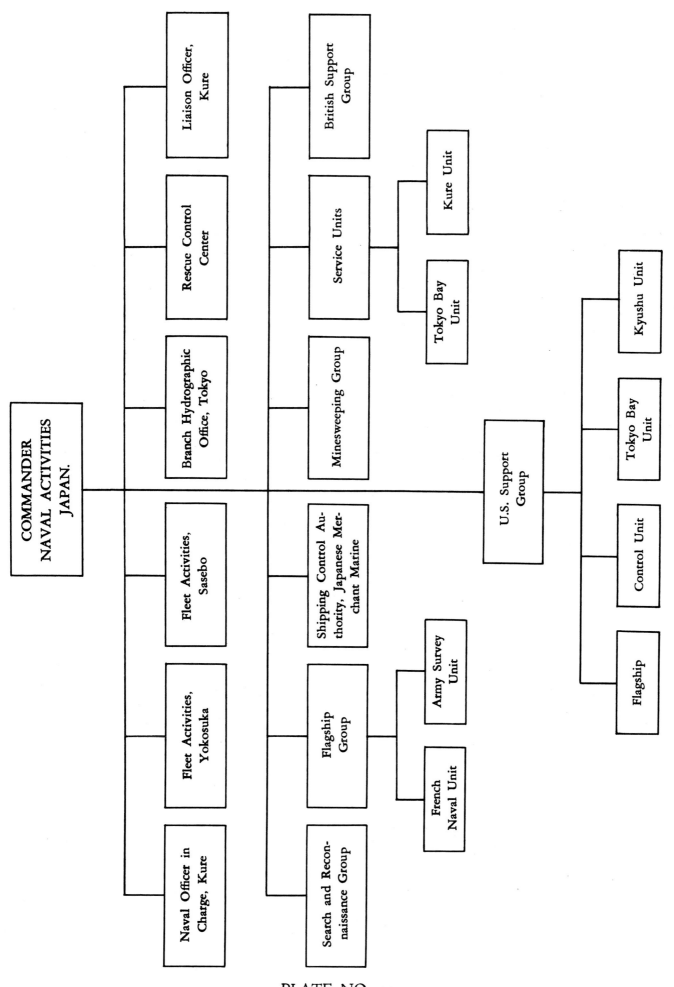

PLATE NO. 91

COMNAVJAP: Task Organization, Task Force 96, 1947

lished on 1 January 1947, Admiral Griffin was redesignated Commander Naval Forces, Far East (COMNAVFE), with the proviso that the title " Commander Naval Forces, Japan," would be used in connection with duties involving the Allied relationships for which Admiral Griffin was responsible to SCAP.[24] On that same date Commander, Naval Activities, Japan, Commander, Naval Operating Base, Okinawa, and Commander, Naval Forces, Philippines, reported to CINC-FE for duty while Commander, Marianas, reported for operational control. CINCFE in turn reassigned these responsibilities to COMNAVFE.[25]

Plans for the landing of Occupation forces, their equipment, and subsequent logistic support entailed the assignment of a large number of amphibious craft to Navy commands in Japan. Following completion of operations, most of the landing craft were returned to the United States by the middle of April 1946. Others were decommissioned and sunk by combat support forces or scuttled after being loaded with Japanese ammunition and poison gas.

Owing to personnel demobilization, transfer and consolidation of Occupation forces, and expansion of Army units in port areas, all port directorates except those at Kure and Kagoshima were abolished on 14 May 1946. Kagoshima controlled a heavy volume of United States and Japanese shipping involved in the repatriation program. The Kobe, Kagoshima, Nagasaki, and Fukuoka offices that reported ship movements were all closed by August when Army authorities assumed control of port operations.

The Port Director's office at Kure was established by the U.S. Navy, but when southern Honshu was turned over to the British Commonwealth Occupation Force (BCOF) in March 1946, functions of the port director were assumed by the Royal Navy.[26] The British Naval Officer in Charge, Kure, and all British naval units under his command were under the operational control of COMNAVJAP. In accordance with the provisions of SCAP Occupation Instructions, the former Japanese naval yard at Kure remained under United States control.[27] The COMNAVJAP liaison officer in charge supervised scrapping

---

23 (contd.) NAVTECHJAP completed its work in Japan on 11 March and transferred its headquarters to Pearl Harbor. On 18 March COMNAVJAP assumed all naval responsibilities held by Fifth Fleet incident to the enforcement of surrender terms and control of Occupation forces with the exception of mine-sweeping which Commander, Fifth Fleet, retained until his departure on 25 March 1946.

24 See Ch. III.

25 COMNAVJAP, Comd Narr, 21 Jan–1 Oct 46 [C], pp. 3, 4. SCAP Occupation Instructions set forth the basic mission of COMNAVJAP as follows: (a) control the coastal waters of Japan; (b) continue responsibility for all naval activities ashore in Japan; (c) continue to supervise Japanese mine-sweeping as directed; (d) continue control of Japanese naval vessels; (e) continue surveillance and inspection to verify the execution by Japanese naval forces of disarmament and demobilization and compliance with directives of SCAP; (f) continue to operate Japanese shipping and provide port direction as required; (g) continue to control all naval and merchant shipping in the area of Japan as required for safe navigation, furnishing proper routing and other advice as expedient; (h) assume operational control of such Allied naval forces as may be provided for enforcement of surrender terms in Japan; (i) continue to perform air-sea rescue as required, in coordination with Commanding General, Pacific Air Command, U S Army; (j) coordinate with Commanding General, Eighth U S Army, in plans to alleviate human suffering and preserve order in the event of disaster and to quell incipient disorder riots, or other disturbances which might endanger lives or property of Allied nationals; (k) secure and safeguard intelligence information of value to the Allied Powers and arrange with Commanding General, Eighth U S Army, and Commanding General, Pacific Air Command, U S Army, for mutual exchange and unrestricted access to matters of interest thereto.

26 See Ch. II.

27 SCAP Occupation Instns No. 3, 12 Feb 46 (R).

of former Japanese naval vessels.[28]

Drydock and limited repair facilities at Kure, Sasebo, Yokosuka, and Maizuru were retained. By March 1948 approximately 11,000 Japanese workers were employed at Kure, Sasebo, and Maizuru. Almost 30 percent of these were actually engaged in ship work. Approximately 1,000 Japanese were employed by Fleet Activities, Yokosuka, for work in the ship repair department.[29]

Fleet Activities, Yokosuka and Sasebo

The largest shore establishments under COMNAVJAP were Fleet Activities, Yokosuka, and Fleet Activities, Sasebo, both located on the sites of former Japanese naval bases. Fleet Activities, Yokosuka, was responsible for general administration of the Yokosuka Naval Base, Yokosuka Marine Air Base, and Kisarazu Naval Air Base, and for control of the United States personnel in communities adjacent to these establishments. Other duties included demilitarization, inventory, and disposition of enemy equipment in its area of responsibility in accordance with current instructions, operation of Radio Tokyo (Station NDT)[30] and other communications facilities located in the Yokosuka area; assistance in the logistic support of fleet units based at Yokosuka and naval units ashore in the Tokyo Bay area; and administration of Port Directors at Yokosuka, Yokohama, and Tokyo. By inspection and surveillance, control of all former Japanese naval vessels in Japanese ports east of longitude 138° was maintained.

With the surrender of the Japanese, the U.S. Navy was assigned Yokosuka as its zone of authority.[31] The Japanese had evacuated hastily before the Allied landings and left the base in complete disorder. Demilitarization was begun immediately and was completed within the first year. Ninety percent of the former arsenal was returned to the people for reindustrialization.[32]

Yokosuka Base repaired ships supporting the Occupation, became the supply center for the U.S. Navy ashore and afloat in Japan, and governed the city of Yokosuka. The military government of Yokosuka was integrated into the Base organization instead of being a separate command.

The area of responsibility and scope of

---

28 According to a plan prepared by COMNAVJAP and approved by SCAP on 2 April 1946, all former Japanese Navy combatant ships larger than destroyer class, which could be operated or towed, were to be completely scrapped within one year of their release from the repatriation service. It was also planned to sink wrecked and heavily damaged ships in deep water, and to dispose of all submarines afloat. Eighteen Japanese scrapping companies were assigned the job of scrapping the major ships. This tremendous task of disposing of the Japanese Navy was assigned to COMNAVJAP and was declared completed as of 15 January 1949. In all, 415 vessels were destroyed: 35 major vessels, 128 minor vessels, 42 submarines, and 106 midget submarines were scrapped, and 104 submarines were sunk; 190 vessels were distributed as reparations, and 80 remained in Japan subject to reparations. (Tokyo, *Pacific Stars and Stripes*, June 4, 1949, p. 9.) See Ch. V.

29 COMNAVFE, Comd Narr, 1 Oct 47 to 31 Mar 48 (C).

30 Physical control of Radio Tokyo (NDT) was transferred from Yokosuka to HQ COMNAVFE in Tokyo on 4 Feb 47.

31 Commodore O. O. Kessing, USN, was placed in command of Fleet Activities, Yokosuka, on 8 September 1945. He was relieved by Capt H. M. Briggs, USN, on 23 November 1945. Capt B. W. Decker, USN, replaced Capt Briggs on 3 April 1946. One of the outstanding accomplishments of the U S Navy in Japan was the industrialization of the former secret city of Yokosuka. Under the able leadership of Capt Decker, the ex-Japanese naval base became one of the most progressive communities of Japan.

32 Commem Prog, Flt Activ, Yokosuka, Japan, Navy Day, 27 Oct 48.

Japanese destroyer *Okake* is disarmed for conversion to troop
transport duty, Maizuru Naval Base.

Yokosuka Naval Base drydocks service an American destroyer.   Completely repaired,
these drydocks offer modern service to ships in port.

PLATE NO. 92
Fleet Activities, Japan

command of Fleet Activities, Sasebo,[33] were considerably smaller since the greater part of Sasebo Naval Base was then under the jurisdiction of the Second Marine Division, operating under Eighth U.S. Army control.[34]

Mine-sweeping Operations

Prior to the end of the war, U.S. mine sweepers had been engaged in clearing the mine fields in the East China Sea. Upon cessation of hostilities, this operation lost its importance and sweeping operations in the East China Sea southwest of Kyushu were suspended. All mine craft were returned to Buckner Bay (Okinawa) for regrouping and preparation for their new tasks incident to the evacuation of Allied military personnel and the entry of Occupation forces.[35]

More than 3,700 acoustic, approximately 2,500 pressure type, and 4,500 magnetic mines had been laid in Japanese waters during the war. Samples of United States mines had been recovered by the Japanese, analyzed, and means devised for removing them. They developed effective sweeping for ground mines of all types and for acoustic mines. While their methods of sweeping influence (pressure type) mines were not as effective as those of the United States, they reported that before the end of hostilities they had swept 1,250 United States influence mines; they also reported that 623 of their ships were either sunk or damaged by mines during the war period.[36]

The immediate task assigned was the clearing of navigable channels, through Japanese and American mine fields, into certain key Japanese ports to secure the landing of Allied Occupation units; this was to be followed by additional clearance of channels and harbor facilities to insure safe entry for the supply vessels brought in to maintain the troops ashore. The secondary tasks assigned were the sweeping of sea lanes around southern Kyushu and between the Japanese ports of occupation so that United States ships could move without restriction between these ports, and providing mine-sweeping units for task groups of Fifth Fleet.

Early in the Occupation, the Japanese were instructed by Commander Fifth Fleet to supply information on mine fields and safe channels for the ports of Sendai, Nagoya, Kobe, Osaka, Kure, Hiroshima, Nagasaki, and Wakanoura. Arrangements were made to have the Japanese meet United States forces and assist in sweeping operations which began 12 September 1945. Japanese coastal defense vessels were used as additional mine sweepers and were controlled by Commander Minecraft, U.S. Pacific Fleet (COMINPAC), through a Task Group Commander established in Tokyo, and through U. S. Sweep Group commanders in the field. Japanese sweepers not operating directly under local U. S. commanders were controlled from Tokyo where COMINPAC's representatives issued the necessary directives

---

33 The duties assigned to Fleet Activities, Sasebo, included security, direction of recreational facilities for use of Fleet units based at Sasebo and shore and naval personnel, operation of Radio Sasebo and other available communication facilities, logistic support for shore based naval units and for the 2d Marine Division insofar as practicable, operation of boat pools, and supervision of harbor services and Fleet post office facilities. Fleet Activities, Sasebo, was also responsible for maintaining contact with all former Japanese naval vessels in ports of Kyushu and Shimonoseki. Port Directors, Sasebo, Nagasaki, and Fukuoka were supervised by Fleet Activities, Sasebo.

34 See Ch. VII.

35 Rpt (C), COMINPAC to CNO, 29 May 46, sub: Mine-sweeping Opns Supporting the Occupation of Japan and Korea, 31 Aug 45 to 7 Mar 46.

36 *Ibid.*

to the Japanese mine-sweeping central authority. Where practicable they were assigned tasks directly in support of United States interests; these tasks included entry into Japanese ports, freedom of movement on the high seas for United States shipping, and elimination of floater sources. After completing such tasks Japanese naval units were employed to assist the Japanese repatriation program, then to sweep Japanese ports which appeared desirable for Japanese use and might later be desirable for the use of United States vessels. Since Japanese mine-sweeping vessels were equipped to sweep for moored mines only, they were assigned to areas which were sown with this type of mine. Later when United States vessels conducted magnetic and acoustic exploratory sweeps of these waters, no mines were found.[37] Progress made during the initial mine-sweeping operations is shown in Plate No. 93.

The U.S. Navy mines laid in Japanese and Korean waters were almost exclusively influence mines containing firing mechanisms which had been modified; pressure and low frequency acoustic mines were an exception. Since standard mine-sweeping gear and procedures were of reduced effectiveness against these modified mines, new gear and procedures were instituted at the earliest possible stage of the mine-sweeping campaign. No pressure sweeps were available in the forward area for use during the earliest sweeping in connection with the Occupation of Japan, and entry of transports heavily loaded with men presented a serious problem involving poten-

tial casualties. Even though the entry channel was swept for all other types of mines, and chosen for probable lack of pressure mines, some means was obviously desirable to avoid risk. " Guinea-pig " ships were obtained and fitted out for this purpose. While sweeping, these ships were operated by skeleton volunteer crews. All personnel remained top-side, operating the ship by remote engine-room controls. Precautions were taken against personnel casualties by padding decks and overheads and by providing crash helmets. " Guinea-pig " ships were not used until after the completion of the magnetic and acoustic sweeping. In planning the mine-sweeping operations in Japanese home waters, an effort was made by choice of harbors and channels to avoid as much as possible those areas sown with pressure mines. The sweeping of ports mined with large numbers of pressure mines was deferred sufficiently to allow a high percentage of these mines to become sterilized.[38]

On 25 March 1946 a total of 328 Japanese vessels and 9,064 Japanese personnel were engaged in mine-sweeping duties.[39] The last moored mine-sweeping tasks were completed in August 1946. As the sweeping progressed, vessels and personnel were released so that by the end of 1948 less than 1,500 Japanese personnel and only fifty-two vessels were engaged in mine-sweeping. Major ports of Tokyo Bay, Nagoya, Nagasaki, Sasebo, Kobe, and Osaka were completely cleared of mines and were declared open to all shipping. Operations were continued in the Inland Sea and the Shimonoseki Straits between Kyushu

---

37 *Ibid.*

38 The initial Occupation sweeps were completed about the first of November 1945. Channels had been cleared in the Tsugaru Strait, Tokyo, Nagoya, Sendai, Chosi, Wakanoura-Kii Suido, Kochi, Shikoku, and Bungo Suido in the Honshu area, and in harbors of Kagoshima, Nagasaki, Sasebo, Arcadia, Van Diemen Straits, and Kadoura in the Kyushu-Korea area. In the second phase of the mine-sweeping operations, additional Japanese ports required for occupation or repatriation were opened, and facilities of ports already opened to Occupation traffic were expanded.

39 In October the figures had been reduced to 161 vessels and 4573 personnel. (Rpt [C], COMINPAC to CNO, 29 May 46, sub: Opns of Minecraft 5th Flt for Period 31 Aug 45 to 7 Mar 46).

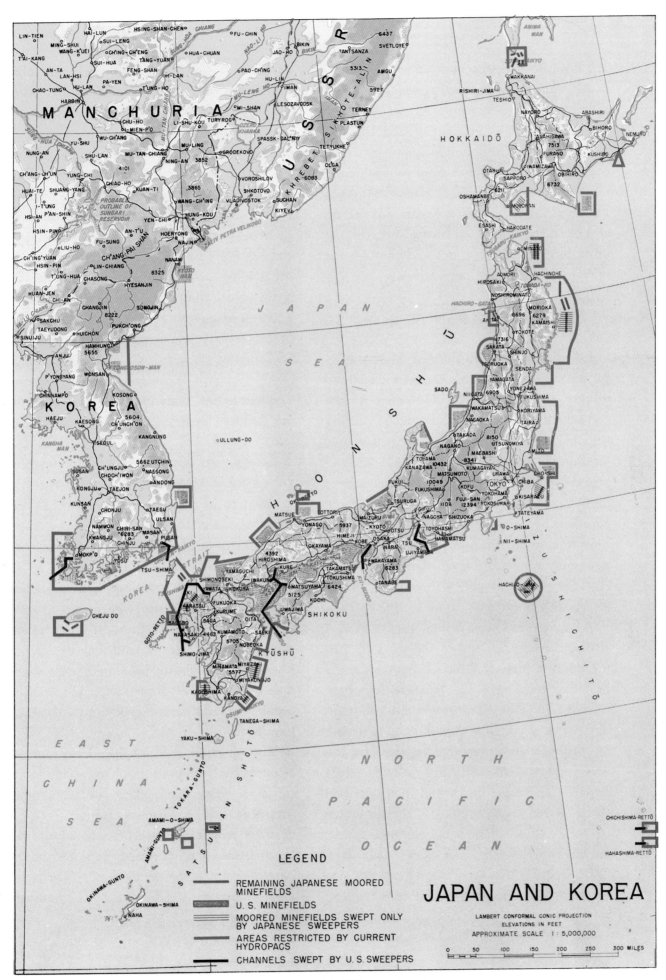

LEGEND

REMAINING JAPANESE MOORED MINEFIELDS

U. S. MINEFIELDS

MOORED MINEFIELDS SWEPT ONLY BY JAPANESE SWEEPERS

AREAS RESTRICTED BY CURRENT HYDROPACS

CHANNELS SWEPT BY U. S. SWEEPERS

JAPAN AND KOREA

LAMBERT CONFORMAL CONIC PROJECTION
ELEVATIONS IN FEET
APPROXIMATE SCALE 1 : 5,000,000

0   50   100   150   200   250   300 MILES

PLATE NO. 93
Mine Situation in the Western Pacific, 20 February 1946

and Honshu.[40] (Plate No. 94)

As mine-sweeping tasks were completed, small craft were returned to the Japanese Home Ministry for civilian use and listed as available for repatriation. Converted merchant ships and hospital ships were similarly returned to the Japanese Home Ministry. Hull and engine repair for boats was set up at Yokosuka, Sasebo, and Kobe so that small boats could be repaired and sold through the Foreign Liquidation Commission.

SCAJAP—Merchant Shipping

In order to simplify the task of operating the Japanese Merchant Marine most efficiently, trained civilian Japanese ship management and operational personnel, as well as existing shipping and related civilian organizations, were used. Representatives of the civilian Japanese ship industry and related fields were formed into a group known as the Civilian Merchant Marine Committee (CMMC) to provide a simple medium through which the Administrator, U.S. Naval Shipping Control Authority for the Japanese Merchant Marine (SCAJAP), could act.

As a result of the natural confusion and chaos following the end of the war and during the first phases of the Occupation, many problems concerning the Japanese Merchant Marine had to be met through improvisation. The crews of all ships were directed to remain on board their respective vessels, but the question of replacements and qualified reliefs arose. Perishable goods and foodstuffs had to be moved. Stock piles for civilian industry were rapidly diminishing or nonexistent. Repair facilities were idle from bomb damage. Spare parts were lacking and machine tools for their manufacture had been assigned

to the war effort. Fuel oil, coal, and lubricants were deficient and were badly distributed. Civilian shipping organizations had been fully mobilized for the war effort at the expense of the basic national economy. Labor was scarce and the enormous problem of repatriating over six million nationals required prompt action. Since many Japanese merchant vessels had suffered from bomb damage and required voyage repairs, which were delayed by lack of acilities and spare parts at the repair yards, additional shipping for repatriation was required. Therefore, various United States vessels, principally Liberty ships and LST's, were delivered by the Administrator, SCAJAP, to the Japanese Civilian Merchant Committee for manning and operation by the Japanese under SCAJAP operational control.[41]

On the third anniversary of the Occupation, 2 September 1948, SCAP directed that the initial steps be taken to decentralize the Japanese Merchant Marine. Each agency of the government would control the Government owned special type vessels required by its missions: patrol, training, research, and weather ships. Private owners would take over vessels such as tugs, salvage vessels, dredgers, small ferries, and floating cranes. Owners of fishing and whaling vessels would take control of their ships subject to the supervision of the Fisheries Agency of the Japanese Government.

This directive reduced the Occupation interest in the foregoing group of vessels to little more than maintenance of an accurate inventory. The directive further provided that the remaining vessels, which were in fact the true merchant marine carrying freight and passengers, were to remain under charter to the government's CMMC. The charters,

40 Tokyo, *Pacific Stars & Stripes*, October 24, 1948, p. 10, and June 4, 1949, pp. 8, 9, 11.
41 COMNAVJAP, Comd Narr, 21 Jun to 1 Oct 46 (C), pp. 19–20.

MOORED MINES SWEPT

OPERATIONS	OVER-ALL SWEEP- ING DATES	MINES LAID	MINES by US	SWEPT by JAP	AV. SIZE US	AV. SIZE JAP	FORCE JAP	AREA SWEPT	SWEEPER DAYS	REMARKS
Tsugaru	7 Sep–18 Oct 45	3195	945	0	12		0	1125 sq mi	504	*Roche* (DE 197) damaged by floating mine 27 Sep 45.
Tokyo	28 Aug– 3 Sep 45	250	74	0	25		0	150 sq mi	96	
Sendai–Choshi	10 Sep–15 Sep 45	820	264	0	16		0	192 sq mi	24	
Wakanoura	11 Sep– 2 Oct 45	630	384	0	46		6	524 sq mi	594	1 Jap ship reported mined on 2 Sep 45.
Kochi	8 Sep– 8 Nov 45	420	185	27	8		2	103 sq mi	78	
Bungo Suido	22 Sep–31 Oct 45	3640	1687	222	39		2	360 sq mi	1360	
Nagoya	28 Sep–26 Oct 45	170	0	0	66		6	121 sq mi	360	
Kagoshima	1 Sep– 8 Sep 45	320	166	88	8		not listed	164 sq mi	48	Includes 2/3 of Fukae Shima–Nomo Misaki mine lines. 125 of mines swept were dummies.
Nagasaki	9 Sep–16 Sep 45	694	278	0	7		0	436 sq mi	72	Includes remainder ot mines north of Ikitsuki Shima. One Jap ship reported mined 28 Oct 45.
Sasebo	9 Sep– 4 Oct 45	1114	396	58	50		12	162 sq mi	924	
Arcadia	1 Sep– 7 Sep 45	1068	31	0	21		0	600 sq mi	135	
Van Diemen	15 Sep– 1 Dec 45	780	80	0	11		0	1291 sq mi	112	Plus 3 obstructors.
Kadoura	24 Oct–29 Nov 45	120	73	0	6		0	75 sq mi	23	US sweepers checked Jap sweeping.
Omai Saki	18 Nov–31 Dec 45	290	13	229	4		13	612 sq mi	30	*Bridge* (AF 1) mined 1 Nov 45. *Daito Maru* mined and sunk while sweeping 16 Nov 45.
Tsushima	12 Oct–14 Apr 45	6196	3001	478	19		9	1108 sq mi	412	*Kanshu Maru* mined and sunk 9 Oct 45. *Minivet* (AM 371) mined and sunk 29 Dec 45.
Tachibana	14 Dec–26 Jan 46	480	16	310	2		10	595 sq mi	138	Japanese reported 52 mines swept prior 8 Sep 45. 2 Jap landing craft mined. US sweepers checked Jap.
Rickshaw	19 Oct– 1 Dec 45	4966	511	0	24		0	2565 sq mi	194	
Klondike	27 Oct– 7 Nov 45	1500	411	0	26		0	1371 sq mi	216	
Skagway	27 Oct– 9 Nov 45	3700	896	0	26		0	3960 sq mi	550	
Reno	2 Nov–28 Nov 45	1400	619	0	24		0	1475 sq mi	75	440 mines swept by US forces in Aug 45.
Total		**31,753**	**10,030**	**1,412**				**16,989 sq mi**	**5,945**	

INFLUENCE MINES SWEPT

OPERATIONS	OVER-ALL SWEEP- ING DATES	MINES LAID	MINES by US	SWEPT by JAP	AV. SIZE US	AV. SIZE JAP	FORCE JAP	AREA SWEPT	SWEEPER DAYS	REMARKS
Tokyo	29 Aug– 3 Sep 45	26	3	0	25		0	21 sq mi	36	Japs reported 12 mines swept previously of total 26 laid.
Bungo (Hiro)	22 Sep–31 Oct 45	86	33	0	39		45	152 sq mi	230	Japs reported 10 mines swept previously. LSM 114 fired a mine on 31 Oct in shallow water.
Nagoya	29 Sep–14 Dec 45	45	6	0	66		0	81 sq mi	1900	Two mines fired on second coverage. M5 (b) sweep fired mine near reported pressure stick.
Sasebo	14 Sep– 4 Oct 45	60	2	0	50		0	150 sq mi	260	One of these on second coverage. Japs reported 5 influence mines swept previously.
Kobe	28 Nov– 9 Mar 46	659	2	0	56		14	34 sq mi	4850	Japs reported 27 mines swept in Kobe channel previously. Mine fired by GP *Marathon* on 20 Jan, may have been magnetic outside swept channel. 9 Jap ships mined in Izuminada after 1 Sep 45.
Kure-Otake	27 Oct 45–26 Feb 46	571	12	0	26		17	420 sq mi	1331	Japs reported 4 mines swept in Kure channel previously.
Fukuoka	13 Oct 45–11 Jan 46	306	0	0	28		8	19 sq mi	1445	3 Jap ships mined in Fukuoka Wan after 1 Sep 45.
Fusan	28 Sep 45–29 Jan 46	197	4	0	18		6	5 sq mi	260	Japs reported 39 mines swept prior to 28 Sep. Jap GP *Kure* mined and sunk outside swept area on 9 Oct 45. 4 other Jap ships mined in Fusan after 1 Sep 45.
Total		**1950**	**62**	**0**				**882 sq mi**	**10,312**	

PLATE NO. 94

Moored and Influence Mines Swept: August 1945—April 1946

however, were to be changed from " bare boat " to time charters ; this thrust the responsibility of manning, supplying, and repairing ships on the owners. The entry of private enterprise into these fields was expected to reduce the drain on the national economy and prepared private companies for eventual full control of their ships. SCAP designated SCAJAP, which continued to operate as a staff section of COMNAVFE, to implement this program, regulating its progress to the ability of the shipping industry to assume responsibilities.[42]

Repatriation

One of the largest tasks performed by the Navy in Japan was the repatriation of Japanese nationals from all areas of the Pacific and the return of aliens in Japan to their homes.[43] Responsibility for the operational control of repatriation shipping and the supervision of its maintenance was vested initially in Commander, U.S. Fifth Fleet, insofar as it concerned former Japanese naval ships, and in FLTLOSCAP for former merchant ships. Repatriation was under way when the Shipping Control Authority for the Japanese Merchant Marine (SCAJAP) was formed.[44] SCAJAP was continued as a task group of COMNAVJAP. By the end of 1946 mass repatriation was completed from all areas except those controlled by the U.S.S.R. SCAJAP vessels continued to be available to repatriate the thousands of military and civilian personnel believed held in these areas.[45]

Suppression of Illegal Traffic

A considerable amount of unauthorized waterborne traffic was conducted between Korea and Japan, consisting mainly of Japanese attempting to return to Japan and Koreans attempting to return to Korea with more than their authorized allowance of personal effects as well as extensive commercial smuggling. In order to prevent these activities and the introduction of contagious diseases by illegal entrants rom Korea, Occupation forces maintained beach and off-shore patrols to intercept such traffic.[46] Destroyer patrols operated in Korean waters from the cessation of hostilities until January 1947 under Commander, Seventh Fleet, and after that date under Commander Naval Forces, Far East, (COMNAVFE) ; in addition, intermittent patrols were maintained off the coast of Honshu and Kyushu.

It was recognized from the start that the suppression of illegal sea traffic in Japanese and Korean waters should eventually become the responsibility of the Japanese and Korean governments. Japan, however, did not have a coast guard organization prior to the war ; the coast guard functions were performed by the Imperial Japanese Navy. Korea was in the initial stages of achieving national sovereignty. A small operating coast guard consisting of former United States vessels was

---

42 COMNAVFE, Comd Narr, 1 Apr–30 Sep 48 (C). Responsibility for the operation of certain categories of vessels was returned to their owners in February 1949, through the General Maritime Bureau, Ministry of Transportation. COMNAVFE, however, retained administrative control over these vessels. (COMNAVFE, Comd Narr, 1 Oct 48–31 Mar 49 [C].)

43 See Ch. VI for details of repatriation program as it operated under G-3, GHQ, SCAP.

44 See p. 287.

45 Tokyo, *Pacific Stars & Stripes*, May 29, 1949.

46 COMNAVJAP Opn Plan 3–46, Annex C (C), 8 Jul 46.

established in Korea.[47] In Japan, twenty-eight patrol craft formerly engaged in mine sweeping were allocated to the Japanese Coast Guard because it was felt that activation of the Coast Guard would reduce U.S. Navy patrol tasks. This added new responsibilities to the U.S. Navy in the form of supervision and direction of the coast guard operations.[48]

In order to coordinate better the work of various agencies formerly concerned with maritime matters and to provide a firm foundation for the development of a Japanese Coast Guard, the Japanese Diet passed the Maritime Safety Authorities Bill. This law became effective on 1 May 1948, establishing a Maritime Safety Board under the Ministry of Transportation.[49]

Miscellaneous Naval Activities: 1946—1948

Branch Hydrographic Office: On 1 July 1946 Branch Hydographic Office, Tokyo, was established with Commander E. B. Dodson, USN, in charge. He also assumed direction of the Japanese Hydrographic Office which had formerly been under the supervision of SCAP through the Army Engineer Corps. The mission of the Hydrographic Office at Tokyo, in addition to services to United States and Allied shipping, was the reorganization of Japanese hydrographic facilities and resumption of hydrographic work in Japanese waters. When the U.S. Office was closed in 1948, work was continued by the Japanese Office.

Support Groups: United States and British Naval Support Groups were assigned tasks that backed the U.S. Army and Navy and Allied units in their control of the Japanese Empire. They conducted inspections of Japanese shipping including suspicious vessels encountered at sea, controlled movements and inspections of ex-Japanese naval vessels and shipping, performed escort duties, and assisted in air-sea rescue operations. Units were maintained in the Yokosuka and Sasebo areas available to meet emergencies and frequent

47 An intensive training program was set up and supervised by the US Coast Guard personnel at HQ, USAFIK. On 1 September 1947 the newly organized Korean Coast Guard assumed responsibility for the illegal shipping patrol in Korean waters, and the US naval forces assigned to COMNAVFE were accordingly reduced by three destroyer escorts. US and British units continued to operate out of Sasebo, Japan, on intermittent patrol for the purpose of interdicting such illegal shipping of southwestern Japan and in Tsushima Strait, and also stood ready to operate in Korean waters if required.

48 After 1 June 1948 operational control of the Japanese Coast Guard was vested in the Maritime Safety Board, operating under the guidance of the Public Safety Division.

49 (1) Its functions were: to enforce laws and orders pertaining to safety of vessels, to establish the qualifications and number of ship's officers required, to assist vessels in distress, to investigate marine disasters, to prevent and suppress crime at sea, to provide service concerning waterways and navigational aids, and otherwise to insure maritime safety. In addition, this bill placed under the jurisdiction of the Maritime Safety Board all former functions of the Secretariat of the Minister of Transportation, the Director General's Secretariat (under General Maritime Bureau), the Maritime Transport Bureau, the Ship Bureau, the Seamen's Bureau, the Commissioners of Marine Courts of Inquiry, the Lighthouse Bureau, and the Hydrographic Bureau. It provided for a fleet of vessels not to exceed 125 in number and limited to a total tonnage of 50,000 gross tons, with no individual vessel having a displacement greater than 1,500 tons or a speed in excess of fifteen knots, and for a total personnel strength not exceeding 10,000, only 720 of whom might be assigned to duty aboard ships. (COMNAVFE, Comd Narr, 1 Apr to 1 Sep 48 [C].) (2) After passage of the Maritime Safety Authorities Bill, COMNAVFE exercised no operational control over the Maritime Safety Board (MSB) except in the custody of ex-naval vessels and mine-sweeping operations. These were only temporary functions of the Maritime Safety Board; control was therefore retained through SCAJAP which functioned as a staff section of COMNAVFE.

visits were made to all ports open to United States shipping to observe conditions and inspect Japanese shipping. Each group contained one cruiser and four destroyers. The U.S. Group had three additional destroyer escorts assigned primarily to perform patrol duties in Korean waters. During 1947 and 1948 Support Groups continued assigned tasks. The British Group operating under COMNAVJAP was dissolved on 30 November 1947 and in its place a unit consisting of three destroyers was formed to operate as a part of the U.S. Support Group.

Naval Air Units: In February 1946 COMNAVJAP had under his control one Marine Air Group, MAG 31, composed of 116 aircraft of various types.[50] The Naval Air Base at Kisarazu serviced the needs of Naval Air Transport Service (NATS) until it was decommissioned in May 1946 and the NATS detachment was moved to Atsugi Airfield; Air search and reconnaissance functions were operated directly from Headquarters COMNAVJAP, with air facilities provided by Fleet Air Wing One. The boundaries of search and reconnaissance, including search and rescue functions, were defined by CINCPAC and the ports of Yokosuka and Sasebo were selected as seaplane bases. Ready duty destroyers, fleet tugs, and seaplanes were used singly or in coordinated action in rescue search missions at sea. These missions included searching for downed planes, removing sick patients from ships, and towing disabled Allied and Japanese vessels.

Communications: Communications for GHQ and the Navy Liaison Office were handled by the USS *Teton* upon arrival at Yokohama in August 1945. When the Army Mobile Radio was set up in Tokyo, a mobile communications unit set up transmitting and receiving stations to handle the Navy communications for GHQ. Later, this unit was dissolved and Radio NDT at Yokosuka took over the guard for SCAP, SCAJAP, FLTLOSCAP, and the Port Directors in this area. In early 1947 physical control of this unit was transferred to Headquarters, COMNAVFE. At the end of the year the Army receiver station located on Tsushima Island near Tokyo took over the receiving side of the Guam-Tokyo radio teletype circuit, making possible the joint use of facilities and personnel. A joint emergency transmitter station was constructed at Totsuka which furnished emergency service requirements of GHQ, FEAF, Army Air Communications Service, and Eighth Army Headquarters.[51]

The cooperation of Navy and Air components with the Army ground forces made it possible for the Occupation of Japan to proceed in an orderly, efficient manner. From the very beginning, when individual and coordinated missions were outlined, through the initial landings and later when the Occupation was established, the contribution of each of the forces in carrying out its assigned missions was a tangible element of the success of the Occupation.

---

50   MAG 31 was ordered to return to the US in June and by October the total aircraft assigned COMNAVJAP had been reduced to only six.

51   COMNAVFE, Comd Narr, 1 Apr to 30 Sep 48 (C).

EPILOGUE

The fourth anniversary of V-J Day found the character of the Occupation changed through gradual evolution from the initial stern quality of a military operation to the friendly guidance of a protective force. Japan was well on the road toward becoming a sovereign nation once again. (Plate No. 95)

The Prime Minister spoke for his people in conceding progress toward economic recovery :[1]

In the economic field, we have started well on the road of stabilization. ....Our budget is balanced. The administrative readjustment program is nearing completion. ....the government is now engaged in the formulation of a plan for tax reform and tax reduction that will ensure equity and efficiency to our tax system. ...

In pursuance of its economic stabilization policy the government will continue to strive to effect further retrenchment in expenditures. We intend to simplify and stream-line our administrative machinery still further, while taking adequate measures for unemployment compensation and relief. We are vigorously pushing forward to promote enterprises, large and small, as a means of providing jobs to the unemployed, at the same time of enhancing the nation's economic power.

To that end it is imperative that we expand our export trade and import raw materials and technology as well as capital from abroad. We must also establish firmly law and order, assure the world of our social and industrial stability, and give proof of the soundness of our economic policy and practices. ....a great deal has been accomplished—largely, however, with Allied assistance. But a great deal more remains yet to be done—done more by our own initiative and efforts.

In a parallel statement made on this same anniversary, General MacArthur summarized the progress of the Occupation and expressed his belief that Japan was ready to shoulder a major part of the responsibility for her recovery :[2]

Today marks the fourth anniversary of that historic event on the Battleship Missouri in Tokyo Bay when the warring nations of the Pacific entered into solemn covenants designed to restore the peace. The four years since passed have been fruitful years here in terms of human progress, as the Japanese people have fully and faithfully observed their surrender commitments and advanced steadily and progressively along the road of spiritual regeneration and physical reconstruction. Today Japan might, indeed, be viewed as a symbol of hope for less fortunate peoples overwhelmed by the despotic rule of coercive force. For, despite the continued presence on Japan's soil of an occupation force from beyond the seas, the Japanese people in their enjoyment of full personal freedom know that by their skill and their industry they serve no other cause but their own. They, themselves, plot the ultimate course of Japan's destiny within the family of free nations.

The past year has witnessed accelerated progress in every phase of Japan's reconstruction. True, as elsewhere, there have been assaults upon the integrity of the democratic process by the small existent Communist minority, but these assaults were effectively repulsed—not by the repressive force of police power but by the weight of an increasingly informed and active Japanese public opinion aroused to meet the threat to their free institutions. As a result, the threat of Communism as a major issue in Japanese life is past. It fell victim of its own excesses. The

---

1   Radio Address by Prime Minister Yoshida, 2 Sep 49.
2   GHQ FEC PIO, Press Release, 2 Sep 49.

Nippon Times

昭和二十四年八月十四日　　TOKYO, SUNDAY, AUGUST 14, 1949　　第三種郵便物認可

Nippon Times

Published by
The Nippon Times, Ltd.
KIYOSHI TOGASAKI, President

TOKYO OFFICE:
1. Ichome Uchisaiwai-cho, Chiyoda-ku. Central P. O. Box 144, 352, 358.
Telephone: Ginza (57) 303, 403, 5857, 5858, 5859, 7003.
Telegraphic Address: "Times Tokyo-yubin".

OSAKA: Dojima Bldg. Tel.: Horikawa (35) 177.

SUBSCRIPTION RATE:
¥ 2.945 per copy, ¥ 0.055 charges incidental to sales tax. Thursday issue with supplement ¥ 4.905, ¥ 0.095 charges incidental to sales tax. One month ¥ 89.00, ¥ 1.65 charges incidental to sales tax. Obtainable directly from all newspaper agents in Japan. By mail ¥ 104.5 per month, ¥ 1.79 charges incidental to sales tax. For foreign countries postage ¥ 150.00 per month extra.

TOKYO, SUN., AUGUST 14, 1949

Years of Progress

The four years following the end of hostilities in the Pacific on August 15, 1945, have been fruitful years of progress for Japan. As compared to the war-battered, bewildered nation which accepted unconditionally the Potsdam agreement, Japan today can look with justifiable pride upon the present progressive state of the nation. Indeed, the four years have been years of achievement as seen from forward steps taken toward rebuilding the country not as another military machine but as a nation pursuing those high concepts of peace and democracy.

The task is not over yet. Far from it. But even the most severe critic must admit that tremendous progress has been achieved. Compare the food situation four years ago and today. The rations of staple food at that time were not only meager but more often their distribution was delayed for days and weeks. Today vast improvements have been made, thanks to the Occupation and the efforts of the nation's farmers, and no longer do urban citizens take long treks into the countryside to grub for food.

Four years ago cities were almost completely levelled and the housing shortage was something beyond imagination. Housing is still an acute problem, but the war devastation has almost been obliterated with houses and buildings rising in mushroom fashion. The people are better dressed. Progress in health and sanitation are keeping them in better health. Serious epidemics are almost nonexistent. Transportation facilities have shown tremendous improvement. No longer do passengers enter and leave trains through the windows, and they do not ride the connecting rods between trains. The rampant waves of burglary, murder, and other serious crimes have been halted. Four years ago honest citizens could not walk the streets of their cities at night without risking their lives and limbs.

The nation's economy has been placed on the road to recovery and on a stable basis. The streamlining of industrial and business activities with the stress on efficiency and economy is, of course, bringing the problem of unemployment to the fore. But the progress made in production from the utter ruin of four years ago must be considered almost a miracle. The adjustment of government personnel and the balanced budget promise a more efficient administration at lower operating costs.

Aside from the physical progress achieved, a most remarkable transformation for the better has taken place in the mental outlook of the people. No longer are they the cringing subjects of a militaristic police state. They now have the freedom to think and speak as their conscience directs them. This and other freedoms granted the people under a democratic regime naturally led to initial excesses. But the people are now finding their equilibrium. As proof of this happy development, the weight of public opinion recently prevented the Government railway workers from resorting to illegal tactics and made possible a personnel retrenchment program which the people believed necessary for the ultimate welfare of the nation.

Credit for the remolding of a war-shattered nation into a shape from which she may soon become a contributing member of the international society must go to the benevolent policies of the Occupation as well as to the diligence of the Japanese people as a whole. Too much credit cannot be paid the unexcelled statesmanship of General MacArthur and the excellent deportment of the members of the Occupation Force who brought with them practical examples of the democratic way of life.

The past four years since the fateful surrender date have been years of progress. But it is to be hoped that the years to come will see no slackening of the pace in the forward surge of the Japanese people toward the attainment of a peaceful, democratic nation—one which will be able to ward off any attack by those believers in false gods. Holding firm to the lessons learned in the past four years, the Japanese nation with competent leadership and a responsible citizenry can face the future with hope and optimism.

PLATE NO. 95
Japanese Newspaper Editorial Summarizes Four Years of Occupation, 1945—1949

Japanese mind penetrated the hypocrisy supporting its position. This test of strength, while disturbing to orderly progress, served to bring to light for the first time the full latent power of the Japanese devotion to the concepts of freedom and the integrity of their constitutional processes. Therein lies encouragement of Japan's potential strength as a bulwark of human freedom.

Politically, progressive gains have been made in the fabrication of a system of government truly representative in character. The lines of separation between the three great branches, executive, legislative and judicial, as provided by the constitutional design, have found strength in healthy public discussion of the vital issue of constitutional interpretation, and as a result the affairs of government have advanced with a minimum of overlapping friction and increasing inter-branch cooperation.

The development of the desired autonomous responsibility in the conduct of local affairs has been retarded somewhat by the need for rationalization in the field of government finance to permit local revenues to support local government. A remedy for this difficulty is now being evolved, providing hope that the coming year will produce the legal basis fully to sustain the severance of pre-existing centralized controls and support the development of a political and social system resting upon interrelated and self-sustaining segments at the community level from which the national government may draw its power and direction. Therein will lie the safeguard against the re-emergence of autocracy as the prevailing philosophy of government in Japan.

Probably the most significant political development of the past year has been the growing consciousness of individual responsibility in the conduct of public affairs. This has been given emphasis by a popular demand for higher standards of public morality, keynoted by action of the electorate in rejecting for return to elective office public officials whose public record was compromised by the exposure of corruption in government. Administrative and judicial action in the investigation of the stewardship of public responsibility and vigorous prosecution, without fear or favor, of violators of the public trust, not only have served to safeguard the public interest, but have

given vital reality to the constitutional assurance of " equality before the law ". There is thus rapidly taking form the ethical base upon which the pillars of a free, responsible and representative government safely may rest.

Socially, the Japanese people are wearing well their constitutional mantle of personal liberty and individual dignity. Apart from the growing consciousness of individual responsibility in the conduct of public affairs, there has been a sharp revulsion against persons who have failed to abide the law, with a resulting decisive drop in the incidence of private crime. The basic causes of social unrest throughout Asia have largely been eradicated in Japan by a redesign of the social structure to permit the equalization of individual opportunity and personal privilege. This is having a profound influence upon the economic potential, thereby fortifying the spirit against radical designs of either extreme to suppress freedom.

Substantial progress has been made in the building of an effective police system based upon the statutory principle of decentralization in the exercise of the police power. Increasingly the Japanese people are coming to understand that this power rests in their hands, rather than in the hands of any ruling clique, and provides the legal weapon for the preservation of the local security by their direction. They realize that the maintenance of internal order in the nation as a whole, subject to the safeguards provided by law, is dependent upon the manner in which each community administers the police power corresponding to its local responsibility. Here, too, difficulties are being experienced due to the present maladjustment of government finance, but this problem, as pointed out, is in process of solution. Apart from this, progressive strides have been made toward implementation of the new concepts embodied in the police law, and the police services are being administered with restraint, tolerance and commendable efficiency. The danger that a police state will re-emerge or that the police system as now constituted and manned will fail to maintain reasonable law and order is non-existent. Progress of trade unionization during the past year, despite a degree of freedom unsurpassed in modern civilization, has been somewhat impeded by the machinations of an irresponsible union leadership, but

293

its rank and file are showing an increasing awareness of this threat to labor's legitimate objectives and are moving to insist upon moderation and objectivity. Workers in the public service, through the functioning of a modernized and enlightened civil service system established by law, for the first time in Japan's history find protection of their rights and interests adequately provided for, without continuous struggle on their part, with machinery established for the hearing and adjudication of individual or collective grievances. This has resulted in a marked uplift in individual morale and greater attendant efficiency in the conduct of the affairs of government.

The enfranchised women of Japan are exerting an increasingly beneficial influence upon Japan's political, economic and social life. They are responding magnificently to the challenge of the attending responsibility and give every promise of proving a powerful and effective force in the shaping of Japan's peaceful destiny.

Economically, Japan is still in transition from an economy of survival to one of health, but the past year has witnessed significant progress along a broad front. Foremost of the gains made lies in the development of a more positive leadership and an increasingly informed public opinion.

Both leaders and people are coming to understand that representative democracy draws its strength from the support of a broad majority of the people imbued with the belief that under it they may attain a standard of living commensurate with the capabilities of modern civilization—that a prerequisite to that condition is individual freedom of activity in the field of economic enterprise, for no individual bound in economic thralldom can be politically free. Thus, for the vast majority of those who earn their living in industrial and commercial pursuits there could be no political freedom so long as their economic destiny was determined by decisions made in the closed councils of the few families which formerly controlled the vast bulk of the productive and financial resources of Japan. Nor could there be any political freedom for those who work the soil so long as they were economic serfs under a feudalistic system of land tenure. The fruition during the past year of the plans laid down by the Occupation and carried out by the Japanese Government to remove, through the Economic Deconcentration Program on the one hand and the Land Reform Program on the other, these barriers to the existence of a free society, has established in Japan the economic basis for the existence of a broad middle class which, having a stake in the economic well-being of the country, will support the ideal of democracy as their way of life and will reject with scorn any will-of-the-wisp economic utopias which require the surrender of the individual's freedom to the State.

With patience, fortitude and self-discipline the Japanese people withstood the privations of the immediate postwar period. With comparable energy, industry and hope they are now launched on the huge task of making Japan once again self-supporting among the family of nations. On the way to that goal great obstacles have been overcome, although some still remain. Since the summer of 1945, when productive activity in Japan was utterly paralyzed, the production of commodities and goods for home consumption, for industrial use and for export has risen steadily until now it is rapidly approaching the average level for the years 1930 to 1934, prescribed by the Far Eastern Commission as an interim standard. Coal, basic to so much of Japan's industry, is now being produced at a monthly rate of 3.2 million metric tons as contrasted with less than 1.7 million metric tons in 1946. Electric power, another basic ingredient of industrial activity, has attained a monthly volume of 3.2 billion KWH, as compared with 2.8 billion one year ago. Production of chemicals, necessary both for industrial uses and for the protection of the public health, has attained a volume of 105% of the 1930–34 average, as compared with 76% one year ago and 21% in January 1946. Equally significant advances have been made in other fields of economic activity, such as in the construction of dwellings and business buildings to replace those destroyed by war, and in the production of an increasing variety of goods both for home consumption and sale overseas.

To acquire the raw materials needed to feed her industrial machine as well as to overcome the deficit in her indigenous food production, Japan must export a large volume of goods and services. Despite *existing handicaps, chiefly the limited availability of raw materials from those sources which customarily supplied Japan in the prewar years, progress in this direction has been heartening. In 1946, Japan's total exports were $103,000,000.00; in 1947, $173,000,000.00; in 1948, $258,000,000.00, and in the first six months of 1949, exports had already exceeded the total for the full year 1948 by a sizeable margin.*

In the past twelve months two significant decisions to promote the economic rehabilitation of Japan were taken by the Government of the United States. One was that of May 1949, to cease the removal of industrial plants for reparations. This action dispelled the pall of uncertainty which had previously paralyzed entrepreneurial initiative and restored the incentive to the investment of capital in the rehabilitation and construction of capital plant and equipment. The second was the authorization by the Congress of the United States of limited budgetary appropriations for financing the importation into Japan of materials needed for rehabilitation purposes in addition to the appropriations previously made for the importation of primary necessities such as food, fertilizer and medicines to protect the Japanese people against widespread suffering and disease.[3]

The enactment by the Japanese National Diet in the spring of 1949 of a national budget which for the first time in many years achieved a true balance, and subsequent action to sharply curtail the cost of government by streamlining its structure and reducing its personnel, have struck at one of the contributing factors in the postwar inflation and are gradually effecting greater stability. To prevent the specter of inflation from rising again, a firm and determined course based upon sound fiscal and financial policies is now being pursued by the Japanese Government. This, accompanied by maximum utilization of indigenous resources and efficient employment of the manpower of Japan in the useful pursuits of peace, will speed the day when the Japanese economy will be stabilized and its dependence on American subsidy eliminated.

To stimulate productive endeavor and to strengthen the foundations for the growth of free private competitive enterprise in Japan, the economic controls necessitated by the war-generated shortages of critical materials have been removed as fast as the availability of adequate supplies has obviated their necessity. The timing of progressive further relaxations will, of course, depend on the progress of the transition from an economy of scarcity to one of normalcy.

Since October 1, 1945, nine and one-half million people have been added to the population of Japan—five million by repatriation and the rest

---

3 In his support of appropriations for the fiscal years of 1949, 1950, and 1951 for economic aid to the Japanese, Mr. Joseph M. Dodge, well-known Detroit banker and former financial advisor to the American Military Government in Germany who had visited Japan to survey economic conditions and foreign trade procedures at the request of General MacArthur, testified before the National Advisory Council Staff Committee about the importance of such aid and how effectively it was being utilized in Japan :

" The actual and projected appropriations for the fiscal years 1949, 1950 and 1951 for economic aid for Tri-Zone Germany are approximately twice that for Japan. On a population basis for Germany of something more than half that of Japan, the appropriations for Germany are over three times the amount for Japan per captia. The proposed FY 51 appropriation for Tri-Zone Germany is more than twice that of the amount of economic aid requested for Japan.

" We should note the substantial progress that has been made in Japan on relatively modest appropriations. Effective financial stabilization substantially has been achieved. There has been an increasing transfer of responsibility from the Occupation to the Japanese Goverment and to the Japanese people. There has been a substantial increase in exports and industrial recovery has proceeded at a heartening pace and is now at almost the level of the 1932–1936 period. For the first time (in 1949) there is a reduction in the foreign trade deficit.

" In no other nation has so much been accomplished with so little.

" The FY 51 appropriation request for Japan has been reduced substantially. On a basis of $ 320 million for Japan and the Ryukyus, the reduction for FY 51 from FY 50 is 33.6%. In economic aid requested for Japan there is a reduction of 35%. This compares with a proposed reduction for FY 51 in the ECA total of 21.4% and for Tri-Zone Germany of 21.7%." (Statement by Mr. Joseph M. Dodge before National Advisory Council Staff Committee on 12 January 1950, p. 2.)

through natural increase. Yet there has been no mass unemployment, no social unrest and no large-scale dole. In June 1949, persons reported as totally unemployed were fewer than 400,000. Further, despite recent reductions in the number of government employees in the interest of governmental economy and efficiency and the current rationalization of industry necessitated by the adoption of a single foreign exchange rate for foreign trade and the transition from subsidized to competitive industry, total unemployment by the end of August 1949 is estimated not to exceed one-half million persons. During the twelve months ended June 30, 1949, the total number of persons at work in any given week averaged over 34.5 million, as compared with 32.9 million in the preceding twelve-month period, or an average increase of 1.6 million in the total number of persons at work. In June 1949, the total number of persons at work stood at an all-time high of 37.4 million. These figures reflect an orderly absorption of the working energies of the increasing population in an expanding number of employment opportunities in industry, agriculture and small scale family enterprises. Unemployment, therefore, presents no major problem at the present time, and the expanding areas of employment in the work of reconstruction will stand safeguard against any acute unemployment problem in the foreseeable future.

Since the full employment of Japan's industrial potential requires a vigorous revival of her foreign trade and since among her chief customers in the past were the countries bordering on the Pacific basin, the question as to whether Japan will regain her traditional trade with China, despite the stranglehold of Communism upon that tragic land, has been mooted with increasing frequency. This question is largely academic. Foreign trade requires production in excess of domestic needs. Human experience demonstrates with striking clarity that the further removed a people become from the economic philosophy of free enterprise in like ratio does its productive capacity deteriorate. This deterioration proceeds until, as under Communism, with incentive completely lost, the human energy and individual initiative which find their expression in production give way to indolence and despair. In such unhealthy climate industry and commerce cannot thrive and realism warns that the potentialities of trade with any people under the strictures of a collectivistic system must be discounted accordingly. For the time being, therefore, and for some time to come, Japan must look elsewhere for the sources of her needed imports and the markets for her manufactures. Against this need Japan has already initiated foreign trade with 113 other countries and territorial areas.

I dare say that no operation in history has been subject to such extraordinary divergence of opinion carried in the media of public expression than has Occupation of Japan. Some writers have been extravagant in their praise, others no less extravagant in their criticism. The truth, awaiting the judgement of history, will rest somewhere in between.

Nor has there been any operation subject to such a variety of influences and pressures—the ideological protagonists, the special pleaders, the vindictive and the lenient—many seeking to influence public opinion through prevarication of the truth. In the search for sensationalism, incidents in Japan, elsewhere scarcely worth the public notice, have been exaggerated out of all proportion to their true significance, with the serenity and order and sincerity of purpose normal to postwar Japan all but ignored. And time and again simultaneous attack has been leveled against Occupation policy, by the leftists as too reactionary and by the conservatives as too liberal. Such an atmosphere, while giving assurance that our moderate course is well charted, does not contribute to an objective public appraisal of the situation.

The great and noble effort by the American people, with the wholehearted support of other Allies, toward the reorientation and reconstruction of postwar Japan, beyond peradventure of doubt, will prove eminently successful. Long hence history will record of the Occupation that its greatest contribution to the progress of civilization was to introduce into Japan the great concepts of personal liberty and individual dignity and to give the Christian ideal the opportunity to advance into Asia.

Of the Japanese people I can pay no higher tribute than to repeat that they have fully and faithfully fulfilled their surrender commitments and *have well earned the freedom and dignity and opportunity which alone can come with the restoration of a formal Peace.*

In a previous message to the people of Japan on the second anniversary of their new constitution the General had forecast the future in a policy of progressive emancipation :[4]

While insisting upon the firm adherence to the course delineated by existing Allied policy and directive, it is my purpose to continue to advance this transition just as rapidly as you are able to assume the attending autonomous responsibility. Thus progressive latitude will come to you in the stewardship of your own affairs.

One of the most important elements in relaxation of controls was a plan for the gradual deactivation of forty-seven prefectural civil affairs teams,[5] culminating in the absorption of their duties and responsibilities by only seven regional and the Hokkaido (District) civil affairs teams, announced by GHQ, SCAP, on 28 July 1949. The remaining teams were to be maintained at approximately their former strengths but were to be staffed primarily by civilians trained in economics, education, welfare or some other of the civil affairs departments, with a minimum number of military personnel for administrative purposes. The plan further provided for the discontinuance of the Civil Affairs Section of Eighth Army and the establishment of a small Civil Affairs Section in GHQ, SCAP ; the transition was to be completed by 31 December 1949.[6]

This progressive relaxation of controls was designed to permit the local Japanese officials to assume more and more responsibilities in their respective fields as rapidly as they demonstrated their capacity to undertake them.[7]

---

4 GHQ FEC PIO, Press Release, 2 May 49.
5 In keeping with the changing aspect of the Occupation, designation of " Military Government Section " was changed to " Civil Affairs Section " and its prefectural units deactivated. (GHQ SCAP & FEC Staff Memo No. 26, 21 Jun 49. AG 323.3, 20 Jun 49)
6 GHQ FEC PIO, Press Release, 28 Jul 49.
7 GHQ FEC PIO, Press Release, 15 Aug 49.

REPORTS OF GENERAL MacARTHUR

VOL   I: The Campaigns of MacArthur in the Pacific
VOL   I: Supplement: MacArthur in Japan: The Occupation, Military Phase
VOL II: Japanese Operations in the Southwest Pacific Area

". . . This report has been prepared by the General Staff to serve as a background for, and introduction to the detailed operational histories of the various tactical commands involved.

The pressure of other duties having prevented my personal participation in its preparation, it has been entrusted by me to that magnificent staff group which actually conducted the staff work during the progress of the campaigns. They speak with that sincere and accurate knowledge which is possessed only by those who have personally participated in the operations which they record . . ."

Preface by General Douglas MacArthur.

Senior Commanders: South West Pacific Areas

Gen W. Krueger: Sixth Army; Lt Gen R. L. Eichelberger: Eighth Army; Gen Sir Thomas Blamey: Aust. Imp. Forces; Lt Gen G. C. Kenny: AAF; Adm T. H. Kinkaid, USN: Seventh Fleet

The General Staff: GHQ: South West Pacific Area

Lt Gen R. K. Sutherland, CofS; Maj Gen R. J. Marshall, D CofS; Maj Gen C. P. Stivers, G–1: Maj Gen C. A. Willoughby, G–2; Maj Gen S. J. Chamberlain, G–3; Maj Gen L. J. Whitlock, G–4; Maj Gen S. B. Akin, CSO; Maj Gen W. F. Marquat, AAO; Maj Gen H. J. Casey, CE; Brig Gen B. M. Fitch, AG; Brig Gen L. A. Diller, PRO.

Editor in Chief

Maj Gen Charles A. Willoughby, G–2

Senior Editors

Col E. H. F. Svensson, G–2; Gordon W. Prange PhD; Mr. Stewart Thorn

Associate and Contributing Editors

Brig Gen H. E. Eastwood, G–4; Col F. H. Wilson, G–2; Col R. L. Ring, G–2; Col W. J. Niederpruem, G–3; Lt Col M. K. Schiffman, G–2; Maj J. M. Roberts, G–3; Capt J. C. Bateman, G–2; Capt Mary Guyette, G–2; Capt John L. Moore, G–2; Lt Stanley Falk, G–2; Mr. Jerome Forrest; Mr. Kenneth W. Myers; Miss Joan Corrigan.

Translation–Interrogation–Production

Lt Col W. H. Brown, G–2; Louis W. Doll, PhD; Capt E. B. Ryckaert, G–2; Capt K. J. Knapp, Jr., G–2; Lt Y. G. Kanegai, G–2; Mr. James J. Wickel; Mr. John Shelton, ATIS; Mr. Norman Sparnon, ATIS; SFC H. Y. Uno, G–2; Mr. K. Takeuchi; Mr. S. Wada.

INDEX

Aburayama, 108n
Administrative and Executive Group, FEC, 84
Admiralty Islands, 179, 275
Aeronautical Chart Service, USAF, 275
Africa, 95
Agriculture, 212–213
Agriculture–Commerce Ministry (Jap.), 23
Aichi, 97n
Air Defense Command, 17
Air Division, 1st, 86
Air Forces
    Fifth, 14, 17, 29, 44, 58, 62, 268–270
    Seventh, 14, 17, 268, 273
    Thirteenth, 14, 17, 270
    Twentieth, 88, 94–95, 97
    Far East, 6, 7, 16–17, 24–25, 35, 38, 45n, 73, 86, 88,
        94, 97, 104
        air traffic handled, 275
        communications, 290
        initial operations, 268–270
        joins USAF, 273
        maintenance in Japan, 273
        mapping and photographic activities, 275
        number of personnel, 273
        number of units, 270
        organization and missions, 270–273
        surveillance missions, 268
        training, 273
        transport mission, 270, 275
        types of units, 275–277
    Strategic, 7, 10, 17, 96, 271
Air Transport Command, 17, 24, 94, 113, 268, 273, 275
Airborne Division, 11th, 6n, 7, 14, 17, 24, 27–32, 36,
    38, 41–44, 53, 55, 65, 94, 268
Aircraft types. *See individual types of planes*
Airlift operations 7, 14, 17, 27–28, 32, 38–42, 94–96,
    268–270
Airways and Air Communications Service Wing, 7th,
    273
Alaskan Department, 7
Aleutian Islands, 277
Allied Council for Japan: 69–71, 77, 82, 157, 161, 179,
    183
Allied forces, 34
Allied Translator and Interpreter Section, SCAP, 256,
    260
Amapoora, 178

American Red Cross, 52, 105. *See also* International
    Red Cross
Amoy, 173
Amphibious operations, 29
Ancon, 100
Antiaircraft artillery units, 60
Aomori, 42, 44–45, 60, 90, 120, 138, 270
Area of Initial Evacuation, 19, 21, 28, 35, 42–43
Arisue, Lt. Gen. Seizo, 24–31
Armies
    First, 1, 7, 14
    Sixth, 1, 6–17, 36, 45–47, 56–60, 75, 93, 102, 109,
        119, 122, 136, 140, 152n, 154, 195–198, 227, 277
    Eighth, 1, 6–10, 14–17, 24, 28, 35, 31, 34, 36, 41–45,
        51–65, 71–75, 86, 89, 93, 104–113, 119, 122, 152n,
        154, 195–201, 214, 223, 226–229, 260, 268, 277,
        283, 290, 297
    Tenth, 7, 10, 14, 17
Army Forces, China Theater, 172, 277
Army Forces in Korea, 86, 151n, 157, 165, 277
Army Forces, Middle Pacific, 7, 14, 82, 152
Army Forces, Pacific, 4, 7, 14, 17, 23–31, 35, 42, 67,
    71–76, 82, 96, 105, 113, 119, 131, 151, 158, 198, 268
    271
Army Forces, Southeast Pacific, 7
Army Forces, Western Pacific, 7, 10, 14, 16, 60, 93, 152,
    168–169
Army Service Command—C, 16, 58, 60, 199
Army Service Command—I, 14
Army Service Command—O, 16, 60
Arms, personal, surrender of, 244
Army Air Communications Service, 290
Army Air Forces
    troop strength, 58
    units in support of occupation, 16–17
Army Air Forces Weather Control, 270
Army Mobile Radio, 290
Arsenals, location, 134n
Asahi Shimbun, 238
Asano, 31
Asian mainland, 149
Assault plans, 1–2, 12
Atomic bombs dropped, 12
Atsugi airfield, 19, 21, 24–31, 34–35, 38–42, 53, 55, 89,
    113, 268, 290
Auchincloss, Col. S. S., 25n

Australia, 104, 113, 115, 179
  RAAF Command, 17
  U.S. troop strength, 1942, 1n
  in war and occupation, 1, 19, 32n, 201, 267
Australian Air Force, 267
Australian Military Forces, 151–154, 157, 179
Australian units, 62–64

B–29's 27, 32, 94–95, 270
Back, Brig. Gen. George I., 73n
"Baker" series, implementation of, 7, 17
Ballentine, Rear Adm. J. J., 277
Bank of Japan, 223
Banks. *See* Financial institutions
Bataan, 102, 106
Beary, Rear Adm. D. W., 278
"Benevolence," 100
Berkey, Vice Adm. Russell M., 278
Bern, 94
Besson, Gen. Frank S., 73n
Biak, 271
Billeting, 55
Bismarck Islands, 179
Black market operations, 209–211, 213, 217, 238, 241
BLACKLIST, 2, 4, 11–12, 28, 47, 89–90, 97, 116, 231–
  232, 255
Board of Information (Jap.), 238
Boeki Oho (Board of Trade), 217–219
Bombardment Wings, 97
Bomber Command, V, 58
Bonin Islands, 17, 82–86
Borneo, 62, 178
Bouchier, Air Vice Marshal C. A., 62
Bowers, Maj. F., 25n
Branch Hydrographic Office, Tokyo, 289
Brisbane, 244
British Commonwealth JCS in Australia, 74
British Commonwealth Occupation Force, 19, 32n, 34,
  60–65, 71, 73–74, 84, 86, 102, 199, 201, 227, 267,
  280, 289–290. *See also* United Kingdom
British Commonwealth units, 64, 86
British Naval Officer in Charge, Kure, 280
Broadcasting Corporation of Japan, 34, 208
Buckner Bay, 283
Bungo Suido, 278
Burma, 113, 159, 178, 193
Byrnes, James F., 106n

C–46's, 24–25
C–47's, 25
C–54's, 25, 27, 113
CAMPUS, 4
Canada, 69, 102, 111, 113, 115
Canton, 23, 155, 173–174

Caroline Islands, 88
Cavalry Brigade, 2d, 39
Cavalry Division, 1st, 6n, 14, 32, 38–42, 53, 55, 64,
  112, 138
Cavalry Reconnaissance Troop, 302d, 39
Cavalry Regiments
  7th, 39
  8th, 38, 41
  12th, 38, 41
  112th, 6n, 14, 32, 36
Celebes, 166
Censorship, civil, 73, 206–208, 232–233, 236–241
Central Liaison Committee, 195
Central Liaison Office (Jap.), 73n, 81, 227
Central Pacific, 117
Changchun, 174
Chase, Maj. Gen. William C., 32, 39
Chiba, 19, 36
Chiba Prefecture, 42, 62
China, 2, 19, 67, 69, 82, 95, 99, 113, 136, 145, 147,
  151–159, 164–168, 170–176, 191, 214
Chinese Communists, 158–159, 170, 174, 176
Chinese Naval Air Training Base, 111
Chitose, 111
Chofu airfield, 38–41
Choshi, 19
Civil affairs, administration of, 57, 297
Civil Affairs Section, SCAP, 198
Civil Communications Section, SCAP, 80
Civil Information and Education Section, SCAP, 75,
  80–81, 205–206, 255
Civil Intelligence Section, SCAP, 62, 79–80, 222, 233–
  238, 243–247, 255, 257, 260, 264–265
Civil liberties, safeguarding, 220
Civil Property Custodian, SCAP, 82, 223–226, 241, 255
Civil Service (Jap.), 257
Civil Transportation Section, SCAP, 81
Civilian internees, non-Japanese. *See country of na-
  tionality*
Civilian internees, UN (*see also* Prisoners of war, UN)
  nations represented, 113
  number detained, 104n, 149
  relief and repatriation, 89–116
Civilian Merchant Marine Committee, 145, 286
Civilians, Japanese. *See* Japanese nationals
Clarification of Censorship directive, 238
Closed Institutions Liquidating Commission, 224
Coast Guard (Jap.). *See* Maritime Safety Service
Coast Guard, U.S., 289n
Coast defenses, 134
Collaborators, internment of, 232, 236
Combat Cargo Group, 2d, 16
Command structure, 67–88

Commander in Chief, Pacific (CINCPAC), 4, 10, 18, 82, 88, 151n, 152, 158, 168–169, 273, 277, 283, 290
Commander in Chief, Pacific Advance, 99
Commander, Marianas Islands (COMMARIANAS), 88, 280
Commander, Minecraft, Pacific Fleet, 283
Commander, Naval Activities, Japan (COMNAV JAP), 73–74, 81, 88, 147, 154, 278–281, 288, 290
Commander, Naval Forces, Far East (COMNAVFE), 86, 88, 280, 288, 290
Commander, Naval Forces, Japan, 280
Commander, Naval Forces, Philippines (COMNAV-PHIL), 88, 280
Commander, Naval Operating Base, Okinawa, 280
Commanders, U.S., missions in occupation, 4, 10–11, 25–27, 35, 42
Commerce, rehabilitation of, 217–219
Communications
    establishment with Japan, 12, 25
    Japanese, surveillance of, 241
    in occupation forces, 55–56, 290
Communist infiltration, 187–191, 239, 241, 255, 258, 263–267. See also Subversion, internal
Compilations Branch, SCAP, 256–257
Coronet, 1–2, 6, 16, 58, 60, 270
Corps
    I, 6n, 14, 45, 47, 64–65, 86, 201, 227, 245
    IX, 6n, 14, 17, 42, 44–45, 53, 65, 86, 201, 227, 245
    X, 6n, 14, 45, 47
    XI, 6n, 7, 14, 32, 38–39, 42, 45
    XIV, 6n, 7, 14, 42, 44–45, 53
    XXIV, 7n, 14, 16, 86, 93, 102, 162
Corps Artillery, XI, 135
Corps of Engineers, 275, 289
Corregidor, 106
Corsair aircraft, 24
Counterintelligence. See Security and intelligence
Counterintelligence Corps, 34, 36, 45, 73, 233, 254–256, 260, 264–265
    41st, 74n, 233, 235, 241–244, 254–260
    mission, 254
    number of field units, 245, 267
    in repatriation program, 258–260
    Training School, 244
Courts, surveillance of. See Juridical system, surveillance of
Cowan, Maj. Gen. D. Tennant (Brit.), 64
"Crescent," 95
Criminal Investigation Division, SCAP, 254
Customs, surveillance of, 222
Czechoslovakia, 113
Dai Nippon Seijikai (Political Association of Greater Japan), 231

Daily Life Security Law, 209
Dairen, 159, 174, 181
Demobilization and disarmament
    achievements summarized, 131
    aircraft, number disposed of, 136
    disarmament process, 134–135
    disposal of materiel, 136
    disposal methods, 140–142
    fleet units, disposal of, 143–147
    general program, 117–120
    home forces demobilization, 120–123
    Japanese plans, 120
    Japanese role in, 2–4, 11, 27, 34–36, 65, 118
    materiel returned to Japanese, 142–143, 147
    number of persons demobilized, 122, 123
    of overseas forces, 123
    rate of progress, 127–134
    reorganization of system, 126–127
    weapons reported, disposed of, destroyed, returned, 136, 138, 142n
Demobilization Board, 126, 127
Demobilization Commissioner, 122
Derevyanko, Lt. Gen. Kusma N. (USSR), 184
Diet (Parliament), 38, 209, 249, 289
Diplomatic missions, foreign, 82
Diplomatic Section, SCAP, 77
Disarmament, Japanese. See Demobilization and disarmament
Dodge, Joseph M., 295n
Dodson, Comdr., E. B., USN, 289
Domei news agency, 23, 34, 238
Downfall. See Assault plans
Duke of York, 32n
Dunne, Col. D. M., 25n

East China Sea, 283
Economic and Scientific Section, SCAP, 75, 77–79, 81 214–219, 241, 257, 265
Education, civil, 205–208
Education Ministry (Jap.), 205–206, 263
Education Mission, 206
Educators, screening of, 205–206
Ehime Prefecture, 64
Eichelberger, Lt. Gen. Robert L., 12, 14, 24, 28–29, 36, 39, 44, 58, 109, 112, 198
Eiho Maru, 189
Elections, surveillance of, 220
Electric power, 214, 294
Emperor of Japan. See Hirohito
Enoshima Maru, 173
Enemy Property Custodian (Jap.), 226
Epidemics, control of, 60n. See also Prisoners of war
Eta Jima, 142
European Theater of Operations, 44

Evacuation Hospital, 54th, 105n
Exports. *See* Imports and exports

F6F's, 24–25
Facilities Allocation Board, 55
Far East Air Materiel Command, 271
Far East Air Service Command, 271
Far East Command
   air and naval forces, 86–88, 268–290
   establishment, 82–84, 278–280
   forces included, 82, 86
   GHQ command structure, 84–88
   mission, 84–86
Far Eastern Commission, 69, 71, 76, 81, 145, 294
Fighter Command, V, 58
Fighter Groups, 16
Fighter Wing, 85th, 17
Financial institutions, control of, 222–224
Financial restrictions, 224
Finland, 113
Finschhafen, 271
Fire fighting, 249–254
Fire Prevention Week, 254
Fire Research Institute, 251
First Demobilization Ministry (Bureau), 120, 123–127
Fisheries, 213–214
Fisheries Agency (Jap.), 286
Fleet Activities, Sasebo, 281–283
Fleet Activities, Yokosuka, 281–283
Fleet Air Wing One, 290
Fleet Liaison Officer, SCAP, 152, 154n
Fleets
   Third, 17, 28, 31, 99–100, 277–278
   Fifth, 17, 140, 150, 152, 154n, 277–278, 283, 288
   Seventh, 17, 25, 277–278, 288
   Pacific, 277
Fletcher, Adm. Frank J., 19, 277
Food Supplies, civilian, 24, 44
Foreign Liaison Section, SCAP, 82n
Foreign Liquidation Commission, 60, 286
Foreign Office (Jap.), 90
Formosa, 2, 99, 155–158, 166–170, 173–174, 178–179, 191
Fort William McKinley, 270, 271
France, 69, 113, 170, 173
Fraternization, 51–52
Freedom of Speech and Press directive, 236
Fuchishima, 44
Fuchu, 251, 271
Fuji trust, 224n
Fukuoka, 97n, 108n, 134, 270, 280
Fukuoka Prefecture, 47
Fukushima, 97n
Fukushima Prefecture, 53

Fusan, 174
Fushiki, 90
Futsu-saki, 28

General Accounting Section, SCAP, 81
General Headquarters, SCAP. *See* Supreme Commander, Allied Powers
General Hospitals
   42d, 32n, 60, 105, 112–113
   120th, 115
General Maritime Bureau, 145
General Order No. 1, SCAP, 32–34
General Procurement Agent, SCAP, 81
General Procurement Board, 227
Geneva Convention, 89, 96
Gerusalemme, 178
Ginza, The, 51
Glider Infantry Regiments
   187th, 31, 41
   188th, 31
Government Section, SCAP, 80, 219, 255
Graves Registration Service, 115
Great Britain, 69, 102, 113, 115, 145, 147, 158–159, 173, 176–178. *See also* British Commonwealth Occupation Force
Greece, 113
Grew, Joseph C., 106n
Griffin, Vice Adm. R. M., 278, 280
Guam, 2, 14, 88, 96, 106, 113, 166, 271, 290
Gumma Prefecture, 42

Hachi-nohe, 45
Hachioji, 39
Hadano, 42
Hagashi-Kuni, Prince Naruhiko, 23, 38
Hainan, 173–174
Haiphong, 155
Hakata, 90, 126, 127, 176, 191
Hakodate, 90, 97n, 109, 126, 127, 191
Hall, Lt. Gen. Charles P., 38
Halsey, Adm. William F., 17, 99–100, 277
Hamamatsu, 109
Hara-Machida, 32, 39, 41
Harada memoirs, 257
Harbin, 174
Hawaii, 14, 35, 113, 158, 193
Hayama, 31
Hiratsuka, 39
Hiro, 64
Hiro Bay, 278
Hirohito, Emperor of Japan, 4, 12, 23, 27, 34, 38
Hiro-saki, 45, 138
Hiroshima, 12, 97n, 108n, 127, 223, 283
Hiroshima Prefecture, 267

Hodge, Lt. Gen. John R., 12, 14
Hodges, Gen. Courtney H., 14
Hokkaido, 7, 19, 42, 44, 53, 69, 89, 97n, 111, 120, 123, 201, 213, 275, 277–278, 297
Home Depot Division, 130
Home Ministry, 126, 127, 140, 235, 286
Hong Kong, 23, 106, 143, 170, 173, 239
Honshu, 7, 17, 19, 44–45, 53, 55, 65, 69, 89, 97, 99n, 108, 120, 149, 164, 267, 277–280, 288
Hulutao, 158–159, 174
Hutchinson, Col. C. R., 25
Hydrographic services, 289
Hyogo, 97n

Ibaraki Prefecture, 42
Iceland, 113
Ie Shima, 268
Imperial Army Air Headquarters, 21
Imperial Army Headquarters, 21
Imperial General Headquarters, 21, 23, 34, 36, 41–42, 118–120, 122, 143
Imperial General Staff, 21, 27n, 122
Imperial Government, 36
Imperial Japanese Army. See also Demobilization and Disarmament; Japanese armed forces
    First General Army (Group), 36, 120, 122
    Second Area Army, 120
    Second General Army (Group), 36, 120, 122
    Fifth Area Army, 120–123
    Eleventh Area Army, 120
    Twelfth Area Army, 120
    Thirteenth Area Army, 120
    Fifteenth Area Army, 120
    100th Air Brigade, 119
    major commands and stations, 120–122
    number of troops in home islands, 4, 27, 95, 118–120
    number of units, 120
    number of verified dead and missing, 130n
    total number and location, 117, 122
Imperial Japanese Navy. See also Demobilization and disarmament; Japanese armed forces
    Fleet Headquarters, 122
    Naval Force Headquarters, 122
    Southeastern Area Fleet, 122
    Southwestern Area Fleet, 122
    civilians employed, 123
    major commands and stations, 122
    number in home islands, 123
    number verified dead and missing, 130n
    total number and location, 117n
Imperial Mint, 223
Imperial Naval Air Headquarters, 21
Imperial Naval General Staff, 36
Imperial Naval Headquarters, 21

Imperial Navy Ministry, 27n, 90, 118, 120, 122, 126, 154, 278
Imperial War Ministry, 27n, 90, 118, 120, 122, 126
Imports and exports, 217–219, 295
Inchon, 174
India, 69, 95, 113
Indian units, 62–64
Indochina, 155, 170, 173, 178
Indonesia. *See* Netherlands East Indies
Industry, rehabilitation of, 214–217
Infantry Divisions
    American, 6n, 14, 39–41, 53, 112
    6th, 6n, 14
    7th, 14
    24th, 6n, 14, 65, 138
    25th, 6n, 14, 64
    27th, 6n, 7, 14, 17, 24, 39, 41–42, 44, 53
    32d, 6n, 38, 45n, 47
    33d, 6n, 14, 47
    40th, 14
    41st, 6n, 14
    43d, 6n, 14, 42, 44–45, 131
    77th, 6n, 14, 42, 44, 53
    81st, 6n, 14, 42, 44–45, 53
    96th, 14
    97th, 44, 53
    98th, 14, 47
Infantry Regiments
    105th, 39, 41
    106th, 41
    127th, 38, 45n
    132d, 39–41
    158th, 6n, 14, 45, 53
    164th, 41, 44
    182d, 41
    306th, 53
    307th, 53
    321st, 45
    322d, 45
    323d, 45
Inflation, control of. *See* Price controls
Information, civil. 206–208. See also Civil Information and Education Section, SCAP
Initial Occupation Area, 44
Initial Post-Surrender Policy, 195, 205
Inland sea, 134, 277, 284
Intelligence measures. *See* Security and intelligence
Interior Ministry, 209
International Military Tribunal for the Far East, 76–78, 233
International Prosecution Section, SCAP, 77
International Red Cross, 90, 96, 99–100, 104, 106, 111, 113

Irumagawa airfield, 44, 58
Ise, 147
Ishioka, 19
Italy, 113
Itazuki, 58
Iwakuni airfield, 62
Iwo Jima, 99n, 136
Iyo Nada, 278
Izu Islands, 17

Japan Air Materiel Area, 271
Japan Communist Party, 191, 263–265
Japanese armed forces
   aircraft, number in homeland, 134
   arsenals and ordnance depots, location, 134n
   definition, 135n
   demobilization and disarmament. *See* Demobilization and disarmament
   number overseas, 123
   prisoners of war. *See* Prisoners of war, Japanese
Japanese Facilities Agency, 56
Japanese Hydrographic Office, 289
Japanese Liaison Group, 56n
Japanese nationals
   employment by U.S., 60
   reaction to occupation, 49–53, 131–134
Java, 178
Jinsen, 23
Joho Kyoku news agency, 34
Joint Chiefs of Staff, 4, 67, 69, 71, 88n, 157, 172, 178–179, 194
Joint Strategic Plans and Operations Group, FEC, 84
Jones, Capt, C. B., USN, 25n
Junod, Dr. Marcel, 96, 97n
Juridical system, surveillance of, 220
Justice Ministry, 251
Justice, surveillance of administration of. *See* Juridical system, surveillance of

Kadena airfield, 94
Kagawa Prefecture, 64
Kagoshima, 109, 126, 191, 280
Kagoshima Prefecture, 47
Kaiwan, 108
Kamada, Lt. Gen. Senichi, 24
Kamaishi, 109
Kami-Shibai, 263
Kanagawa, 97n
Kanagawa Prefecture, 42, 49, 53, 199, 201
Kanoya, 23, 38, 45n, 268
Kanto Plain. *See* Tokyo (Kanto) Plain
Karafuto (Southern Sakhalin), 7, 120, 122–123, 159, 161
Karenko, 173

Kashiwazaki, 44
Katsuura, 41
Katsuyama Bay, 41
Kawabe, Lt. Gen. T., 19n, 23
Kawasaki, 31, 100, 106
Kawasaki trust, 224n
Kazo, 131
Keijo, 270
Kempei Tai (Military Police), 231, 235
Kenney, Gen. George C., 14, 270, 271
Kido diary, 257
Kiefer, Brig. Gen. H. W., 45n
Kiirun, 155, 173
King George V, 32
Kinkaid, Adm. Thomas C., 17, 277
Kinki, 65
Kisarazu Naval Air Base, 32, 281, 290
Kobe, 45, 47, 60, 90, 109, 111, 150, 229, 239, 280, 283–286
Kochi, 64, 108, 278
Kochi Prefecture, 64
Koku Sui-to (Extreme Nationalist Party), 231
Kokura, 229
Kokuryu Kai (Black Dragon Society), 231
Korea and Koreans, 19, 34, 82, 84, 86, 95, 99, 152, 157–159, 181, 270. *See also* Army Forces in Korea
   areas planned as objectives, 2, 4–6
   armed Japanese in, 4
   crime rate among, 262
   education of, 262–263
   epidemics among, 162, 165
   Japanese evacuation from, 161–164
   minority problem in Japan, 260–264
   nationalistic organizations, 263
   number in Japan, 262
   return of nationals to, 164–168, 174, 178–179, 183, 191, 262
   total U.S. forces, use in, 7
   troop strength assigned, 6, 14–16
   troop units assigned, 7, 14
Korean Residents Union, 263
Korizama, 44
Krueger, Gen. Walter, 12, 14, 45, 47
Kumagawa, 19
Kumagaya, 42, 131
Kumamoto, 223
Kumamoto Prefecture, 47
Kure, 60, 62, 126, 145, 150, 191, 229, 280–281, 283
Kurihama, 226
Kurile Islands, 7n, 17, 122, 159
Kyoto, 45, 47, 60, 229
Kyushu, 1, 7, 17, 23, 45, 65, 69, 97, 108, 120, 134, 149, 164, 270, 277, 283, 288

Labor Ministry, 216
Labor, rehabilitation of, 216–217, 296
Labor Standards Office (Jap.), 217
Land Reform Program, 213, 294
Law enforcement, 254–256
LCM's, 136
League of Koreans Residing in Japan, 263
Legal Section, SCAP, 78, 235, 255
"Lewisite," 65
Leyte, 24, 168, 271
Liaison and Coordination Office (Jap.), 73
Liaison measures, 64
Liberty ships, 154–155, 158, 176, 179, 286
Lipa, Luzon, 14
Local Assistance Bureaus, 126, 127, 130
Local Autonomy Bill, 127
Loyalty checks, 255–256
LST's, 154–155, 162, 164, 170, 176, 286
Luzon, 39, 115, 168
Luzon Area Command, 14

MacArthur, Gen. of the Army Douglas. *See also*
    Supreme Commander, Allied Powers
  arrival in Japan, 21, 28–29, 31, 268
  arrival in Tokyo, 39–41, 44n
  basis for plans, 2–4
  on British-held POW, 159, 178
  directive to Imperial Government, 36
  estimate of force required, 56
  and fraternization, 52
  governmental authority of, 195
  issues GO No. 1, 32–34
  named CINCFE, 82
  named CINCAFPAC, 67
  named SCAP, 12, 67
  occupation policies, 23–24, 56–57
  on return of Koreans, 165
  on Soviet-held POW, 161, 179–186
  speeds demobilization, 131
  summarizes progress, 291–297
MAGIC CARPET, 278
Maibara, 106
Mainichi Shimbun, 238
Maizuru, 126, 127, 150, 189, 191, 281
Malaya, 113, 159, 166, 178
Malta, 113
Manchuria, 117, 130, 158–159, 162, 166, 170, 174, 176
Mandaluyong Hospital Center, 115
Mandated Islands, 88
Manila, 12, 19, 27, 35, 90, 94, 113, 115–116, 122, 123,
    143, 168, 268
Manufacturing, rehabilitation of. *See* Industry, re-
    habilitation of
Manus Island, 34

Mapping program, 275
Marcus Island, 17
Marianas Air Materiel Area, 271
Mariana Islands, 17, 82, 84n, 86, 94–95, 99n, 112, 155,
    166
Marianas—Bonins Command (MARBO), 86, 88
Marigold, 32n, 105, 111–112
Marine Air Group 31, 290
Marine Amphibious Corps, V, 6n, 14, 16, 47
Marine Divisions
  2d, 6n, 14, 47, 65, 283
  3d, 14
  5th, 6n, 14, 47
  6th, 28, 44
Marine Regiments
  2d, 65
  4th, 17, 28, 32, 44
Maritime Bureau, 127
Maritime Safety Authorities Bill, 289
Maritime Safety Board (Jap.), 254, 289
Maritime Safety Service (Jap.), 254, 288–289
Maritime Training Institute, 254
Marquat, Maj. Gen. William E., 212n
Marshall, Gen. of the Army George C., 159
Marshall Islands, 88
Mashbir, Col. Sidney F., 19n
Matsushima, 44
Matsuyama air base, 138
McGinley, Brig. Gen. Eugene, 55
Medical Clearing Company, 608th, 113
Medical services, 60
Meiji Inner Shrine, 39
Melbourne, 193
Merchant marine, Japanese, 154, 286–288
Mexico, 113
Military government, 74–75
  concept of, 194–198
  credit for success, 230
  Economic Division, 212–219
  Finance and Civil Property Division, 222–227
  formative phase, 198–201
  functions of staff sections, 201–203, 230
  Legal and Government Division, 219–222
  organization, evolution of, 201–203
  prefectural teams, 203–205
  procurement demands and procedures. *See under*
    Occupation forces
  Procurement Division, 227–230
  regional organization, 199, 201, 267
  Social Affairs Division, 203–212
  staff sections, agencies and units, 195–227
Military Government Companies, 201n
Military Intelligence Company, 319th, 245
Military police, 73, 254, 267

Military Railway Service, Third, 229
Military Security Law, 257
Mindanao, 168
Minesweeping operations, 277–278, 283–286
Mining industry, rehabilitation of, 213
Misaki, 31
Missouri, 17, 32
MIS–X Section, SCAP, 96
Mito, 135
Mitsubishi trust, 224n
Mitsui trust, 224n
Miyagi, 97n
Miyagi Prefecture, 42
Miyazaki Prefecture, 47
Moji, 126
Moscow Meeting of Foreign Ministers, 69
Mount Futabi, 106
Mukden, 174
Muratsuka, 44
Mutsu Bay, 45n

Nagano Prefecture, 42
Nagaoka, 44
Nagasaki, 12, 23, 47, 90, 97n, 109, 280, 283–284
Nagasaki Prefecture, 47
Nagoya, 58, 90, 97n, 120, 127, 191, 223, 229, 283–284
Nakhodka, 145
National Congress of Industrial Unions, 264–265
National Reference Library, 257
Natural Resources Section, SCAP, 79
Naval Air Transport Service, 290
Naval Security Corps, 24
Naval Task Forces
  First Carrier, 28
  Second Carrier, 28
  31st, 99
  33d, 32
  35th, 41
  36th, 109
  38th, 28
  39th, 28
Naval Task Group 30.6, 100
Navy Ministry. See Imperial Navy Ministry
Navy, U.S.
  air units, 290
  Branch Hydrographic Office, 289
  civilians employed, 281
  command structure, 277
  communications, 290
  illegal traffic, suppression of, 288–289
  initial operations, 277–278
  merchant shipping, control of, 277–278, 286–288
  minesweeping operations, 277–278, 283–286
  miscellaneous activities, 289–290

  organization and missions, 278–281
  role in occupation, 4, 7n, 10, 17, 21–23
  role in Japanese repatriation, 288
  role in UN POW relief, 99–102
  support groups, 289–290
  transport operations, 278
Netherlands, 69, 102, 113, 115, 179
Netherlands East Indies, 17, 34, 60, 84n, 115, 166,
  178–179
New Britain, 179
New Guinea, 179
New Ireland, 179
New Zealand, 69, 113
New Zealand Air Force, 62, 267
New Zealand Army, 267
News, dissemination of, 34–35
Nichols Field, 115, 271
Niigata, 44, 90
Niigata Prefecture, 53
Nimitz, Fleet Adm. Chester W., 17, 100
Nippon Shimbun, 187
Nippon Times, 238
Nishima, 19
North Pacific Force, 19, 45n, 277
Northcott, Lt. Gen. J. (Aust.), 62
Norway, 113

Oahu, Hawaii, 14
Objectives of occupation, 10–11, 57–58
Occupation forces
  air units, role in, 268–277
  arrival of, 24–32
  behavior of troops, 49–51
  control by, completed, 53
  cooperation, key to success, 290
  economic benefits derived from, 291–297
  military government administration. *See* Military
    government
  movements, dispositions, locations, 28–66
  Navy's role in, 277–290
  number in forces, 56–58, 265–267
  objective areas planned, 2–6
  objectives, 10–11, 57–58
  procurement demands and procedures, 55–56, 227–
    230
  recreation, 52–53
  reduction in, 47–49, 57–58
  roles and missions, 7–10
  security and intelligence measures. *See* Security
    and intelligence
  stabilized, 65–66
  troop strength allocated, 2, 6, 14–16
  troop units available, 6n, 14
Occupied Japan Export-Import Revolving Fund, 79

Odawara, 31, 41
Office of Civil Property Custodian, SCAP, 81
Office of U.S. Political Advisor for Japan, 77
Office of War Information, 35
Ofuna, 100, 102–104, 106
Oita Prefecture, 47
Okayama, 45, 65
Okayama Prefecture, 64
Okazaki, 58
Okinawa, 14, 17, 24, 27, 38–39, 41, 94, 99n, 109, 113, 136, 158, 162, 169, 268, 271
Okuno Shima, 65
OLYMPIC, 1, 2, 6, 11–12, 16, 60, 270
Ominato, 44, 45n, 150
Omori, 100, 102
Omuta, 108
Onda, 102n
Operational Engineering Section, SCAP, 95
Operations, concept of, 4–10, 12n
Orders, implementing, 12, 17
Ordnance depots, location, 134n
Organization for occupation, 12–19
Osaka, 23, 45, 47, 65, 97n, 150, 223, 226, 229, 239, 254, 267, 270, 283–284
Otaru, 42, 53
Otsuki, 19

Pacific Air Command, U.S. Army, 271, 273
Pacific Air Service Command, 271
Pacific Command, 84n, 151
Pacific Fleet Liaison Group with SCAP, 277–278, 288, 290
Pacific Ocean Areas, 2, 10, 67, 152, 158, 166, 168
Pacific Theater, 67
Parachute Infantry Regiment, 511th, 29–31
Paris, 94
Park, Col. L., 25n
Peace Preservation Law, 257
Peiping Headquarters Group, 172
Percival, Gen. Arthur E. (Brit.), 90
Philippine Command, 86–88
Philippine Islands Treaty, 271
Philippine Military Advisory Group, 88n
Philippine Military Assistance Agreement, 88n
Philippine Scouts, 86–88
Philippines, 14, 17, 34, 47, 69, 82, 84n, 86, 88, 93–95, 115, 136, 152, 155, 158, 168, 235, 268
Photography, aerial, 275
Picnic Bay, 143
Planning phase, 2–11
Point system, 47n, 53, 58
Poland, 113
Police, civil, 36, 51, 220, 235–236, 249–251, 267. *See also* Public safety
Political parties, surveillance of, 220

Population increase, 295
Port Arthur, 159, 174, 181
Portable Surgical Hospitals,
    5th, 105n
    30th, 113
Portugal, 113
Postal savings offices, rehabilitation of, 224
Potsdam Conference and Declaration, 12, 38, 67, 75, 77, 117, 157, 161, 181, 184, 194, 205
Precious minerals, custody of, 223, 226, 241
Presque Isle, Maine, 94
Press, attitude of, 51–52, 190
Press censorship. *See* Censorship, civil
Press Code for Japan, 236
Price controls, 217–219
Prime Minister. *See* Higashi—Kuni, Naruhiko; Shidehara, Kijuro
Prisoner of War Information Bureau (Jap.), 90
Prisoners of war, Japanese
    Communist infiltration among, 187–191, 265–267
    epidemics among, 155, 158, 173–176, 193
    evacuation from Australian areas, 179
    evacuation from China Theater, 170–176, 191
    evacuation from Korea, 161–164, 179–181
    evacuation from NEI, 191
    evacuation from Philippines, 168–169
    evacuation from POA, 166–168
    evacuation from Ryukyus, 169–170
    evacuation from SEAC, 176–179, 191
    evacuation from Soviet control, 123, 127–131, 149, 159–161, 179–186, 191
    evacuation from Western Pacific, 191–193
    organization for repatriation integrated, 172
    medical relief, 151
    Navy's role in repatriation, 288
    number overseas, 149
    number returned, 149, 191, 193
    phases of repatriation, 149–150
    rate of processing, 149
    reception centers, location, 191
    repatriation and processing, 64, 123–126, 143, 149–193, 211–212
    SCAP plan for, 151–152
    SCAP policies, 151
    screening by CIC, 258–260
    transportation allocated, 150, 154–155, 158–162, 166, 168, 170, 172–174, 176–184, 191–193
    U.S. commanders involved, 151n
Prisoners of war, non-Japanese, 154, 157, 164–165, 170, 173n, 191
Prisoners of war, UN. *See also* Civilian internees, UN
    airdrop operations, 94–96
    atrocities against. *See* Recovered Personnel Section, SCAP

Prisoners of war, UN—Continued
  camps, location and supply, 96–99
  concern for, 89
  dead and missing, procedure regarding, 114–115
  definition, 89
  list of camps, 108n
  medical relief, 109–113, 115
  nations represented, 113
  number interned, 90, 97n, 99
  number released, processed, evacuated, 102n, 113,
    115–116
  processing for home, 112–116
  recovery teams, functions of, 92–94
  relief and repatriation, 21, 34, 44, 89–116
  SCAP directives regarding, 90–92
  Operation "Swift Mercy," 99–102
Prisons, Japanese, 60
  inspection of, 220
  labor force from, 216
  reform in, 251
Propaganda leaflets, 2n
Property
  looted, restitution of, 227
  private, policies regarding, 224–226
  public, seizure and custody, 226
  UN and Axis, protection of, 226–227
Provost courts, 65
Provost Marshal, SCAP, 254
Provost marshals, 73
Public health, 208–209
Public Health and Welfare Section, SCAP, 80, 119,
  155, 208
Public Relations Office, SCAP, 238
Public safety, 73, 244–254
Public Safety Commissions (Jap.), 247–249
Public Safety Division, SCAP, 216, 220, 233, 244–254
Public welfare, 209–211
Publications Section, SCAP, 257
Purge, directives on, 220–222, 245

Quarantine, 119n, 155, 158, 162, 165, 176, 193

Rabaul, 179
Radio Code for Japan, 236
Radio Tokyo, 238, 281
Real estate projects, 230
Recovered Personnel Section, SCAP, 102–113
Redeployment to ZI, 58, 152
Regimental Combat Teams. See Infantry Regiments
Relief, civilian. See Public welfare
Reparations procedures, 214–216
Reparations and Restitutions Delegations, 81
Reparations Section, SCAP, 81–82
Reparations Technical Advisory Committee, 81

Repatriation Liquidation Bureau, 127
Repatriation Relief Agency (Bureau), 126, 127
Replacement Command, 115–116
Replacement Depots
  4th, 58
  5th, 115
  11th, 58
  70th, 105n
Replacements, 58, 65–66
Requisition procedures, 55–56
Rescue, 109, 112
Resources, natural, 212–214
Restitution Advisory Committee, 81
Richardson, Lt. Gen. Robert C., 14
Robertson, Lt. Gen. H. C. H. (Brit.), 62
Royal Navy. See British Commonwealth Occupation Force
Ryder, Maj. Gen. Charles W., 53
Ryukyu Islands, 14, 17, 82, 84n, 86, 152, 157, 159,
  166, 168, 191
Ryukyus Command, 86

Saga Prefecture, 47
Sagami Bay, 19, 25, 28, 31–32, 100, 278
Sagamigahara Air Unit, 25
St. Luke's International Medical Center, 60
Saionji, Kimmochi, 257
Saipan, 14, 35, 95–96, 113
Saishu, 162
Saitama, 97n
Saitama Prefecture, 42
Sakhalin, 8n, 159. See also Karafuto
Sambongi, 138
San Fernando, Luzon, 168
San Francisco, 35
Sanjo, 44
Santo Tomas University, 115
Sapporo, 42, 53, 60, 223, 229
Sasago, 109n
Sasebo Naval Base, 23, 47, 126, 127, 143, 150, 173,
  176, 191, 278, 281, 283–284, 286, 289–290
SCAPIN, defined, 73
Schmidt, Maj. Gen. Harry, USMC, 47
Schools, civilian. See Education, civil
Sebald, William J., 183, 186
Second Demobilization Ministry (Bureau), 120, 123,
  126, 127, 145
Security and intelligence, 21, 23, 41, 51
  arms, personal, surrender of, 244
  censorship procedures, 232–233, 236–241
  CIC mission, 233
  CIC regions and units, 245
  Civil Censorship Detachment, 236
  communications means, control of, 241

Security and intelligence—Continued
  information, processing, 241
  intelligence, civil, evolution of, 233–244
  law enforcement, 254–256
  loyalty checks, 255–256
  police agencies, directives concerning, 235–236
  postal system, control of, 238
  propaganda, interception of, 239
  in public safety, 244–254
  publishing industry, control of, 239–241
  radio broadcasts, control of, 239
  repatriates, screening of, 258–260
  responsibilities, assignment of, 231–232
  subversion, surveillance of, 256–258
  surveillance measures, 254–256
  violations, number of, 244n
Sendai, 41–42, 60, 90, 97n, 109, 229, 278, 283
Senzaki, 126, 127, 191
Service units, 58–62
Shanghai, 23, 145, 172–174
Shidehara, Kijuro, 126, 127, 291
Shikoku, 7, 17, 45, 64, 69, 89, 97, 108, 120, 138, 267, 277
Shikoku Prefecture, 65
Shimane Prefecture, 64
Shimbara, 108
Shimonoseki, 45, 90, 120, 126
Shimonoseki Strait, 284
Shinagawa, 99–100, 102, 108
Shintoism, state, 205
Shiogama, 109
Shipping Control Authority (SCAJAP), 154–155, 166, 168, 173
Shipping Control Authority for the Japanese Merchant Marine, 74, 278, 286–288, 290
Shipping resources, 58, 149, 150
Shizu-oka Prefecture, 201
Showa airfield, 38
Siberia, 159, 161–162, 186
Signal Corps, 55
Singapore, 23, 106, 145
Skymasters, 24, 268
Skytrains, 24, 268
Smuggling, suppression of, 64, 165, 262, 288–289
"Snowball," 94
Social Affairs Division, SCAP, 206
Solomon Islands, 117, 179
South Pacific, 84n
Southeast Asia, 149, 151, 157–159
Southeast Asia Command, 151–152, 154, 176–179
Southern Islands Area Command, 14
Southwest Pacific, 84n, 117
Southwest Pacific Area, 7, 14, 34, 67
Soviet Union, 12, 69, 123, 145, 151, 154, 157, 277

Spain, 113
Special Higher Police (Jap.), 235, 257
Special Procurement Board (Jap.), 229
Special Projects Section, SCAP, 257–258
Special Services, 52–53
Spruance, Adm. Raymond A., 17, 277–278
State Department, 88n, 106n
Statistics and Reports Section, SCAP, 81
Stettinius, Edward R., 106n
Stilwell, Gen. Joseph W., 12, 14
Styer, Lt. Gen. Wilhelm D., 14
Subversion, internal, 256–258. See also Communist infiltration
Sugamo, 60
Sugi, 168
Sumatra, 178
Sumitomo trust, 224n
Supply services. See also Occupation forces, procurement demands and procedures
  problems of, 16n
  reorganization of, 58–62
  troop strength, 60
Support Area, FEC, 86
Supreme Commander, Allied Powers (SCAP), 35, 64, 131, 147. See also MacArthur, Gen. of the Army, Douglas
  civil staff sections, 75–82
  communications, 290
  Directives Nos. 1 and 2, 119, 143
  establishment, 67–69
  functions of GHQ, 73–75
  functions of staffs and agencies, 73, 118n
  GHQ established, 75
  naval forces, control of, 74
  organization of GHQ, 71–73
  special staff sections, 76–82
Surrender, Japanese
  ceremony of, 32–34
  events leading to, 11–12
  Japanese delegation, directive to, 19–23, 31–34
Swatow, 173
Sweden, 90
Swift, Maj. Gen. Innis P., 45
Swing, Maj. Gen. Joseph M., 28–31
"Swift Mercy," 99–102
Switzerland, 90, 99, 104

Tachikawa airfield, 38, 41, 271
Tacloban, 168
Takada, 44
Takamatsu, 119, 228
Takao, 168, 173
Takasu, 23
Tama River, 31

Tanabe, 191
Tangku, 172, 174
Tank Destroyer Battalion, 637th, 135
Tass news agency, 186
Tateyama Bay Naval Air Station, 31–32, 36
Tax collections, 223–224
Tench, Col. Charles P., 24–25
Teton, 277, 290
Thailand, 178
"Thought control," 209n, 235
Tishibana Maru, 2n
Tochigi Prefecture, 42, 53
Tojo, Gen. Hideki, 235
Tokumu Kikan (Secret Intelligence Service), 231, 235
Tokushima Prefecture, 64
Tokyo, 4, 7, 12, 17, 21, 31–32, 35, 39–42, 44, 55, 60, 64, 71, 94, 97n, 100, 102n, 108n, 138, 145, 199, 223, 226, 229, 251, 254, 265, 268, 271, 283, 299
Tokyo Area Government Railway Workers Union, 265
Tokyo Bay Area, 7, 17, 19, 24, 28, 31, 38, 99, 105, 112, 134, 135, 143, 277–278, 281, 284
Tokyo conferences, 154–155, 166, 169, 172, 178, 181, 183
Tokyo Economics Board, 23
Tokyo (Kanto) Plain, 1, 7, 24, 38
Tokyo Prefecture, 42, 53, 199, 201
Tokyo Rose, 256
Tokyo Shimbun, 24, 52
Tonari Gumi (Neighborhood Associations), 209
Tone, 147
Totsuka, 290
Tottori Prefecture, 64–65
Townsville, 271
Trade, rehabilitation of. *See* Commerce, rehabilitation of
Transportation Ministry, 127, 145, 154, 278, 289
Troop Carrier Groups, 16
Truman, Harry S., 12, 106
Tsingtao, 23, 145, 174
Tsu-chiya, 45
Tsugaru Strait, 277–278
Tsuruga, 90
Tsurumi, Ken, 24
Tsushima Island, 290
Tsushima Strait, 277
Typhoons, 24, 270

Ube, 102n
Umezu, Mayor, 49
Unemployment, 296
Union of Great Korean Republics Residing in Japan, 263
United Kingdom. *See* Great Britain

Uraga, 126, 127, 155, 168, 176, 191, 193
Uraga Peninsula, 41
Uraga Strait, 28
Urdaneta, Luzon, 105n
Utsunomiya, 45
Vietnam. *See* Indochina
Volcano Islands, 17, 84n, 88

Wainwright, Gen. Jonathan M., 90, 115n
Wakanoura, 283
Wakayama, 45n, 47
Wake Island, 102, 106
War criminals, 233–235
War Department, 157, 181, 235, 257
War Ministry. *See* Imperial War Ministry
War Shipping Administration, 155, 158
War trophies, 138n
Warburton, Col. E. K., 25n
Washington, D.C., 94, 97
Weather Wing, 43d, 273
Welfare Ministry, 126, 127, 151, 208, 211
Western Pacific, 149, 150, 154, 191
Western Pacific Base Command, 95
Whitehead, Lt. Gen. Ennis C., 271
Whitney, Brig. Gen. Courtney, 219n
Willoughby, Maj. Gen. Charles A., 19n, 73n
Wilmington, Del., 95
Women's Replacement and Disposition Center, 115
Wurtsmith, Maj. Gen. Paul, 271n

Yalta Conference, 7n
Yamagata Prefecture, 213
Yamaguchi Prefecture, 47, 64, 102n, 267
Yamanashi Prefecture, 42, 53
Yamazumi, Capt. Chuzaburo, 24
Yasuda trust, 224n
"Yellow List," 97
Yokohama, 29–32, 34–41, 44–45, 49–51, 53n, 55, 58, 60, 90, 102, 105, 109, 111–113, 126, 145, 229, 251, 254, 268, 277, 281, 290
Yokohama Canal, 38
Yokohama Liaison Office, 55
Yokosuka Naval and Air Base, 17, 19, 21, 28, 35, 42, 49, 53, 99–100, 135, 145, 150, 281, 286, 289–290
Yokota airfield, 38
Yomiuri-Hochi, 23–24, 52, 238
Youth Organization for the Reconstruction of Korea, 263
Yoyogi Parade Ground, 39
Yuta Island, 119

Zaibatsu (financial trusts), 224
Zama, 41, 58
Zone of the Interior, U.S., 44–45, 47, 53, 58, 65, 66, 152, 229, 270

☆ U.S. GOVERNMENT PRINTING OFFICE: 1994 360-579

PIN : 071856–000